THE CHURCH ON THE MOVE

The Characters and Policies of
Pius XII and John XXIII

W. A. PURDY

The Church on the Move

THE CHARACTERS AND POLICIES OF PIUS XII AND JOHN XXIII

THE JOHN DAY COMPANY
NEW YORK

Nihil obstat JOANNES M. T. BARTON, S.T.D., C.S.S. *Censor deputatus.*

Imprimatur PATRITIUS CASEY, VIC. GEN.

Westmonasterii, die 2ª Novembris 1965

The Nihil obstat *and* Imprimatur *are a declaration that a book or pamphlet is considered to be free from doctrinal or moral error. It is not implied that those who have granted the* Nihil obstat *and* Imprimatur *agree with the contents, opinions or statements expressed.*

Library of Congress Catalogue Card Number: 66-25867

MANUFACTURED IN THE UNITED STATES OF AMERICA

Contents

AUTHOR'S PREFACE, 7

1. Prologue, 11
2. The War Years, 26
3. The Church and Modern Democracy, 46
4. The Papacy and Politics: Concordats, 58
5. Communism and Socialism, 87
6. The International Community, 121
7. Modern Warfare, 143
8. Lay Status and Station in the Church, 156
9. Court, Curia and Council, 191
10. Social Theories and Conflicts, 218
11. Catholics and Jews, 246
12. Separated Brethren and Religious Liberty, 270
13. Bible, Bureaucrats, Bishops, 295
14. Liturgical Revival, 307
15. Conclusion, 324

APPENDICES, 335

BIBLIOGRAPHY, 343

INDEX, 347

ACKNOWLEDGEMENTS

The author gratefully acknowledges permission to quote from the following publications:
From *The Government of Republican Italy*, J. C. Adams & P. Barile, by courtesy of George Allen & Unwin Ltd.; from *Church and State in Italy 1850-1950*, A. C. Jemolo, by courtesy of Basil Blackwell & Mott Ltd.; from *Church and Sex*, R. Trevett, *Cardinal Gasquet*, S. Leslie, and a *Concilium* article, Diekman, by courtesy of Burns & Oates Ltd.; from *The Social and Political Doctrines of Contemporary Europe*, M. Oakeshott, by courtesy of Cambridge University Press; from *The Church and Industrial Society*, G. Siefer, by courtesy of Darton, Longman & Todd Ltd.; from *Revolution and Papacy 1769-1846*, E. E. Y. Hales, by courtesy of Eyre & Spottiswoode (Publishers) Ltd.; from *Letters from Vatican City*, X. Rynne, by courtesy of Farrar, Straus & Giroux Inc.; from *Il Clero di Riserva*, G. Poggi, by courtesy of Giangiacomo Feltrinelli & C.; from *The Cardinal Spellman Story*, R. Gannon, by courtesy of Doubleday & Co. Inc.; from *Gregory the Great*, F. Homes-Dudden, by courtesy of Longmans, Green & Co. Ltd.; from *The Catholic Church and Nazi Germany*, Guenter Lewy, (copyright © 1964 Guenter Lewy), by courtesy of McGraw-Hill Book Company; from *Modern Catholicism*, W. von Loewenich, by courtesy of St. Martin's Press Inc.; from *Church and State in Fascist Italy*, D. A. Binchy, by courtesy of the Royal Institute of International Affairs and Oxford University Press; from *Christian Democracy in Western Europe*, M. P. Fogarty, by courtesy of Routledge & Kegan Paul Ltd.; from *Le Vicaire et L'Histoire*, J. Nobécourt, and from *Pie XII et le Troisième Reich*, S. Friedlander, by courtesy of Alfred A. Knopf; from *The Mystery of the Kingdom*, R. Knox, by courtesy of the literary executor and Sheed & Ward Ltd.; from *Theology for Today*, Charles Davis, © Charles Davis 1962, by courtesy of Sheed & Ward, Inc., New York.

Author's Preface

FEW WOULD QUESTION that the death of John XXIII in June 1963 moved the world genuinely and profoundly. Yet though it is true that the world entered uniquely into the long last agony that ended the short pontificate, it is easy to forget that less than four years earlier Pius XII had died amid hardly less remarkable, if less intimate signs of respectful mourning. In the autumn of 1958 the world showed little doubt that one of its great ones had departed, and none showed less doubt than Angelo Roncalli.

But it is not perhaps given to men to hold a great office for twenty disturbed years, twenty years of rapid change, and yet leave a reputation permanently immune from debate. Least of all is this possible for popes. In proportion as rulers are placed beyond open discussion they are the more freely made the subject of rumour, speculation and fancy in private; and it has been part of the defensive mentality of the Catholic Church in the past century to put popes beyond public discussion. This is not a traditional procedure, though in fact the popes of the past hundred years would on the whole have earned favourable report in the most candid of earlier ages.

It was the highest Authority that bade the apostles be wise as serpents and simple as doves, and great churchmen are nearly always to be assessed in terms of a balance and tension between these two attributes. But the attributes are not antithetical—though those who despise intelligence suspect the serpent, and those who overvalue it despise the dove. Pope Pius XII had the dove in his coat of arms: his detractors have seen nothing of the dove in him, his hagiographers too much. Neither have served him well.

The case of Pope John XXIII is if anything even less straightforward. People who attract a vast spontaneous personal affection rarely invite level-headed judgements, least of all in an age of rapid and ready publicity. Either they are credited with implausible and superhuman qualities and achievements, or they are by reaction dismissed as myths; the creations of popular legend in whose most trivial action deep wells of significance are imagined. They are judged to be either super-serpents disguised as doves or endearing doves mythologized as serpents. Neither of these extremes is plausible for a great churchman; they will not place him in the apostolic succession even though he be Pope.

Though this seems to me a valid historical generality I have not used it as a presupposition in writing this book. I have merely examined a number of facts and pronouncements which, insofar as they can be understood at this stage of history, seem to bear it out. It is sometimes said that most of what has been written about the Second Vatican Council is elementary epic—contrasts of cowboys and Indians, villains and heroes, princes of darkness and princes of light though all dressed in crimson; but doves and serpents rarely lend themselves to epic.

After some doubts I have used the term *integralist* throughout to designate a persistent and troublesome element in Catholic life;[1] it is not to be identified with 'conservative' as opposed to 'progressive', because men may wish to conserve a variety of things without repudiating progress, and many of those churchmen commonly labelled 'progressive' today are chiefly moved by a desperate desire to conserve, though the chance layers of history may make them seem innovators. The integralist is a different kind of animal; being rarely concerned merely with eternal values,[2] he is too prone to see these threatened by any change of their temporal embodiment. The great churchmen of history commonly spoke of 'despising' the world they did so much for, but were rarely afraid of change, because they did not confuse the eternal with the immobile. Fruitful dying and resurrection are integral to Christianity: ossification is not; but the integralist thinks to preserve only by ossification. Attachment to the outward form commits him to much that alienates the world he is there to save—makes his good news sound like a stale and repetitious story.

But to repudiate integralism is not to repudiate the old and the enduring. It is only to repudiate what has ceased to have touch with life. Of this truth, it seems to me, Pius XII and John XXIII

[1] But one which has encountered very severe, perhaps decisive, attacks in the Second Vatican Council.

[2] Hence the paradoxical alliance of a generation or more ago between French-Italian integralism and the atheist Charles Maurras.

were deeply possessed, though each expressed it after his own manner; John XXIII perhaps more rapidly and instinctively, with less intensity of searching. The magisterial manner of Pius XII sometimes expressed, sometimes distracted attention from a keen restless mind, such as sees things dialectically, even with a certain innate scepticism, though this was overborne by a profound faith and a piety unsparing of self. Whatever integralists read into his utterances it is practically impossible for a pope to be an integralist. Contrasted though they are, Pius and John seem to me to be much further removed from that position than they are from each other.

W. A. PURDY

Rome, July 1965

I

Prologue

On May 28, 1917, a gilt baroque coach drove Eugenio Pacelli, the recently created titular Archbishop of Sardes, through the streets of Munich to the court of Ludwig of Bavaria, to present his credentials as Vatican envoy. The last of the Wittelsbachs, the family that had begun to rule Bavaria in 1180 and had given its share of trouble to the medieval popes, had rather less than eighteen months left to reign. Bavaria, the most independent of the German states, retained its own diplomatic service, and Pacelli's object, which he was to achieve, was to negotiate a concordat between it and the Papacy. This historic Catholic state had recently produced Döllinger, bitterest opponent of papal infallibility, and in the three years following the Great Definition it had expelled the Jesuits and the Redemptorists from its confines. There was scope for negotiation.

The gilt coach passed through a rather drab, war-worn city, still retaining then its baroque splendours but full of strained and hungry citizens. It was already a world of contrasts, but the imminent end of the old Bavarian order could not have been easily guessed as the Archbishop drove up. The Russian Revolution had a few weeks earlier weakened the Allies; the spring offensive on the western front had failed; the sapping of Italian morale that led to Caporetto was already well advanced; inadequate British forces were doing badly in Palestine. If, as has been said, war offensives are aimed at the minds of rulers then Germany, and Bavaria with it, were still immune. But two days after the Archbishop's call on the king, General Pershing was appointed commander of the American Expeditionary Force. Pacelli was to stay in Munich more than long enough to see the complete turn of the tide, and all the problems that came with it. As an ecclesiastical peacemaker Pacelli, who was only just forty-one, was plunged in at the deep end; it took him five difficult years to complete the job. But during the time he was already getting on with others; a month after arriving in Munich he was in Berlin, talking to Bethmann-Hollweg the Chancellor and to the Kaiser, who gave the famous impression of him: 'Pacelli is an attractive and distinguished man, of high intelligence with very fine manners: he is the perfect model of an eminent prelate of the Catholic Church'.

There is a touch of the world of the gilt coach about the description. Pacelli was well equipped to negotiate concordats in the old world of the seventeen German states. He spoke German so well that it became almost his second tongue. Later, when he was Pope, the German Ambassador at the Vatican, Von Bergen, one day came out of an audience exploding with irritation: 'Why does he insist on talking French [the official diplomatic language] when he speaks German as well as I do?' Pacelli came of a family which had been in legal service to the Papacy for a century; he was born into the world of the *aristocrazia nera* when it was still smarting after six years of Piedmontese liberal government. The purpose of a concordat is to secure the essential bases for Catholic life and action; Pacelli may well have relished better the taking up of this challenge in a world of seasoned dynasties than in one of upstart régimes tinged with all the errors of the *Syllabus* (see page 77).

But in Protestant Berlin his business was not concordats for the moment; he was there to press the Vatican peace plan on the Prussians. Like most belligerents who think they are going to win, the Kaiser was lukewarm about neutral peace plans, and Pacelli returned empty-handed to the Munich nunciature. Where did his personal sympathies lie? Before patriotism (fervent enough with him, as will be seen) had weighted them with the entry of Italy into the war, he had been coupled with Benedict XV by Don Gregory of the British Legation as the only genuine neutral in a mainly pro-German Vatican. When the Kaiser's war broke out the Allies were decidedly at a diplomatic disadvantage in the Vatican compared with the Central powers. There was no French ambassador, and it was not until December 1914 that England sent a mission under Sir Hubert Howard, which later under Count de Salis became a modest Legation. At the conclave which elected Benedict XV, Aidan Gasquet, a John Bull set down in the Roman Curia, had had to listen to Italian cardinals telling him that 'the war was entirely made by English and French Freemasonry, which was striving to drag Italy into a war which would overwhelm the Church'. (Shane Leslie, *Cardinal Gasquet*, p. 235.) In March 1915, when a new Belgian ambassador to the Holy See was announced, the *Osservatore Romano* caused a diplomatic incident by commenting that 'he was coming to pursue his policy of anti-Germanism at the Curia'. (*ibid.* p. 240.) Gregory was not even satisfied with the Pope's attitude, reading him lectures on the deplorable effect of papal silence about German atrocities in Belgium, and asking rhetorically what Gregory VII or Innocent III would have done in a similar case. It was a lesson that Pacelli may have recalled a quarter of a century later—that those who normally take least notice of popes are in times of stress most demanding that popes should assume a medieval grandeur in their interests.

Back in Munich from Berlin, the Nuncio had another lesson which left its stamp on him—his first experience of Marxist revolution. The German collapse brought the barricades, with crates of Soviet pamphlets, to the baroque city; age-old privilege, gracious living were suddenly on the run. One day Pacelli found his reception room filled not with deferential couriers or diplomats but with ruffians bristling rather awkwardly with small arms. They were ambitious to steal his carriage, which in fact he had been using mainly to distribute relief in the poorer quarters of the city. He seems to have conducted himself with aristocratic dignity and calm, and no harm came to him, but he was shaken, and before the brief revolution was over Gasparri, the Cardinal Secretary of State, had ordered him to rest in Switzerland—in the convent at Rorschach, where he was first looked after by Sister Pasqualina. Munich and the Nuncio quickly recovered and it was with something of the old style that he was seen off to Berlin in July 1925, the Bavarian Concordat skilfully achieved.

His task in Berlin was altogether weightier and of wider scope, and its execution has been generally regarded as a masterpiece of diplomatic technique. But it was the diplomacy of a great churchman, not merely of a professional: apostolic diplomacy. Pacelli certainly set up a brilliant establishment in Berlin, and drew every advantage from it. Hindenburg, the British Ambassador Lord D'Abernon, Dorothy Thompson, then a foreign correspondent in Berlin, have all been cited in witness of his skill and of his exact and copious information. He made in fact a major contribution to the favourable image of Vatican diplomacy that was established between the wars. But what was said by the Roman diplomatic corps to Archbishop Montini when he left Rome for Milan could eminently have been said to Archbishop Pacelli when he left Berlin for Rome—'behind the diplomat we have always discerned the priest'. He was not a Vatican envoy of whom only diplomatic and social circles were aware. He was tireless in addressing every kind of audience, and whether in the Rhineland or in Protestant Prussia (especially perhaps in the latter) his theme was the Catholic and Latin origins of German civilization. St Boniface was the protagonist of most of his discourses.

If he carried through a concordat with the Prussia of Bismarck and Hegel in the teeth of the most virulent Protestantism in Europe, it was not by muting the trumpets that had sounded in the Vatican of 1870 and grated on the ears of Bismarck. An interesting essay remains to be written on what Pacelli's sojourn in Germany contributed to German ecumenism, considered afterwards so daring and advanced by many who regarded Pius XII as something of a symbol of intransigence.

The present writer well remembers the buzz of interest that accompanied the return to Rome of Archbishop Pacelli, who everyone knew was shortly to be cardinal and Secretary of State. Physically and morally his presence dominated the Vatican and St Peter's. What one remembers most is the gravity and the striking absorption in prayer. As archpriest of the basilica he would often be found kneeling, unnaturally still, saying his prayers there. The magnetism was quite unstudied and there was then of course none of the intensity, the tremendous gestures which became so marked in later years. (I remember noticing this contrast sharply during a public audience in the Holy Year of 1950, and reflecting that this was not altogether the man I remembered.) The only figure that invited comparison was Merry del Val (Secretary of State and closest collaborator of Pius X in the stormy Modernist days), who was older, whose star was no longer in the ascendant and who certainly gave no impression of a comparable potential. By contrast other Italian cardinals left little imprint on the memory.

A personal contact with this seemingly austere, hieratic personage was an experience to astonish. A group of us, raw young students, once served his Benediction at the Lucchesi convent. We were given wine and biscuits by the nuns afterwards. The Cardinal Secretary of State came and sat among us, and when we had got over our astonishment we chattered away, doing most of the talking while the great man gave every evidence of being interested only in what each of us was saying. It was one of those impressions that stick firmly over the years. There can have been few men it is less satisfactory to read about, or to read, or even to contemplate the public image. The personal contact was decisive. The personal attraction was, moreover, in its strength and in its limits, that which goes with an interior life—a dwelling apart from a world with which one is by training and tasks deeply involved.

A fair amount had been happening in the world of Rome during Pacelli's absence in Germany. In January 1922 the tough, scholarly, authoritarian Lombard Pius XI had succeeded to the papal throne, and to a Vatican treasury almost emptied by the charities of his predecessor, and in October of the same year Mussolini's Fascists had marched on Rome. The interval between this and the formal assumption of dictatorial powers by the one-time Socialist agitator (January 3, 1925) offered an interesting picture of the two-generations-old Italian state and a no less interesting temperature chart of Church-State relations. The novelist Bacchelli, a year before the March, had noted that 'Italy abhors dictatorship to the same degree that she needs it'. Giolitti had managed a degree of concealed dictatorship, but he could no longer conceal the bankruptcy of the immature laic inheritance of 1870. There were plenty of Catholics, clerical and other, to point this out and to indicate even more sinister strains in Italian liberalism, but the obvious Catholic alternative, Don Sturzo's *Partito Popolare*, was hardly more welcome in clerical circles and itself exemplified the seemingly inevitable fissiparous character of Italian political association. That ecclesiastical, and papal, coolness froze the Popular Party to death in those vital years seems established beyond reasonable doubt. The memories of two generations of anticlericalism, of Modernism (cf. p. 296) too (Murri, one of the priest pioneers of popularism, had ended as Modernist), made the Church unable to contemplate a Catholic party free of clerical leading strings. Yet the very existence of the Popular Party bore witness to the fact that Italian Catholic opinion had never been unanimous in its rejection of the *Risorgimento*. 'The Italian Church,' Binchy has said roundly, 'was a house divided against itself on the whole question.' The tragic extent to which the policy of *non possumus* had weakened Catholic influence in Italian public life was revealed for all to see in the months of political vacuum that made Mussolini's career possible. Not the least feature of the tragedy was that there were so many churchmen so obsessed with other (admittedly real) dangers that they were ready, then and subsequently, to take Fascist protestations at their face value.

Not that the clerics were alone in failing to grasp the implications of Fascism. Even the murder of the Socialist Matteotti (following on the equally brutal though less publicized murder of the priest Don Minzoni) failed to drive many liberals from the government, though it prompted De Gasperi to outline a formula of co-operation between popularism and moderate socialism, aimed at forcing Mussolini's departure. But the press law of July 1924 suppressed Sturzo's *Il Popolo*, the Socialist *Avanti* and the radical *Il Mondo*, and Pius XI set his face firmly against De Gasperi's proposal, in a speech interesting to compare with post-war ecclesiastical (though not papal) pronouncements on *centro-sinistra* policies: '. . . the collaboration of Catholics with Socialists in other countries is mentioned; but because of lack of practice in making distinctions two quite different cases are being confused. Aside from the difference of environments, in their historical, political and religious conditions, it is one thing to face a party that has already come to power, and another to open the way for this party and give it the possibility of arriving; the matter is essentially different.'

Expressing his pain at the idea of splitting Catholic unity in the name of *aconfessionalità*, the Pope went on: 'But neither is it for Catholics to erect violence into a system, or perpetuate the threat of it. . . . Would it not be more fruitful, indeed necessary and proper, for all Catholics to put the great principles of faith and religion, which they profess and from which no part of their life can or should be exempted, at the basis of every activity of theirs, even political?'

It may well have been that at that point De Gasperi's proposal was a desperate and Utopian expedient, but if Catholics were also to avoid connivance in 'erecting violence into a system', it is hard to see what *political* alternative remained to them. The Pope's last paragraph hardly represented one. In any case the matter was soon to become sadly academic: less than four months later Mussolini shed the rags of the parliamentary cloak and shortly afterwards the accession of the brutal Farinacci to the party secretariat fixed the fundamental character of Fascism once for all.

A good deal of post-war writing about the Fascist era consists, of course, of being wise after the event. It is regrettably easy nowadays to make anthologies of silliness culled from ecclesiastical publications and speeches during the years between the opening of the negotiations that led to the Lateran pacts and the issue of *Non Abbiamo Bisogno*, and again later under the patriotic stresses induced by war. But other people were making fools of themselves over Italian Fascism at the same time, even in England. Nevertheless, it is hard to avoid embarrassment at the reactions of much Italian Catholicism to the Fascist régime. They were much conditioned by the prevalent old-womanish attitude to liberal anticlericalism, which tended to exaggerate greatly the hardships which the Church had suffered since 1870. Binchy has shown convincingly enough that, as he puts it, 'all the noisy demonstrations of "militant atheism" and secularist zeal were merely froth on the surface of Italian life'. The Italians are in day-to-day relations a kindly and tolerant folk, and to speak of 'persecution' during the pre-Fascist era is as Binchy quite rightly says 'fantastic'. The real criticism of the Piedmontese governments was that they consistently neglected their own principle of '*libera chiesa in libero stato*' (free Church in free State), interfering with ecclesiastical appointments, etc. On the other hand, far more ecclesiastics were to be imprisoned during the ten years following the 'reconciliation' with the Fascist régime than during the entire period between 1870 and 1929.

Cardinal Pacelli did not become Secretary of State until a year after the signing of the Lateran pacts, but his own brother, the distinguished lawyer Francesco, was one of their architects and there is little doubt that the Nuncio in Berlin was intimately aware of the negotiations. He shared with the Pope, otherwise so contrasted a character, a strong patriotism which he was rarely at much pains to conceal. Binchy has in fact argued that Pius XI would have settled the Roman Question with any government—his ambition to do so was clear months before anyone could have foreseen the Fascist seizure of power. It has often been said that the reconciliation was the work of two authoritarians, but though the manner in which it was carried out and sprung on the world certainly suggested this, it did in fact reflect the wishes of the overwhelming majority of Italians.

But if a few churchmen more exuberant than perceptive saw themselves basking in a new Christian Empire, there is no reason to suppose that the principal actors had many illusions. Mussolini of course was the supreme Italian opportunist, fundamentally irreligious, sceptical in everything except belief in himself and his star. Cardinal Gasparri, the Secretary of State who signed the pacts, was an inscrutable character, at heart very strongly anti-Fascist, concerned in the tradition of his department to strike the best bargain for the Church. Of Pius XI, one or two unhappily worded utterances (notably the one following the end of the Ethiopian War) are familiar quotations with unsympathetic writers, but it was never supposed in the Rome of those days that he harboured any illusions. On the day of the signing he was due to address the parish priests and Lenten preachers of Rome, and offered them his own account of what had been done. He accepted full personal responsibility. To those who spoke of guarantees he offered 'Our own consciousness of the rightness of Our cause, the sense of justice of the Italian people, a trust in divine providence. . . . Future dangers are no greater than they were before,' he said, 'and no better guide to conduct. What will the morrow bring? The answer is, we do not know. *Fiat voluntas tua!*' This was hardly the voice of gullibility; it was a pity perhaps that two days later the Pope saw fit to supplement it by talking to (ironically enough) Father Gemelli's young men from Milan about providence having ordained a meeting with a man free of the prejudices of the liberal school, and about God having been given back to Italy and Italy to God. Yet even here, allowing for some rhetoric, one reflects that every concordat involves *some* willingness to believe well of the other side. Generosity hardly weakened the papal position; rather it lent strength to every succeeding protest against Fascist duplicity. Of these the first came after just three months, and it touched the crucial issue between Fascism and the Church—education. In a debate on the treaty in the chamber, which produced, as well as some interesting speeches, an orgy of Fascist self-praise and pseudo-Dantesque mystical nonsense about the eternal destinies of Rome, Mussolini uttered this threat: 'In this matter we are inflexible. Education must be our liability. These children must be brought up in our religious faith, but we must complete their upbringing, we must give these young men a sense of manhood, of power, of conquest.' And he concluded with a blustering passage, aimed clearly at the Pope, to the effect that

'Big Brother is watching you'. It is interesting to reflect on this speech as one contemplates the middle-aged Italian of today, with his mainly Left inclinations. Any Italian between the ages of thirty and forty-five received his early education under Fascism, but for the most part he suggests the achievement of neither of the dictator's avowed aims: he is neither religious nor bellicose.

The Pope was prompt to react to the speech; on this and subsequent occasions, as Jemolo has shrewdly pointed out, Mussolini's blustering simply offered Pius an opportunity to re-assert the terms of the pacts and the Church's primacy in more and more uncompromising terms. From the standpoint of today, there is something invigorating about those months which culminated in the issue of *Non Abbiamo Bisogno*—a touch of Ambrose, of Hildebrand, of Innocent III, sharply in contrast with the Byzantine atmosphere which at times weighed like a *sirocco* on the country between 1931–8 and again during the war years.

'To militant Catholics the world of pure politics had become a stable world with which they no longer needed to concern themselves. They had no obvious political problems to contend with; they had only a religious task to fulfil. So it was that men of transparent piety had not the slightest scruple about editing Catholic daily newspapers in which three pages out of four bore the unmistakable imprint of the Ministry of Popular Culture, being filled with the *bourrage des crânes*, with all the obligatory hate propaganda directed against the democracies, with eulogies of the war-like spirit and so forth, while the fourth page was devoted to pious reflections and religious gossip. They never suspected for a moment that they were doing anything wrong, and they would never realize why, sixteen years later [after the war] a few anti-Fascists with long memories were wont to eye them with suspicion.'—Jemolo, *Church and State in Italy*, p. 259.

This account is the more devastating for its moderation. The uncritical attitude of Italian Catholicism as a whole to Fascism was the bitter fruit of years of practical estrangement from public life and of a far too academic approach to political thinking.[1] During the Ethiopian and Spanish wars this uncritical attitude grew into a

[1] Jacini, speaking of the *Partito Popolare* programme said, 'If there is one comment to be made today (1951), in the light of experience on this list of demands, it is that which appeared repeatedly from the start in the Liberal press; it was too complete, one might almost say too stuffed.'

patriotic euphoria which produced some utterances that make very depressing reading now. It was not until Mussolini embarked on his culminating peacetime folly of trailing after the Nazi racial policies that the native Italian sense and moderation began to reassert itself, and even then there were some pretty silly things said and written by Catholic public figures, not least by Father Gemelli, rector of the Catholic university of Milan. The Pope spoke firmly against this new Fascist fanaticism more than once, but many writers have felt that the Vatican might have been firmer in disciplining priests and Catholic notabilities who compromised the Church by even qualified approval of racism.

It was widely believed that Pius XI, in the speech he was to deliver on February 11, the tenth anniversary of the Lateran Treaty, intended a full-scale denunciation of current Fascist policies. But he died the day before. '*Finalmente . . . quel vecchio ostinato è morto* (At last . . . the obstinate fellow's dead,)' Bruno Mussolini reported his father as saying. It was one of the most eloquent tributes paid to Pius XI: in seventeen years Mussolini had not encountered nearly enough Catholic obstinacy.

Few students of the period have found it easy to assess the rôle of Cardinal Pacelli in the decade preceding the outbreak of the Second World War, the decade during which he was Secretary of State. He was an exact and tireless worker, and like so many busy men found time to do other things as well—more specifically priestly tasks. He was to all appearances a punctilious collaborator of Pius XI, and enjoyed his complete confidence in the policies just briefly sketched. The late Cardinal Tardini has illustrated how Pius XI was convinced that Pacelli would succeed him. Of his various travels, to the Americas and to France, Pius XI said to Tardini, 'I send him about so that the world may know him and he know the world—he'll make a fine pope'. When the conclave met following Pius XI's death, Pacelli was invited to address the Sacred College, for their guidance, on the policy of the late Pope, and the result was that, with notable speed they elected the Secretary of State.

Yet the contrasts between the two men were more marked than their affinities. Tardini has well expressed this. Pius XI 'at least outwardly enjoyed a fight. Pius XII quite visibly suffered'. Once Pius XI had made up his mind, he was no longer open to persuasion and even inclined to cut people off before they could embark on it.

By contrast 'Pius XII was, by natural temperament, mild and rather timid. He was not born with the temper of a fighter. . . . The same tendency which led him to prefer solitude and quiet disposed him rather to avoid than to confront the battles of life. His great goodness inclined him to satisfy everybody and upset nobody, to prefer the ways of sweetness to those of severity, persuasion to imposition.'

He loved, Tardini went on, to 'sugar the pill'—it was his own phrase—and often when his convictions forbade him to say 'yes' his temperament made it hard for him to say 'no'. It would be tempting, though risky and unprofitable, to consider Church-State relations in the Italy of the pre-war decade in the light of these contrasting and complementary characters, Pope and Secretary. The more pacific Cardinal had closer links with and a more intimate knowledge of Roman life and society than the Lombard Pope, and the patching up of the rupture which culminated in *Non Abbiamo Bisogno* may well have been largely his work: he is said to have seen Mussolini before the better-known, very strained and frigid meeting between Pope and Duce took place.

The Encyclical was the high moment of Pius XI's reign; he obviously enjoyed writing it and it bore very much his personal stamp, quite different from the conventional Vatican style; Binchy has quoted a foreign non-Catholic witness that it 'simply took the Italians' breath away' and it brought in a great volume of foreign approval and congratulation. The funniest comment came from the notorious Monsignor Cornaggia Medici, Canon of St Mary Major, of whom it was said that he could see no difference between a Catholic and a Fascist: 'You do not realize that under all the strong words there was love . . . and joined to the love a precious paternal declaration regarding the substance of Fascism.'

The Fascist authorities themselves proved less perceptive than the Monsignor. Violence was switched on like a tap, but very soon switched off again. A complete rupture was not in the government's interest; nevertheless settlement of the quarrel was a compromise. Catholic Action retained its unique position as the only institution in Fascist Italy able to recruit and operate free of the totalitarian machinery, but it was more rigidly confined than ever to religious activity and diocesan control. As will be seen, this had two interesting consequences for post-war Italian history: it ensured that some form of Catholic organization was there to make its contribution to salvaging the state from the wreck of Fascism; it ensured at the same time that this same tradition should have a strongly clerical colour—something which constituted one of De Gasperi's major problems, and which was aggravated after his death. Italian public life still suffers from the malnutrition and stunted growth of the Fascist era.

If one can only suspect that there was more of Ratti than of Pacelli in Vatican-Fascist dealings down to 1939, it is much easier to assess Cardinal Pacelli's influence in Vatican dealings with Germany and with nascent Nazism. Here the Secretary of State was the acknowledged expert. The Concordat signed with the Third Reich in the first months of Hitler's power was simply the culmination of efforts Pacelli had begun long before with the Weimar republic. Hitler no doubt, like Mussolini, saw kudos to be gained by doing in a few months what had not been done before in years, without binding on himself any burden heavier than his own estimate of the seriousness of contracts. On the other hand there was hardly a man in Europe less likely to have illusions about Nazism than Pacelli. The Concordat provided no more than an essential basis for action and protest; even less than in Italy did it provide secure and healthy environment for Catholicism. Much of Pacelli's remaining time at the secretariat of state was to be taken up in addressing protests to Germany. His part in the Encyclical *Mit Brennender Sorge* has been recently confirmed by the publication, in the Italian paper *Concretezza*, of a facsimile showing substantial corrections in his hand. The present Italian Minister of Defence, Andreotti, in the same issue has a note claiming that the Italian government archives show Pacelli as the instigator of the Vatican boycott of Hitler's visit to Rome in May 1938: a surprising reversal of the characteristic rôles of Pope and Secretary. The papal household left for Castelgandolfo, where Pius XI told an audience that 'this is not the time and place, this feast of the Holy Cross, to see raised in Rome another cross which is not the cross of Christ'. It was sad that in other parts of Italy timid Catholic press comment could be summed up as, 'What a pity our friends the Germans are being so tiresome towards the Church.'

In the autumn of 1936 Cardinal Pacelli had spent a month in the United States, the first papal Secretary of State to go to North America. Beginning as an invitation to a holiday at the Long Island home of the famous Duchess Brady, the visit, stage-managed by the then Auxiliary Bishop of Boston, Francis Spellman, who had served part of his time in the Vatican Secretariat of State as a clerk under Pacelli, developed into an intensive tour of the States and ended with a call upon Roosevelt. At that time dislike of Hitler was by no means universal in America, where many German immigrants had sharp memories of the humiliations and hardships following Versailles but little knowledge of the real nature of National Socialism. Six months later, Cardinal Mundelein of Chicago made his 'paperhanger' speech to the clergy of his archdiocese, which sent Von Bergen, the German chargé d'affaires at the Vatican, hot-foot to the Secretariat of State with a protest. Pacelli answered that he did not comment on speeches without seeing the full text, and countered by asking what the Nazi government was doing about the German press campaign of calumny against priests and religious, apart from encouraging it. A further German protest was answered equally firmly, and in the following November the American hierarchy in unison sent a long and resounding message of encouragement and solidarity to their German counterparts.

The weight of these *démarches* was the greater in that they came from the great home of anti-Communism, and Hitler was at that time beating the anti-communist drum busily, not without effect on ordinary American opinion.[1]

In July 1936 Cardinal Pacelli had gone as papal legate to the consecration of the vast, ugly new basilica of St Thérèse at Lisieux. During the visit he attended a number of official functions in Paris and preached a memorable sermon in Notre Dame. The visit elicited a good deal of abuse from the Nazi press, which charged the Church with making common cause with the Popular Front and a policy of encircling Germany.

When Cardinal Innitzer, the Sudeten German Archbishop of Vienna, spoke an incautious welcome to the German Anschluss in March 1938, he was summoned at once to Rome where he had interviews first with Pacelli and then with Pius XI. (The French Ambassador, Charles-Roux, reported that Pacelli for once spoke with real bitterness of this lapse), Innitzer was ordered to sign an

[1] Robert I. Gannon (*The Cardinal Spellman Story*, p. 177) tells how during this visit 'someone at Mrs Brady's dinner-table had asked His Eminence in an off-hand way about the situation in his beloved Germany. At the moment he was laughing heartily at an Americanism he had just learned, but when Germany was mentioned a cloud passed over his face, he raised his slender expressive hands in a gesture of helplessness and answered—"Everything is lost".'

annulment of his declaration and to go back to Vienna and face the music properly, which he did.

These highlights of Cardinal Pacelli's dealings with Nazi Germany as Secretary of State are a necessary preliminary to any judgement of Pope Pius XII's attitudes during the war. (Cf. below, pp. 41 *et seq.*, and also Chapter 11.) They need to be supplemented too by the consideration that, over and above constant diplomatic activity, he kept a close hand on the considerable *Osservatore Romano* and Vatican Radio output dealing with Germany. Without exaggerating the international impact of these labours, they provide more than enough evidence that the future Pope had no tenderness towards National Socialism. That he had strong German sympathies need hardly be questioned. He had spent many happy years there; he spoke the language perfectly, he liked having Germans about him. German ways suited his very precise temperament. As much could be said for hundreds of people in England, whose patriotism nobody felt the need to question during the war. The same facts hardly provide better ground for questioning the genuineness of Pacelli's impartiality, or the disinterestedness of his subsequent efforts for peace.

Reference to these Vatican activities during the years of pre-war dictatorship should not end without notice of something much less obtrusive, but perhaps in some ways of more consequence for the future. In the Vatican Library during those years worked the Austrian-educated Tridentine and old enemy of Mussolini, Alcide De Gasperi. About the time Hitler came to power, De Gasperi began to write a political commentary in the fortnightly *Illustrazione Vaticana*, and continued to do so for the five years until the paper disappeared in 1938. An admirer of the German Zentrum (cf. Chapter 11), he rejected the neurotic anti-liberalism which distorted so much Catholic political thinking at the time, not least in Italy. For too many Italians, among whom clerics were prominent, the word 'liberal' simply summoned up nightmares of Garibaldi, freemasons, international Jewish financiers and *carbonari.* Though he believed that the welfare state must be accepted in a moderate degree if Christian and not Marxist ideals were to control the future of democracy, De Gasperi was strongest in insisting on the importance of liberty as a Christian and human value: 'Although the co-operation of public powers is always desirable, what is important in contemporary life is that the Catholic Church enjoy that degree of ordered liberty that would permit her to live her own religious life *publicly and integrally* and to exercise her peaceful spiritual ministry.' (Italics mine.)

Pre-war history clearly revealed, from 1929 in Italy and from 1933 in Germany, the dangerous paradox of existence under concordats in authoritarian states (cf. Chapter 4): that it tended to undermine the appetite for that fullness of liberty which the concordat was designed basically to secure. De Gasperi wrote the above passage as early as 1935, and he was still insisting on the same theme at the fourth congress of Italian Christian Democracy seventeen eventful years later: 'The conclusion to which experience has led us today is this: the dictatorships of the past, the dictatorship threatened for tomorrow [Communism], the unavoidable pressure of the state bureaucracy and of systematic state intervention, have brought to the fore—*whatever any theory*, reflection or discussion may conclude—the need to insist on freedom, personal and political.' (Italics mine.)

In 1935 De Gasperi was hardly even a voice crying in the wilderness, but it was something—a better illustration perhaps of the real value of the independence created by the Lateran pacts than much official Vatican activity—that the future Prime Minister was able, until a little before Pius XI's death, to give expression to these ideals, even in what Webster[1] calls 'the cautious muffled tones of Vatican journalism'. For they were not fashionable in that hey-day of the Axis, even in the Vatican. De Gasperi was later to remind us that he never set foot in the Secretariat of State during his years in the Vatican.[2] It was to be the achievement of John XXIII, certainly no 'Liberal' in any sense given to the word in Italy since the *Risorgimento*, to make the world wonder whether in the Vatican the last fears of liberty might not be on the brink of exorcism.

[1] *Christian Democracy in Italy, 1860–1960*, Richard Webster.

[2] Cf. Chapter 4 where this theme is developed at greater length.

2

The War Years

ROME IN FACT presented a rather depressing spectacle at the death of Pius XI. Instead of the thunders he was hoping to be spared to deliver, there appeared, on the tenth anniversary of the Lateran Treaty, the first number of *Illustrazione Romana*, a glossy periodical full of advertisements of Catholic banks and insurance companies and having a variety of contributors whose only common bond was, as Webster (*op. cit.* p. 120) puts it, 'exalting the Vatican, the Monarchy and the Régime in one breath'.

This represented a breaking into the open of Clerico-Fascism, a term which was and still is used as a vague term of abuse by the Italian Left, but which truly describes a precise and quite limited current whose lay members were mostly drawn from among the rich. Such people inclined to view even the last and worst aberrations of Fascism more in sorrow than in anger, inclined as they were temperamentally to regard 'strong government' as the natural ally and prop, not so much of the Church as of ecclesiastical organization. Anyone who passed through his impressionable years at this time and who knew Rome well will find memory a better guide than any amount of reading to the peculiar atmosphere that existed: a better guide, too, to much of Church-State relations in the late fifties and to many attitudes revealed at the Second Vatican Council among older conservatives. One well-known English Jesuit then lecturing at the Gregorian had to be transferred a very long distance, so intolerable did he find the atmosphere. That this atmosphere was also to be found among the rank and file of careerists in the Vatican it would be naïve to doubt.

It was in such an atmosphere that the conclave met to select a successor to Pius XI. There is no evidence that the totalitarian powers showed any special interest in the election, nor any special emotion at its result, though this is unlikely to have been popular with the Nazis. Oddly, the German Ambassador Von Bergen happened to be doyen of the diplomatic corps at the Vatican, so by protocol he spoke the sympathies of the diplomats to the college of cardinals. Apart from a reference to 'a new world' and 'the ruins of the past' his speech was the customary string of sonorous commonplaces.[1] Everybody must have realized that it was less likely than ever that any but an Italian would be chosen at this moment; any other choice would have set the world by the ears—and Mussolini had no cause to be dissatisfied at the choice of an Italian. There were several he might have preferred to Pacelli, but on the whole he could reflect that the latter's influence on Pius XI (the *vecchio ostinato*) had been generally moderating, in that concordatory tradition which Pius XI had established (he had in fact signed such instruments with no less than thirteen nations) but which temperamentally did not altogether suit him. It is true that Ciano's paper *Il Telegrafo* placed Pacelli at the head of a list of 'political' or anti-Fascist candidates (Ciano had never got over the fact that a cameraman once caught him kneeling beside the Secretary of State with his hands flat-joined in prayer)[2] but the head of the information bureau at the Ministry of Press and Propaganda eventually told reporters that the choice 'might have been worse'—by which perhaps he meant that it might have been Cardinal Mundelein.

The German press, which had been specially annoyed with Pacelli since his Notre Dame sermon eighteen months earlier, was naturally more violent, describing him and caricaturing him as the 'Popular Front candidate'; but after the election Von Plessen, Chancellor at the German Embassy, contented himself with saying that 'a careful diplomat is undoubtedly better than an impulsive, irascible old man'.

All this made not the slightest difference to the conclave, which was the shortest since 1623. It made other records by electing the first Secretary of State since 1775 and the first native of Rome since 1721. When on the eve of his coronation the new Pope appointed the cheerful Neapolitan Luigi Maglione to the Secretariat of State

[1] Yet Padellaro, the Italian biographer of Pius XII, managed to read it (1956) as an 'outrageous' invitation to the sacred college 'to elect a pope in the image of Hitler'!

[2] The photograph is reproduced in Tardini's *Pio XII*.

(he was a former Paris nuncio and a reputed Francophile) there was a general feeling that the Axis had been reasonably snubbed[1]—a feeling that some of the foreign press, especially in France, indulged so robustly that the *Osservatore Romano* felt obliged in the interests of neutrality to sprinkle a little cold water. Germany alone sent no special representative to the coronation.

Two of Pius XII's leading characteristics, his extraordinary capacity for work and his immense estimate of the dignity and responsibility of his office in every field, were given dramatic scope at the outset of his reign. In Europe it was a time of intense diplomatic activity overshadowed by the sense that time was running out. There was complete continuity between the action of the Secretary of State who had been chief prop of the aged and sick Pope, and the new Pope who now became virtually his own Secretary of State. Less than a month before he died, Pius XI had received Chamberlain and Halifax; in an interesting speech he had spoken of his satisfaction that Europe had been spared war but went on: 'But the sincerity due to Our apostolic responsibilities and Our age compels Us to add that We hoped this happy success [Munich] would serve not only the general peace of Europe and the world but the internal peace, the peace of soul and of conscience of the millions of Catholics in Germany whose heavy tribulations We follow and share every day—who in obedience to their cardinals and bishops do not mix in politics but pursue the sanctification and salvation of their own souls according to the teaching and laws of Christ, in that way making the most solid contribution to the welfare of their country. And this must be said of the Catholics of all countries, including—first and foremost in fact—this Italy of which you are such welcome guests. We are sure that you are reliably informed of this, though every day downright calumnies are put out to persuade the world otherwise. . . .'

Whatever the accuracy of this comprehensive account of the demeanour of Catholics in Axis countries, it was a clear expression of the conviction that Munich had not done much for them; privately Pius XI, less oracularly and more characteristically, had described Munich as 'not ever a capitulation but a *capitombolo*'

[1] This did not prevent Von Bergen sending a despatch saying Maglione was really pro-German. Cf. Friedlander, *Pie XII et le IIIe Reich,* who calls this the 'true meaning of the appointment'!

(somersault). He further told Chamberlain that he (Pius) was not in the habit of exaggerating, that there was real persecution in Germany and, in effect, that any 'peace' which turned a blind eye to it was a mockery. Chamberlain said he fully agreed, but doubted whether much was to be hoped from periodical formal protests: Hitler took little notice of these, especially from people who were not in his good graces, and British prestige did not stand very high with Hitler at that moment! His government would do its best for Catholics and Jews in Germany when the occasion offered. It was to be a long time before it did—too long for thousands of Catholics and Jews.

This was the last meeting of Pius XI with any head of government. With his death a certain edge went out of the papal voice, perhaps. In the rather slow, deep-voiced discourse of Pius XI there was nearly always an element of improvisation—he rarely wrote down more than notes, and his salty Lombard humour would break in here and there. Pius XII's speeches were altogether more deliberate and carefully planned. He did not use a manuscript, except in later days at the microphone, but he wrote the speech out in full and, having a phenomenal visual memory, soon had it by heart. 'He was well aware,' wrote Tardini, 'that he lacked the gift of improvisation,' and always tried to avoid the need of it. He had earlier suffered from a slight stammer, which he could counteract best by a somewhat declamatory delivery.

From the moment of his first broadcast, made from the Sistine Chapel the day after his election, March 3, until the outbreak of war, the Pope continually made exhortations to peace, and supplemented these with considerable diplomatic activity. But though the latter, naturally, was aimed at forestalling the outbreak of hostilities, the speeches never suggested that peace could be bought at any price, or that *any* kind of postponement would suffice. The first broadcast referred to 'integral peace', and mentioned, first, peace of conscience, second, peace among families and, only last, peace among nations, to be based on mutual help and collaboration in the interests of the human family as a whole. At Easter (April 9) he again spoke of peace being sought where it was not to be found, while solemn agreements and the pledged word had lost their security and value. At the end of April the Pope approached Mussolini—through the Jesuit Tacchi-Venturi who was sympathetic to the régime and had ready access to the Duce—with a suggestion for a five-power conference 'to find a solution of the questions which exposed the world to the danger of war'. Mussolini's comment was, 'Germany cannot delude herself that she will succeed in doing with Poland what she did with the others without bloodshed. Poland will resist; she will be overcome by superior German strength and we shall have the beginning of a European war.'[1]

The general reaction to this papal initiative was to express appreciation of its motives and avoid any commitment. The Vatican had to be satisfied with counselling calm and moderation and declaring itself ready at any time for any intermediary function. But there was no blinking at the facts—no hope or aspiration for another 'somersault'. On the contrary, at the beginning of July Maglione, by order of the Pope, asked the Italian Ambassador to the Vatican on two separate occasions (July 3 and 6) to convey to his government and through them to Germany that 'the representatives of France and England had left no doubt of their countries' determination to go to war should Germany try to resolve by violence its territorial dispute with Poland'.

It is against this background that Pius XII's peace broadcast of August 24, 1939 should be understood, and particularly its most frequently quoted sentence, 'Nothing is lost by peace; everything may be lost by war.' In those last days before the war it was capable of being misinterpreted, and was. To those who felt that peace as it had been understood since Munich was nothing but continuous subjection to blackmail, the epigram seemed very disputable. This sort of peace, far from losing nothing, seemed to involve a piecemeal giving away of everything. But nothing the Pope had ever said about peace suggested that he saw it as an inert persistence of the *status quo* of 1939.

The epigram was to the dictators a flat negation of their basic beliefs. 'Empires not founded on justice are not blessed by God,' said the Pope in the same speech. This mild echo of St Augustine's *City of God* (which speaks more bluntly of a 'great piracy' in allusion to the earlier Roman Empire founded in Africa) was clearly enough applicable to the conqueror of Ethiopia who was hoping for still easier pickings from a well-calculated jump on to the Nazi triumphal car.

[1] Friedlander (*op. cit.* pp. 32–3) says astonishingly that Giovannetti 'mentions no *démarche* of the Pope to Mussolini'. The French edition has a detailed description, pp. 54–6, by Tacchi-Venturi of his talk with the Duce.

But bellicosity, if of a less discreditable sort, was mounting among the democratic peoples too. I remember an intelligent priest exploding at the time against a Catholic editor who had written 'war settles nothing'. War is an unhappy and cruel way of settling things: it has not always, as a matter of history, been an ineffective one. For us in the 1960's the question is no longer whether war settles anything, but whether there is any conceivable issue that would be worth settling at the price of such a war as would be fought today. This was not so clear in 1939. The present dilemma, and one which caused Pius XII increasing anguish as the years passed, is that the second half of his antithesis must perhaps now read 'everything *will* be lost by war', while the first half is less than ever true if 'peace' be taken as the mere absence of hostilities. No one of course understood or proclaimed this more than Pius XII himself in the years following the war.

The last week of August was spent by the Vatican in desperate attempts through its nuncios to induce a settlement of German-Polish differences. Attention was switched to the question of minorities and their treatment: Hitler had told Henderson that this, not Danzig and the Corridor, was driving him to military measures. The Nuncio in Warsaw, Cortesi, was instructed to suggest that the Poles should undertake to avoid ill-treatment of German minorities if Germany would reciprocate the undertaking. Colonel Beck, the Polish Premier, answered that this would be tantamount to admitting the German accusations, and said any invitation by the Holy See should be made simultaneously to both powers. Cortesi suggested to Rome that this might take the form of a proposal for international control, but only the preliminary soundings had been made by the rather cautious Vatican procedure before August 31. Mussolini was approached again, and suggested that the Pope might counsel Moscicki, the Polish President, to cede Danzig and treat directly with Germany over the rest.[1]

The last Vatican effort was made on August 31, when Maglione called the representatives of the five powers together, and asked for the avoidance of incident and provocation between Germany and Poland. Next morning early the German troops crossed the Polish frontier.

In a somewhat frigid editorial the *Osservatore Romano* wrote: 'The unhappy event, to prevent which, with the unanimous

[1] For the Vatican's following-up of this suggestion see Friedlander *op cit.* pp. 40–43.

consent of all peoples, the most generous efforts were directed in recent days, has nevertheless happened. Two civilized peoples cross swords, shed blood, launch a war of rival interests, in spite of a truce that had still five years to run, and though it was declared that the rivalries could be composed without an armed conflict. To avoid resort to force is a principle not only of Christian civilization . . . but of political wisdom. Yet the twenty centuries since the Christian proclamation of human brotherhood show that force has always been the sower of force, blood of blood, offence of reprisal.' This pointed, thus early, a problem with which neutrality is constantly faced, especially if it is not a silent neutrality: does it entail blaming both sides, or is it consistent with recognizing the facts of aggression? If Germany invaded Poland, could it be said that *two* civilized peoples had launched a war?

Addressing the Belgian Ambassador a fortnight later, the Pope outlined his programme for the war he had been unable to prevent: to restrict its evils. He hoped to see civilian populations shielded from direct military operations; to see the lives, property, honour and religious feelings of occupied peoples respected; to see prisoners humanely treated and not denied the ministrations of religion; to see gas and germ warfare banned. This was in the venerable tradition of the truce of God and the peace of God—the medieval devices by which the Church had sought to mitigate the regular activities of a warrior class. A fortnight later still, with politicians, soldiers and map-makers already carving up Poland yet again, the Pope lamented the lot of the hundreds of thousands of victims of 'this war which We strove so obstinately, so ardently but alas so vainly to spare Europe and the world'; he spoke in general terms, but perhaps it was hardly necessary to add that the overwhelming majority of these victims were Poles. To Cardinal Hlond and a group of Polish refugees the Pope spoke with warm eloquence through which it seemed easy to discern his true feelings, though the preoccupation with neutrality produced what seemed in the context slightly odd, apologetic turns of phrase: 'You have come to Us for a word of comfort. Our Father's duty is to give it to you, and no one surely could have any right to be surprised.' And again 'There remains to you the radiance of a military valour which has filled even your adversaries with admiration, and to which they have faithfully rendered homage.' After saying 'We would like to hope, in spite of good reasons for doubting based on the too well known designs of the enemies of God, that Catholic life will continue deep and fruitful among you,' the speech ended movingly: 'We say not to you, Dry your tears! Christ, who wept at the death of Lazarus and the ruins of His fatherland, will gather up, to recompense one day, those tears which you pour out over your dear ones dead, over that Poland which cannot die. For the Christian, who knows their supernatural value, tears themselves have their sweetness.' And there was a reference to Chopin's skill in distilling joy from tears—a human art which the wisdom and goodness of God can surpass.[1]

Monsignor Giovannetti comments thus on these events surrounding the outbreak of war: 'Some historians have asked how far the hardening of the attitude of the Polish government and particularly of Colonel Beck *immediately* decided the declaration of war. The question exceeds the limits of these notes. What is certain is that the Holy See vainly pressed councils of moderation on both sides. And it is evident that the Holy See counted on these being received with favour by a government not hostile to itself as the Nazi government was.'

He goes on to defend Pius XII from the charge of speaking 'too late' or 'tepidly' against the violation of Poland. He argues that an interdict, for example, would have done no good to the Poles and merely put thirty million German Catholics in a dilemma of conscience, in which they must either obey the Church and risk death or annihilation of Christian life in central Europe, or obey the State and sustain a schism, equally to the ruin of Catholicism in Germany. Pius, he adds, lost no opportunity of affirming that he had children everywhere and that in both camps there were high-minded men revolted by all injustice. But to state the dilemma in terms of an interdict is perhaps to state it too sharply.

Turning to later phases of the war and to the outcome of Vatican moves to humanize it, Giovannetti (whose own sympathies seem reasonably plain) makes it absolutely clear that the German authorities were almost completely uncooperative with Vatican efforts on behalf of prisoners of war—even their own. The Nuncio in Berlin was rebuffed when, on his own initiative, he asked the government in November 1939 to enquire seriously into charges of S.S. cruelty to civilians in occupied territories. He acted in

[1] For an interesting account of Pius XII's concern with an abortive plot to depose Hitler between October 1939 and February 1940, c.f. Nobécourt, *Le Vicaire et L'Histoire*, p. 194.

response to representations made at the nunciature by German clergy, professional men and Protestant leaders. The *démarche* and response were reported to the papal Secretary of State.

In his Christmas address of 1939, the Pope spoke of 'a series of deeds irreconcilable either with natural law or with the most elementary human feelings. . . . In this category falls the premeditated aggression against a small, hardworking and peaceful people, under the pretext of a "threat" non-existent, not thought of, not even possible.' These words could be taken to refer to any or all of three countries recently invaded: Czecho-Slovakia (March), Poland (September), and Finland (November 30); but only the Finnish war was still undecided. Monsignor Giovannetti asserts that they were intended to apply to all three. But it was perhaps a little too easy for anyone whose conscience was likely to be troubled to suppose otherwise. Monsignor Giovannetti is conscious of the difficulty: 'In the face of the spiteful bearing of the contending parties or of those ready to join in, the Holy Father, though accusing nobody by name and avoiding casting the blame for the war on one or another, set out the causes of trouble for each to ponder. It was his intention not to embitter further minds already exacerbated, but rather to lead them to reflection; and if he protested and condemned, he did it with gentleness, with that love for the humble and the weak, for justice and charity, which fits the mission entrusted by Christ to his Church.'

It was possible to reflect further, of course (as some did) that Christ Himself and some past popes had occasionally considered justice and charity to demand harsher words. Another pope—a surviving Pius XI, for example—might have interpreted the situation of 1939 differently. But it is not easy even now to decide who would have been right.

'The failure of efforts for peace had for Pius XII one explanation above all—mistrust,' says Monsignor Giovannetti, and adds the explanation: 'it was the mistrust of others for the word of the German dictator.' (Giovannetti, *Il Vaticano e la Guerra, 1939-40*).

In March 1940 Ribbentrop visited Rome for consultations with the government, and asked for a papal audience. He also had two conversations amounting to an hour and a quarter with Maglione, in which he received a rough handling. He was observed to come out looking pale and angry, and Giovannetti's entertaining account of the conversations makes it easy to see why. The maladroit

Ribbentrop began with a blustering tirade about the certainty of Nazi victory, which imperfectly engaged his audience's attention. He passed on to some stock grumbles about the German clergy interfering in politics: Maglione asked him to furnish details of names and occasions, and countered with an imposing list of Catholic complaints against German administration. Ribbentrop interposed that he had not been informed of all this; Maglione answered that he had given the Ambassador a full memorandum some months earlier, and supplied a copy on the spot.

Both Pope and Secretary also harried Ribbentrop on the question of German conduct in Poland, and pressed the demand for permission to send an apostolic visitor there. (This was continuously evaded and in July the German Ambassador summoned the nerve to ask for the appointment of German bishops in Poland, Bohemia and Moravia. This request, renewed a year later and extended subsequently to Alsace-Lorraine, Luxembourg and the Austrian territories annexed from Jugoslavia, was always flatly refused by the Vatican.)

The Berlin Nuncio reported that accounts of the interview had circulated in Germany much to Ribbentrop's annoyance. There had even been exaggerated talk of a Canossa. Ribbentrop's own account had been that the Pope had made 'an extraordinary, even overwhelming impression', on him,[1] but that in the Cardinal Secretary of State he had encountered an enemy of German National Socialism. It was, says Giovannetti, a title of honour for Cardinal Maglione.

On May 10 Germany invaded Holland, Belgium and Luxembourg. Pius XII, who had warned Princess Marie José, Belgian wife of the Italian Crown Prince, of the invasion in an audience four days earlier, gave orders to the Secretariat of State for an official protest but anticipated this by typing and sending off telegrams to each of the three rulers. On June 29, after the Franco-German armistice had been signed in the forest of Compiègne, the Pope sent a noble message of encouragement and of confidence for the future of France to the French bishops.

He had just encountered a major discouragement himself, with the entry of Italy into the war on June 10. Six months earlier he

[1] Friedlander (*op. cit.* p. 56) speaks of Monsignor Giovannetti's curious reticence about this interview. But he himself gives only Ribbentrop's version of it which, if no better than his accounts of his interviews with Maglione, is valueless.

had spoken hopefully to the new Italian ambassador to the Vatican, Alfieri, of 'the wisdom of the rulers and the intimate impulse of the people which have so far kept Italy from being involved in the war'.

A few days later the King and Queen of Italy visited the Vatican, and again, in a brief speech, Pius XII said in effect: Italy is lucky to be out of the war—let her stay out and make her contribution to the peace. On his return visit to the Quirinal he urged the opportunity for Italy to earn greatness, respect, real strength by keeping the peace. On April 24 he wrote with fervour and flattering warmth to Mussolini, hoping that his 'firmness, initiative and Italian feeling would spare Our and your beloved country from so great a calamity'. Mussolini answered cordially enough but was 'unable to guarantee that the present state of things would last to the end'. (Giovannetti, *op cit.*, p. 166). A last and eloquent public plea was made by the Pope in Santa Maria sopra Minerva on May 5, 1940, five weeks before war came.

The Pope had many reasons for wishing Italy to remain out of the war. In the first place undoubtedly, his horror of war combined with his patriotism to make him anxious to spare his countrymen an enterprise for which few of them had any enthusiasm. He was convinced from the beginning that the war would be a long one. Tardini recalls how the Italian Ambassador told the Pope in August 1940 that the war was already won: The Holy Father fixed him with one of those searching looks, which knew so well how to express surprise, dissent, interrogation, and answered simply 'Really—it's won?' From the tone in which the words were spoken the diplomat, a very intelligent person, grasped that his optimism had carried him a little too far and tried to rectify it: 'It's won——virtually'. Pius XII often recalled the incident and smiled over that 'virtually'.

The Pope also hoped that abstention from the war might check the growing subservience of Italy to the Nazi policy. Distaste for this had grown both in the Vatican and in the country as a whole ever since the racial policy had been launched. A few clerical publicists might lean over backwards to squeeze a little Catholic sense out of Fascist extravagance, but the common attitude was better expressed by the thrifty onlookers who, watching troops self-consciously doing the goose-step (re-christened *passo Romano*) down the Via dei Fori Imperiali, observed that it would wear out army boots more quickly and so further burden the poor old taxpayer.

Last but by no means least, the entry of Italy into the war was likely to pose considerable problems for the functioning of the Church's administration and diplomacy. Article 12 of the Lateran Treaty laid down that 'envoys accredited by foreign governments to the Holy See shall continue to enjoy within the Kingdom of Italy all the prerogatives and immunities enjoyed by diplomatic agents under international law, even in the event of their states not being in diplomatic relations with Italy. . . .' The article went on to guarantee 'always and in all circumstances freedom of correspondence for all states including belligerents, with the Holy See and vice versa, as well as free access for bishops of the whole world to the Apostolic See'. And finally, 'the diplomatic representatives of the Holy See and all diplomatic mail forwarded in the name of the Sovereign Pontiff shall enjoy on Italian territory, even in time of war, the treatment that is due under international law to the diplomats and diplomatic mail of other foreign powers'.

As Binchy has pointed out, this by no means provided clearly for all contingencies likely to arise out of the peculiar position of the Vatican state as an enclave set in the heart of a belligerent nation. In 1915 the Law of Guarantees had quite failed (as many of its original devisors had foreseen) to cover the situation, and the Vatican envoys of Italy's enemies had departed to Switzerland.

In the weeks preceding Italy's entry into the war, Vatican relations with Fascism reached their lowest ebb. From the moment of Mussolini's meeting with Hitler on the Brenner, March 18, it was clear that the end of non-belligerence was only a matter of time. Nine days later even the optimistic Monsignor Borgongini Duca was asking Cardinal Maglione to pray for him since he stood in great need of it. Talk of peace became increasingly unwelcome in Fascist circles, and the staid *Osservatore Romano*, which had been reporting the war with great objectivity, enjoyed its finest hour, being accused of playing the democratic game, putting God on the side of the English and French and of international Jewry, and having its distributors threatened with revolvers. On April 25 Giunta, an official of the Fascist grand council, referred to the Vatican as 'the chronic appendix of Italy'—this in the presence of the Duce and to the applause of Farinacci and his crew.

On May 14 Alfieri, the Italian Ambassador to the Holy See, who had been transferred to Berlin, came to make his farewells to the Pope. He took this rather odd occasion to say that Mussolini had been very annoyed by recent papal activities which suggested an attitude hardly friendly to Italy. He specified the telegrams to Holland, Belgium and Luxembourg and the sermon in the Minerva.[1] The Pope answered rather neatly that even Germany had not reacted to these things, and that they really hardly concerned Italy. He then added the celebrated words, 'Whatever happens, We have nothing to reproach Ourself with and We are not afraid even to go into a concentration camp.'[2]

Even Borgongini Duca, protesting verbally to Ciano about the treatment of the *Osservatore*, and being asked whether the Pope and Cardinal Maglione were upset, answered 'Yes—they're upset for you, because it is you, the Italian government, who are making fools of yourselves before the civilized world.' (May 17) However well this point may have been taken, the attacks on the *Osservatore* were in fact switched off. The Pope's words in particular made an impression, and whether or not they were taken as a hint that he might leave Italy in the event of war, the last thing Mussolini wanted was to enter the war in the middle of a first-class row with the Vatican. It was finally agreed that the enemy envoys to the Vatican should take up residence there; they did so on the day war was declared by Italy and ironically, just as the enemy ambassadors to the Quirinal were departing, Count Wladimir d'Ormesson presented his credentials at the Vatican as the new Ambassador of France. There were wild rumours of a projected Fascist raid on the Vatican on the same day, but four days later the government instructed its ambassador there to deny them 'in the most absolute manner'.

The Pope gave strict instructions that everybody in the Vatican state, diplomats included, should be meticulously correct in behaviour, and high standards of austerity were set. The *Osservatore Romano* ceased to publish allied communiqués.[3] Elsewhere in Italy

[1] The latter had this pointed passage: 'God, the Lord of the universe, from whom empires depend and who alone raises up thrones and casts them down and renders vain the thoughts of men, looks down to see if there be a man who contemplates such ruin and whose heart is touched, and who stretches his hand to justice that calls for peace.'

[2] He added that if he had anything to reproach himself with it was perhaps having been too discreet about what had happened and continued to happen in Poland. (Giovannetti, *op. cit.* p. 285).

[3] This, Padellaro quaintly explains, was 'so as not to embarrass the Italian press, which was almost certain to distort them according to the accepted usages of war.' Another illustration of the problems peculiar to Vatican neutrality.

Catholic press and publicists had hardly been conspicuously independent even in peacetime, and their conventional patriotic rhetoric represented no great change or inconsistency. Yet Jemolo has recorded the impression that '. . . one no longer sensed the upsurge of genuine enthusiasm which had characterized the similar demonstrations of solidarity five years before, when the troops were leaving for the war in Africa'.

The truth is that relations between Catholicism and Fascism had always been a good deal more formal and superficial than the more quotable printed evidence might lead the Left-inclined outsider to suppose. Academic persons might (like the Gemellis and the Fanfanis of those days) be bemused by theorizing about the corporate state, or by a romantic version of history which freely mythologized about Constantine, Dante and the divine destinies of imperial Rome; administrators might sometimes find their path made easier, or even be beguiled by native exuberance into pipe-dreams of a grand alliance between Throne and Altar. But for the Catholic of independent mind and shrewd observation there were reminders frequent and clear enough that in the last analysis he was caught between two irreconcilable doctrinal systems. The real Fascist was never more than a formal Catholic, ready to dress up and carry a flag when a bishop or other ecclesiastical personage paid a visit, but largely a stranger to regular local Catholic life. Equally the real and active Catholic remained very much on the fringe of the Party. Fascism, always a more flexible system than Nazism, made a place for the Church, within the system and on the system's terms, in a way which beguiled some of the more simple churchmen; but a few shared ideas and a shared aversion to Communism were not enough to create a Cesaropapist idyll in Italy. Himmler is said to have warned the Italian Ambassador in Berlin in 1941 that Italy was exposed to a twofold danger—the action of the Catholic Church and an attempt upon the Duce's life. He calculated that ninety per cent of the German clergy and sixty per cent of the Italian were out of sympathy with the ideas of their government. 'After the war we shall have to make a clean sweep of them.' The average Italian was far too intelligent not to realize and fear what a Nazi victory would mean for the future pattern of Italian life.

If so much could be said of the average Italian, it was certainly to be said of the brilliant and widely-experienced Pius XII. He was a genuine patriot, but he had higher motives for discretion than the average Italian. His was the crushing responsibility of spiritual fatherhood over all Catholics, wherever they were, however their judgements were distorted or their passions inflamed by war. One wonders how much his attitude to decision, his sense of its incalculable consequences, of its loneliness, was annealed in those months, when the diplomat's training conditioned the anxieties of the universal pastor. What would Angelo Roncalli, then among the obscure Vatican diplomats, have made of this situation?

The war was a heavy spiritual affliction to Pius XII, and at the same time accentuated some of the leading elements in his character. He was naturally sensitive, fastidious, appalled by disorder, suffering and irreligion. He had lived much of his life among the elaborate courtesies, the orderly subtleties and nuances of diplomatic intercourse. Widely travelled and a linguist (though this last accomplishment has, as commonly with popes, been exaggerated), he was cosmopolitan by inclination, and so exceptionally aware of a world divided and embittered. His own intense spiritual life, his pastoral zeal previously so cramped in scope by circumstance, his exalted, dramatic sense of his office all combined to make him see it as his vocation to assume this great burden of catastrophe in a way at once universal and lonely. For the duration of the war, and hardly less afterwards, he was above all the vicar of the Christ of Gethsemane.

Hence the paradox that the Pope who was perhaps the most accessible in history to crowds and casual visitors was within his own court the most solitary and detached. *Segregatus in evangelium Dei*—it was a vocational enlargement of a natural disposition. 'By nature,' Cardinal Tardini has written, 'he was almost irresistibly driven in on himself, withdrawn from others. He loved study intensely; he was happy when seated at a desk, among books, reviews, documents . . .' exercising his remarkable powers of assimilation and synthesis. He was embarrassed by the need for rapid decisions; given time, his decisions took meticulous account of the facts.

He ate alone. He saw his family once a year, Romans though they were—for an hour or two at Christmas. His relations with the papal court inclined to the formal, even to the authoritarian, except for his few familiars, who were mostly either Germans or layfolk. When Maglione died in 1944, no Secretary of State was appointed, but two pro-secretaries, one of whom at least was told, 'I do not want collaborators but executors.'

It is scarcely possible to speak to anyone, Catholic or not, who came into close contact with Pius XII, especially during the war, who was not sharply struck with this impression of an intense, remote personal life, which was yet completely impersonal in the sense of being wholly immolated, given over to the office, to the Church, to that humanity which is the concern of the office and the Church.

One often comes across the word 'mystical' in reading of Pius XII. The word is commonly used with great vagueness and for many it probably points confusedly to a contrast between his manner of self-dedication and that of John XXIII. If the word suggests some antithesis with 'practical' it is surely inapt. Pius was not content to enter 'mystically' into the sufferings of wartime. The impressive tale of Vatican relief and humane activities has often been told and need not be rehearsed here. The Christ of Gethsemane was also the Christ who 'went about doing good,' and Pius XII was his worthy vicar in this too. He saw no limit to his responsibilities to the world, and he had a capacity for work which his doctors once, rather to his pleasure, described as 'inhuman'. The somewhat ornate and copious character of his oratory, which has rarely benefited by translation, can easily obscure for the English mind (more sympathetic to understatement) what in fact it faithfully reflects—an apocalyptic conception of the war and an almost obsessive ambition to enter into the tribulations of all involved in it. He saw the war as destructive at once of the juridical order and of charity. Towards restoring the former, or restricting its violation, he could only exhort; the decline of charity he could compensate not only by exhortation but by extending and intensifying his own. It was probably this as much as a diplomatic preoccupation with the demands of neutrality that made him often shy of explicit condemnation and so caused many a dilemma.

These considerations seem an indispensable preliminary to an estimate of Pius XII's attitude to the dictatorships. What he thought of National Socialism (as distinct from the Germans) was made clear enough in 1945. The same statement gives some account of his reasons for not speaking equally explicitly at an earlier date. But it should not be supposed that his utterances were always obscure, least of all to his immediate hearers. On December 7,

1939, he spoke to the Italian Ambassador some formal courtesies about the 'happy circumstances' of the Lateran Treaty and the wisdom of the Italian government in keeping out of war.[1] These are often quoted. How much less often one hears another passage from the same speech: having spoken of justice being forgotten in 'a false train of thought that deifies the human and degrades the divine to human terms', he went on: 'Each of these errors, as is the way with error, has its time—its time of increase and its time of decline; its meridian, its twilight, its rapid setting. Two times—the time when the heady poison of seductive doctrines carries away, infatuates and enchains the masses, and the time when the bitter fruits ripen and the eyes of the masses, or of the most reflective, look at these teachings in terror, recalling the calculations and promises, now clearly fallacious, which first lead them into error. Toady, how many eyes hitherto closed are opened!'

To such a listener, at that lowest moment of Italian subservience to Nazism, there was hardly need for dotting 'i's and crossing 't's. The speech has a clear echo in one made six years later, to an audience in St Peter's Square (March 18, 1945): 'To those who allowed themselves to be seduced by the apostles of violence, who are now beginning to waken from their illusions, shocked to see where their servility has led them, there remains no way of salvation but to foreswear once and for all the idolatry of absolute nationalism, the pride of race and blood, the lust for mastery in the possession of the world's goods, and to turn resolutely to a spirit of sincere brotherhood, founded on the worship of the divine Father of all men.'

Sometimes accusations by name were equivalently made, as when at Christmas 1940, he spoke of his efforts on behalf of prisoners being 'frustrated in some countries' and went on to mention those countries in which they had been successful! Pius was not unaware of the difficulties of this self-imposed discipline of anonymity: in the Christmas broadcast of 1941 he said: 'We love, God is Our witness, with equal affection all peoples without exception and to avoid even the appearance of bias we have so far imposed on ourselves the maximum reserve. But the extent of the persecution of the Church is such that we feel obliged in the name

[1] It was at this time that Cardinal Tisserant made his appeal to Pius for an encyclical on the duty of obeying conscience, the failure of which led to his famous letter to Cardinal Suhard of June 11, 1940.

of truth to speak a word, lest bewilderment should be occasioned among the faithful.' The same speech contained an eloquent apostrophe of Christian Rome—'a city eternal in time more because of Christ than because of the Caesars'; a plain enough contradiction of that Fascist mystique of Imperial Rome to which even clerical publicists had occasionally lent their voices.

It was not until 1945, when there was no longer danger that his words might bring reprisals and aggravate the sufferings of the helpless, that the Pope spoke explicitly and at length on Nazism; it was a comprehensive survey, altogether more pungent in style than many of his utterances and revealing his consciousness of many familiar criticisms; it should be quoted at some length. He described National Socialism as 'a conception of state activity that took no account of the most sacred feelings of humanity and trod underfoot the inviolable principles of the Christian faith. The consequent ruin We saw from afar, and none has watched with greater tension the approach of the inevitable fall.

'For twelve of the best years of Our life We lived among the German people. With the freedom that the conditions of that time allowed, We applied Ourself to consolidating the position of the Church in Germany. We had every chance to get to know the great qualities of that people. It is this that gives Us confidence that they can raise themselves again to new dignity, new life, once they have pushed aside the satanic spectre of Nazism, and once the guilty have (as We have said before) expiated their crimes.

'While there remained any spark of hope that the movement might take a different, less pernicious direction, whether by the weight of its more moderate members prevailing or by the effective opposition of the German people, the Church did everything in her power to set up a barrier to the spread of those violent doctrines.[1] In 1933 the German Government asked the Holy See to conclude a concordat with the Reich; the German episcopate and most Catholics supported the request: neither the existing partial concordats with the Länder (Bavaria, Prussia, Baden) nor the Weimar constitution seemed to them adequate guarantees for Catholicism. Since the Reich proposed the agreement, the Holy See

[1] Those who, not having lived through the early thirties or having conveniently forgotten them, find this a surprising confession, should read Dr Brigitte Granzow's *A Mirror of Nazism* to discover what was being written by the best English papers at the time.

would have been responsible for the consequences (to German Catholics) of a refusal.[1] The Church neither nourished excessive hopes nor intended any approval of the doctrine and tendencies of Nazism—as We Ourself explained in the *Osservatore Romano* of July 3, 1933. Yet it must be admitted that in succeeding years the Concordat brought certain advantages, or at least prevented greater evils. Though often violated, it did give Catholics a legal ground of defence, a platform from which to resist as long as possible the tide of persecution.'

The Pope went on to give details of this persecution, and of German Catholic resistance, and continued: 'Unhesitatingly the Holy See multiplied protests and pressure on the German government, strenuously and clearly recalling it to the obligations derived from natural right and confirmed in the Concordat. Finally, on Passion Sunday 1937 it launched the encyclical *Mit Brennender Sorge*.[2] Some thought this too strong, many were shaken by it.

'Would it have been possible at that moment, by political measures, to bridle this brutal violence and put the Germans in the way of casting off the tentacles which gripped them, and so save Europe and the world from an immense tide of blood? No one can safely say. But no one can blame the Church for not having denounced in time the true character of Nazism.

'From that moment persecution was intensified, down to the last moment when the Nazis were still hoping, after victory, to finish once for all with the Church. For this we had unshakeable authority—if events in Austria, Alsace-Lorraine and Poland were not proof enough.

'Continuing the work of Our Predecessor, We never ceased during the war (especially in broadcast messages) to oppose to Nazi doctrine and practice the unshakeable laws of humanity and Christian faith. This was for Us the most suitable, We may even say the only effective, way of proclaiming in the sight of the world the unchangeable principles of the moral law among so much error and violence, to confirm the minds and hearts of German Catholics in the higher ideals of truth and justice. Nor was it without effect. We know in fact that Our broadcasts, especially that of Christmas 1942, were in spite of every prohibition and obstacle studied by diocesan conferences and expounded to the people.'

[1] For an account of the negotiations see G. Lewi, *The Catholic Church and Nazi Germany*, Chapter 3.

[2] For Pius XII's own part in the authorship of this, cf. p. 22.

The Pope concluded with some statistics concerning Dachau over the preceding five years. Of 2,800 Polish ecclesiastics who had entered during that time, only 816 were still there in April 1945; the rest, except for two or three transferred, were dead. In 1942 480 other ministers of religion were in the camp, of whom 435 were Catholics. Many others followed in subsequent years, yet at the beginning of 1945 there were only 350. Others were there from Holland, Belgium, France (including the Bishop of Clermont), Luxembourg, Slovenia and Italy. One of them had been subjected to a parody of the Scourging and Crowning with Thorns.

3

The Church and Modern Democracy

THE CATHOLIC CHURCH has frequently stated that she is not committed to preferring one form of government before another. Real absolutism, of course, that is, any government which claims an authority independent of God and His law, is incompatible with Catholicism. It involves a non-Christian conception of power. For the Christian, power can come only from God, though how it is derived from Him and by what means it is conferred have been matters for legitimate difference of opinion among Christian thinkers. There are absolutist threads in the complex historical web of Western kingship, and they have at times threatened to dominate. When they have done so they have encountered the resistance of the Church, vigorous in proportion to the Church's health at the time. The alliance of Throne and Altar is not entirely a conservative myth, much less a Fascist one, but it has generally been a very uneasy alliance.

Democracy on the other hand has very old Christian roots. Insofar as the term stands for an effort to bring responsibility home to rulers, to make government a service rather than an exploitation, to establish the rule of law, it has been very prominently the work of Christian thinkers and hardly less prominently the work of churchmen. If these exalted the sacred character of monarchy they did so, in pre-Reformation times at least, mainly as a means of increasing the ruler's sense of responsibility, of vocation. They frequently lent their support to monarchy in times of difficulty and disorder or when kings were weak or minors; they as frequently headed movements to check the pretensions or abuses of monarchy. The reign of King John in England and the period of disorder immediately following it—the minority of Henry III—shows them doing both in quick succession.

The Church too has contributed notably to the shaping of democratic institutions, especially in their early stages—whether these have taken an explicitly political form or not.

These are the commonplaces of history. The great principles of government by consent, of responsibility, of the rule of law, far from being modern secularist inventions or sitting uneasily with Catholicism, are a necessary corollary of it. Complaisance or subjection in the face of absolutism—the sort of pusillanimity for instance that led to the suppression of the Jesuits in 1773—is consistently typical of the weakest phases in the history of Western Catholicism. When churchmen are heard sighing for some Saturnian age in which Throne and Altar were in Utopian harmony, they are at best bad historians; at worst they are sighing for a state of affairs in which ecclesiastics, of the higher ranks at least, had more privileges than were usually good for them.

Unfortunately the history of modern democratic movements has tended to obscure these simple truths. With the French Revolution and subsequent outbreaks under the same inspiration, resistance to absolutism was associated with aggressive anti-clericalism of various kinds. The Italian *Risorgimento*, which overthrew various monarchical régimes in Italy, was of course affected with this spirit, though by no means wholly. There were other and more respectable currents in the movement—aspirations towards reforms which were certainly clamorously necessary, not least in the Papal States. Unfortunately, since the papal monarchy was one of those overthrown by the *Risorgimento* (the one indeed whose overthrow attracted most attention) Italian independence and democracy were born directly of a major quarrel with the Church: in this respect it was historically thoroughly uncharacteristic. None realized this better than Gioberti, the spiritual father of the Italian neo-Guelph movement (which captured the passing interest of the future Pius IX). Gioberti with many others saw the Pope as the most likely and natural leader of a national movement against the Austrian hegemony.

But Pius IX's early enthusiasm for neo-Guelphism turned, after he came back from his flight to Gaeta, to aversion, and the Roman tradition became one of distrust of 'liberalism' (one has to be very careful with this word in Italy, especially among ecclesiastics) and democracy, and a strong bias towards *identifying* it with the more virulent forms of anti-clericalism, secularism and conspiracy against the Church—everything summed up (rather misleadingly for the Anglo-Saxon) in the Italian word *laicismo*.

A good deal that is rather imprecise has been said, both by sympathizers and by critics, about the *Syllabus of Modern Errors* of Pius IX. Some people at the time even read it as condemning railways. This document in brief, uncompromising propositions stated in extreme form the prevailing ideas of the secularism of the day. It added of course that nobody could hold these propositions and remain a good Catholic. It did not say that all who were in sympathy with modern democratic aspirations, or even with that complex movement the Italian *Risorgimento*,[1] necessarily held all or any of these propositions. To put it another way, the *Syllabus* was not a 'blanket' condemnation of liberal democracy or 'modern thought'. It condemned what it said it condemned, neither more nor less.[2] It condemned propositions, not persons, but it is an inevitable drawback of this form of pronouncement that the over-zealous or vindictive heresy-hunter who invokes it against X or Y tends to assume in doing so the same authority as the document itself, to the embarrassment or indignation of X or Y as the case may be. Similarly, those who were anxious to hold the *Syllabus* up to ridicule would in various ways exaggerate the scope of its anathemas. Partly as a result of this kind of abuse, the *Syllabus* made its contribution to that atmosphere of siege which prevailed in the Italian Church until the days of Fascism, and which even the great Leo XIII was not able to dispel.

It is of the first interest to contrast this history of the relations between the Church and Italian democracy with the history of Church-State relations in North America, which was to become in the period this book deals with the most powerful of the free nations. American democracy began as a religious protest against absolutism. Not however against secularist absolutism, but against the absolutism of a religious establishment. The Pilgrim Fathers of New England and Lord Baltimore's Catholic colonists in Maryland had this in common, that they were minorities finding refuge from religious persecution. In these first generations Catholics, who, except in French Canada, remained a small minority, found the

[1] The *Syllabus* was in fact a digest of documents originally issued mainly in an Italian context.

[2] But cf. the account of propositions 16 and 79 in Chapter 12, pp. 291-2.

New World a much less secure refuge from persecution than did Protestants. It was the intolerance of the puritan revolutionary Congress towards Canadian Catholicism that helped to keep Canada within the British Commonwealth—Britain, from opportunism more than conviction at that time, proving more accommodating to the Church, and ignoring loud American protests.

Nevertheless, for many reasons, not the least of which was the difficulty of federating states which already had differing established religions, religious tolerance came to be written into the American Constitution. Whether or not there was any church predominant enough to become an establishment, none did; churches and state were separated.

But this was not the tolerance of secularist indifference. The one sentence of the *Declaration of Independence* that everybody knows contains the phrase 'endowed by their Creator'. Whatever the American Revolution borrowed from the French, it did not borrow irreligion; but neither did it borrow intolerance from the Catholic or Protestant states of the *Ancien Régime*. True, Catholics were to suffer a great deal from bigotry in America during the nineteenth century, especially after the vast Irish immigration had swelled their numbers so as to alarm the older inhabitants. The *Awful Disclosures* of Maria Monk were invented in those crude times, and they were only the most garish manifestation of a deep suspicion which has been seen even in the present century, as when the electorate were told in 1928 that the entry of Al Smith into the White House would mean a private telephone line from thence to the Vatican. (In fact it was some years before a Catholic president was able to install such a hot line, and then it was not to the Vatican.) Many consider that the educational disabilities of Catholics in America are still at bottom a witness to this ancient rancour. But in spite of all this the fact remains that the liberal democracy enshrined in the American Constitution has provided the necessary basic freedom for the Church to grow in America in the remarkable way she has. So conscious of this were some at least of the American bishops, and so enthusiastic about it, that their own more conservative brethren, as well as French and Italian critics accustomed to a very different sort of democracy, suspected them of being tainted with secularism and indifferentism, and in 1899 Leo XIII was induced to condemn a number of propositions under the general heading of 'Americanism'. The label was an odd one in the sense that no reputable American Catholic left the Church, or would have dreamed of doing so, in advocacy of any one of these propositions. They represented rather the most pessimistic European diagnosis of the tendencies in the less conservative wing of the American Church.

In spite of this, Leo XIII was much impressed by the advantages the Church enjoyed under the American Constitution and the lack of conflict with the State there. This considerably influenced his policy of *ralliement* in France, where however the character of the Republic and its relations with Catholics were sadly different.

America was at this time still regarded as a missionary country. It was not until 1908 that the affairs of the Church there were administered from Rome in the ordinary way and not by the missionary Congregation of Propaganda. Satolli, a Roman curial official, had spent the years 1893–6 there as Apostolic Delegate, beginning as an enthusiast for liberal policies but being frightened off and eventually sponsoring the condemnation of Americanism. The Lateran Treaty redirected attention to a feature of American relations with Rome which by 1929, with the rapid advance of America, had come to seem an anomaly: the United States, in spite of its large Catholic population, was not represented diplomatically at the Vatican. That moment, a year after the anti-Smith campaign and its bedtime stories, was not a propitious one for raising the subject, but the election of Roosevelt, civilized above the average of American politicians and himself related to the saintly Mother Seton and to a former president of Fordham, changed the atmosphere, or at least made it of less consequence.

In 1936 Cardinal Pacelli made his crowded month's stay in America. It created plenty of speculation, but Bishop Spellman, the tour manager, true to his Vatican training, kept the press so effectively at bay that Pacelli's diplomacy was hardly severely tested, publicly at least. This in spite of the fact that the visit coincided with the peak of Father Coughlin's campaign against the New Deal and all its works and pomps.

The Cardinal and his advisers took the temperature very shrewdly, ignoring the turbulent priest: anything else would have smartly united all parties in a clamour against Vatican 'interference' in American domestic affairs. Roosevelt romped home, the 'National League for Social Justice' committed a reasonably dignified *hara-kiri*, and two days after the election the Cardinal Secretary of

State dined at the White House and had a long private conversation with Roosevelt. While not as bad as a sub-Atlantic tunnel to the Vatican,[1] it all doubtless made the Know-Nothingers and the American Protective Association turn in their graves, as they would again when, in February 1937 Bishop Spellman, staying with the President, said Mass in the Monroe Room of the White House.

Alarums and excursions apart, the enduring effect of all this was probably much greater in the Vatican than in the States. Whether the U.S.A. had a diplomat in the Vatican or not was perhaps, as Cardinal O'Connell and others argued, not of the first importance; that the acute mind of the future Pope had taken the American pulse at such a moment certainly was. The Catholic Church in America was not an intellectual force[2] but it was generous, compliant, vigorous and commanded considerable material resources. All these characteristics combined to make easy the forging of more and stronger links between Rome and this vast, rich expanding country in which the Church had previously developed with the minimum of Roman control. The effect was to be clear enough at the beginning of the Second Vatican Council, when the American hierarchy appeared as the most completely attuned to the ideas, aims and even prejudices of the Roman Curia. On the other hand, as the Council developed, other American characteristics and sentiments began to tell in the opposite direction. The bishops of a people so steeped in the pioneer qualities of enterprise, independence, adaptability, directness and impatience of flummery could hardly fail to respond to the multiple signs of a new spirit and outlook in the Church—even if it involved the canvassing of ideas that many of them were neither at home with nor powerfully equipped to handle.

Where the forging of links above referred to aroused no enthusiasm, especially when it seemed to overstep the bounds of internal Catholic affairs, was with American Protestantism. When Roosevelt finally sent Myron C. Taylor to Italy, everything possible

[1] This was one of the electioneering scares put out in 1928.

[2] There is food for thought in the fact that K. S. Latourette, dealing with the U.S.A. in Vol V of his *Christianity in a Revolutionary Age*, under the impressive sectional heading 'The Roman Catholic Response to the Intellectual Currents of the Age', treats only one individual even at the length of a paragraph: Joseph Clifford Fenton. Only two other names are mentioned—John Courtney Murray and Gustave Weigel, who 'were also eminent but they and Fenton did not entirely agree'. This at least deserves immortality as an understatement.

was done to sugar the pill. Taylor was already serving as Roosevelt's personal representative on an intergovernmental committee for political refugees, and had been in touch with the Vatican in this work, and a presidential memo to Cordell Hull represented the Mission as no more than an extension of this. Taylor was to be 'President's representative with the rank of ambassador', was to live in a villa he already had in Florence except when business required him in Rome, and was not intended to function beyond the duration of war. None of this prevented the move stimulating a brisk flow of bigotry which continued intermittently through the ten years of Taylor's mission and culminated when Harry Truman 'drove a sword deep into the heart of Protestant America' by nominating (abortively) General Mark Clark as U.S. Ambassador to the Vatican.

The Vatican must have seen here some of the virtues of American democracy. Even if Protestant noise could put a halt to the designs of what it called 'Spellmanism', this was only because by the same token Spellmanism could grow in this free air. And if being a 'good American' could become a dangerously absorbing and narrowing preoccupation for a Catholic it was a vast deal less unhealthy than trying to be a good German under Nazism or a good Italian under Fascism. In any case, American Catholicism and American democracy were well safeguarded from too enervating a state of continuous marital bliss. The perennial problem of confessional education in an a-confessional state soured relations between Catholics and others during the post-war years. It brought Cardinal Spellman into conflict with Mrs Roosevelt, the voluble, rather anti-Catholic widow of the President under whose roof Spellman had said Mass. Tension was not eased when the same roof came to shelter its first Catholic president. Was it a violation of the First Amendment, a compromise of the separation of Church and State, the thin end of the wedge of Establishment, if the authorities paid Catholic children's school bus fares? It was a point on which the Cardinal and many Protestant good Americans differed, strongly but not silently.

But they could differ, and they could say what they thought. On the other side of the world, they were acutely aware, lived millions who could not. The relations of Communism and Catholicism belong to another chapter, but American reaction to what Cardinal Spellman vigorously called 'the God-hating, freedom-hating

Communist puppets now terrorizing, brutalizing and tyrannizing half the world and openly ambitioning, with the help of traitors, many even within our own country, to enslave the rest of the world' was creating dilemmas in the minds of many American Catholics. This was especially true of the activities named after Senator Joe McCarthy, whose name set up highly exaggerated Catholic associations in the public mind. The Brooklyn *Tablet* and the kind of uncomplicated minds it catered for might perceive no dilemma and root for the man from Wisconsin; others wondered whether his methods were not perhaps as prejudicial to the American way of life as the subversive activities against which they were directed.

In all these matters the Vatican wisely preserved silence, but Cardinal Spellman's views were as clear and forthright as those of his former colleague in the Secretariat of State, Cardinal Ottaviani, and always expressed with a refreshing lack of cotton-wool wrapping. They were expressed fairly widely, too—as when at Brussels (October 1953) he delivered a long and spirited apologia for America and current American policies.

The advantages and dangers of one kind of democracy could thus be clearly seen in what was now the most powerful and rich of democratic states—a state moreover which was no longer, to the Vatican, a distant, raw protégé of Propaganda but a great country whose multiple ties of blood with the Old World were complemented by heavy commitments in Europe and considerable influence in Rome.

As a result, in some cases, of this American weight, after the war, some form of democratic régime existed this side of the Iron Curtain in every European country except those of the Iberian peninsula. But a unified judgement on democracy in Europe, especially from the point of view of Church-State relations, was of course no easy matter to anyone who knew anything about it.

In England the situation invited certain obvious comparisons and contrasts with America. Just as it was absolutism that had brought death, exile or crippling disabilities to Catholics under the Tudors and Stuarts, so it was in the long run the revival of democratic freedoms that brought relief, though Protestantism of a fairly robust kind remained by law established. If Catholics were able eventually, within certain limits, to establish themselves (in fact, not in law) on their merits, it was because of the progress of democratic institutions and the growth of a tolerant public temper not wholly traceable to the growth of religious indifference. British Catholics, in fact, had no reason to feel any tenderness to authoritarian régimes, though you might not always have thought so from reading the Catholic press. Occasional and local bigotry, the incompetence and harshness of the government's record in Ireland, whence so many Catholics in Great Britain took their origins, the asperities of the education question, all have contributed to obscure the broad basic truths set out above.

In Ireland British rule had indeed been a mockery of democracy —a generally stupid and heedless overlordship which had nevertheless in the end given way freely to the pressure of reality, and not before democracy had allowed the Irish members to play ducks and drakes with the Mother of Parliaments for a generation. Irish Nationalism, closely bound to religion yet strongly laced with the nineteenth-century liberal tradition, then produced a political system which was democratic without making serious inroads on the power of the clergy.

It is matter for speculation how far all this was understood in the Vatican, where British opinion was not very broadly represented.

In France democracy was the child of the Revolution and had the most serious record of anti-clericalism, culminating in the Combes laws (cf. Chapter 11, pp. 249 *et seq.*). Yet on a narrower front the Church was vigorous, not least intellectually. It offered a challenge weightier than any other to secularism, which itself was perhaps strongest in France. The record of the clergy in the First World War, both as pastors and as soldiers, was good enough to diminish anti-clericalism notably. But there was a great shortage of priests, and French Catholicism was chronically at odds with itself. Action Française was a chief cause of division between the wars, being condemned by Pius XI in 1927. During the Second World War, in 1943, a book by Godin and Daniel, *La France, Pays de Mission?* gave a startling picture of the decline of religion. The enterprises which grew out of this book, and other related ones, will be discussed elsewhere (see Chapter 10). As far as French democracy was concerned, it had done little for the Catholic faith, but it had not prevented the emergence of some remarkable men and movements, of mainly non-political character.

The Belgian Church, dominated in the first quarter of this

century by the gigantic figure of Mercier, flourished under a constitutional monarchy, while Holland, a Protestant country more than one third Catholic, offered perhaps the best example of how the Faith could prosper in a free, pluralist society. In Switzerland, where Catholics were also a substantial minority, religious freedom now made the old distinctions between Catholic and Protestant cantons less rigid.

These last three countries make up, together with Austria and parts of Germany, France and North Italy, what Professor Fogarty has called 'the central belt of high religious observance' in which Christian Democratic movements, Catholic and Protestant, have chiefly flourished for some years. These held in 1955 nearly two-fifths of the seats in lower houses of Parliament in these countries. Christian Democratic trade unions held a majority over the Socialist unions in Holland and Belgium, fell short of the Communists but substantially exceeded the Socialists in Italy and France, and constituted an appreciable and organized minority in Switzerland, Austria and Germany. Christian Democratic organizations had a substantial footing among farmers and the smaller employers, and at least a foothold among larger firms. Massive youth and family movements (not to be confused with the ordinary Church youth and women's movement) gave Christian Democracy and Christian Action a strong position among these groups as well. And the Christian Democratic movements had the help of a strong press, of the Protestant and Catholic universities and schools and of a variety of research and other service agencies.[1]

Continental Christian Democracy, Fogarty adds, has up to the present been identified with the idea of the specifically Christian party or social organization, whereas elsewhere (in Anglo-Saxon countries for instance) Christians have tended to work through established, strictly non-confessional parties or institutions. The ideal of this movement, to insist on the value of the free and reasonable personality, with an eternal destiny and inalienable rights, is plainly in line with or derived from the classical social teaching of the papacy, and represents a continuous protest not only against any form of totalitarianism but also against secularist liberal capitalism as it has developed in Western Europe.

It is a striking fact that a high percentage of those bishops who have made a strong impact on the Second Vatican Council exercise

[1] M. P. Fogarty, *Christian Democracy in Western Europe, 1820–1953*, p. 8.

their office within Fogarty's 'central belt': Alfrink (Utrecht), Bekkers ('s-Hertogenbosch), Suenens (Malines), De Smedt (Bruges), Frings (Cologne), Döpfner (Munich), Liénart (Lille), Weber (Strasbourg), Guerry (Cambrai), Charrière (Lausanne), König (Vienna), Gargitter (Bressanone), Lercaro (Bologna), not to mention Cardinal Bea and Popes John XXIII and Paul VI who were all born within the area.

Nor have the leading principles of Christian Democracy been without their influence in the Council. For instance, in the debate on the relations of episcopate and Curia Cardinal König explicitly invoked the principle of subsidiarity, or 'horizontal pluralism'. This insists that larger and higher forms of authority and organization should not usurp the functions of the lower and more restricted. It is a corollary of 'personalism'—a way of guarding against the swamping of personality by organization. So is 'vertical pluralism'—the habit of respecting the integrity of other groups with different ideas and aims, while maintaining one's own. The principle has naturally commanded attention in countries where different religious traditions have had to learn to exist side by side, or where the Church has had to coexist with secularism without enjoying special privileges. Vertical pluralism is very much what is commonly meant by tolerance—a word Fogarty does not like, thinking it inadequate and 'Laodicean' in flavour. Ecumenism, certainly a movement beyond tolerance, flourishes in most of the 'central regions' of Christian Democracy (cf. Chapter 12, pp. 270, *et seq.*).

Fogarty does not overstate of course when he says that 'the churches which inspire Christian Democracy have often shown this kind of pluralism little respect', but this has not always been a matter of ill-will. Putting aside for the moment thorny theological questions about 'the rights of error', tolerance carries its own logical and practical difficulties: 'A group which proposes to disturb public order or decency or to avoid its members' normal civic obligations —to violate, that is, the natural law which is common ground for Catholic, Protestant, humanist and all men of good will—puts its claim for freedom to develop its own ideals out of court. So does a group which sets out to destroy the principle of vertical pluralism itself. Christian Democracy does not admit that there is freedom to destroy freedom.'[1]

[1] Fogarty, *op. cit.* p. 44.

On the other hand, the kind of activity which aims to restrict the 'freedom to destroy freedom' is difficult to keep within precise and reasonable bounds. McCarthyism, censorship, the handling of proselytism—all have reflected this dilemma. The price of liberty is higher than Disraeli's eternal vigilance—it includes the inevitability that either some things will escape your vigilance or else your vigilance will itself become insupportable. It is a dilemma which legally trained administrators, not least in the Church, sometimes seem unable to appreciate. But it is getting a pretty fair airing, one way or another, in the Rome of Vatican II (cf. Chapter 12). Bishops have warned their fellows in public session that Catholics should not appear solicitous for freedom only when they are in a minority.

4

The Papacy and Politics: Concordats

ONE COULD SAY of John XXIII that he was by nature and temperament a pluralist, not least of the 'vertical' kind (see p. 56.) His inclination was certainly to leave those below him to get on with their appointed job, provided they were doing that and no more, and doing it properly. His handling of the Second Vatican Council was notably more restrained and surer than Pius IX's handling of the First. It was still more vividly his inclination to respect, not to say love, the integrity of persons and ideas. Juridical niceties, the detailed problems arising from broad conceptions and generous principles, even the complications which were so often alleged to follow his warm and robust impulses, all worried him less, though he had a very sure flair for handling the concrete situation when necessary.

Pius XII, a lawyer by background and training, a diplomat of a quite different mould from his successor, a more deeply reflective and erudite pope, also reigned a great deal longer and through a greater variety of hazards and problems. The problem of right-wing dictatorship for instance had, if not entirely disappeared, narrowed enormously (except in the minds of a few fanatics) by John's accession, and even that of Communist dictatorship did not present itself in precisely the same terms as it had in the immediate post-war years, though if the menace was less acute, the problem of handling it was perhaps more subtle. It was arguably, of course, the merit of John and his advisers to see this more clearly than many in the Curia or in the Church at large, but this must be left for consideration elsewhere (see Chapter 5, pp. 87 *et seq.*). If John exploded a revolution in his short reign, Pius lived through a longer and more complex one with which he made indefatigable attempts to grapple, at least intellectually. The attempts were given copious verbal expression, and it is time to trace their course, beginning with problems arising directly out of the political and other events and conditions so far reviewed.

In his first Encyclical, *Summi Pontificatus* of 1939, Pius XII singled out two 'leading errors' as characteristic of that time of universal anxiety and unrest. The first was forgetfulness of that 'law of human solidarity and charity which is dictated and imposed by our common origin and by the equality of rational nature in all men, no matter to what people they belong, and by the redeeming sacrifice of Jesus Christ'. The earth is, he added, an inheritance of which all men can by natural right avail themselves. It was a theme to which he was often to return. It reminds us of the common roots which Christian and modern liberal social thinking share: it smacks more of the *Declaration of Independence* than of *La Dottrina del Fascismo*, *Mein Kampf* or the *Marxist Manifesto*. It foreshadows that interest in the ideal of a world community which was to figure increasingly in Pius XII's pronouncements over the succeeding twenty years. It is a catholic ideal consonant with the Catholic conception of man's nature and destiny, and a law which cannot be put aside in the name of any limited loyalty or ambition. Thus the first leading error is linked with the second, the claim to a civil autonomy independent of divine authority and law. To condemn this error is not to assert pretensions to theocracy. But while liberal democratic régimes may insist on separation of Church and State, and even unduly restrict the former's authority on certain disputed ground, it is the authoritarian states, above all those based on 'organic' theory, that have traditionally accused the Church of directing her teaching and activity against civil authority. Hence when the same Encyclical says 'against such suspicions We solemnly declare with apostolic sincerity that any such aims are entirely alien to that same Church which spreads its maternal arms to the world not to dominate but to serve . . .' it is to the dictators it is chiefly addressing itself. It is the canon law, the *jus publicum* of the Church, which lays down that the state like the Church is a *societas perfecta*, that is, an organization naturally endowed with all the means necessary to the achievement of its proper ends, and hence enjoying autonomy within the scope of those ends.

If anything has brought this principle into dispute, it is not Catholic teaching but the crude necessities of modern life in a world where the problems of survival and sustenance can no longer be plausibly seen as confined within national boundaries (see Chapter 6, p. 121, *et seq.*).

But if the Church condemns false theories of the State, she does not exaggerate the extent to which these 'party' theories grip the mass of people. Hence the 'optimism' behind the policy of concordats, which imply no condonation of error but offer the Church a minimal basis for appealing to and working on those right instincts which survive: 'We do not of course fail to recognize that, fortunately, false principles do not always exercise their full influence, especially when age-old Christian traditions, on which the people have been nurtured, remain still deeply, even if unconsciously, rooted in their hearts.'

Here was a diagnosis applicable in varying degrees to Russia, Germany and Fascist Italy. Speaking to Italian Catholic Action leaders in September 1940, Pius XII exhorted them to 'humility and kindness, patience and mildness, prudence and discretion; a wise charity tolerant of the erring though not of error'. He may be thought to have been exercising these virtues, mixed with a dash of strategy, in reminding the same audience that in Italy the 'wisdom of governors' had made religion 'the foundation and crown of education'. But if this provision of the Concordat reflected no inner conviction of Fascism, at least it was political realism for Italy, and represented for the Church an opportunity she was denied in more grossly totalitarian states. It was for Catholic Actionists, said the Pope, not to exaggerate its value, but to realize that only their own constant energies could produce any fruit from it—make it prevail over the contrary indoctrinating forces so ubiquitously at work.

The deployment of these energies was of course under Fascism excluded from the political field. If prominence seems to be given here to relations between the Vatican and Italy, it is in the conviction that these have very much coloured the Vatican conception both of Church-State relations and of Catholic lay action. Italy, which absorbed the Papal States, is the country on the Vatican doorstep, the country which largely staffs the Vatican. It has been for nearly forty years the country of the concordat *par excellence*—but the country in which the interpretation of the concordat is most influenced by historic theocratic aspirations on the one hand and atavistic anti-clericalism on the other. To concentrate too much on this relationship, with all the peculiar moral tensions it engenders, would obscure (perhaps has obscured) the enduring historic principles emphasized in the preceding chapter. To consider it too little would be no less false to recent history.

Previous to the end of World War II ecclesiastically-sponsored Catholic lay action in Italy traditionally had little connection with politics. It had begun in the late 1860s as a movement of protest against the new state, accepting the *non expedit* as a basic principle, tending to organize Catholic life as a thing apart from that of the nation as a whole, something in a state of siege: an odd state of affairs in a country which housed Rome and the papacy and an ancient and rich Catholic tradition. Catholicism lived at odds with Italian liberalism from the *Risorgimento* to the First World War. This last did something, as wars have commonly done in modern times, to break down the barriers of anti-clericalism, but the opportunity offered by the electoral reforms of 1919 for the emergence of a popular Catholic party was hampered by ecclesiastical mistrust and eventually extinguished by the triumph of Fascism. The brief, sad history of Don Sturzo's enterprise revealed two things: that the Italian Church as a whole was unwilling to support a party which, though of Catholic inspiration, remained non-confessional, while the maintenance of clerical leading-strings was even then enough to lose any such party a decisive number of votes.

Under Fascism the question of the relation of Catholic Action to politics ostensibly ceased to be actual. Article 43 of the Concordat laid down that 'The State recognizes the organizations dependent on Italian Catholic Action, insofar as they conduct their activities, as the Holy See has laid down, unconnected with any political party and in immediate dependence on the hierarchy of the Church, for the realization and diffusion of Catholic principles.'

What the Church had made a matter of policy under Italian liberalism she now accepted willy-nilly in a one-party state, as part of the price of the settlement of the Roman Question. As we have seen, this formal detachment from politics was in no way unwelcome to Pius XI, but (as his frequent protests implied) the climate of Fascism was immensely more restrictive than the formal terms of the Concordat entailed: the Catholic movement was more than ever driven in on itself, more than ever strictly under ecclesiastical control and confined to matters 'religious' in a far narrower sense than the mainstream of Catholic tradition could tolerate.

Nevertheless, the recurrence of abuse and attacks by the Fascists on Catholic Action reflected their shrewd appreciation of the limited force of such paper restrictions. Young men, especially undergraduates and similar types, gathered together in a repressive society, will not be hindered by ordinances from talking politics and harbouring political dreams and ambitions; rather will they be the more stimulated. Pius XI has been called 'the pope of Catholic Action' and also 'the pope of concordats', and he certainly saw Catholic Action as primarily a work of apostolate carried on within the non-political framework provided by the treaties. This non-political framework entailed, down to the end of the Second World War, a general if not uncritical acceptance of the one-party régime. But, as has been seen, in the last year or two of Pius XI's reign this acceptance was more and more strained, and *pari passu* the Catholic Action movement, especially in its intellectual branches, the Laureati and FUCI (undergraduates' federation) became more and more discontented and politically-minded.

In the later phases of the war, when Nazi-Fascist control began to break down, Catholic participation in the resistance was often organized by Catholic Action leaders in co-operation with the lower clergy, while the Vatican and even some of the hierarchy were prominent in helping refugees. When the problem arose of finding leaders for a democratic régime after the war, Catholic Action leaders had at least the advantage of experience in organization, nor were most of them indisposed to enlarge the field of their activities. The historic capacity of the Church to give of her best in crises (one recalls Bismarck's observation that in the French countryside after the Franco-Prussian war 'the only people we found on their feet were the curés') was evident again, and except for the intransigent Left and those 'liberals with long memories' of whom Jemolo speaks, the dubious record of complaisance shown under Fascism by many elements in the Italian Church was at least temporarily forgotten. After all, it had not been the whole story: there had been a great deal of courage and candour which was at least as impressive as the fearlessness of *fuorusciti* who denounced the régime from the safe distance of Paris, New York or London. The inexhaustible charitable energy of Pius XII himself lent a fair aspect to the image of the papacy, while the skill of De Gasperi and his obvious independence of mind lent prestige to the new party and allayed the old suspicions of clericalism.

Yet the unity imposed by crisis, by the common effort against Communism and by the desperate need for reconstruction only masked the difficulties inherent in the Italian situation. Italy was a late arrival in the Christian Democratic field. It was a country where democracy was not well understood. Churchmen shared this limited understanding, and for many of them it went with an equally limited enthusiasm. Yet Rome, the capital of Italy, was also the centre of the Church and the seat of papacy and Curia. Catholic Action, at the very time when its influence, direct or indirect, on Italian politics was strongest, was subjected to a vigorous process of centralization. That dependence on the hierarchy which was essentially part of Catholic Action as described in the Concordat—which was still of course in force—had been its strength under Fascism, and had even suited the Fascist book insofar as it reflected and guaranteed the purely confessional concerns of the Catholic organizations. It had in fact been consistent with a good deal of pro-Fascist flag-wagging. Once Catholic Action became associated with Christian Democracy and a vehicle of political pressure, such dependence could only lead to imputations of clericalism against the Christian Democrats—imputations which were not softened by any feeling that Catholic Action was a fruitful training ground for politics or that Catholic Action as such had anything notable to contribute to the national fund of practical political wisdom.

The architect of the highly centralized and disciplined Catholic Action of the post-war years was Dr Luigi Gedda. He was one of the select group who enjoyed the confidence of Pius XII—a confidence which he exploited freely to create for himself a position of such dominance in the Italian Catholic world that he became popularly known among his critics as the Italian Salazar. He was a most able organizer and administrator and a dynamic personality of unquestioned apostolic zeal, but politically naïve—the supreme example of what has come to be known as an 'integralist'. Not perhaps the man most likely to be over-nice about the delicate distinction between Catholic and political action. He had an exaggerated belief in the value of organization; on one occasion he told a conference of diocesan presidents of Catholic Action: 'The three million members of Catholic Action are a marvellous reality, the more so when we think that to every member there corresponds a membership card, to every membership card a subscription, to every subscription a newspaper, and above all to every card, subscription and paper a trained soul (*un' anima formata*)'. A member of the French Catholic youth movement told his Italian confrères on one occasion: 'You Italians, when you have succeeded in organizing a great meeting in a *piazza*, believe that you have testified to the truth.'

It is not surprising to find Gedda's historical diagnosis of contemporary ills somewhat over-simplified; he told another conference of diocesan presidents: 'It is four centuries since that laceration of Europe from which even today we suffer: a laceration brought about by Protestantism. . . . But see what has happened as the years have passed. Protestantism meant free enquiry (*libero esame*); one might say religious liberalism, and this religious liberalism was not long in becoming political liberalism, the liberalism of the French Revolution, which expressed not the Christian conception of liberty but a so-called liberty to do everything, which in reality is licence . . . and this political current derived from the religious current of Protestantism spread and developed in Europe at a period when economic and social phenomena of the first importance were maturing . . . in the face of these the dominant liberalism repeated the gesture of Pontius Pilate, washing its hands: *Laissez faire*, *laissez passer*. And then you see the social condition aggravated, and the first, romantic socialism come to birth . . . but this socialism matured, and had its doctrine . . . it became a political system, Communism. See how there is a fatal logic of error. . . . From that Protestant revolution there descends over the centuries the Communism of today, and that Protestantism which was originally stopped at the borders of Italy enters now to poison our people through its by-products.'[1] Gedda in fact reflected only too accurately the limitations of Italian Catholic life and education since the *Risorgimento*—limitations of which intelligent Italian Catholics themselves were becoming increasingly critical, and which explained why Italian Catholic impact, so strong in politics after the war for the reasons given above, was so negligible in the field of culture.

Gedda became something of a legend in his time, and it is easy to exaggerate his political importance and that of Catholic Action under him: it was of course always in the interest of the parties of the Left in Italy, and not least of the left wing of the Christian Democrats, to do so. In the crucial election of 1948 he was success-

[1] Quoted by Poggi, *Il Clero di Riserva*, p. 171.

ful in organizing 'civic committees' to mobilize votes for the Christian Democrats. These civic committees, not being officially a part of Catholic Action, evaded the provision of the Concordat which excluded Catholic Action from party politics. It was this success, certainly valuable in keeping Communism at bay, that thrust him to the top of Catholic Action; but he never really repeated it. The 'crusade' he organized in 1950 for the 'great return' of Italian Communists to the Church was hardly political, and was a good deal less successful; so was the *S Plan* to wean the workers from the Communist-controlled General Trades Union. In 1952 he launched 'Operation Sturzo' in the Roman municipal elections—it was the first of several attempts to organize a single anti-Communist front of Christian Democrats and parties to the Right, including neo-Fascists. It drew its name from Gedda's attempt to involve the aged Don Sturzo as a figurehead. The plan was defeated by the resistance of Christian Democrat leaders themselves, and in fact the relations of the party, and especially of De Gasperi, with the 'Italian Salazar' remained consistently cool. One of the most regrettable aspects of De Gasperi's untimely death was that it weakened resistance to the *linea Gedda*, which itself was intensified in the last years as Pius XII's health deteriorated and his detachment grew.

Gedda undoubtedly enjoyed for some time the Pope's confidence, as has been said, but it is doubtful whether he retained it unimpaired, and Pius's many pronouncements on Catholic Action and on the allied questions of Italian Church-State relations by no means add up to an endorsement of the *linea Gedda*. The two men really had little enough in common. They shared a strong belief in authority and discipline and a horror of Communism, but Pius XII could hardly have been further removed from Gedda's exuberant naïveté. One who knew him well said to me of Pius XII that his profound supernatural faith was in fact allied to a natural Roman scepticism, a mistrust of vast and vague ideals, of over-simplification and of the possibilities of manipulating men.[1]

Of the value of the lay *apostolate*, especially where there is a shortage of priests, he showed no doubt from the beginning of his pontificate. In 1939 he said (without any specific mention of Catholic

[1] It is hardly necessary to add that this has nothing to do with the 'cold scepticism' of Herr Hochhuth's travesty.

Action): 'This apostolic work, carried out according to the mind of the Church, consecrates the layman as a kind of *minister Christi* in the sense in which St Augustine explains: "When, brethren, you hear Our Lord saying: where I am there too my servant will be, do not think solely of good bishops and clerics: you too in your way minister to Christ by a good life, by almsgiving, by preaching His name and teaching when you can." '

He certainly repudiated the *post-Risorgimento* Italian tradition of detachment from secular life and siege mentality. In 1939 also the young men of Catholic Action were told that their 'faith must not be kept in ivory towers'. Throughout the war, a concern second only to his efforts to mitigate the effects of war was that the Church should be *ready*, when the end of the war came, to play her part in the new situation: 'It is Our duty, and that of all the faithful, to prepare spiritually, with prayer and example, with purification and penance, work and sacrifice, this future encounter between Christ and a world more than ever needful of His light and His grace.'

In 1946, as post-war problems loomed, he created thirty-two new cardinals (shattering the traditional Italian majority, though not greatly disturbing the balance of the Roman Curia) and said to them as they gathered before him (February 20), 'The Church cannot enclose herself, inert, within the secrecy of her temples, abdicating her divine and essential mission to train the complete man, to collaborate without ceasing in laying solid foundations of society. In this regard the faithful, and especially the laity, find themselves in the vanguard of the Church.

'[The laity] should understand ever more clearly not only that they belong to the Church but that they *are* the Church—that is, the community of the faithful on earth under the direction of the common head and the bishops in communion with him. From the dawn of her history the faithful with the consent of their bishops have entered into associations for the most varied purposes, and the Holy See has never ceased to approve and praise this.'

It is interesting to consider this in relation to some of the things which have been put forth, and received, as startling novelties on the subject of the laity during the present Council. It has of course nothing directly to do with political activity; but it was impossible to ignore at that time the question of political implications, and less than a month later the Pope broached these, giving the customary annual talk to Rome's parish priests and to those appointed to give the Lenten sermon courses. The political future of Italy was still very much in the balance. A people long unused to the exercise of political rights was being besieged from all points of the political compass. On the Left the old cry of clerical interference was being raised. Pius faced squarely the question 'what are the rights and duties of priests in questions concerning public life?' They are, he said,

1. To teach the faithful by word and writing all concerning faith and conduct, and tell them what is incompatible with the Church's teaching whether in religion, philosophy or practical programmes.

2. Voting is a grave responsibility, especially voting for those who make the constitution and laws, particularly concerning religious holidays, marriage, the family, schools, social justice. Hence the Church must explain moral duties deriving from the franchise.

3. Article 43 of the Concordat forbids priests to join or fight for any political party. The Church will faithfully enforce it. But she cannot renounce the rights referred to above, nor allow the State unilaterally to judge the priest in the exercise of his office or apply sanctions.

4. Priests' responsibilities can extend to giving advice and *instructions* even in relation to public life. The civil powers cannot arbitrarily judge abuses of this responsibility under the facile pretext of separating the clergy from politics. Do not forget that the persecutions and police spying of Nazism were conducted in the name of resistance to 'political Catholicism'.

The key word here was the one I have italicized. If it meant instructions how to vote, or even instructions how not to vote, was it compatible with 'not fighting for any political party?' On June 1 of the same year, the eve of the Italian and French elections, Pius XII offered his own practical interpretation of these principles. The question is, he said whether 'these two Latin sisters, with more than a millennium of Christian civilization behind them, will continue to take their stand on the solid rock of Christianity, in recognition of a personal God, on belief in the spiritual dignity and eternal destiny of man, or whether they wish to commit their future to the unyielding power of a materialist state, without an other-worldly ideal, without religion, without God. The answer is in the hands of the electors, and a high and grave responsibility. On the one side, the spirit of domination, the absolutism of a state which claims to hold all the controls of the political, social and economic machine, in which men will be no more than lifeless cogs. On the other side, the Church, calm, resolute, not seeking strife but determined to defend her children.' The only reasonable interpretation of this seems to be that the choice between a vote for the Communist party and any other vote is not a political but a moral one, and hence hardly falls within the terms of Article 43 of the Concordat. After all, even in a state where Christian Democracy exists 'the Church' can hardly be plausibly set up as one side of a *political* choice. But however clear the distinction was here, it could clearly create difficulties in other contexts—as for instance in later years in that of the Opening to the Left. Not, of course that the papacy committed itself to any instructions, or even advice, on this last; but other high ecclesiastics were to prove less reluctant.

Exactly two years later Pius XII reverted to the same theme, in an interesting context; it was a few weeks after the elections of April 1948 in which Gedda's civic committees had operated on behalf of the Christian Democrats, and aroused considerable criticism. Speaking of a 'reawakening of Christian spirit and resolution' the Pope added, 'Catholic forces, while remaining independent of political groupings and tendencies, can sometimes follow a path parallel to these, where common interest suggests it. Parallel but not more—without identification or subordination.'

If this was a justification of the activity of the civic committees, it seemed no less to sanction limited collaboration with secularist parties. True, the Pope went on to condemn Catholics who *join* movements for laicizing and de-christianizing private or public life: but joining involves identification or subordination—not a mere parallel course dictated by a limited common interest. Can it in fact be argued in face of this passage that John XXIII, in tolerating the Opening to the Left, was 'reversing' the policy of Pius XII?

The related questions of the proper limits of Catholic Action and of Church and State continued to occupy Pius XII: he was aware, it seems of divergent currents within the Church, and in particular of contrasts between the Italy of the Gedda period and other parts of the Church. 1951 was a year in which he spoke a good deal on the theme. To the parish priests and Lenten preachers on February 6 he voiced his concern about 'the other Rome'—the non-ecclesiastical Rome which was steadily acquiring the reputation of being one of the most thoroughly materialistic and frivolous cities in the world. It called to his mind the well-known chapter of St Augustine's *City of God* (II, 20) which describes so forcefully the mind and manners of Rome in the last generation before the barbarian invasions.

There are too many circles in Rome, he said, which a priest cannot even enter; add to this the sad lack of Roman vocations, and the inadequate co-operation of the many non-parochial clergy of the City in such things as youth work, and here is a vast field for the lay apostolate: 'in friendly forms', he adds. He goes on to warn the clergy against 'excessive bureaucracy' in the care of souls (even they were being affected by the craze for organization). People should 'feel the goodness and paternal affection of the parish priest, who should have an exact knowledge of his parish, street by street, house by house, and should keep a parish register not as an end in itself but only as an aid to this personal intimacy.'

The anti-Geddan overtones of this become more explicit in an address to Italian Catholic Actionists on April 3: Catholic Action, said the Pope, can have no honorary members; it is not a new organization of apostolic work growing beside the existing ones. However important the Church acknowledges social solutions to be, her religious mission remains for her primary. Catholic Actionists should not think of themselves as cogs wholly dependent on the movement of a vast machine: nor should their leaders see things in this way. He added reminders that Catholic Action should not become an instrument of party politics and that it had no right of patronage over other associations.

When Pius addressed the World Congress of the Lay Apostolate on October 14 of the same year he was obviously still turning over the same questions in his mind. He repeated the basic principle that Catholic Action should not become an instrument of party politics, but added 'just as it is praiseworthy to hold aloof from the contingent quarrels that envenom party strife, so it is blameworthy to leave the field free to the unworthy or the incapable to direct the affairs of the state'. It is difficult, he concluded, to formulate one rule for everybody; circumstances, mentality are not the same everywhere. Did this mean simply that Catholic Actionists could and should, as individuals, play their part in politics, or was it an advance justification of 'Operation Sturzo', which took place some months later? If the Pope saw the undesirability of implicating Catholic

Action and the Church directly in party politics, he was equally sensitive to any hint of confining the Church to the sacristy. 'We congratulate you,' he told the same audience 'on resisting efforts to confine the Church to matters called "purely religious". If the Church is kept in the sacristy anywhere it is by force: she should still be doing all that is possible to extend her influence outside.'

On this and other occasions he launched into historical considerations. He invited his audience not to 'overlook or fail to acknowledge the beneficent influence of the close union which until the French Revolution governed, in the Catholic world, the mutual relations of the two powers established by God—Church and State. The intimacy of their relations on the common ground of public life created, in general, an atmosphere of Christian *esprit* which rendered largely unnecessary the delicate work to which priests and laity today must harness themselves in order to safeguard and give practical expression to the Faith.' But rosy though this picture might be, it was no mere *laus temporis acti*. The Pope went on: 'At the end of the eighteenth century a new factor came into play. On the one hand, the American Constitution, the establishment of the United States which developed very rapidly, with a parallel development of the Church's life and vigour there and on the other the French Revolution and its ramifications came near to detaching Church from State. In varying degrees the logical outcome was to leave the Church power to act, fulfil her mission and defend her rights and liberties by her own means. This was the origin of the so-called Catholic Movements which, under the leadership of priests and laity strongly united and loyal, deployed the mass of believers in the fight for the faith. Was not this the initiation of the laity into the apostolate?'

The assimilation of the Catholic movements of recent history to the lay apostolate is more convincing for some countries than for others. In countries where there is complete religious freedom, in the sense of a fair field and no favour, where Catholics are neither subject to political and civil disabilities nor victims of prejudice or discrimination, a Catholic movement may conceivably be apostolic in its main purpose. But such Utopias were rare at the time when the Catholic movements were launched. In countries where Catholic life involves a struggle with the powers that be or with social hostility or ostracism, the organization and discipline needed to achieve results, or even to survive, is likely to be such as to obscure the apostolic and emphasize the 'political' colour of the Catholic 'movement'. In Italy especially, where the difficulties, often exaggerated, of Catholic life after the *Risorgimento* went with the memory (dear to clerics) of life under the Temporal Power or the Catholic principalities, the Church felt herself especially under siege and embattled against the world, and the emphasis on discipline and close subordination to the hierarchy was paramount in discussion of Catholic association. 'Leadership', 'deployed', 'fight', 'defend' are words used naturally enough by Pius in the context of initiation into the lay *apostolate;* the undertones are of a better world lost and a worse one not yet accepted with resignation.

The same ideas are running through the Pope's mind when four years later he addresses the Tenth International Congress of Historical Sciences, but there is a significant development: 'The Church is not an ideology—"Catholicism"—but as well as being a divine institution she is a historical fact. She has adapted herself, assimilated new things; she has been a faithful advocate of political authority.

'In the pre-Christian era public authority was competent in the sacred and profane fields. In the Christian era the former passed to the Church, and the history of Church-State relations began.' He goes on to quote a passage from Leo XIII's *Immortale Dei* arguing that history shows the Church to have either invented or fostered in political society those developments which have been for the general good—checks on the irresponsible exercise of sovereign power or its excessive interference with local and group rights. Nevertheless, the Church has generally held to the doctrine of the two perfect societies, as set out classically by Leo in the Encyclical quoted, in *Diuturnum Illud* and in *Sapientiae Christianae*.

He reverts to the other side of the picture, quoting Boniface VIII's words to the Hapsburg Envoy in April 1303: 'As the moon has no light but from the sun, so earthly power has nothing but what it receives from ecclesiastical power.' His comment is, 'It was a conception conditioned by the age: it would have been more remarkable had it not appeared.' In the context of the thirteenth and fourteenth centuries, he is prepared to defend spiritual and civil penalties for abandonment of the Faith: 'they were aimed to preserve the religious and ecclesiastical unity of the West'. To non-Catholics, the Church now applies canon 1351—'No one should be forced against his will to embrace the Catholic Faith'—and she considers, he adds rather curiously, that 'their convictions constitute a motive, though not the principal one, for tolerance.'

'The Church does not disguise that she considers unity of people in one faith, and harmony with the State, as the normal condition; but she recognises that for some time events have moved in the opposite direction—towards multiplicity of confessions and conceptions of life within the same nation, with Catholics in a minority of varying strength,' and again he singles out America as a country where the Church has expanded in these conditions (cf. Chapter 12, pp. 289 *et seq.*).

There is a transitional air, an air almost of thinking aloud, about much of this. We detect the voice of the canon lawyer looking to general principles and backwards towards the ideal (if not idealized) relations of the past; but more clear—as proper to such an audience—is (in the above-quoted passage) the voice of the fashioner of concordats, looking around and ahead, recognizing the dynamic character of history, the evolving of a pluralist society, recognizing that ecclesiastical politics are, like others, the art of the possible. Mentioning tolerance, he cites his own famous long speech of December 1953 to Italian jurisconsults. This, with its interesting background, will be discussed elsewhere (cf. Chapter 12, p. 289), for in it Pius treats at large the question of religious tolerance in a context he found congenial—that of the World Community. But in its last section he touches on concordats:

'Concordats are, for the Church, the expression of collaboration between Church and State. In principle, in thesis, she cannot approve complete separation of the two powers. A concordat ought to ensure the Church, *de jure* and *de facto*, a stable position in the state and guarantee her full independence in the fulfilment of her divine mission. It is possible that in a concordat Church and State may proclaim a common religious conviction; but it can also happen that one of the functions of the concordat will be to forestall disputes of principle and remove from the outset matter for conflict. When the Church has signed a concordat, this signature holds for the entire content; but its intimate sense can (by mutual consent) be variously graded. It can signify express approval or mere tolerance.'

This passage justifies a digression. It should remind us of the historical origins of concordats—in that society which Pius has been previously describing, not without nostalgia: a society in which the ecclesiastical power was interwoven with the secular in a way which is quite insufficiently expressed by the modern word 'establishment'.

The various conventions of the early twelfth century which culminated in the Concordat of Worms and settled by compromises the conflicts concerning the investiture of bishops, took this state of affairs for granted. So did later medieval instruments like the Concordat of Vienna of 1448. They were the upshot of lengthy bargaining between two authorities which believed themselves supreme in their respective spheres—spheres which were not easy to keep separate in that society whose roots were feudal.

The French Concordat of July 1801 is of crucial importance as the first effort to codify the relations of the Church with the modern state born of the French Revolution. It is therefore essentially different from those concordats which had merely settled family quarrels usually turning on financially profitable 'privileges' or immunities. It is true that its preamble recognizes 'that the Catholic Apostolic Roman religion is the religion of the great majority of Frenchmen'. But it 'is no longer the religion of the French *res publica*'. Consalvi made strenuous efforts to carry this point, but Napoleon could hardly have yielded without betraying the principles of the Revolution.

The absolutist states of the eighteenth century may have done their utmost to empty the Church's privileges and immunities of content, but they had not generally repudiated them. The 'Gallican' theory of pre-Revolution Church-State relations, often expounded of course by clerics, had in fact insisted strongly on Church rights, though on its own version of them. Now, this state founded on the sovereignty of the people recognized no position of privilege for the Church. If her hierarchy was salaried, it was certainly not by right, but simply by way of compensation, so that the usurpers of Church property might be left undisturbed. The rights of religious orders were totally disregarded—they were banned. A complete reorganization of dioceses—arguably a sensible one—was imposed on the Church. Worst of all, a series of 'organic articles', unilaterally added to the Concordat though not destined to last, imposed the worst excesses of Gallicanism[1] on the papacy. The immediate practical value of the Concordat was melodramatically illustrated during the rest of Napoleon's career by his treatment of Pius VII—one of the nastiest episodes in European history.

Nevertheless it was this document that was of real interest for

[1] Gallicanism was a tendency in the French Church towards greater independence from Rome; the opposing tendency was called ultramontanism (see p. 76).

the future of Church-State relations, and hence indirectly of the Church's relations with other Christian bodies—not the series of old-type concordats which the able Consalvi concluded with the reactionary Catholic signatories of the Congress of Vienna. These looked backwards, and merely perpetuated occasions for the old quarrels and interference. It was unfortunate that the excesses of the revolutionary movement made the Church slow to discern the signs of the times and hesitant to accept the new order of things, which had so many roots in Christian history and thought. Both Pius VII and Pius IX were frightened off liberal sympathies by the harsh course of events, and it came to be accepted as a commonplace that the Church was aligned with the Ancien Régime against 'liberalism'—a term used far too vaguely. It was to be left to the Second Vatican Council in 1963 to present a Declaration on Religious Liberty which, though in many respects it had venerable ancestry could, because of this recent history, be criticized and feared by legal-minded conservatives as 'likely to make future concordats impossible.' (Cf. Chapter 12, pp. 293 *et seq.*).

In 1801 the Church was making a concordat with the modern state in its most secular form—despite all appearances to the contrary. This secular state was based on half a dozen fundamental principles: the natural equality of men and their inalienable right to life, liberty and security; the sovereignty of the people; the right to resistance and revolution (in the name of the people); equality before the law; universal suffrage and representative government; the 'liberties', of conscience, of worship, of speech and the press, saving public order. All of these were capable of Catholic interpretation, some of them found support in Catholic tradition, none was necessarily tied to atheism, anti-clericalism, confiscation or any other of the accompaniments of the revolution that afflicted the Church. But it was, inevitably, these latter aspects of current 'liberalism' that dominated the ecclesiastical mind, so that it was clear that in the Concordat she was tolerating, as the lesser evil, a *fait accompli*—and this to the intense annoyance of many French loyalist bishops and clergy, and the conservative Roman curial officials of the day. She was certainly not accepting the Revolution nor even admitting the possibility of its acceptance.

These two assumptions, that of a strictly-rationed 'tolerance' and that of antipathy and suspicion towards the idea of 'separation' of Church and State as inextricably bound up with the worst excesses of the Revolution, were to lie behind the approach to concordats down to recent times. One of the Church's bargaining counters, it almost seems, is the conviction that she is everywhere entitled to a privileged position, however history may have obscured the title, and that she enters every negotiation as the dominant partner;[1] claims which a Catholic state might be expected to acknowledge, but which rather more surprisingly seem to have been pragmatically accepted by other states. Z. Zielewicz, discussing the unique standing of the Church and the Holy See in the international community, bases it empirically on the *de facto* unique character of Catholic supranationalism and unity under the Pope rather than on any *de jure* claims to be *the* Church. He contents himself with showing that other religious bodies lack the necessary practical qualifications for recognition as subjects of international law.[2]

The French Concordat of 1801 made no allusion to any other religion, but it must have been clear to everybody what was intended. When Napoleon was consecrated and crowned as Emperor by Pius VII in Paris in 1804 his oath included, in the spirit of the revolutionary dogmas, an undertaking to respect and ensure liberty of worship. Recalling the episode later in his famous pamphlet on the *Syllabus*, Dupanloup described how Pius VII was unhappy about this, which he thought smacked of indifferentism; when Consalvi raised the point, the answer was that there was no intention either of sanctioning indifferentism or of denying the authority of the Church, but merely of 'civil tolerance and assurance of personal protection'. The Pope declared himself satisfied and Napoleon took the oath in his presence. It is amusing to reflect that what was thus agreed between Pope and Emperor here was almost exactly the position set out in the Declaration of Vatican II—a hundred and sixty years later, and greeted with similar misgivings from the Right. It may be allowed that it also represents an element of inconsistency on the part of Napoleon, who doubtless at that moment saw himself more easily as heir of Charlemagne than of Robespierre.

Be that as it may, few would now deny that in this first settlement with the modern world it was Pius and Consalvi who were right and

[1] What chiefly made curialists dubious about the declaration of a general right to religious liberty was that it would destroy this 'basis for concordats'—i.e., the Church's claim to a unique sanction for her own freedom as the repository of divine authority on earth.

[2] Quoted Cardinale, *Le Saint Siège et la Diplomatie*, pp. 49–50.

the angry French and curial conservatives who were wrong. If the settlement seemed on the short view, during Napoleon's ascendancy, to lead only to the latest and most unrewarding version of political Catholicism, in the long run it was the starting point for a new genuinely liberal order. This was first sketched out in the 1830s by the group who conducted *L'Avenir*; it was born out of due time, was exaggerated by Lamennais, could not compete with the apocalyptic ultramontanism of De Maistre and in the end largely provoked Gregory XVI's anti-liberal Encyclical *Mirari Vos;* but its influence was not destined to perish.[1]

One of the places where it spread was Belgium, where the 1830 revolution against Dutch rule followed hard on a concordat concluded with the Protestant government by the future Gregory XVI, then Prefect of Propaganda. This was yet another type of concordat—with a country where another religion was established.[2] It presented a paradoxical situation, where the Church was put in the position of saying, in effect; 'We will not merely tolerate your heresy and intolerance, but we will discountenance the resistance of that compact minority of your Catholic subjects which finds them intolerable.' In a less unbalanced atmosphere, a few concessions to 'liberalism' might have seemed less than rash compared with these acrobatics. And indeed, the first Belgian state to emerge from the Revolution—a free church in a free state in a predominantly Catholic country—was given a *nihil obstat* by Gregory, who also treated with *de facto* revolutionary governments in Latin America.

Gregory has been rightly censured for ill-judged and anachronistic fulminations against the political ideas of his day; but what strikes us about the whole period which culminated in the famous *Syllabus*

[1] Hales has trenchantly summed up the mood of the Vatican after 1815: 'The Catholic Poles were told that they must remain quietly obedient to their autocratic and foreign sovereign, the Czar, although he was denying the necessary liberties of their faith. The Catholic Belgians were told to obey the Calvinist King of Holland, although he was doing the same. The Catholic Irish were told that they must not mind having their episcopal nominations vetoed by a Protestant King in London. The French liberal Catholics were silenced, and told to obey their most Christian King, who in fact was an agnostic; everywhere the first principle was legitimacy, and this generally meant absolutism. . . .' *Revolution and Papacy*, pp. 278–9. In fairness it should be added that Gregory XVI in an audience with the Czar spoke so strongly of the latter's treatment of the Poles that the Czar emerged from the audience pale and shaken. Sir John Acton was present at this audience.

[2] It is tempting to speculate what might have happened with a similar arrangement in England. Plans for it, canvassed by Castlereagh in 1814, were defeated by Daniel O'Connell and the Irish clergy.

of 1864 is the contrast between the proclaimed intransigence of the Vatican and the almost mole-like perseverance with which the Secretariat of State under Consalvi and Antonelli collected concordats.[1]

The *Syllabus* was really a sort of tendentious index to the writings of Pius IX (not his own work) which had the effect of inflating his dislike of current events and ideas in Italy into general anathemas. Yet if a liberal solution of the Church-State problem in Italy could have been represented to the patriotic Pius IX as a matter of principle and not of force, and if Cavour had restrained the grosser excesses of the *Risorgimento* movement, it is by no means clear that a settlement other than the disastrous one of 1870 could not have been found. Antonelli would certainly have negotiated such a settlement if so instructed. In the ten years or more preceding Cavour's death the Vatican signed a dozen agreements some of which were with *de facto* revolutionary governments. Yet the threat of the withdrawal of the French garrison from Rome was the last straw which induced Pius to sign the *Syllabus* which ended with the notorious article 80, condemning the proposition that 'the Roman Pontiff can and should reconcile and harmonize himself with progress, liberalism and recent civilization'. This was lifted from the document in which Pius had finally broken off all parley with Cavour about the Temporal Power, just before the latter's death.[2]

Dupanloup, Ollivier and Newman all heroically leant over backwards to defend a moderate interpretation of the *Syllabus*, the first drawing heavily on the distinction between the plane of 'thesis' and that of 'hypothesis' (the ideal state of affairs and the actual) which had originated with the *Civiltà Cattolico* Jesuits, and was, as we have seen, revived by Pius XII in connection with concordats. It was certainly a distinction which made more sense of the internal contrast in papal policy just outlined, and would have made no less sense of a bargain with Cavour over the Temporal Power—though those who on either side accused Dupanloup and Newman of 'watering down' the *Syllabus* plainly failed to grasp the force of the distinction.

In the perspective of today the point of interest (and the justi-

[1] This contrast was to be repeated in relations with Communism after the Second World War.

[2] It thus is a supreme example of giving Italian quarrels a dogmatic-sounding world setting.

fication of this long historical digression) is that in 1953, only a decade before the Second Vatican Council, Pius XII is still arguing in the same terms, as he faces the question of the religious arrangements in a possible international community.

It is a somewhat complex picture that emerges from an examination of Pius XII's attitude, over his long reign, to secular society, the state and the layman. The widely-travelled diplomat and avid reader could not fail to be aware of the world scene and its diversities; but he was also a keen Italian patriot and the son of a Roman ecclesiastical lawyer, steeped in recent Roman ecclesiastical and political history. If he was aware of the pattern of pluralism emerging in the world according to the American style, he was more deeply conscious of the theocratic tradition which had only come to a formal end in Rome a few years before his birth, and which, still dominating the *jus publicum* of the Church, formed the staple of every canon lawyer's training.

We have seen that this cast of mind disposed many Italian ecclesiastics to be, putting it mildly, remarkably long-suffering in their attitude to Fascism. If they would have formally repudiated many of the old-fashioned ideas about 'the secular arm', they were not averse to having their tasks rendered superficially easier by a little Caesaropapism. By temperament, by long experience and by his circumstances as Pope, Pius XII was exempt from this sort of naïveté; but an authoritarian bent and a deep horror of Communism combined to fill him with reserves in his judgement both of political democracy and of independent lay activity. In his Christmas broadcast of 1953 he warned his listeners that 'the weakness of authority undermines a country's solidity more than any other difficulties, and the weakness of one country brings with it the weakness of Europe and endangers the general peace. It is therefore necessary to react against the mistaken view that the just prevalence of authority and law necessarily opens the way to tyranny. We have said before [Christmas 1944] that in a democratic state authority ought to be true and effective. Otherwise the "ideal" of liberty is licence, without responsibility or respect for others.'

He might be thought to be providing a gloss on this in telling the Roman parish priests and Lenten preachers in March 1957 that public opinion should press the government to fulfil its concordatory obligation to preserve the sacred character of Rome, by discouraging pornography in various fields. The instance he primarily cited, that of two outstandingly blatant posters, was clear enough: but it was perhaps not so clear that he fully assessed the dangers of this kind of ecclesiastically-inspired paternalism, the extent to which it could be abused by the clumsy, the fanatical, the ignorant or the merely designing.

He had travelled in America; American influence and personnel increased at the Vatican in his time; curial personalities travelled frequently in the States and American money in one way or another poured freely into the Vatican; every year Pius himself addressed a begging broadcast to the children of America at the beginning of Lent. Yet on the few occasions when, addressing Americans, he referred to their political system and way of life, it was generally the note of warning that was dominant over that of congratulation.

The first year of his pontificate was also the one hundred and fiftieth anniversary of the establishment of the United States hierarchy; his congratulatory Encyclical letter *Sertum Laetitiae* inevitably had much praise for the spectacular progress of the American Church in that period; but it also contained what was for such an occasion a notable amount of admonition, about the ill effects of materialism especially in the American educational system, about the 'plague of divorce', about social injustice manifest in gross inequalities of wealth. No doubt the advice of a hierarchy predominantly of Irish descent and of the very conservative Catholic University of Washington (the only educational establishment the Pope singled out for praise) did something to set the direction of his criticisms, but the censorious note does obtrude. He sounded it again eighteen months later in a broadcast to the Eucharistic Congress at St Paul, Minnesota:

'You live in a country where a tradition of human freedoms allows you to practise your faith without let or hindrance. Your chief enemy is within you—that natural drag of fallen humanity to self-seeking and sin. Self-sacrifice must combat him. . . . You must not forget that you belong to a Church whose Founder and Head was scourged, mocked and crucified, and that His body which is the Church is today being persecuted.'

Many of the Pope's older hearers must have reflected that they could remember something very like persecution, and that self-sacrifice had paid a far from insignificant part in raising the Church in America to its present position.

In his Christmas broadcast of 1944 Pius spoke of democracy as 'an organic unity of persons, not an amorphous mass', in which the moral elevation, practical suitability and intellectual capacity of the deputies is a matter of life and death. People get the government they deserve, he added. Again, Americans (and British) who had just helped to deliver Italy from Fascism may well have been tempted to reflect that in a country which gets, whether deservedly or not, an adventurer as a dictator these things are no less a matter of life and death, but are much more likely to be a matter of death. If a democratic nation finds these qualities too clamorously lacking in its public men, it can at least get rid of them; dictators, in modern times, have proved a fixture short of national catastrophe. Pius indeed recognized these persuasions to democracy as operating after the war, yet the tone of this broadcast is rather that democracy is 'allowed'.

He probably spoke with an eye on Italy, where a second experiment in democracy was about to be launched. He had lived in Rome through the travail of war, with the isolation of Vatican life greatly increased and Italy and its capital dominating his consciousness. The problem of its future, important enough by any standards, he saw as crucial.[1] When a group of people from the Adriatic province of Picenum, working in Rome, sought audience of him in 1958 he told them: 'We should not be afraid of patriotism, or allow local patriotism to overshadow it—especially if the *patria* is Italy. . . . Italy, thought of and willed by God as the land in which the centre of His Church should be sited, was the object of His special love. No people has its destinies linked with the work of Christ as the Italian people has.' Conceding that patriotism can degenerate and become excessive and harmful nationalism, the Pope went on: 'There are those in Italy who raise the alarm that Christianity would take from Caesar that which belongs to him—as though Christ had not commanded otherwise! As though the lawful and healthy lay character of the state were not one of the principles of Catholic doctrine. As though it were not the continuous effort of ecclesiastical tradition to keep the two powers separate yet, according to right principles, united. As though the mixing of the sacred and the profane were not most strongly verified in history when a part of the faithful is detached from the Church.' This last allusion was presumably aimed at Protestant countries, inheritors of the principle

[1] Cf. p. 67), the 'two Latin sisters' speech of June 1946.

cujus regio ejus religio, and perhaps at Orthodox countries. But it could be pointed out that America, where a large part of the faithful is and always has been detached from the Church, the mixing of sacred and profane is not verified at all, whereas in Fascist Italy and in General Franco's Spain this kind of confusion is not unknown. In Christian Democrat Italy a notable example of it, and one which casts a curious light on the Vatican attitude to Italian politics, was to be 'Operation Sturzo', which took place at the Roman administrative elections of April 1952. Alcide De Gasperi's daughter Maria, who often acted as his secretary, has given an account of it in her recent memoir of her father.[1]

When De Gasperi emerged as leader of the new Italian Christian Democrat party after the war, he was able to claim, as he did before a university audience in 1946, that during his long period of asylum in the Vatican he had never as much as visited the Secretariat of State, and had steered clear of practical politics. He was a deeply convinced and devout Catholic, and made no doubt that Catholic principles should direct political and international discussion. He spoke always with reverence and gratitude of the recent tradition of papal social teaching, and not least of that of Pius XII, and was always anxious that his own policies should be clearly understood in the Vatican. But he was no less anxious that the Holy See should not provoke a fresh wave of anti-clericalism by interfering with politicians and party matters, whether directly or through the instrumentality of Catholic Action.

In 1949 he wrote to Pius XII, who was reported 'much perplexed' by the projected collaboration of the Christian Democrats with the Social Democrats (who had split off from the then revolutionary-minded Nenni party and accepted the leadership of the moderate laic Saragat) and the Republican party which enshrined the ideal of the *Risorgimento*. De Gasperi explained to the Pontiff the importance of weaning moderate socialism to a policy of gradual reform, and of winning those moderate anticlericals among republicans who only voted anti-Communist out of fear to a more positive appreciation of Christian Democratic ideals. He defined both clericalism and anticlericalism in terms of lack of respect for consciences. He was aware that the cry of 'clerical interference in politics' was a stock one with persecuting totalitarianism, but he did not regard it as necessarily always and everywhere an unjustified

[1] *De Gasperi, Uomo Solo*, Rome, 1964.

complaint. Moreover, he did not believe that in steering austerely clear of politics Catholic Action cramped its field of activity: rather that it would thereby be left freer to influence society more widely.

He was convinced that to create a confessional common front would simply invite the creation of a contrary, anticlerical common front. The Christian Democrat party could only overcome its internal difficulties and launch an effective programme of reform by strictly political methods—by a cautious and laborious pragmatism. In 1952 he wrote to the Pope in this sense, adding that though papal social teaching always tried to keep ideals and principles within a practical framework, the hard core of its more passionate advocates, especially within the party, often failed to do the same. 'If it is true that we men of action have need of the light and air that comes from ideas, it is no less true that we need understanding and encouragement.' He believed that the unity of the party was vital at that moment, but very much in danger, and appealed to the Holy Father to give his advice and influence towards maintaining it.

The background of this unusual step was of course 'Operation Sturzo'. Gedda, the Catholic Action leader and his associates were trying to achieve a '*unione sacra*' between Christian Democracy and the parties of the Right, including the neo-Fascist *Movimento Sociale Italiano*, to be expressed in the presentation of single voting lists at the administrative elections. The following is Maria De Gasperi's account of the sequence of events. She bases it mainly on the relevant pages of the unpublished diaries of Emilio Bonomelli, manager of the papal villa at Castelgandolfo, which she was allowed to examine.

'On the morning of April 19 the Jesuit Father Lombardi came to Castelgandolfo to speak to my mother. For an hour and a half he mingled blandishments with threats, insisting that Christian Democracy should broaden its front by means of a single voting list extending as far as the extreme Right. He used phrases like this: "The Pope would rather see Stalin and his cossacks in the Piazza S. Pietro than the Capitol won by the Communists at an election. Martyrdom, in fact, would be better". "Be careful!" he went on, alluding to my father. "If the elections go badly we shall force his resignation." '

Account should be taken here of the old Roman trick of making free with the Pope's name for tactical purposes—a trick overworked for instance in the Second Vatican Council. There is no doubt that De Gasperi was convinced that the Pope was behind this pressure on him. But to a supporter who 'allowed himself in his enthusiasm to accuse the Head of the Church of interference in Italian politics my father, stopping him with a gesture, answered, "If it is imposed on me I will break my life and my political work, but I cannot do other than bow the head." The man saw that the eyes of De Gasperi were heavy with tears.'

The original scheme was to present single lists for Christian Democracy and all parties to the Right, using the aged Don Sturzo as a rallying-point and getting him to appeal to the electorate on behalf of the lists. But Sturzo refused to co-operate without written undertakings from the monarchists and neo-Fascists, and when these were overlong in coming Gedda's men decided to present their own, Catholic Action, lists. Monsignor Montini,[1] dining with Bonomelli on April 20 'confirmed that this decision was irrevocable'. Bonomelli's account continues: 'I asked Monsignor Montini if the Pope realized the consequences of such an intervention, which would amount to a repudiation of the Christian Democrat party and would bring about the fall of the government. "It is just that that they want", he answered me. "They have done nothing but repeat for a long time that the party is carrying us to ruin, and they think that Gedda and his Catholic Action is the only efficient force capable of replacing the party and standing up to Communism." '

Monsignor Montini's use of 'they' was of course not without significance. When Bonomelli passed on the news De Gasperi said: 'If what you tell me is true, I am not surprised at your apocalyptic tone. Only now do I realize you were right when you painted such a black picture of the state of mind nourished towards us in the Vatican.'

'I maintain the Holy Father is not well informed,' Bonomelli resumed, 'and that no one has the courage to tell him the truth. I am inclined to go off and try to see the Pope this morning and speak to him straight.' (*a cuore aperto*).

'Thank you, do,' answered De Gasperi.

Bonomelli did not get to the Pope, but saw Count Galeazzi, the architect in charge of the fabric of St Peter's and the Pope's chief Italian lay confidant. Galeazzi said that he shared Bonomelli's anxieties and promised to speak to the Pope. Bonomelli's round-by-

[1] Now Pope Paul VI.

round account of the very Roman scuttling to-and-fro which occupied the rest of the day is too complicated to be worth reproducing; it ended excitingly with Bonomelli waylaying the Count as he was following Prince Pacelli into the lift going up to the Pope's private apartment, and reading him some scribbled notes of De Gasperi's explaining his position:

'Galeazzi took the papers and saluted me with a "let's hope for the best". An hour later, at 21.15, he tried to get me at home but failed. I called him at 7.0 next morning, and he said he had wanted to tell me that there was nothing more to fear from Gedda regarding the presentation of his list. Also that the Holy Father, leaving aside his impression of the manner in which the negotiations had been broken off, was clear that there was now nothing to do but concentrate the Catholic forces on the Christian Democrat list. Galeazzi at the same time said something in Gedda's defence and stressed the need of establishing good relations between the party and Catholic Action.'

Down to the time of De Gasperi's death in August 1954, these 'good relations' remained strictly circumscribed by the Prime Minister's very precise conceptions of the proper limits of party politics and of Catholic Action. De Gasperi's good relations with the Vatican remained even more circumscribed—a month after the events just described he was refused a papal audience for the thirtieth anniversary of his wedding.[1]

It is interesting to recall that nearly thirty years earlier, in July 1924, at the critical moment in the history of the Fascist régime and of the Popular Party, De Gasperi's last-ditch scheme for driving out Mussolini with a combination of popularist and moderate socialist forces had foundered on the rock of Pius XI's disapproval. That Pope, while admitting that it was 'not for Catholics to erect violence into a system or perpetuate the threat of it' had offered them no political alternative, but only the consistent application of 'the great principles of faith and religion'. Pius XI could not be blamed for failing to see then what he was to see only too clearly later—that in the insidious atmosphere of blandishments and bullying which Fascism created for the Church, this consistent application was a hazardous business. It must have seemed odd to De

[1] Yet De Gasperi, in the interests of Catholic solidarity loyally made an appearance with Gedda in the same tribune when the Pope addressed Catholic Action on October 12, the 30th anniversary of ACLI.

Gasperi, when out of Italy's long and bitter travail he had managed to create a political alternative to violence while himself remaining staunch to 'the great principles of faith and religion', to find himself once more being reproached from the Vatican for splitting Catholic unity by resisting confessionalism. 'The wheel is come full circle, I am here,' he might have said with Edgar in *King Lear*, reflecting at the same time that there were at least some Bourbons in the Catholic world who had learned nothing and forgotten nothing in the interval.

Not much more was learned or forgotten until the advent of John XXIII and the Second Vatican Council. What John contributed to the easing of Vatican relations with the Italian political world is discussed below, in Chapter 6. What the Council he created did to revolutionize the broader conception of clerical-lay relations, previously so conditioned by recent Italian history, is discussed in Chapter 8. It has sometimes been suggested that Pope John's policy in these matters (certainly in contrast enough with most of his pronouncements at Venice) represented his long-held views, now unhampered by the need to conform. It seems much more likely that they represented the reactions of an unprejudiced and realistic mind, detached from curial tradition and with post-war experience of the outside world, to the Italian situation as he and his closest collaborators now saw it at close quarters. This was not as the inner circle of high Italian churchmen saw it. John was less inclined than scholastically and canonically trained officials to imagine that a complex historico-political situation would yield to a few burning syllogisms; this has been said often enough; but there is no proof that he was any more inclined to think it would yield to his more pragmatical methods in the time at his disposal.

Here was yet another way in which the Council was of decisive importance, for it at least provided the opportunity to take the whole complex of secular-ecclesiastical questions out of the Italian context that had dominated them since the days of the *Syllabus*. Nowhere was talk of opening windows and fresh air more apposite. It is not possible as this book goes to press to foresee what the final effect of the Council will be in this field. The experimental character and imperfections of the original *schema* on the Church and the Modern World, and the perplexities with which it was received, were themselves eloquent testimony to the immaturity and lagging of received Catholic teaching in what had long been thought marginal matters. Equally, the vigorous and outspoken criticism the *schema* received witnessed to a strong determination in the Church at large to pay more than lip-service to liberty: to end the cult of theocratic amateurism, of an unworldliness which is at the same time prepared to tell the world its business.

Theocracy has throughout history left the Church recurrently unprepared for revolt or revision, and only her divinely-given tenacity has helped her to successive belated adjustments. She has always been at her most creative when her leaders could 'despise' the world they were helping to build, but it is of crucial importance for the Catholic mind to grasp with exactness what contempt of the world means. It certainly does not mean philistinism or amateurism. Nor does proper and necessary engagement with the world mean worldliness. The latter has in fact generally gone with crystallization, formalism, a failure to grapple with the historical process; on the other hand, one of the most famous authors of a treatise *De Contemptu Mundi* was the great Innocent III.

John XXIII seemed to grasp these distinctions instinctively. He was a great priest who was no clerical, a man of simple and unaffected holiness who yet managed to see the world about him, and the men about him, with shrewdness and candour. His own humility was so perfectly tempered that he could see, more easily than is always given to popes, that self-styled emperors, within or without the Vatican, had no clothes. The revelation was healthy and, it is now safe to say, irreversible.

5

Communism and Socialism

IT APPEARS THAT the first mention of Communism in a papal document is found in Pius IX's Encyclical *Qui Pluribus* of November 9, 1846, just over a year before the Communist League asked Marx and Engels to draft the Manifesto. Pius IX described Communism as opposed to natural right and calculated to overturn entirely everybody's rights, goods, property and society itself. The Manifesto duly appeared in 1848, the 'year of Revolutions' which extended to Rome, and the following April the Pope, in another letter, saw 'socialism and Communism' as behind the effort to establish a republic in his city.[1] In a letter to the Italian hierarchy the following December Pius again coupled socialism and Communism, though with a vague allusion to their 'different methods' of subverting the labouring classes: this in contrast to Marx and Engels, who severely criticized the older forms of socialism (Saint-Simon, Fourier, Owen) which, failing to take their stand on the class war, were 'Utopian' and not 'scientific'.

Pius IX did not return to the subject until 1864, the year of the First International which, founded in London, promoted a somewhat heterogeneous series of agitations on the continent culminating in the Paris Commune of 1871; the Encyclical *Quanta Cura* mentioned socialism and Communism again passingly, as bent on secularizing education. The *Syllabus of Errors* of 1864 lumps socialism, Communism, secret societies, biblical societies and clerico-liberal societies all together as 'pestilences'. Up to this time there was no real attempt to distinguish socialism and Communism or to analyse the situation from which they sprang.

In March 1870, at the First Vatican Council, a *postulatum* or

[1] *Quibus Quantisque*, April 20, 1849.

suggestion for discussion was tabled, drawing attention to socialism as a great evil of the time, adding that the reasons for its success were the greed and harshness of employers and requesting that the Council should detail and proclaim the Christian teaching on the relations of employers and workers—a clear advance on earlier papal pronouncements.

The first papal document devoted explicitly to 'socialism, Communism and nihilism' was Leo XIII's Encyclical *Quod Apostolici Muneris* of December 1878. It was still treating them rather on the level of secret societies which the bishops were instructed to tell the faithful not to join or support. In the meantime the 'scientific' socialist movement had split on the question of whether bourgeois states should be taken over and used by the proletariat or destroyed and replaced by popular dictatorships. Out of the quarrel was born the German Social Democratic party, consisting of devout Marxists who yet repudiated proletarian dictatorship and espoused parliamentarism, and were destined to provide the model for many other countries. In *Humanum Genus* of 1884 Leo linked socialism and Communism with freemasonry. In the classical *Rerum Novarum* of 1891 there was a longer but still passing comment, criticizing the socialist solution of the problems the Encyclical dealt with. *Rerum Novarum* is of course a landmark because it offers not merely condemnations but an examination and principles for a solution of the social and economic problems of the day.

Between *Rerum Novarum* and the Encyclical which Pius XI issued for its fortieth anniversary, *Quadragesimo Anno*, papal comment on Communism was very sparing. Benedict XV made only two very brief allusions to it; but during the post-war famine Russia shared in the generosity by which he emptied the Vatican treasury. Robert Graham has described[1] how during the early years of the Revolution, particularly at the 1922 Genoa Conference, White Russians complained of the 'cordiality' of the Vatican to the Bolsheviks, on the strength, of course, of fanciful tales; thus Pius XI, prolonging papal aid to Russia in December 1924, thought it well to remark in passing that this was far from implying any approval of the Soviet régime. Other very brief allusions down to 1931 show a clearer distinguishing of Leninism from other kinds of socialism,

[1] In *Vatican Diplomacy* (Princeton 1959) pp. 349 *et seq.* The author also summarizes the remarkable cloak-and-dagger story of Monsignor d'Herbigny's missions to Russia, aimed at preserving in desperate conditions the apostolic succession there.

and Leninism is what Pius means by communism. Though Communism had not yet assumed full stature as Public Enemy Number One, we are far from the days when it was lumped together with anything from liberalism to Mormonism.

In the forty years separating the two well-known Encyclicals, a great deal had happened to 'socialism'. In Russia the pure Marxist Revolution had taken place, and the 'new civilization' hymned by the Webbs was in process of establishment. Stalin began his great drive for collectivization in the year before *Quadragesimo Anno* appeared. But outside Russia the various 'democratic socialist' parties varied endlessly in their attitudes to Marxism. Hence when Pius announced that 'no one can be a good Catholic and a true socialist at the same time' there was fluttering in many dovecotes. In Fascist Italy the question was academic, and it seemed arguable that, Russia apart, the socialism to which Pius referred was an academic concept or doctrine rather than something identifiable with the existing parliamentary parties that called themselves Socialist: socialism, he said, had a concept of society 'opposed to Christian truth . . . it supposes that human association has no purpose but earthly well-being'. It was very questionable how far membership of many existing socialist parliamentary parties committed anyone to this bald doctrine. Cardinal Bourne declared at Edinburgh the same year that membership of the British Labour Party was not affected by the Encyclical.

The tactics of the *main tendue* and the popular front during the thirties drew sharp reactions from Pius XI (cf. AAS 1936, p. 376) and five days after he had attacked the Nazis in *Mit Brennender Sorge* he followed up with the Encyclical *Divini Redemptoris* in which, recalling previous condemnations since Pius IX and the present insidious ways of Communism, he ended by exhorting the bishops: 'Take care that the faithful do not allow themselves to be deceived. Communism is intrinsically perverse, and no collaboration with it in any field is allowable to those who wish to protect Christian civilization from extinction.' Cardinal Pacelli, then Secretary of State, spoke several times no less absolutely, notably in a discourse at Lourdes in 1935 and again in Paris in 1936.

Divini Redemptoris remained the *locus classicus* of papal anti-communism.

It is not surprising that the Second World War should have overshadowed other concerns during Pius XII's early pontificate. What is striking is the rarity even of allusions to Communism. Neither this word nor the word 'socialism' in fact appear in the index of the *Acta Apostolicae Sedis* between 1937, the year of *Divini Redemptoris*, and 1949 when the Holy Office decree appeared.

Addressing Italian workers in June 1943, Pius spoke of 'false prophets', and went on to say that state capitalism 'compresses and transforms all into a gigantic labour machine. No differently from other systems it marshals and constrains everything into a fearful instrument of war.'

He commended evolution above revolution, adding that neither violence nor arbitrary government action achieve anything worthwhile. These were statements that applied equally to tyrannies of the Right and of the Left, though in the Italian context of that moment they might be taken as chiefly a forewarning against the appeal of Communism.

Speaking to the *corps diplomatique* in February 1946 the Pope explained this long silence: 'We have wished never to say an unjust word, never to fail in Our duty to reprove every iniquity, every act deserving reproof; while avoiding—even when the facts justified it—any utterance likely to do more harm than good, especially to innocent people bowed under the yoke of an oppressor. Our constant aim was to stem a conflict so disastrous to poor humanity. That is why, particularly, We were careful, in spite of pressure, not to let fall one word of approval of the war undertaken against Russia in 1941. Assuredly no one would count on Our silence when the faith or the foundations of Christian civilization were in jeopardy. But there is no people to whom We do not wish with all sincerity a peaceful, dignified, prosperous existence behind their frontiers. We have tried only to lead people from the cult of force to the cult of right.'

He repeated this explanation in a letter 'to the most dear Russian peoples' in July 1952: 'No word came from Us that might seem unjust or bitter to any of the participants. Certainly We reproved iniquity or violation of rights, but so as to avoid (carefully and of set purpose) anything that might bring further hardships on oppressed peoples. And when in 1941 some tried to persuade Us to approve by word or writing war against the Russian people, We never would. Our exhortations, to peace, justice, are addressed to all. All know of Our strict impartiality during the war. The responsibility of Our office compels Us to condemn and reject the errors preached by atheistic Communism; We have had your good in mind in doing this. We know how many of you still nourish the Christian faith in your hearts. We pray it may be strengthened and increased and error repulsed.'

It was not until June 1946, some months after the first of the above speeches, that Pius, addressing the cardinals, spoke directly against Communism: even then it was not named. He condemned rivalries and groupings dictated solely by political and economic interests which submerge Christian charity, before going on to speak of 'the forces of subversion and atheism which are used to lead the insensate herd, the deluded masses, hiding from these the true direction in which they are being led'. The light of the Church is all the more necessary 'to illumine the path and point out clearly the limits beyond which, *to the right and to the left*, the rocks and whirlpools are ready to cleave and engulf the ship'.

This was the same speech that contained the passage about the 'two Latin sisters' (see p. 67). It was prompted by an electoral crisis, Italian and French, which Pius clearly saw as a moral crisis. There was no further allusion, even indirect, to Communism or to Communist countries in any major utterance for over two years, and then the purpose was to comfort the Hungarians. Recalling the Eucharistic Congress he had attended in Budapest in happier days, he lamented their sufferings but urged them to endure: 'The old oak can be buffeted but not uprooted.' A speech to the working men's section of Italian Catholic Action a few months later was a positive discouragement of a 'triumphalist' attitude to Communism: statistics, establishments, publications, he said, are less important than real commitment at all levels: 'Do not judge your successes *modo sportivo vis-à-vis* the Communists; you are not there just because there is an adversary. It is not fear of revolution or of the uprising of the masses that drives the Church to work for the people. It is love, consideration for human dignity.'

Thus far, considering how much he had said in a decade on world order and social and economic questions, Pius XII could hardly be said to have revealed any 'obsession' with Communism. There had been signs in the immediate post-war years, or so some thought, of a thaw in international relations, and no one was readier for hope, even for optimism, than Pius, though never an unrealistic optimism. As early as 1946, in the speech already cited, he had said: 'Without doubt the bitter experience of war, post-war disappointments, the poverty of future prospects, confronts the Church in her work with increasing numbers of men whose strength has been exhausted, their former energy and vigour slackened by extreme hardship. But we must see life steadily and see it whole. To good men we must say: Courage! Your numbers are greater than they seem on the surface; you are stronger than your adversaries in real conviction. God is with you.'

Reports from the world at large convinced him that the Church as a whole stood solid, renewing itself from recent adversities. In works of charity, courage and heroism, he claimed, she compares favourably with the Church of the past. If Pope John's famous 'prophets of doom' matured during these years, they did so with little enough encouragement from John's predecessor.

In the Christmas Eve broadcast of 1948 foreboding sounded: 'We know of the bitter path trodden by many of Our children whom an open system of violence has forced to formal separation from the Church to which inner conviction unites them. We admire the heroism of the few; We see with sorrow and love the anguish of the rest, forced by unjust pressure to a separation which their heart abhors and their conscience rebukes.'

There was an ample background to this. For more than a year a crippling campaign against Catholic activity, educational and other, had gone on in Hungary. Two days after the Pope's speech the arrest of Josef Mindszenty ushered in the worst year in the history of Catholic-Communist relations. Two days later the Consistorial Congregation, in accordance with canons 2343, No. 2 and 2334, No. 2 excommunicated all who had laid hands on Mindszenty and hindered his exercise of his jurisdiction, and declared them 'infamous'. The Pope, speaking to the Hungarian bishops on January 2, exhorted them to be firm and to pray for their persecutors. When the *corps diplomatique* visited him on February 16 to express their sorrow, the note of restraint, the awareness of diplomatic needs, was there in his reply: this 'unique, spontaneous gesture reflects the ideas of the *major et sanior pars*; but it is not a verdict against these invaders of human rights—rather an assertion of solidarity with those who suffer for religion and for the liberty religion entails.'

To a crowd at a Mass of expiation in St Peter's Square four days later the Pope said: 'It is well known what the totalitarian and anti-religious state wants as the price of tolerance and problematical recognition. It wants a Church that keeps quiet when she should speak; that waters down the law of God, adapting it to human tastes, instead of loudly proclaiming and defending it; that detaches herself from the foundation laid by Christ in order to settle on the sands of contemporary opinion or to swim with the tide; that does not resist oppression of consciences or protect legitimate rights and liberties; that slavishly stays shut within the four walls of the Church, forgetting the divine command to go out into the streets. (*Matt. xxii*, 9.)

'Heirs of the martyrs! Is this the Church you love and venerate? Do you recognize the features of your Mother? Can you imagine a successor of St Peter giving way to such demands?' A good passage to go back to when, as does happen, we drink a little too deeply of the heady spirit of accommodation.[1]

On June 20 the Holy Office opened fire by condemning the schismatic 'Catholic Action' operating in Czechoslovakia. The main broadside came on July 1, when a decree declared it unlawful

1. to join or show favour to the Communist party;

2. to publish, distribute, read or write in periodicals which sponsor Communist teaching or action (cf. canon 1399); it added that

3. knowing and free offenders cannot receive the sacraments;

4. those who hold the materialistic and anti-Christian teachings of Communism and especially (*imprimis*) those who defend and propagate these, incur excommunication specially reserved to the See of Rome.

A clarification of August 11 added that No. 3 did not extend to marriage.

This decree was given the widest interpretation: even those who inserted paid advertisements in Communist newspapers were to be excluded from the sacraments; even those who wrote there on sport. The words 'knowingly and freely' applied to the lesser offence and the lesser sanction made allowance for those who might be ignorant, confused in mind or subject to heavy economic or other pressure, while the capital distinction of course was between the first three categories and the fourth. This was important particularly in Italy where a Catholic on whom formal exclusion from the sacraments would bear very hardly might be a member of a Communist trades union for no deeper reason than that in his particular sphere it was the only one that got anything done.

With all these 'interpretations', it remained clear that the decree,

[1] But not one to be used to justify any degree of intransigence.

whatever distensions there had been since *Divini Redemptoris*, returned firmly to that Encyclical. It set out to build a Chinese wall between Catholics and Communists. Yet it was no more than a strict application of the existing law. If a certain relish was detectable in some quarters,[1] the Pope himself showed nothing but sorrow at the tragedy which had forced him to these disciplinary measures. The Holy Office documents were, of course, taken as committing the Vatican to 'political alignment' and the Cold War. But some at least of the same papers would have had much harsher things to say of a pope who refused to speak up for the Hungarians for 'political' reasons.

The Chinese People's Republic, proclaimed in October 1949 with various 'guarantees' of rights and liberties, within the next year and a half organized a ruthless persecution of the Church. In a similar short space the Czechoslovak Communists who seized power in February 1948 launched a full-scale attack on Catholicism. Severe limitations on Catholic life in East Germany were protested against by Cardinal von Preysing in December 1949. It was a black year for Catholics in Poland, too: so was 1953, when the attack on Cardinal Wyszynski began which ended with his imprisonment. 1948 to 1952, when Pius XII wrote to the Rumanian Catholics, were years of persecution there. Sad conditions persisted in the Ukraine.

Altogether, it is doubtful whether any Pope in history had witnessed in four years oppression and suffering on such a scale among his subjects. Yet his dignified and courageous bearing could hardly have been further removed from the anti-communist 'hysteria' which fellow-travellers are always looking for among Catholic churchmen. The Italian writer Giovanni Spadolini noted in 1950 that 'perhaps no paper has condemned the assassination of the Belgian Communist president Julien Lahaut so severely as *L'Osservatore Romano*.'

In his Christmas broadcast of 1953 the Pope discussed calmly the question of coexistence:

'It is hoped that present-day coexistence may bring men nearer to peace. The hope must be justified by coexistence in truth—a bridge between the two worlds which can rest only on the *men* of the two

[1] For the effect of the decree in France, cf. Chapter 10, p. 226; Cardinal Suhard, who had died a month earlier, had written in his *Carnets Spirituels*, 'One does not win souls by excommunicating them, or annexing them by unreasonable means of coercion, even if this be done in the name of Truth.'

worlds, not on their régimes or social systems. While one side tries, knowingly or not, to preserve the natural laws, the other is completely detached from this foundation. Such detachment, whether it derives from "supernaturalism" or from the claim that collectivism is a "historical truth" and therefore in accordance with the divine will, is an uncatholic error. In both camps there are millions who have preserved, more or less actively, the imprint of Christ: they, not less than the faithful and fervent, should be called on to collaborate in renewing the foundation of the unity of the human family. It is true that the voice of truth, love, the spirit is suppressed on one side, and sounds too timidly on the other. Remedies for this, bridge-building, will not come from those who think it the honour of modern man to have no determined ideas or spiritual allegiance.

'But this means responsibility for priests and laity. They must not close eye and mouth to social injustice, and so give occasion for doubting the social efficacy of Christianity. They must not forget that for the Christian the primary social factor is personal responsibility. This is too easy to forget in the impersonal atmosphere of many organs of modern democracy.'

From this time down to the savage suppression of the Hungarian revolt in November 1956 Pius's references to Communism were sparing in number and measured in manner. At Christmas 1955 he confirmed his rejection of the Communist system—it was not to be accepted as a 'providential historical stage'—but at the same time he said, 'We warn Christians in an industrial era not to be content with an anti-communism based on the defence of a liberty empty of content. They should rather build a society in which man's liberty rests on the moral order. Common service is integral to Christianity.' And he told the International Society of Economists the following September that classical economists and Marxists were both at fault in neglecting the possibility of altruism, the force of spiritual values.

The Hungarian disaster roused him to a series of outbursts. He wrote three encyclicals in ten days—something no pope had done before. That of October 28 called for the prayers of the world; that of November 1 celebrated the restoration of Wyszynski and Mindszenty and the seeming break of a new dawn for Poland and Hungary. By November 5 these hopes were shattered, and he spoke sadly of Hungarian blood crying to heaven for vengeance—which history often showed to fall on rulers and nations even in this world.

The slender thread of trust which had begun to reunite peoples and sustain their spirits seemed broken; suspicion and mistrust had dug a deeper abyss of separation. But he still refused to believe peace a vain dream. He called for an effective defence pact of all who sought to tread the path of honour and dignity. This might give the rest pause and rouse the aspirations of their subjects to rejoin the human family.

In his Christmas broadcast he referred to the criticisms of 'realists' who 'blame religion for exacerbating an East-West conflict which a little practical sense would quiet. We, as head of the Church, have avoided calling Christianity to a crusade, but we can understand those who suffer directly thinking in such terms.'

Pius lamented the part played by Catholics, clerical and lay, in the 'befogging tactic' of agitation for conversations and encounters. How reason, he asked, without a common language, where one side rejects the common absolute values, blocking any 'coexistence in truth'. You cannot sit at the table of God and of His enemies. If there seems, understandably, some hardening here as compared with the corresponding broadcast three years earlier, Pius was still far from intransigence; he went on in fact to sketch what have been the main lines of Vatican diplomacy since. We should not cut the bridges; we should maintain mutual relations, but leave it to those competent in Church and State:

'We are bound to speak frankly, but We cannot be reproached with wishing to harden the opposing fronts, or with departing from Our apostolic pursuit of peace. But nothing will be gained if the free peoples try to hide behind one another's skirts, as the prelude to World War II clearly showed. . . .

'A concrete need of the hour is a "fruitful network" which will include Asia and Africa, the Middle East and Palestine. But you cannot build a policy on sentiment, least of all on the sentiment of yesterday or the day before.'

In July 1957 Hungarian priests were forbidden under pain of major excommunication to take active part in politics, and at the beginning of the following year the Congregation of the Council pronounced sentence against three of them.

While there was little room for discussion about Catholic-Communist relations after the Holy Office decrees of 1949-50, the old question of what degrees of socialism and, in the concrete, what socialist parties were compatible with Catholicism was still a burning one, not least in the post-war Italian Republic. The common front of the revolutionary Left which emerged from the Resistance, and which De Gasperi had to reckon with in the critical years during which he was re-establishing the Italian state, no longer presented an immediate revolutionary threat by 1949. Saragat with his Social Democrats broke with Nenni and joined the government coalition, but Nenni and his followers retained close links with Togliatti and the Communists. Was the ecclesiastical ban to embrace them too? Pius XII had said little on the subject of socialism, though whether or not this was because he thought the last word had been said in *Quadragesimo Anno* is not clear. A strict application of *Quadragesimo Anno* certainly precluded *joining* even Saragat's party, though not so obviously any collaboration with it in politics or local administration. As far as Nenni was concerned, down to 1953 his party's ties with Italian Communism were so close that there was little ground for making distinctions. The *Osservatore Romano* a week or so after the Holy Office decree commented: 'Everybody knows that there are many very different forms of socialism. Here it is enough to say that a socialist party which makes absolutely common cause with the Communist parties and links its forces with those of Communism, "favouring" it in explicit fashion, is already condemned in the first part of the July decree. And if its members, moreover, stick to the materialistic doctrine of Communism they clearly fall under the excommunication referred to in the fourth section.'

In the June election of 1953 the Christian Democrats lost their absolute majority, and there arose that problem of coalitions which has plagued Italian politics ever since. In the *Civiltà Cattolica*, conventionally regarded as semi-official in Rome, the very conservative Father Messineo, true to the older traditions of the Jesuit journal, described as 'puerile' Saragat's suggestion of a leftward move and accused the Social Democrat party and its leader of 'feeling afresh the attraction of its natural parentage.' Any truck with Nenni he labelled as 'introducing the Trojan horse into the democratic citadel and opening the gates to Communism.' He went on to offer for the Christian Democrats' consideration a number of 'programmatic propositions' of a strongly paternalist flavour, without explicitly suggesting where they should look for allies to form a majority for implementing them. But since he also explicitly recommended an 'attenuation' of political liberalism (the only moderate party to the right of the Christian Democrats) there was not much choice left. This, which reflected still the mentality behind 'Operation Sturzo' of the previous year, fairly represents what was to be the average ecclesiastical line for the next decade, though it was plentifully criticized from within the Church; e.g., Don Carlo Colombo (who nowadays enjoys the particular confidence of Paul VI) wrote the following September in *Vita e Pensiero* in obvious answer to Messineo: he affirmed that a move to the right would mean finally putting social reforms in cold storage, and deepening the gulf between the workers and peasants and the Catholic party: 'In the long run this would mean inevitably an increase in the strength and attraction of Communism, and might leave us only the alternatives of a democratically elected Left government or a police state; neither is a happy prospect politically or religiously.' Colombo concluded that there was nothing but to look leftwards and try to democratize the socialists.

The left wing of the Christian Democrat party led by Gronchi pressed hard during this period for alliance with Nenni's party, involving neutralism in foreign policy instead of the Atlantic Pact and a stronger socialist-type domestic policy, until in 1955 Gronchi was 'elevated' to the presidency. By this time De Gasperi was dead and with Fanfani as heir apparent the question of the *apertura a sinistra* (opening to the Left) became the great national debate—a debate in which the hierarchy was very far from backward, though the Pope kept out of it. In a Christmas declaration (1955) from Udine the bishops of the Trentino, the old Austrian lands north of Venice, declared: 'It is high time to finish with this amusement of vain words about distension, *apertura*, compromises with the known and professed friends of those who aim at the destruction of the Christian social order, who accept with eyes wide open doctrines which tolerate barefaced violence and terror. . . .'

None was more vocal in his robust opposition to the *apertura* than Angelo Roncalli, the new Patriarch of Venice (cf. p. 103). In a lengthy memorial to his clergy and laity on socio-political matters, dated August 12, 1956, the future author of *Pacem in Terris* seconded his neighbour bishops in castigating those 'deviations from the straight path, those alignments, those dangerous and wicked compromises with ideologies and social structures which are by virtue of their basic assumptions the contradiction and overturning of that human and social order which Christianity brought into the world'. He went on to speak no less harshly of 'subtle humanistic tendencies, ignoring or treating superficially the supernatural', of a 'myopic and laicized conception of life' afflicting especially the young; of the painful spectacle of new theories about total freedom of action and political autonomy in relation to the hierarchy and the organs dependent upon it (this last an allusion no doubt to Catholic Action). Finally, explicitly on the *apertura a sinistra*, he spoke of his bitterness of spirit at the obstinacy of those determined to go ahead with it at all costs, in defiance of the hierarchy, of the transparent words and writings of the Holy Father. (These last would have been difficult to illustrate.) This 'practical sharing of Marxist ideology' he described as bringing us face to face with a grave doctrinal error and a flagrant violation of Catholic discipline.

This and a great deal more which followed gave little foretaste, it must candidly be said, of the spirit which was to animate *Pacem in Terris* and other pronouncements at the time of the Council. But the Holy Ghost makes of popes something very much more than patriarchs.

The elections of May 1958 presented the same political dilemma in aggravated form and elicited the same comment from Father Messineo. Segni, the new Premier, tried to form a government with the support of the Liberals, but it lasted less than a year. During that year Angelo Roncalli became Pope John XXIII. An attempt at a Left-Centre with Nennians merely abstaining also failed. On April 4, 1959, the Holy Office replied to a *dubium* or query: is it allowed for Catholics to vote for parties or candidates who, though they do not themselves profess principles contrary to Catholic teaching, and even call themselves Christians, yet in fact unite with Communists and in action show favour to them? The Holy Office replied that it was not allowed, and drew attention to its own decree of July 1949. Certainly no new era was dawning yet.

The bishops of the Marches and finally Cardinal Montini (though in a markedly restrained and considered fashion) came out against the alliance with socialism. The *Osservatore Romano* was no less uncompromising: in an article of January 1960 it even dismissed talk of a possible democratization of the Socialist party and its weaning from Communism as 'the barren illusions of confused minds'. On the same day Cardinal Alfredo Ottaviani of the Holy Office preached a sermon in St Mary Major in the same sense. All this was excited by the prospect of President Gronchi's visit to Moscow, postponed for what was thought diplomatic influenza but eventually carried out in February. Gronchi's somewhat unpresidential behaviour there and the reaction against the cabinet's sympathy for the Left led to Segni's resigning, and on March 25 Tambroni, a right-winger, formed a one-party or *monocolore* government which in fact could only survive with Fascist support, notable during a vote in April which resulted in the resignation of three of Tambroni's ministers.

The next May an even more pugnacious *Osservatore* editorial, the famous *Punti Fermi*, aroused very critical reactions outside Italy. Deploring a 'great confusion of ideas' and an 'unwholesome secularist theory' which proclaimed an 'absurd distinction between a man's conscience as a Catholic and his conscience as a citizen' the article went on to lay down four 'firm positions': the first, stressing the full jurisdiction of the Church as a *societas perfecta* concluded, 'In every sector of his activity [a Catholic's] conduct both private and public must be motivated by the laws, orientation *and instructions* of the hierarchy.' The second point, starting from the premise that 'the politico-social problem cannot be separated from religion', asserted that 'The Church has the right and duty to enter also this [the political] field, to enlighten and aid consciences to make the best choice according to moral principles and Christian sociology.' The third point came to the heart of the matter: 'The problem of collaboration with those who do not recognize religious principles might arise in the political field. It is then for the ecclesiastical authorities, and not for the arbitrary decisions of individual Catholics, to judge the moral lawfulness of such collaboration. A conflict between such a judgement and the opinion of the faithful themselves is *inconceivable* in a truly Christian conscience. In any case it must be solved in obedience to the Church, as the guardian of truth.' The fourth point simply reaffirmed an 'irreducible antithesis' between the Marxist system and Christian doctrine.

The writer went on to deplore the temerity of those who presumed to judge these matters for themselves, and called upon all to align themselves with the 'thought and directives of the hierarchy of the Church, which *alone*, as we have already pointed out, can judge *in a particular social and political situation* whether the higher principles of the religious and moral order are involved or threatened. Every Catholic has a duty to conform to these directives and judgements in the political field.'

Putting the sting in the tail, the article ended by quoting what the Pope when Patriarch of Venice had written against the *apertura a sinistra*. The more naïve took this, as they were intended to, as an indication that the Pope was behind the article. It would be of great interest to know the effect of this tactic; it may well have been the exact opposite of what the compilers intended. In this field at least, what has been called the 'Johannine age' may have begun from that day.

The Dutch Dominican journal *De Bazuin* commented that the *Punti Fermi* could only be fully accepted in a 'clerical, feudal and medieval' society, and that nowadays no Catholic north of the Alps could accept them either in theory or in practice. The Jesuit *De Linie* and the Catholic daily *De Tijd* also, more moderately, rejected the article. De Linie surmised that it might cause embarrassment to Mr Kennedy. *Time* dotted the 'i's: 'Although the editorial was specifically designed to warn Italian Christian Democrats against allying themselves with Marxist groups, its general implications applied also to Kennedy.'

The more conservative Catholic papers in non-Catholic countries reassured their public in embarrassed and slightly tortuous terms, while Pierre Salinger, Kennedy's press secretary, issued this laconic statement: 'The American office-holder is committed by an oath to God to support and defend the Constitution of the United States, which includes Article I providing for the separation of Church and State. Kennedy's support of this principle, he added, is 'not subject to change under any condition'.

The *Osservatore* article illustrated the pitfalls inseparable from Vatican comment on Italian politics, which ever since the days of the *Syllabus* had been subject to transposition into a world context. It also exemplified a favourite controversial tactic among Roman conservatives, of setting up an extreme laic position, demolishing it easily and with an air of simply repeating orthodox commonplaces, but in fact leaving the real problem untouched. The underlined phrases point to the extreme theocratic tone of the article. Nobody pretends that a Catholic can 'separate' his Catholic conscience from his political conscience, but was it possible to derive from this truism a justification of the sort of clerical interference which was, at all levels except the very highest, increasingly bedevilling Italian politics? It was not merely a question of justifying the article, as many Catholic papers abroad uneasily did, by saying that it applied only to the peculiar conditions of Italy. The question was, were those conditions too 'peculiar' to be tolerated as reconcilable with Catholic teaching on the proper limitations of the clerical and lay spheres? The ecclesiastical attitude to socialism (or at least the majority one) seemed to many to be determined by very different standards from those used to judge Fascism in its hey-day, when a few more *Punti Fermi* might with profit have been driven home.

The *Osservatore* leader was designed to precede closely the National Council of the Christian Democrats in Rome. It was a challenge which the party secretary, Aldo Moro, a product of the University Catholic Federation and of Catholic Action, who had since learned politics in the hard school of experience, took up in a 45-page report. Left-wing comment alleged that it had originally been 47 pages: the last two, announcing and explaining his resignation, provoked by *Punti Fermi*, he had been induced to withdraw. He gave a reasoned exposition of the moderate Left-Centre viewpoint, distinguished it from that vast and vague Opening to the Left feared by Father Messineo (whose first article he clearly alluded to). The long and patient way in which he spelt out the political ABC of the matter hardly suggested that he took seriously the extravagant claims to political judgement made in the *Osservatore* article. Though subsequent speakers in all sectors of the party spoke with formal respect of the weight and importance of Church guidance, it was obvious enough that in its present form this was adding considerably to their already sufficient embarrassments.

A few weeks later, when the neo-Fascist MSI, emboldened by their hold over the caretaker premier Tambroni (who depended on their votes), flouted their opponents by arranging their annual congress in Cardinal Siri's Genoa, a city proud of its fame for anti-Fascist and anti-Nazi resistance, severe rioting broke out there and elsewhere, which the Communist party of course exploited, and Tambroni was forced to resign. The *fatti di Luglio* (events of July), as they came to be called, frightened the Italians and restored temporarily a spirit of collaboration, so that Fanfani was able to form a ministry on a programme of reform supported by a *convergenza* of the Liberals to his right and the Social Democrats to his left, with the Nennians abstaining.

There was no question that this turbulent year, which revealed many of those attitudes of mind among Italian churchmen which were to become widely recognized during Vatican II, did little to improve the image of the Church in Italy.

During 1961, with Fanfani still Prime Minister, aspirations towards an understanding with Nenni continued, especially since, following the administrative elections of November 1960, it proved impossible in many places to form local councils without Christian Democrat-Socialist combination. It was possible even to find towns where a town council was Communist-Socialist and a provincial council Christian Democrat-Socialist, or *vice versa*. Nevertheless, clerical reaction was, on the whole, more restrained than in the previous year, apart from one or two extravagances like the Bishop of Pesaro's pastoral exclamation '*Domine salva nos*, *perimus*!' (Lord save us, we perish). When Moro, defending a *Centro-Sinistra* coalition in a television interview in November, was asked, 'What about the hierarchy?' he answered in substance (though in about ten times as many words), 'Christian Democracy is a Catholic party with Catholic aims and interests, but not an expression of the hierarchy's will.' When someone pressed, 'But supposing you have a clash with them?' he answered ambiguously, 'Our position is too firm, clear and considered for that.' But by Moro's standards this was bold.

It was widely believed in Rome that John XXIII had been quietly discouraging Italian episcopal exuberance in giving political directives.[1] It was noticeable in view of the vigour of his views at Venice (see p. 98), that apart from signing the Holy Office declaration in April 1959 he had avoided pronouncements on Communism. People outside Italy have a habit of talking rather imprecisely about 'the Holy See' saying this or that, even when it is not by any means clear, as for example with an *Osservatore Romano* article, that it has papal approval; and this is a vagueness which lesser Vatican personnel do not always find unwelcome. But in the two years that separated the Holy Office declaration (April 1959) from the Encyclical *Mater et Magistra* (May 1961), again the words Communism and socialism were neither of them to be found in the papal *Acta*.

In *Mater et Magistra* Communism is not mentioned by name, but is alluded to in the fourth section. The occasion being the seventieth anniverary of *Rerum Novarum*, the Encyclical, like *Quadragesimo Anno*, was partly commemorative, but also an advance. Vital social relationships need adjusting to the conditions of each age, the Pope argued, in order to make them more balanced and human.

[1] Parish priests were often much more exuberant: at least one in a small place south of Rome made a habit until quite recently of demanding to see the ballot papers after an election, and then offering pithy comments on them.

Of the many much-publicized theories on how this is to be done, some have already vanished as mists dispersed by the sun, *some are today quite changed from what they were*, while others become steadily less acceptable in general. It is easy to see why this should be so. These vulgarized and fanciful notions fail to see man whole and leave out of account his more important attributes. Moreover they ignore obvious weaknesses of human nature, such as sickness and suffering, and it is patent that no economic and social system, however cunningly devised, can provide a complete remedy for such ills. Besides, men everywhere are guided by an intrinsic and invincible religious instinct which no amount of violence can destroy or cunning stifle.

Indeed it is a very mistaken popular notion that the religious instinct planted in man is some sort of hallucination or a mere fiction: and that it ought therefore to be rooted out of men's minds as an anachronism.

In only one paragraph out of two hundred and sixty-four is persecution mentioned, and then the concern is to emphasize less the wickedness than the folly, the hopelessness of ordering social relations on a mistaken conception of man. The dignity of man separated from God rests on shifting sands. When those who deny God persecute those who proclaim him, there is no question where dignity lies.

The whole thing is given a broader, serener setting, away from that obsession with the Italian political context which had recently been too prominent.

The Christmas before, the Dutch bishops had issued a pastoral letter on the Second Vatican Council. Among other things they said: 'In these days, when history is becoming for the first time a great world story, when movement is towards a worldwide organization of temporal society, the catholicity, the universality of Christian charity also has for the first time a great chance to be exercised with full modern efficiency and fruitfulness.

'Technical advances are giving a new dimension to our life on earth, and this challenges us to find how our profane tasks can be brought into perspective with the "one thing necessary" without compromising it. The Church is confronted with Marxist, humanist, existentialist philosophies which call themselves atheist or agnostic. Even if, as believers, we cannot possibly accept these philosophies we should see what is the nucleus of truth contained in these movements, a nucleus which is perhaps their most powerful force.

'In this spirit Cardinal Tardini[1] has declared that "the Council is not directed against anyone—man or movement—but wishes to attract rather than condemn whoever is outside the Church." '

In 1962 this letter was translated into Italian in Turin and Venice. The withdrawal from circulation of these translations at the request of the Holy Office occasioned, it was said, a scene at a meeting of the Council's Central Preparatory Commission, when Cardinal Gracias, supported by Cardinals Döpfner, König and Liénart, protested in very harsh terms against the action.

Nearly two years separate *Mater et Magistra* from *Pacem in Terris:* two of the most eventful years in the modern history of the Catholic Church. The lengthy discussions that led up to the Naples congress of the Christian Democrat party (which itself made history by launching the Left-Centre coalition) found Cardinal Siri of Genoa, President of the Italian bishops,[2] joining in a pessimistic chorus with Signor Scelba, but both of them were now singularly out of tune with the *Osservatore Romano*. On December 12 it sounded a warning against 'a climate of extremism, of intolerance and false zeal which is weakening and discouraging. Every Catholic should take care of unity in essentials, even if this involves reasonable concessions, give and take in matters of opinion. . . . The Church's magisterial authority gives us the highest security. . . . Unnecessary dissensions should not be provoked among Catholics; our judgements and words on men and matters should be carefully weighed, the Pope has told us, so that understandable passions and convictions should neither upset those within nor alienate further those without the fold.' The paper quoted *Mater et Magistra*: '[In application of social principles] there can arise differences among upright and sincere Catholics; when this happens they should not fail in consideration and mutual respect. They should not become bogged down in interminable discussions nor, under the pretext of waiting for the better or the best, fail to do the good which is here and now possible and therefore a duty.'

Whatever the degree of inspiration behind this (and few doubted whence it was inspired), it was startlingly enough contrasted in tone with *Punti Fermi;* it must have had some effect at Naples on the

[1] At that time Secretary of State.

[2] Now replaced in that office by a triumvirate of cardinals, Urbani (Venice), Colombo (Milan), and Florit (Florence).

Right-Centre waverers and given heart to the architects of the new experiment.

When Fanfani remodelled the administration on the basis of the Naples resolution, pious conservatives waiting, fingers in ears, for the explosion were eventually forced to recognize that things were going on very much as before—rather too much, since what was needed was a vigorous reforming programme. As La Malfa, the best economist in the Italian chamber, pointed out, measures which had been the commonplaces of even conservative administrations for years in northern Europe were being viewed with old-maidish tremors in the Italy of the economic miracle. Conservative churchmen had to shoulder some of the blame for this. Though they paid lip-service to the idea of social reform they had long implacably frowned on what most Catholic political leaders believed necessary political means to achieve it.

The first test of the new experiment came on June 10 with administrative elections in Rome; the *Osservatore* returned to base with a leader which came as near as possible to being an order to vote Christian Democrat. But the habits of thought behind this article were on the eve of a historic shake-up. Within four months the Second Vatican Council had assembled, and from that day to this Roman diehards have had other iniquities than those of Moro, Fanfani and Nenni to occupy their minds.

When John XXIII set out by train for Assisi and Loreto to pray for the success of the Council—the first pope since Pius IX to travel more than ten miles from Rome—the moderately conservative *Giornale d'Italia* wrote in a leader: 'In the Italy united by the *Risorgimento*, after years of incomprehension and strife, the Pope is free, acclaimed, venerated. . . . By means of the Council John XXIII wants to come out, wants to open a great, popular, direct discussion with the Catholics of every country, with the separated brethren, with everybody irrespective of ideologies. It is like a huge effort to throw off a too tight belt—to get out and travel towards the world of our time. The world exists. Every problem not stated with that fact in mind is a problem badly stated and therefore without solution. . . . Pope John seems to have an acute and profound sense of this reality.'

Giuseppe Saragat wrote in his party's paper: 'The struggle against the totalitarian state in our time has led the more thoughtful non-practising Catholics to regard the historic office of the Church with a mind very different from that of traditional anti-clericalism.'

One reason why Communism had made headway in Italy was because it had often seemed to the uninstructed only a rather more practical version of just that 'traditional anticlericalism', and clerical warnings against it no more than the traditional echoes of the *Syllabus*. Here was a lesson that those who cry too loud about lesser or imaginary evils risk not being heard when they protest against greater. Pope John's voice as he opened the Council struck notes very different from the notes of those who cry 'wolf', and he was not slow to point the difference with his reference to prophets of doom.

But neither was he slow to stress the other kind of obstacle to his pacific and constructive aims. Those who were tempted to over-stress the significance of the presence at the Council of Russian observers (it was in any case a brilliant success, achieved with an appropriate touch of mystery and drama) were kept with feet on the ground not only by the Pope, who spoke sadly of those bishops who were forcibly kept away, but also by *Pravda*, which wrote on October 13: 'No matter what decisions are taken by the Council it is clear that the Catholic Church is on the decline. The Vatican of our days represents a living corpse and nothing can resurrect it.' Comment in the Catholic satellite states was more tactful—in Poland and even in Hungary; in Czechoslovakia and Bulgaria it was less so.

The important fact remained that Bishops were there from these countries. If the master achievement of John XXIII was, through the Council, to bring the bishops together and open a window on the world for all of them, it was an achievement nowhere more important than with those men from Communist-controlled Churches. Some of them served on conciliar commissions—occasions of much greater intimacy with the bishops of the free world. With a few practical strokes, in fact, the eighty-year-old Pope had done more than could be accomplished by half a dozen encyclicals rehearsing yet again those errors of which, as he had said, men were already well aware.

Events followed one another quickly in the last year of Pope John's life, and the world, knowing him to be mortally ill, followed them tensely. The release of Archbishop Slipyi was announced on February 9. In March the nomination of the Pope for the Balzan Peace Prize brought a message of appreciation from Khrushchev for John's efforts for peace. The Cardinal Secretary of State replied briefly to the Balzan committee: 'The Church, which works actively as guardian and promoter of evangelical virtue in order to establish brotherhood among men, is pleased by this high honour.' About the same time the East German bishops in a Lenten pastoral enlarged on the need of taking Christianity whole and entire: 'Deceptive attempts to take one principle of Christian teaching out of its context and adapt it to other ends, ignoring its significance in Christian doctrine as a whole,' was what they criticized, and they chose as their example the Christmas message of *Peace on Earth*.

On March 7, a few hours after the tenth anniversary of Stalin's death, Khrushchev's daughter and son-in-law were received in the Vatican by John XXIII. The visit was preceded by a week or so of rather comical manoeuvring, hints and rumours; everything possible was done to strip it of official character and to achieve a neat blend of publicity and casualness; a good deal of covering fire was put out by Vatican radio, analogous to that put out by *Pravda* when the Russian observers were allowed to go to the Council. The Communist leopard could not change its spots, the broadcaster maintained, and the not very tactful or engaging Mr Adzhubei on the whole obligingly illustrated this. In Rome he spoke of the Ukrainians having 'got what they deserved' and of Pius XII having 'blessed the swastika' and (worse shock for the formal Italian mind) turned up at a Press Club dinner without a tie, having come straight from a drinking party with the faithful comrades at Frascati. In Naples he made it clear that it would be foolish to read too much into such things as his father-in-law's birthday message to the Pope.

But the world obstinately persisted in regarding all this as nothing beside the fact that the encounter took place. It was horrifying or exciting according to taste, but it was not trivial.

The private encounter in the Pope's library was, according to the account given some time afterwards by the Pope's Private Secretary, Monsignor Capovilla, genuinely human and moving, at least as far as Mrs Adzhubei was concerned, and showed the special power of John XXIII's personality at its highest. Afterwards, when the Russians sat in special chairs at what was professedly a press conference, the Pope's speech was equally a small masterpiece. He had been given a peace prize, and he passed the prize on to the Church. The Church's function (he had said it before) is to *make* peace. You have to make peace. It is not a negative function, a 'neutrality' of watching events in silence, or even of telling people not to fight. It is the ceaseless hammering at an ideal of harmony rooted in the exercise of the virtues: of the theological virtues of faith, hope and charity certainly, but also of homely virtues: serene and courteous language, discipline in the assertion of rights.

The Italian party chiefs, and some of the honorary party chiefs who wore cassocks, were inclined to sigh, 'All very well, but for every Italian who reads or understands these careful words, fifty will see pictures of Khrushchev's relations coming out of the Vatican, smiling and blinking in the sun. What *will* happen to the elections?'

Exactly five weeks later the Encyclical *Pacem in Terris* appeared. Against this background it had little chance of being read coolly. 'In two thousand years,' trumpeted Radio Prague, 'this is the first time an official document of the Catholic Church faces up to the problem of peace and war.' The comment stupefied even hardened anticlericals in Italy, but to hear some other western commentators you might have thought it was true. This said more for the power of Pope John's personality than for the intelligence or learning of the commentators.

The title words are also the first words of the three-line opening paragraph of the letter: 'Peace on earth—most ardently in every age all men have longed for it; but there is clearly no way of securing it, no way of guaranteeing it, except by the scrupulous preservation of divinely established order.' The letter was called *Peace on Earth*, and it was addressed to 'all men of good will'. Those who knew their liturgy, or even their Christmas carols, doubtless recognized these as the second and third phrases of a well-known liturgical hymn; the first was 'Glory to God in the highest'. If this was a novel Catholic way of approaching the problem of peace, then the *Gloria* deserved a place among the Top Ten.

But there were novelties, and interesting ones, as will appear.

Pacem in Terris was a set of symphonic variations on the conventional scholastic definition of peace as *tranquillitas ordinis* which went back to St Augustine. The thematic material was not particularly new: Pius XII was quoted about thirty times. There were five parts. The first dealt with order between men; the second with orderly relations between the state and its subjects; the third with orderly inter-state relations; the fourth with the relationship of men and states to the world community. The last, which attracted the lion's share of attention, consisted of 'Pastoral Exhortations'.

Communism was not mentioned, nor even very pointedly alluded to; but the whole structure of the document, the ideal it so calmly elaborated, was a silent reproach, more eloquent than a dozen diatribes, of any authority which, disregarding its derivation from God, goes on to disregard the dignity of man.

Authority, the Pope said, is necessary, providential, but limited. The test of state authority is whether its ultimate purpose is to augment freedom.

'Hence a régime which governs solely or mainly by means of threats, intimidation and bribery provides men with no effective incentive to work for the common good. And even if it did, it would certainly be offensive to the dignity of free and rational human beings. Authority is above all else a moral force. For this reason the appeal of rulers should be to the individual conscience, to the duty which every man has of voluntarily contributing to the common good. But since all men are equal in natural dignity, no man can force internal compliance on another. Only God can do that, for He alone scrutinizes and judges the secret counsels of the heart.

'Hence representatives of the State have no power to bind men in conscience unless their own authority is tied to God's authority and is a participation in it. . . . Obedience to civil authorities is never an obedience paid to them as men. It is in reality an act of homage paid to God. . . .'

This was a judgement on any abuse of authority; hence it applied notably to Communist régimes, but not to them alone. And though it was written explicitly about states, the Vatican Council had already focused attention, and was to focus more, on the question of wielding ecclesiastical authority with due regard for human dignity.

It is also possible, the Pope went on to show, for authority to offend human dignity by defect as well as by excess. The state must promote men's rights, not merely make pious noises about them:

'Heads of states must make a *positive* contribution to creating a social climate in which the individual can safeguard his own rights and fulfil his duties, and can do so with ease. For if there is one thing we have learned in the school of experience it is surely this: that in the modern world especially political, economic and cultural inequalities among citizens become more and more widespread when public authorities fail to take appropriate action in these spheres. This renders human rights totally ineffective.

'The public administration must therefore give considerable care and thought to the question of social as well as economic progress, and to the development of essential services to keep pace with the expansion of the productive system. Such services include road-building, transportation, communication, drinking-water, housing, medical care, ample facilities for the practice of religion and also recreational facilities. The government must also see to the provision of insurance facilities, to forestall any danger of a citizen's being unable to maintain a decent standard of living in the event of some misfortune or great additional responsibility. The government is also required to show no less energy and efficiency in the matter of providing opportunities for suitable employment graded to the capacity of the workers. It must make sure that working men are paid a just and equitable wage and allowed a sense of responsibility in the concerns for which they work.'

This might give any government cause to think, but it would have been especially interesting to sit any post-war Italian administration for an examination on the paragraph. Just over a fortnight after the Encyclical captured the attention of the world the Italians, going with remarkable calmness to the polls, handed over another million and a quarter votes to the Communists. People who should have known better raised their voices in unison with those who could hardly know at all to blame this on the Pope's recent activities. But in the long television campaign which had preceded the election, the Communists had done virtually nothing to exploit the Pope's alleged 'softening' towards them. They had concentrated on national administrative abuses, which were not in short supply. If there was a paragraph in *Pacem in Terris* which did anything to help the Communists, it was much more likely to be the one just quoted. The *Messaggero* noticed an absence in the campaign of 'resounding appeals to great principles'. The new race of Italian subtopians had ears long dulled by repetition of these. *Pacem in Terris* was built on great principles, but it also spoke of houses and medicine and drinking-water. The Communists, no less shrewd, and having rejuvenated their party leadership since 1958, made deep inroads into the young voters enfranchised since that year. 'Communism Offside' was a Christian Democrat election slogan; the election merely lighted up for all to see the long hard road that Italy had to travel before this could become more than a slogan—before, that is, Italy could be the sort of modern democracy outlined in *Pacem in Terris*.

Communist gains had been fairly consistent for more than a decade. La Malfa, the gifted outgoing economic minister, explained this well enough. After the early post-liberation governments had set the country on its feet, he pointed out, laying the real foundation of the economic miracle, the centrist governments of the past ten years had allowed this rapid advance to take place in an atmosphere of anarchy and aimlessness, typified by the disorderly mushroom growths on the outskirts of cities, hardly more edifying than the shack-towns of a gold rush. Economic planning, he argued, had begun at least five years too late, when the major impulse of expansion had already subsided.

This was yet another gloss on paragraphs 63–4 of *Pacem in Terris*, and he might have added a good deal more. If there is one place where *aggiornamento* is needed it is inside the Christian Democrat party. But its traditional ecclesiastical advisers are not those most interested in *aggiornamento*.

The last word may be left with Giuseppe Saragat, then leader of the Social Democrats (highly successful at the election), now President of the Republic: 'The Communists are still outside the democratic field. Certainly some of their practical suggestions, considered separately, are acceptable: but there is one point that utterly divides us—liberty. We may say of them what Napoleon said of the Czar Alexander: "An excellent man—a pity he strangled his father".'

This brings us to the famous (one had almost written notorious) passage of *Pacem in Terris:* paragraphs 158–160, in the fifth section, 'Pastoral Exhortations'; 158 'It is always perfectly justifiable to distinguish between error as such and the person who falls into error, even in the case of . . . religion or of the highest ethical standards. A man who has fallen into error does not cease to be a man. He never forfeits his personal dignity; and that is something that must always be taken into account. Besides, there exists in man's very nature an undying capacity to break through the barriers of error and seek the road to truth. . . . Catholics who, in order to achieve some external good, collaborate with unbelievers or with those who through error lack the fullness of faith in Christ, may possibly provide the occasion or even the incentive for their conversion to the truth.

159 'Again, it is perfectly legitimate to make a clear distinction between a false philosophy of the nature, origin and purpose of

men in the world, and an economic, social, cultural and political programme, even when such a programme draws its origin and inspiration from that philosophy. True, the philosophic formula does not change, once it has been set down in precise terms, but the programme clearly cannot avoid being influenced to a certain extent by the changing conditions in which it has to operate. Besides, who can deny the possible existence of good and commendable elements in these programmes, elements which do indeed conform to the dictates of right reason, and are an expression of man's lawful aspirations?'

The first of these paragraphs presents little novelty, and little difficulty, as the matter-of-fact tone suggests. It is also an optimistic tone—the tone the Pope had already set for the Council whose first session had ended four months earlier. The 'prophets of doom' he had referred to on that occasion, the people who so enjoyed deploring and condemning, were the same people who were inclined to use such confusing anthropomorphisms as 'error has no rights'. Men are the subjects of rights, and of those rights which belong to them by nature, as men, they remain the subjects so long as they remain men. The Pope adds the consideration that men, *all* men, remain fundamentally good and the subjects of divine solicitude.

This is a statement of true humanism, which is not dogmatic secularism; it is a repudiation of the sectarian spirit, a basis for the widest kind of ecumenism. There is no 'eirenical' vagueness, no blurring of the firm lines of truth, no indifferentism. But there is realism and charity, and exhortation to act on these virtues.

The novelty is not in the substance but in the bold simplicity of statement.

It was the next paragraph, 159, which was generally taken as pointing principally to the subject of our present chapter. Proportion may be better preserved if it is remembered (the focusing of journalistic interest at the time made it hard to remember) that it is not exclusively applicable to Communism. It could apply to Fascism—in which case undoubtedly many of those who praised it would condemn it, and *vice-versa*. It applies to many aspects of public policy in liberal capitalist democracies. Most Catholics in most countries spend much of their time co-operating with people whose philosophy (in the sense of basis assumptions about the nature and destiny of man and the world) they most certainly reject. The capital difference is that they do so without suffering grievous disabilities in the process, as they do in Communist countries. But they may well be exposed to more subtle and no less grave dangers; though they remain free to be materialists or Christians, they can for that very reason easily be enslaved by materialism, even if it is not of the dialectic kind. If a society were conceivable in which, without their suffering grievous disabilities, the differences between them and materialists were habitually more clearly marked and more candidly declared, they would arguably be much better off. (This is not of course to imply that living in a secular humanist society is all danger and no profit or opportunity for the Christian: one of the aims of the Vatican Council has been to get us away from that unfruitful illusion.)

If there is anything in this line of thought, then it may well be that a valuable gloss on paragraph 159 is provided by Pope John's quip in a letter written to Slavonic Christians on the eleventh centenary of their founding apostles, SS Cyril and Methodius: 'We hope, indeed We are confident, that the blizzard [of Communist tyranny] may become a gentle breeze.' A gentle breeze of opposition may be better than an enervating calm.

It may be said that Catholics behind the Iron Curtain will not find this a very cogent line. Supposing this to be true (and it is not at all clear that it is) the matter may be approached from another direction by asking what are the alternatives before the Roman Church in regard to the Catholics behind the Iron Curtain? Journalists sometimes put them to us very simply, in stock terms: 'Are you going to stick to the crusading mentality, or is co-existence possible?'

But coexistence is a somewhat vague word. Pius XII sketched an ideal of coexistence in truth (p. 94) but as he describes it, it might clearly be better realized in a professedly atheist society which maintained full religious liberty than in a more comfortably humanist society which constantly tempted Catholics to blur vital distinctions. But there is a large assumption here. The granting of full religious liberty would not be consistent with classical Marxist-Leninist atheism. So long as it remains the purpose, however muted, of a government to *promote* the decay or destruction of religion or of any Church, talk of coexistence will be a mere form of words. A mere dogma that religion is *bound* to wither away would be quite different, and harmless; such belief is held by many benevolent western humanists. It can safely be left to empirical verification, or the test of time.

I believe that here is the point of paragraph 159. If there is one respect in which it is supremely relevant to draw the distinction between Marxist philosophy and Marxist practice (or to aspire to draw it) it is in this matter of religious liberty. If you like, it is the distinction between 'crusading' Marxism and philosophical Marxism. Pope John clearly believed that it might at some time be possible to draw it.

On our side what is called the crusading mentality[1] (as distinct from an actual crusade, which is something nobody who knows a little history would want to embark on, even if he had never heard of nuclear bombs) rests on the assumption that you cannot trust Communists. Nothing they say or do means what it seems to mean. They never tell the truth, except tactically. They thrive on spreading optimism as well as fear and despair, and so on. Now this is a view with sound empirical backing. It is a perfectly good ampliative induction from the history of Communism. But your real crusader will say it is more than that. He will point to the Communist texts as the fundamentalist used to point to the Bible, and argue that he is thereby raising the induction to the level of a logical entailment. It must be this way, always. The book says so. It is precisely the validity of this step that the Encyclical is questioning. Nor is it merely repeating the truism that there is a distinction between living men and a dead document, useful truism though it is. It is acclaiming the enduring attributes of human nature in the face of conditioning. It was a quaint coincidence if it was a coincidence that, in the same week that the Adzhubeis visited the Pope, the Italian television, reviving a series of Garbo films, chose *Ninotchka*. Lubitsch, in his frivolous way, was acclaiming precisely the same thing. Pius XII had done no less (p. 94). The evidence may seem to point the other way. A certain type of evolutionary theory might suppose that humanity, conditioned ruthlessly enough for long enough, would cease to show those characteristics which tradition has called human. The Catholic can never believe this. '*Naturam*

[1] When this phrase was being bandied about at the time of *Pacem in Terris*, the *Osservatore Romano* pointed out very properly that it was Communists who crusaded, even with tanks, against Catholics and not *vice-versa*. But the test of the crusading *mentality* is not what you do but what you would do if you could. The modern popes emerge from this test pretty well. Not so all other ecclesiastics.

expellas furca, tamen usque recurret'[1], said the pagan poet. The Church makes this her own, adding God's sustaining love as the sublimest reason.

What *Pacem in Terris* implies is that even if, contrary to its exhortations, you make your 'cynical' judgements of Communism unalterable judgements about all *men* in Communist countries, forever, you have achieved nothing. What you may gain in 'vigilance' or 'realism' you lose in futility, despair, the abandonment of belief in the power of good to overcome evil except by wholesale destruction. You are throwing away the very ground of that positive peace which is rooted in the rationality and goodness of the nature that God created and sustains.

It is not a luxury the Church can afford. She is charged with the salvation of all men. Coexistence which shut her in one of two armed fortresses, a 'peace' that involved her turning her back on millions of the human race, many of them her baptized subjects, would be an abdication of part of her mission. Even the present state of affairs is better than that—as the Vatican showed clear signs of thinking in its recent slender agreement with Hungary. A high Vatican official, asked what was its status, answered: 'It is not even a *modus vivendi*—it is a *modus non moriendi*.'

Paragraph 160 of *Pacem in Terris* goes on:

'It may sometimes happen, therefore, that meetings arranged for some practical end, though hitherto they were thought to be utterly useless, may be fruitful at the present time, or at least offer prospects of success. But whether or not the moment for such co-operation has arrived, its manner and degree in attaining social, economic political and cultural advantages, these are matters for prudence to decide. . . . As far as Catholics are concerned, the decision rests primarily with those who take a leading part in the life of the community, and in these specific fields. They must however act in accordance with the principles of the natural law, and moreover observe the Church's social teaching and the directives of ecclesiastical authority. For it must not be forgotten that the Church has the right and duty not only to safeguard her teaching on faith and morals, but also to exercise her authority over her sons by intervening in their external affairs whenever a judgement has to be made about the practical applications of this teaching.'

[1] 'You may pitch out nature with a fork; she will always come back.' Horace, *Epistles*, i; 10, 24.

Again the Italian scene seems to be in the forefront of the Pope's mind. The words 'directives' and 'intervening' perhaps suggest slightly stronger claims than the Latin intends. There is certainly no abdication of the Church's claim to pass moral judgements over political action; but the whole context shows that the claim, thinly disguised in *Punti Fermi*, to a right of veto over political combinations is abandoned. Moreover the general acceptance of the possible value of 'dialogue' makes no exception for Communism: significantly there is no reference to the crucial passage of *Divini Redemptoris* (cf. p. 89).

A good sample of the ferment of ideas which has resulted in Italy may be seen in the March 1964 issue of *Testimonianze*, a Catholic intellectual monthly published with ecclesiastical approval, one of whose editors is the well-known broadcasting priest Father Ernesto Balducci.[1] This issue is a symposium under the title '*Communists and Catholics: What Kind of Dialogue?*, One of the symposiasts quotes the French Dominican Yves Jolif who was one of three religious allowed by Cardinal Feltin to attend a *Semaine de la pensée marxiste* in Paris. Talking of 'spiritual emulation' as a possible aim of such dialogue, Jolif says: 'We cannot cancel the existence of Marxism, any more than Marxists can cancel the existence of some hundred million Christians, least of all at a time when the renewal of the Christian communities is so evident. We need to exorcize fear and recognize reality: in contemporary history there are Marxists and there are Christians; both are active in a world which is the same for all. What I call spiritual emulation will be achieved when Marxists and Christians give up the idea (God grant that it never becomes a reality) of suppressing a large part of humanity.'

Whatever be thought of this, the startling thing is that it should be quoted with approval in an Italian Catholic publication which is in good standing. How recently this has become conceivable readers may judge from this chapter. But it should not be thought that the symposium is either reckless or vague. It spends much time saying what sort of dialogue is not possible: not one with the tactical political purpose of opening the way to Communist participation in Italian government; not one based on false eirenicism, or on any suggestion that Christian and Marxist views of man can be reconciled; not one aiming at some kind of Catholic-Communist popular

[1] Since the above was written, determined attacks have been made on this group in the Italian and Vatican press, though without mention of names.

front. All the same, strange-sounding phrases are heard in Italy nowadays: talk of the 'de-mythologizing of Marxism', of a 'pluralism of positive ideals'. Communists can, it seems, be heard in private conversation jocosely describing the Ilichev Report (a crude revival by a man of low intelligence of the old anti-God commonplaces) as 'atheist clericalism'. And of course audiences in Communist suburbs sit in reverent and absorbed silence through the Communist Pasolini's universally praised film of *The Gospel according to St Matthew*.

It is easy to be too impressed, or too alarmed, by all this. But there is no doubt that since the Chinese a little over two years ago chose the tenth National Congress of the Italian Communist Party as the stage for their first great row in the West with Russia, the tendency has increased to represent Italian Communism as a new type of Titoism: to talk of 'the Italian way to socialism'.

It is easy to be too alarmed because the relation between Catholics and Communists in Italy is quite different from anything that minority Catholics living in a non-Catholic country with a tiny Communist party can picture. It has nothing whatever in common with the boot-licking attitude to Communism so long common form among left-wing intellectuals in England. Italians are inveterately shrewd bargainers, with a recent political history which does not incline them to extravagant risks. Those who are ready to use a vote for Communism as a stick to beat the government with do not belong very convincingly to the 'deluded masses'.

Was there anything so very revolutionary in *Pacem in Terris*, as far as Communism was concerned? Broadcasting to the German *Katholikentag* at Cologne on September 2, 1956, Pius XII, whose long pontificate was very much more sorely tried by Communism than Pope John's, referred to his earlier observations on 'coexistence in truth': 'We only add these remarks: The Catholic Church does not force anyone to belong to it. For itself it asks freedom to live in the state according to her constitution and her laws, to minister to her faithful and to be able to preach openly the Gospel of Jesus Christ. This We say is its indispensable basis for any honourable coexistence.'

Robert Graham comments on this: 'In other words, the Church does not demand that the State necessarily modify its own official ideology as a condition for normal relations. Even from the atheistic Soviet Union it does not exact as a condition *sine qua non* the ending of Marxist-Leninism.' And he quotes Count dalla Torre, former editor of the *Osservatore Romano*, writing in 1949, the year of the Holy Office decree: 'The Catholic Church asks from the Communist countries nothing more nor less than it asks from other countries where separation of Church and State exists.' (*op. cit.*, pp. 383–4).

There is no trace of the 'crusading mentality' in all this. But in 1949 and for a decade afterwards there was a great difference between this tone of Vatican diplomacy abroad and the tone of pronouncements on politics in Italy, where, as many thought, Church and State were not sufficiently separate. John XXIII's 'revolution' was to reduce this contrast, and also to introduce the bold notion that if you were unobtrusively bargaining diplomatically with the Communist states, there was no harm, without sacrifice of principle, in an occasional lapse from apocalyptic and triumphalist language. Eventually, this habit seeped down: in November 1963, during the second session of the Council, when Pope John was dead, a Socialist-Catholic coalition was in prospect. The Italian hierarchy chose the moment to issue a pastoral, which contained this passage: 'We would like to be understood: we have no wish to offend anybody. On the contrary we would like to think that the first to understand our observations correctly might be those Communists who are said to be in good faith. We speak of atheistic Communism, of its erroneous doctrines, of its system which, being anti-religious, is at odds with the rights of man. And we would like, with sincere respect and with great charity, to invite those who allow themselves to be attracted by the materialistic mirage to reflect on and accept our word: this *is* a mirage.' Nothing substantially new here: but the tone made every Italian commentator on public affairs rub his eyes as he read.

Two recent commentators on Italian politics[1] have contrasted strongly the two types of Italian Communists—the party militants and the party voters: 'If the militant Communist becomes disillusioned with the party, tremendous social pressures keep him from breaking with it, for the renegade Communist is as anathematized as the unfrocked priest. The Communist voter's attachment to the party is not nearly so strong. He might be weaned from the party were two things to occur: the first is the creation of a strong constitutional radical party capable of attracting the proletarian vote; the second is a general improvement in the Italian administra-

[1] *The Government of Republican Italy*, by J. C. Adams and P. Barile, p. 152.

tion and a lessening of the prevailing clerical influence in government such as to cause the Communist voters to find a guide in the present government rather than an oppressor.'

The writers saw little sign of these changes early in 1961, but they might well be accelerated if the new attitude of the Italian Church develops further, as under the present Pope it shows every sign of doing.

6

The International Community

THE AGE OF the sovereign state in Europe largely coincided with the eclipse of papal international authority as that had been understood in pre-Reformation times. Thomas Hobbes's *Leviathan*, to a large extent an anti-ecclesiastical work, appeared in 1651, three years after the Peace of Westphalia. If this be taken as the extreme statement of the characteristic post-Renaissance view of state sovereignty as it emerged from the weariness of the Thirty Years War and the collapse of even the shell of a united Christendom, it was a view hardly seriously challenged in practice until The Hague conferences at the turn of the present century, as far as international relations were concerned. Advocates of the divine right of kings might unite with advocates of the divine right of freeholders in raising horrified hands against Hobbes's cynical contention that the State guarantees a quiet life to each man only by creating power sufficient to keep all in awe; but the behaviour of states towards each other suggested that on the international plane *The Leviathan's* diagnosis was only too sound, and that Hobbes was further justified in drawing the conclusion that only an all powerful world state could maintain permanent peace.

Marxism and the socialist international were a radical challenge to the Hobbesian theory, but they too were destined to receive serious practical embodiment only later, also in the twentieth century.

At the threshold of modern times, on the eve of the disruption of a united Christendom, the voyages of discovery provided an occasion for the papacy to make one of its last appearances as the natural international arbiter in the interests of peace. In July 1493 Alexander VI divided the New World by papal bull between Spain and Portugal. Historians have sometimes hailed this as a triumph of peacemaking, though in fact it may well have been done by the Borgia Pope at the prompting of the Spanish government; it had to be clarified a year later by an ordinary treaty and it did little really to determine the future of the New World.

The vigour of the Counter-Reformation and the outward splendours of baroque Rome masked the divorce of the papacy from many of the intellectual and material forces that were to make the modern world, though its historic seat was in the heart of that country which then led European civilization. Yet if in Europe the Holy See was losing the universal rôle that had for long been acknowledged even when resented, geographically vast accessions to the Catholic world in America and the spread of Catholic missions elsewhere were already laying the foundations for a new type of papal authority, more far-reaching than before. During the Thirty Years War, which was virtually to put an end to the old religious Europe, the foundation at Rome of the Congregation of *Propaganda Fide* (1622) for organizing missionary activity, and of the missionary college of the same name five years later, was an important indication of this new direction, though the seventeenth-century papacy might arguably have spent more money on these activities and less on display.

The path of transition from the headship of Christendom, recognized though found irksome by princes, to a limited moral authority, neutral and bent towards pacification, was a long and hard one for the papacy, though its problems were not altogether shirked. The story is told of Urban VIII at the death of the Swedish Protestant champion Gustavus Adolphus, that as head of the Catholic Church he ordered *Te Deums* in all the churches but as enemy of the Hapsburgs he said a private Mass for the repose of the Swedish king's soul. This curious blend of triumphalism and ecumenical spirit well illustrates the ambiguities which dogged papal policy from the time its international prestige was compromised by involvement in Italian dynastic politics and war. Richelieu, though not from the highest motives, was ahead of the papacy in learning the lesson of tolerance. An international policy of neutrality in the interests of its own integrity and of its subjects on both sides of quarrels was gradually seen as the only possible one at the Vatican, but was often carried out maladroitly.

It was the Turkish question that kept papal activity alive on the international plane and gave it some consistency and dignity. Otherwise the two centuries that followed the Peace of Westphalia are those in which papal standing reached its nadir; if the bottom of the graph be looked for it may well be found in the suppression, at dynastic bidding, of the Society of Jesus by the unlucky Clement XIV in 1773. Earlier, Innocent XI (1676–89) had worked hard, in a better tradition, trying to persuade warring Catholic sovereigns to unite in the interests of Christendom against the Turkish threat; he has been described as the real architect of Sobieski's victory in front of Vienna in September 1683. His sense of Christendom also expressed itself in his strong support of toleration as against Louis XIV's revocation of the Edict of Nantes. Clement XI (1700–21) during the War of the Spanish Succession further developed the new papal tradition of peacemaking, though against heavy odds, states taking a long time to get out of the habit of thinking of the papacy as another European Power; thus the Peace of Utrecht was a heavy diplomatic defeat for the papacy. Bullied by the rival Catholic Powers during the war, the Pope appeared to the Protestant-dominated peace congress as not only having failed in neutrality but also having changed sides, and they ignored his claims both as to the Papal States and on behalf of Catholics in other countries concerned in the settlement.

Benedict XIV (1740–58) summed up the papal position at mid-eighteenth century when he said he could write a book on *The Martyrdom of Neutrality*.

Yet by the time Clement XIV suppressed the Jesuits in 1773 Europe was already on the eve of a decisively new phase in her history and the golden days of those arrogant powers that were arraigned against the Society of Jesus were numbered. The papacy on the other hand, so often defeated on the old fronts, had been quietly developing, outside Europe, resources which were to nourish a revival of its prestige and moral force in the post-revolutionary world. Pius VII (1799–1823), though he did not manage to set the Church permanently on a new path, did make the important Concordat of 1801 with Napoleon, and his dignity and forbearance in face of French ill-treatment earned him an international prestige at the time of the Congress of Vienna which finds no parallel except among the medieval giants like Innocent III and among the greatest popes of recent times. Yet though this prestige and Consalvi's skill brought the papacy well out of the Congress, the Pope remained neutral; if he had little sympathy for liberal, revolutionary ideals, he had none either for the creaking system of the Holy Alliance.

The last years of the Papal States are not thought of as a great period in Church history. While schemes for reform of the government of the patrimony foundered on reactionary curial opposition, after the death of Pius VII and the fall of Consalvi rigid conservatism and undiscriminating dislike of new ideas marked the policy of the popes in Europe. Yet even Gregory XVI, so often judged a mere reactionary (which he largely was), envisaged a native clergy and even native bishops in the mission fields.

To concentrate on the papacy's reaction to the *Risorgimento* and the unification of Italy, and the pronouncements evoked by these events, is to get a distorted view. Though the history of the post-*Risorgimento* papacy can be viewed from one standpoint as a history of withdrawal, of defensive strategy, of an increasingly confessional approach to new problems and a lack of sympathy with new ideas, it was also a time of expansion for papal diplomacy; this was continuous down to the period after World War II, when it reached a climax. Leo XIII's efforts here were so notable that they were strongly opposed by France in the non-Christian world, especially in the Far East. Even Pius X, whom the French and other liberals liked to describe as a 'religious' pope, did not abandon this policy. It has often been complained that the associations of the very word 'diplomacy' are out of harmony with the spiritual aims of the papacy, and that since (at least) 1870 all reason for it has evaporated. The view was aired at the Second Vatican Council. But the reigning Pope is among those who have answered such criticisms. Speaking on April 25, 1951 at the 250th anniversary of the Roman Accademia (where prospective clerical diplomats were trained), 'Monsignor Montini conceded . . . that these objections have a certain foundation of truth but that they do not translate the complete reality of the situation and reveal, in fact, an inexact conception of diplomacy. This he defined as "the art of creating and maintaining international order, that is to say, peace." It is the art of establishing humane, rational and juridical relations among the peoples of the world, not by means of force or the balancing of material interests but by means of open and responsible settlements. If this is the definition of diplomacy (said the future Pope) then it is entirely appropriate to the Catholic Church, which strives to achieve true peace in the world. "If civil diplomacy," he commented, "tends to the unification of the world by making reason prevail over force, and to the growth of individual states in the harmonious concert of an ever larger international organization, it finds in ecclesiastical diplomacy almost a model towards which it can look with assurance; not so much because of any technical proficiency that the Church might display, or any success attending its efforts (for both of these elements may be lacking) as because of the ideal from which it takes its departure and towards which it tends, the universal brotherhood of men." '[1]

These words are specially significant as uttered by one who was as close as possible to Pius XII, one of the most celebrated of modern Vatican diplomats, in the crucial post-war years. They are an excellent commentary on the way in which the papal presence on the international scene has acquired new importance in the present century, when the characteristic trend in international affairs has been away from the Hobbesian notion of sovereignty, which had held the field for two centuries and a half. There can be no question of the sympathy the papacy has shown for this trend over the past quarter of a century especially.

International law has of course long coexisted with the modern sovereign state. Nor is the popular, cynical notion, often encouraged by publicists, that states largely ignore it, born out by history or legal learning. On the contrary, in peace time the level of observance of international law is very high: self-interest often dictates it.

Discussion of the nature and sources of international law has not always been carried on with clarity by jurists or moralists, both of whom have tended to treat it as a Cinderella. For instance the *De Jure Belli et Pacis* of Grotius (1625) generally accepted as a classic in the field, came to be talked of loosely as a treatise on international law, whereas it was really about something much wider. The term *Jus Gentium* (which with the Romans had a precise practical meaning as well as a more general theoretical one) comes nearer to describing Grotius's concerns, but has not been used wholly consistently in modern times. Sometimes it is used virtually as a synonym for international law, but Catholic writers have generally agreed to regard it as some type of law intermediate between 'natural' and positive law, based on the general free consent of men prompted by nature, and therefore needing no

[1] Robert Graham, *Vatican Diplomacy*, p. 32.

'laying-down'. Consent is the condition of such institutions as comprise the *Jus Gentium*, but once that consent is evident the resultant obligation derives from natural law. The *Jus Gentium* is not universal and immutable like the natural law; e.g., it would become different if the world ceased to be divided into independent sovereign states.

Grotius had no doubt that such law was derived from nature. He cited four basic principles of natural law binding equally nations and individuals; principles forbidding aggression, expropriation, disregard of treaties and crime. But he admitted that where there is no machinery for judging such offences, war is the appropriate settlement for nations to have recourse to.

The Jesuit theologian and jurist Suarez, writing in the hey-day of sixteenth-century absolutism, based the need for international law on that unity of the human race which no development of sovereignty could wholly obscure (*De Legibus*, II, c. 19).

The horrors of the Thirty Years' War did much to focus interest in international relations on the problem of permanent peace. Grotius's attempts, begun in 1612, to effect the reunion of the Christian churches reflected the current conviction that religion was the greatest source of dissension among men, but he lived to see more secular motives dominating the long struggle, and died (1645) three years before the Peace of Westphalia. His contemporary the French monk Emeric Crucé (1590–1648), author of *Le Nouveau Cynée*, was an early advocate of international arbitration, in which he envisaged a prominent rôle for the papacy as well as (ironically enough) for his own government.

The English quaker, William Penn, a great seventeenth-century champion of religious toleration, wrote an essay *Towards the Present and Future Peace of Europe* in 1693, and twenty years later the French Abbé Castel de Saint-Pierre, present at the negotiations for the Peace of Utrecht, published there in 1713 his *Projet de Paix Perpetuelle*, a work which greatly influenced Rousseau. Saint-Pierre was hardly a typical Catholic thinker: he was typical rather of his age with its complacent belief in the possibilities of human progress, and he anticipated many of the Liberal aspirations of the following two centuries. It is a sad commentary on the spirit of their times that most of these writers were either ignored or treated as oddities and bores. Even when great writers like Kant (*Essay on Perpetual Peace*, 1795) and Bentham (*Principles of International

Law, 1787–9) turned to such themes the results were hardly accorded a leading place among their work.

The two great problems of international law have been those of devising adequate institutions for it and (the crucial problem with all systems of law but most of all with this) equipping it to control the use of physical force. The further problem of codification may be added. In none of these was significant progress made until within the past hundred years, and even since then it has been pathetic compared with the immense multiplication of non-political international relations. International institutions for limited purposes—telegraphs, post, agriculture, radio—began to appear in the nineteenth century, but it was only the advent of world wars that brought both problems into focus. The Hague Conferences of 1899 and 1907, though they discussed schemes of arbitration, were still aiming at the humanizing of war on the assumption that it was a predominantly gentlemanly business and the natural way to settle international differences. Such phrases as 'the profession of arms' expressed the prevailing feeling; they linger on still in the memoirs of elderly generals, but any lingering notions that war is romantic were stifled in the mud of Flanders and Picardy, though they have occasionally flickered again.

International law had existed for a long time, even been written into the constitutions of some states, without attempting to limit the use of war as an instrument of policy or even to give judgement on just and unjust wars; but in 1918 a decisive step was taken when the League Covenant aimed to restrict the *right* to wage war.

If the papacy, whose neutralism was, we have seen, misunderstood, was excluded from the peace negotiations of that year, Benedict XV nevertheless gave his blessing to the League in principle. He could hardly have done otherwise: the central idea of the movement was that aggressive war is a crime against humanity as a whole, and that humanity as a whole should do something about it. It was an idea which only philosophers and moralists had previously aired. Statesmen and lawyers had for the most part quietly ignored it, though Gladstone during the Franco-Prussian war in 1870 said, 'The greatest triumph of our time will be the enthronement of public right as the governing idea of European politics.' Asquith pursued this idea in 1914: 'What does the idea of public right mean? It means . . . perhaps . . . by a slow and gradual process, the substitution for force, for the clash of competing ambitions, for groupings and alliances and a precarious equipoise, of a real European partnership based on recognition of equal rights and enforced by the common will.'

Yet so far was Europe from such a common will that men, including Christians and even churchmen, often treated the League with cynicism. Astute enemies of peace exploited it. Its mistakes and failures are familiar enough. But it was the sign of a decisive stage in history and the Kellogg-Briand pact was an even clearer sign. If World War II was the sad sign of the failure of the League it was no less a proof, especially after Hiroshima, that if the ideas behind the League were abandoned humanity might well now despair.

They were not abandoned. The United Nations rose from the ashes of the League. There rose also a new spirit. The same broad principles lie behind the charter, but other ideas are increasingly at work. It is the paradox of our time that, while peace has become a necessity for survival, the traditional instruments for preserving it—diplomacy (peace by accommodation), collective security, limiting of armaments without limiting of sovereignty—are no longer thought adequate. There is a new awareness of the unity of mankind: not a Christian awareness, but something more than the idealist, optimistic notions generally ignored or derided in the past. Already in March 1936, after Hitler's occupation of the Rhineland, Winston Churchill, hardly a dreamer but not much listened to in those days, said:

'If the League of Nations were able to enforce its decree upon one of the most powerful countries in the world found to be an aggressor, then the authority of the League would be set upon so majestic a pedestal that it must henceforth be the *accepted sovereign authority* by which all the quarrels of people can be determined and controlled. Thus we might upon this occasion reach by one single bound the realization of our most cherished dreams.

'But the risk! No one must ignore it. How can it be minimized? There is a simple method: the assembly of *an overwhelming force, moral and physical, in support of international law*.'

Scepticism was general, and majority Catholic opinion, still cluttered by nineteenth-century neuroses about freemasonry and vaguely-conceived 'liberalism', was in the sceptical van. But Churchill bravely added two years later: 'What is there ridiculous about collective security? The only thing that is ridiculous about it is that we have not got it.'

Pius XII's pontificate covered the collapse of the semblance of international order, the war, the advent of the atomic age and thirteen years of the struggle for peace. In no aspect of the life of his time did he show such sustained interest as in the growth of the idea of a world community, the attempt to find adequate institutional forms for that healthy shift, so marked in our time in the field of international law, away from the merely external regulation of the relations of sovereign states towards the laborious business of the growth of an international community and to the well-being of persons. Paragraph 139 of *Pacem in Terris* was to say: 'The common good of individual states is something that cannot be determined without reference to the human person, and the same is true of the common good of all states taken together. Hence the public authority of the world community too must have as its special aim the recognition, respect, safeguarding and promotion of the rights of the human person.' This is one of a great many passages in the fourth part of the Encyclical which can be more or less paralleled in the writing and speeches of Pius XII. The theme became habitual in his Christmas broadcasts, and the sheer volume and tenacity of his comment is impressive. It was as though he determined to carry the papacy by storm back to the position of world arbiter it had once held.

The new international ideas found echoes in the papal diplomatic tradition. Whatever the defects of modern papal diplomacy, they were not (as we have seen Monsignor Montini pointing out) those of ordinary diplomacy. Even where there had seemed excessive concentration on the Church's rights and immunities to the neglect of broader considerations, negotiation without threats had been necessarily the rule. The Church was committed by nature to 'peaceful means', and from 1870 onwards by circumstance too. It is a commonplace that she has gained thereby. Stalin's famous question to Laval, 'How many divisions has the Vatican?' has been generally thought a damp squib, and Churchill's own comment, that Laval 'might certainly have mentioned a number of legions not always visible on parade' is representative. By contrast, conventional diplomacy, even when making use of such organs as the League, has increasingly looked like that of 'the smiler with the knife under the cloak'.

Pius XII's diplomacy in the months surrounding the outbreak of World War II has been variously judged, as we have seen, and the materials for a final judgement are still not to hand; but for the twenty years following that time he increasingly supplemented, if he did not replace, diplomacy by open pronouncement and exhortations on international relations and on the growth of the world community. As good a way as any of rendering manageable this vast bulk of material is one which will also serve the purpose of this book—to take those parts of *Pacem in Terris* which deal with these two themes (Parts III and IV) and match them with Pius XII's statements. The universal regard for Pope John and the world-wide sense of new ways within the Catholic Church over the past half-dozen years has given to *Pacem in Terris* a certain lapidary status, but these two sections will be found to contain little that cannot be parallelled in the preceding pontificate. Part III in fact begins by saying, 'In the international field, We wish to lend the weight of Our own authority to the constant teaching of Our predecessors.'

Part III turns out to be largely a résumé of material from the three Christmas broadcasts of 1939, 1940 and 1941, with some additional material from those of 1947 and 1948. John began by reaffirming that nations like men have reciprocal natural rights and duties; this principle had formed the basis of the 'five peace points' of Christmas 1940 and the 'five evils to be excluded from the new order' of Christmas 1941.

Public men, John went on, remain men, with dignity and moral responsibility, especially to tell the truth; Pius XII at Christmas 1947 had spoken more strongly of 'modern Herods', condemning insincerity as the stigma of our time; lying, travesty of words and facts, deceit, are become the classical offensive weapons, he said. The following November he told the International Congress for Federal Union in Europe: 'Europe cannot build only on an abstract idea [that of "the common heritage of Christian civilization" which had recently been invoked at The Hague]. It needs living men. Who will they be? . . . the most pressing appeal for European unity comes from family men of order and calm, not *déracinés* [the rootless].'

Authority, went on John, is subject to the moral order and the common good; Pius, as we have seen, in his first Encyclical singled out as a leading error 'forgetfulness of human solidarity', and his fifth peace point at the ensuing Christmas was that 'the spirit of Christian charity, ideals, responsibility must inform the letter of ordinances'.

There must be no domination by superior nations, said John; all are equal in natural dignity. Peace Point No. 1 in 1939 had been the rights of nations without distinction: 'The will to live of one should not be sentence of death for another'; the first 'evil to be banished' of 1941 was 'harming the integrity and security of any nation whatever its size or armaments'.

On June 2, 1945, during the San Francisco Conferences Pius spoke up strongly for the rights of small nations, and in October 1947 he expressed approval of the United Nations having provided a 'rostrum' for them.

John's paragraph on international justice simply cites the 1939 Christmas broadcast. John on minorities and their rights only repeats Point 4 of 1939 and Point 2 of 1941.

In paragraphs 98–100 John speaks of *active* solidarity among nations—collaboration and the pooling of resources: '. . . this is already happening in our own day in the economic, social, political, educational, health and athletic spheres—and with beneficial results. We must bear in mind that of its very nature civil authority exists, not to confine men within the frontiers of their own nations but primarily to protect the common good of the nation, which certainly cannot be divorced from the common good of the entire human family.' He goes on to say that states should positively encourage every kind of advantageous interchange between peoples. Pius XII had dwelt much on this theme in the late forties; he inclined to make less of state initiative and more of private initiative. At Christmas 1947, while he spoke of 'a titanic struggle between two opposite spirits that dispute the world' he disclaimed any commitment to one camp, one 'bloc' or the other, evoking rather the classical Augustinian distinction between the Two Cities: 'To be with Christ or against Christ—that is the whole question.' 'If all honest men would unite, how near would be the victory of human brotherhood and the healing of the world! They form a considerable part of public opinion and give proof of humanity and political wisdom.'

He was fond of condemning the egoism of states—thinking perhaps of that *sacro egoismo* which, born in the days of Giolitti, had been a Fascist cliché—and clearly saw internationalizing tendencies as Catholic in spirit with the large as well as the small 'c': 'Catholic doctrine on state and civil society has always been based on the principle that by divine will the peoples of the world form a community having a common purpose and duties. Even in times when proclaiming this principle aroused very sharp reactions, the Church refused to accept the idea of absolutely autonomous sovereignty exempt from social (i.e., supranational) obligations. The Catholic Christian, convinced that every man is his neighbour and that every people has equal rights of membership in the family of nations, joins forces with all who oppose that egoism which must be conquered if the world is to be saved' (Christmas 1948). He re-emphasized this a year later on the threshold of the 1950 Holy Year in which international crowds of pilgrims mingling together would, he hoped, be the vanguard of a crusade for peace.

A good half of what *Pacem in Terris* has to say about economically under-developed countries (para. 121–5) is a direct quotation from Pius XII's Christmas broadcast of 1941. There Pius had listed third among the evils to be banished from the new order 'that egoism which excludes nations less favoured by nature from the world's economic resources'. In the passage quoted by John, Pius argues that the freedom, neutrality and economic initiative of small nations must be respected, and John adds the gloss that even aid to them must be administered scrupulously in this spirit. Pius in fact had gone further: in the last months of his reign, he told African delegates to a Roman conference that in the modern world financial and technical aid to underdeveloped countries was a condition of their achieving liberty and should be regarded as urgent for that reason.

The rest of Part III of *Pacem in Terris* deals with the problem of disarmament and will be treated separately. Part IV goes on to deal with the 'relations of men and political communities to the world community', something which had occupied Pius XII for many years.

John begins (para. 130–1) by pointing to the present interdependence of states—cultural and economic, in security and social progress: Isolationism he says, is no longer practical politics. Towards the end of the war Pius had been mainly concerned with peace and security, the future of which he declared at Christmas 1944 to depend on the democracies regarding 'the unity of the human race and of the family of peoples as a morally necessary completion of social development'. A society must develop, he argued, in which 'democracy could penetrate into the thorny field of foreign policy!' A great broadcast on world hunger in April

1946 gave scopc to his liking for viewing social-economic problems supranationally yet practically: 'The bitter certainty forces itself on the experts as they bend over their growing columns of statistics: the sinister shadow of famine hangs over a quarter of the population of the globe; it threatens to destroy numbers beside which those killed in the war will seem insignificant.'

Summarizing details and listing practical remedies he goes on: 'There is no room for isolationism or enjoying the privileges of the conqueror. This has been well understood in America. In the great world offensive against hunger the U.S.A. have generously put themselves at the head, redoubling their production efforts. Canada has followed the same path with traditional liberality. Great Britain has called an international conference in London on victualling, and has maintained war-time rationing. Even a little, hardly noticeable rationing by the better endowed nations would bring a notable relief to the less fortunate,' and he turns his eyes confidently to Latin America—to Argentine and Brazil which are potentially 'true world granaries'. 'It is time to listen to the reproof of Christ to those who from egoism or indifference fail to come to the relief of their neighbours; He condemns equally those agitators who exploit hunger and those who by scandalous luxury and waste aggravate it.' 'Every mouthful of bread you give to the poor is given to Christ; every mouthful you deny them is denied to Him,' and he ends with unaccustomed terseness, quoting the relevant passage of the Sermon on the Mount (*Matt. v*).

The general welfare can no longer be assured, *Pacem in Terris* goes on (para. 132–7), by the traditional methods of diplomacy and international conferences. Sovereign states cannot cope in these ways with the world-wide problems of today. The common good now requires an authority co-extensive with these problems, supranational, world-wide.

During the war years, the world problem which had most occupied Pius XII's thoughts had been that of peace, and at Christmas 1944 he considered how a world peace organization could 'avoid the defects of its predecessors'.

'The outlawing of war is a duty which permits of no delay, hesitations, evasions. Only a general firm determination can escape previous failures.' He considered that such a peace organization should command economic sanctions and even be armed. But his deep conviction that the essence of peace lay in the mind and spirit made him sceptical of all practical projects which struggled for existence in a world of warring ideologies. At Christmas 1950 he said: 'A strict union of all peoples who are masters of their destiny, joined in mutual confidence and mutual help, is the best guarantee of the re-establishment and defence of peace. Instead, in recent weeks the line of cleavage has gone deeper.'

Yet schemes for world government fascinated him, and any congress with this scope meeting in Rome could be sure of a sympathetic reception at the Vatican. An international congress of the Movement for World Federal Government met in Rome in April 1951. Launched at a Luxembourg conference in 1946, this had reached its peak membership of 67,000 in 1949; it was two-thirds American and the other third was largely British. Pius addressed it warmly:

'Your movement sets itself to realize an effective political organization of the world as a whole. Nothing is more in agreement with the traditional doctrine of the Church; nothing squares better with her teaching on lawful and unlawful war, especially in the contemporary situation. An organization of this kind *must come*, when there is no alternative but a recourse to armaments which for some decades have been driving people to ruin.

'To be effective it must be federal, you say. If you mean not tied to a mechanical uniformity, you are again in accord with the firm social and political principles of the Church. No organization will be viable which does not harmonize with the sum of natural relations, the organic natural order. The first care must be solidly to re-establish this; first, nationally and constitutionally: a man must not be thought of as a mere vote; second, economically and socially: the cash nexus and class must no longer be thought of as the staple factors; third, culturally and morally: individual liberty divorced from natural ties, from rule, from objective social values is nothing but mortal anarchy, especially in the training of the young.' Moral firmness, intelligent foresight, suppleness of adaptation would be needed, the Pope concluded—and above all, creative imagination.

The following Christmas he firmly placed the Society of States alongside the family and the nation as naturally adapted to perfect ordering of human society: 'The indissoluble union of states is a natural postulate, a fact which imposes itself, to which, however hesitantly, states must submit as to the voice of nature and try *to embody in a stable organization*. The Church is the reflection and the inspiration of this idea. Once it is realized, even just war will finally be seen as superfluous.'

This matching of the world community with the Church is always at the heart of Pius XII's thinking. Perhaps the memory of the acute difficulties of papal diplomacy during the Nazi-Fascist epoch, the hazards of neutrality, the dilemma so often posed between denunciation which would endanger some of his flock and silence which would embarrass others, made attractive the idea of a world organization with which the papacy could find natural alignment.

When the fifth national congress of Italian Catholic jurists, meeting in Rome in December 1953, chose as its theme 'Nations and the International Community', Pius took the occasion to give an address which became celebrated and was often under discussion at the Second Vatican Council because it reviewed in this context the question of religious freedom (see p. 289); but it also marked a further stage in the Pope's thinking about the world community, this time in its juridical aspects: 'It is no accident that such congresses multiply. Technical progress and the penetrating action of *an immanent law of development* combine to make every day more urgent the regulating of international relations, private and public. History might suggest that a juridical community of states is a Utopian ideal; but practical sense—the desire for peace—urges it and perhaps stirs among men a latent faith in their divinely ordained unity of nature and purpose. This rather than the will of nations must be the norm.'

Against this, and against those fundamental rights which he adduces as flowing from it, there is no absolute sovereignty, Pius argues. But such a community of states would raise new and difficult problems, not to be answered by a simple yes or no. There are conflicting tendencies innate in states as in persons: assimilative, absorptive, exclusive, isolationist, expansionist, power-seeking; only God unites in Himself all that is good. The visionary and the lawyer-diplomat are always seeking a balance in Pius XII; but there is an increasing breadth and hopefulness about his utterances on this international theme. He was convinced that the 'old rise and fall of empires, the alternate conquest and submission' was passing once for all, and that its passing would release afresh in men 'an intimate impulse deriving from their common origin, nature and purpose'; increased communications and exchanges among peoples, he believed, were merely the occasion for the expression of this permanent impulse—itself the real cause of world community movements. The Italian Society for Fostering International Relations heard him say in October 1955, 'It seems the time has arrived when advanced peoples must ask themselves frankly the question: must they resign themselves to what hitherto has seemed the hard law of history, (tension, dispute, war) or try new ways . . .?'

To a *Pax Romana* congress in April 1957 Pius made perhaps his most considered declaration that the world community is a profoundly Christian thing, to whose evolution the Christian cannot remain indifferent. What then, he asked, if the movement take place in a non-Christian cadre? His answer perhaps links him as firmly as anything with the next pontificate and the Council: in the relief of material want, in basic education, in all manner of help to the poor and disinherited the Christian must be prompt to co-operate, hoping to expand humanitarianism into a Christian notion of community which is beyond time; for service at personal sacrifice is the very image of God made man. It was a theme constantly resumed in the Council, notably by Cardinal Lercaro, Cardinal Gerlier and the leaders of the newly-awakened Church of Latin America.

In an address of great eloquence to Italian Catholic youth on March 19, 1958, a few months before his death, Pius took as his theme the passage from the *Song of Songs*, 'Now the winter is past, the rain is over and done,' and this was his central argument: 'For the first time men are aware, not only of their growing interdependence but of their astonishing unity. This means that humanity will grow ever more ready to feel itself the Mystical Body of Christ. So will the Christian solution to the problems that weigh on the world appear steadily more evident.'

It is not given to one man, or to one generation, to accomplish everything; this might well seem the point at which Pius handed over the torch, however unwittingly, to his successor, whose simple directness of genius was to make the intellectual vision of Pius seem a near-tangible, almost homely reality.

The last paragraphs (142–5) of *Pacem in Terris* consider the United Nations Organization and its specialized agencies. Very briefly it gives qualified praise to the *Declaration of Human Rights* of December 1948, and concludes: 'It is therefore Our earnest wish that the United Nations Organization may be enabled progressively to adapt its structure and methods of operation to the magnitude and nobility of its tasks. May the day not be long delayed when every human being can find in this organization an effective safeguard of his personal rights. This is all the more desirable in that men today are taking an ever more active part in the public life of their own nations, and showing an increased interest in the affairs of all peoples. They are becoming more and more conscious of being living members of the universal family of mankind.'

That an organization whose avowed primary purpose is the maintenance of international peace and security should command papal approval is hardly startling, and there is nothing new in John's brief statement, except perhaps just its unqualified brevity, and the emphasis on the safeguarding of personal rights. UNO had been born and endured its early trials under Pius XII. Already in 1944, as we have seen, Pius had his observations to make about the new project: it chimed with 'what We have long maintained, that the notion of war as a suitable and proportionate means of resolving international conflict is already out of date'. He was for arming the United Nations, economically and militarily. Security measures against those judged responsible for war he thought 'difficult to avoid', but they should not deny the victims hope of eventual admission to the community of nations. Punishment for war crimes should be directed to individuals, not communities.

By the following Christmas the Charter had been signed. The Pope commented: 'Unprecedented experience, good will, political wisdom and organizing power are going into the task, itself unprecedented in size and complexity, of reconstructing the peace. We propose, as in the past, only to reiterate the necessary moral presuppositions.' Quoting *Proverbs*, *xx*, 9–10, he condemned the 'abomination' of the double standard; the use of vast resources to mould public opinion regardless of truth; the 'cruel and bloody irony' of the totalitarian state which 'adds up to a system contrary to the dignity and well-being of the human race and represents a continual threat of war.'

It was at this time that he announced his first consistory, in which out of thirty-two cardinals only four were Italians and eighteen nations were represented. There was possibly an undertone of consciousness of wartime criticisms when he said, 'For Our part We are anxious to make this house [the Church] ever more solid, more habitable for all without exception. For this reason We want to neglect nothing that can express the supranational character of the Church. . . .

'It is an attempted sacrilege and injury to the human race to try to confine the Church as the prisoner of a particular people or banish her from a particular country.'

He contrasted the universalism of the Church—not imperialism, not exploitation but a force for cohesion and balance working within man—favourably with the successive attempts of liberal humanism and totalitarianism to create an alternative unity in disregard of or opposition to the Church. If there is a note of what would now be called triumphalism here, he offsets it by declaring that the Church is, like all social forces, subsidiary in that its purpose is to sustain its members, not destroy or absorb them; its universalism is not at the expense of roots, of tradition, the necessary foundations of human dignity.

By the following Christmas the early frustrations of the Security Council were being received rather pessimistically: 'When the Charter was first signed, all people listened. At last they could breathe again. What remains of it today?' and a year later still, as the rift between East and West widened and the use of the veto increasingly hampered the Security Council, Pius's comments were increasingly anti-Communist and he inclined more to look to European unity. There is always a certain tension between the universalism of the Church and the fact that her historic heart lies in Europe and the Mediterranean: a tension which Pius at this period inclined to reflect. By Christmas 1948 he had restored the accent to the world community, and was hoping that UNO could become a full expression of 'solidarity of peace, cancelling every vestige of its origin, which was solidarity for war'.

The Christmas broadcast of 1956, following hard upon the rebuff to the Security Council at the Hungarian crisis, dwelt on UNO:

'Although the programme on which UNO is based envisages applying absolute values to international relations, the recent past has shown false realism prevailing in not a few of its member states, even when there is question of re-establishing those human values openly trodden under foot. A unilateral outlook determined only by interest and force causes different charges of disturbing the peace to be treated very diversely and absolute standards are thus overturned.

'No one expects or asks the impossible even of UNO. But we

might have expected that authority would have its weight at least through the presence of observers in those places where essential human values were in extreme danger. However worthy of recognition it is that UNO should have condemned grave violation of the rights of men and of entire nations, it could have been wished that States which refused admission to observers—thereby showing themselves to have a conception of sovereignty which undermines the foundations of UNO—had been denied their rights as members of the Organization.

'UNO should have the right and the power to prevent every military intervention of one state within the boundaries of another, under whatever pretext, and also to undertake, with a sufficient police force, the keeping of order in a threatened state. If We make reference to these threats, it is because We wish to see the authority of UNO reinvigorated, above all by the achievement of general disarmament.'

He went on to reaffirm his belief that only within the ambit of UNO could this take place with international law and be effectively controlled.

This is hardly a complete vote of no confidence. The Pope could not be expected to be any more satisfied than the rest of the civilized world at what the outcome of the Hungarian crisis augured for the future of the world community. The first stage of United Nations intervention was no more than another illustration of how the operation of the veto made a farce of the Security Council. But the Pope's implied criticism of the General Assembly seemed to make rather light of the dilemma which confronted that body. Granted that a firm and courageous application of juridical logic would have entailed the suspension or expulsion of the U.S.S.R.: it would also have entailed that the UNO ceased to be even formally a world authority and appeared as merely an instrument of the Western Powers, so that what modest restraining influence it could have on Communist designs would have ceased. The investigation, report and reiterated condemnation carried out during 1957 absolved the organization from any charge of silent condonation of the Hungarian outrage. The unpleasant choice between a policy of *fiat justitia ruat coelum* (justice at any price) and a policy of making the best of a bad job was one which Pius had been forced himself to make in face of the Nazis during the war, and the UN could hardly be criticized for making the same choice as he had made.

In fact his criticisms were never extreme: he remained deeply convinced that the world community was in process of evolving and that (as he said perhaps most clearly to *Pax Romana* in April 1957) essentially it was a profoundly Christian thing to which no Christian could remain indifferent. He would have subscribed to the opinion, widespread enough at the time of his death, that though UN ambitions had been circumscribed and rendered less immediate by cruel fact, the organization was, if weak as an instrument of government, not unimportant politically. If its voting system entailed anomalies, it yet gave the smaller nations a voice they could not have had in mere power politics, while its specialized agencies kept its prestige alive against the day when it might play a weightier part. The medieval French monarchy was an institution which had survived a similar early history to play a great rôle.

Pius was generally keen in his support of the specialized agencies and anxious to develop Catholic international organizations in co-operation with them.

One is left with the impression that, insofar as comparison is possible in this field between the brief pontificate of John and the long and disturbed one of Pius, it is in personal approach and method that they differed. There was a note of the enthusiast in Pius XII's utterances, but also, blending with this sometimes uneasily, a note of the academic and the jurist. John's approach was instinctively welcome in a scientific humanist world as being more empirical and open. Pius, in considering anything, never went far without asking, and answering, the question: is this accommodated easily within the existing total Catholic scheme of things? No one could have been more ready and anxious to be aware of what was stirring in the world, but always it was to be judged by Catholic standards which were at once fixed and very comprehensive. There was little notion of Catholics and others beginning a modest exploration from common ground. Thus an attitude of mind possibly appropriate in the field of strict dogma was often extended into fields where a more empirical mood was called for, in which it would have been more encouraging and relevant, to the outsider at least, to say '*we* are all feeling our way together towards common solutions' than '*you* are feeling your way towards solutions to which *we* can perhaps award a *nihil obstat*'. Thus utterances which were in fact remarkably positive and encouraging towards modern movements (compared say with the rather self-regarding jeremiads of the mid-nineteenth-century papacy) could sometimes fail to strike the sparks of sympathy for which Pius XII so passionately hoped.

John XXIII, by contrast, seemed disposed by nature to meet men first as men, to search out and come down on to common ground, without fearing that the *magisterium* would be thereby compromised. It is quite certain that this was what primarily moved him in producing *Pacem in Terris*.[1] He was convinced that his intervention in the Cuba crisis had been strongly influential if not decisive in the turning-about of the Soviet ships, and this not least because of some personal feeling he had aroused in Mr Khrushchev.

Considering what more he might do to further the cause of peace, he conceived the idea of an Encyclical which should start from propositions about the human person which no one could reject, and so illuminate the broad and open character of the concept of peace. He would insist strongly on the dignity and rights of men, without distinction, as human beings, rights which necessarily called for recognition in any peaceful order of things. 'If you first talk about their rights,' he said, 'they may listen when you begin to talk about their duties.' These are rights which a man cannot lose in any condition. His destiny is to live together with others in truth, justice, charity and freedom: this remains unaltered in whatever condition he finds himself—whether he belong to a great nation, a small nation, a poor nation, an underdeveloped nation, a nation organized for war, a defeated nation, a revolutionary nation or no nation at all. Any system of relations of man to government, any system of international relations which fails to take account of all this stands condemned, and there is no need for the Pope to dilate upon the condemnation. States too have rights. They have a right to be sensitive of honour—but this is not a right to be trigger-happy; that is not a grown-up notion of honour. If nations have no purpose but to serve the common good, to serve men, they can hardly do so on principles flatly different from those that bind men. The idea of reasons of state, in the sense of needs which justify men in behaving as they would never behave in home or club or pub, this idea is at last due for burial.

The need for world economy, taking into account the underdeveloped nations, the need for a condemnation of war, and for disarmament, the need for a world authority—these needs all spring

[1] I owe much of what follows here to an absorbing conversation with Monsignor Pietro Pavan.

not from Utopian dreams but straight from the dignity and rights of man and from the need of preserving and advancing these in a world like the present one: the real world.

The final paragraphs of *Pacem in Terris* stress that the building of a new world order is an immense task, to be achieved only little by little. Here again John is able to quote Pius XII at length: 'There are indeed some people who in their generosity of spirit burn with a desire to institute wholesale reforms whenever they come across situations which show scant regard for justice or are wholly out of keeping with its claims. . . . We would remind such people that it is the law of nature that all things must be of gradual growth. If there is to be any improvement in human institutions, the work must be done slowly and gradually from within. Pius XII expressed it in these terms: "Salvation and justice consist not in the uprooting of an outdated system, but in a well-designed policy of development. Hot-headedness was never constructive; it has always destroyed everything. It has inflamed passions but never assuaged them. It sows no seeds but those of hatred and destruction. Far from bringing about the reconciliation of contending parties, it reduces men and political parties to the necessity of laboriously redoing the work of the past, building on the ruins that disharmony has left in its wake." '

His chief message to his own flock is that, spurred on by love, they must firmly identify themselves with 'men of high principle' who are shouldering this enormous burden. 'Everyone who has joined the ranks of Christ must be a glowing point of light in the world, a nucleus of love, a leaven of the whole mass.'

It has sometimes been said that Pope John and Khrushchev found affinity in their common peasant origin. The salty realism of John, his capacity for going to the heart of things, might suggest the peasant. But there was nothing of the hardness, the suspicion, the narrowness, the *campanilismo* (parish-pump mentality) of the peasant about John's serene vision of the world. It was Catholicism liberated and literally translated, embracing the grandeur of the liberal aspirations of two centuries without their cloudiness and excess of optimism: embracing even what was good in the Marxian apocalypse. To all of them he said, 'God is not what you have turned away from, perhaps through our fault; there—see for yourself—God is what you are looking for.' Not a new sermon. It echoes St Paul among others. But it was delivered in an accent, a language and tone which fell on men's ears anew and echoed remarkably.

7

Modern Warfare

A FEW WEEKS before Eugenio Pacelli was elected Pope, a younger native of Rome created a somewhat more limited stir in Washington, D.C. Born in Rome in 1901, Enrico Fermi studied science at Pisa and lectured in Florence and Rome until he tired of Fascism and went to America in 1939. By that time he was already a Nobel prizewinner for atomic research. On January 26, 1939, addressing a conference on theoretical physics in Washington, he made the suggestion that the reaction known as 'fission' might release neutrons in sufficient quantity to initiate a chain-reaction in 'burning' uranium. He threw the meeting into an uproar, and eminent physicists rushed out to telephone like reporters in American crime films, to instruct their laboratories to start the search for neutrons.

In the year of Pius XII's death, 1958, the United Nations General Assembly held a second Atomic Energy Conference at Geneva, bringing together over seven thousand people from forty-eight governments and six international organizations. Earlier in the year a petition signed by 9,235 scientists from forty-three nations, urging an immediate international agreement to stop the testing of nuclear weapons, had been handed to the United Nations Secretary General by Linus Pauling, a Nobel prizewinner for chemistry. The signatories included thirty-five other Nobel prizewinners.

The first nuclear chain reactor had operated as predicted at an experiment at Chicago University on December 2, 1942. The first sustained, controlled production of atomic energy was accomplished. 'It was a triumph of experiment, deduction and theory to which many scientists, engineers and technicians had contributed,' as the laconic reports had it. But whereas in that year, when calculations were being made as to the effect of atomic bombs, not a millionth of a pound of the relevant materials existed and there was no knowledge of processes for producing them in quantity, by 1958 the annual production of uranium in U.S.A. alone was stated to be 15,000 short tons. At the same time it was said by the U.S. Federation of Scientists that, with the stockpile of nuclear weapons then existing, it was possible to cover the earth with a radiation level which for ten years would remain high enough to prove fatal to all living things on land.

In the same year of cheerful prognostications, it was said that a major attack on U.S.A. would, without precautions, kill ninety million people; with maximum warning and precautions, between five and twenty-five millions.

Two other interesting pronouncements belonged to the same year. The British White Paper on defence said: '. . . the democratic nations will never start a war on Russia. But it must be well understood that, if Russia were to launch a major attack on them, even with conventional forces only, they would have to hit back with strategic weapons. In fact, the strategy of NATO is based on the frank recognition that a full-scale Soviet attack could not be repelled without resort to a massive nuclear bombardment of the sources of power in Russia.'

President Eisenhower's State of the Union message (January 9) said: 'The most powerful deterrent to war lies in the retaliatory power of our Strategic Air Command and the aircraft of our navy. They present to any potential attacker the prospect of virtual annihilation of his own country. Even if we assume a surprise attack on our own bases, our bombers would immediately be on their way in sufficient strength to accomplish this mission of retaliation.'

All this within one pontificate. It dwarfed all other developments under Pius XII. No other pope had had to live for so long with so appalling a new problem—and one which was aggravated at so dizzy a rate. If he did not 'solve' it, he cannot be said to have neglected it. A writer in *Encounter* for January 1965 remarked that 'The extreme rigour with which the Church has developed the moral theology of sex has been unfavourably contrasted with her remarkable casualness about the morality of war.'[1] However true this may be of English Catholic thinking (which the writer was mainly concerned with) as an account of Pius XII's voluminous utterances it could hardly be further from the truth, unless a man

[1] Bernard Bergonzi, *The English Catholics.*

can still be regarded as casual about a problem after talking about it for twenty years.

On September 14, 1939, a fortnight after war had broken out, Pius told the Belgian Ambassador his own programme regarding it: to do what he could to mitigate and confine its evils. This he saw chiefly as shielding civilian populations from direct military operations and the banning of gas and germ warfare. These were applications of the traditional teaching on the just war; Suarez, enlarging on St Thomas's requirement of '*recta intentio*', had spoken of '*debitus modus*', the proper way of waging war. This language still seemed appropriate in 1939, though its appropriateness was even then increasingly questioned. For example, Martin D'Arcy in his *Christian Morals* published two years earlier set out the pacifist argument for the intrinsic unlawfulness of war waged by modern methods, and described it as 'very powerful indeed', though containing an 'element of exaggeration'. During Pius XII's reign exaggeration in this field was to become impossible.

Broadcasting on the first Christmas Eve of the year, Pius made his second peace point, 'freedom from the slavery of the arms race', which he saw as one of the chief causes of the current conflict. A peace concluded without mutually agreed, organic, progressive disarmament *actual and spiritual*, must in the end, he said, prove inconsistent and lifeless.

The italicized words should be noted, though 'deterrents' had not then been heard of and nuclear weapons were still a matter of theorizing, though in fact even the 'fusion' process which was to produce the real monsters of today was recognized by scientific opinion as a possible source of energy as early as 1934. Nevertheless, at Easter 1941 the Pope broadcast: 'We beseech belligerents to abstain finally from the use of yet further murderous weapons. Every novelty of this sort invites as reprisal the use of the same or worse by the other side. If *already repeatedly the limits of what is permissible in a just war have been passed*, would not further "progress" transform war into an inconceivable horror?' The Christmas following he named five things for which no place could be found in 'a new order based on moral principles' (the implied judgement on the existing order was damning enough): the fourth of them was 'total war and an unrestricted armaments race'. All this hardly amounted to 'casualness about the morality of war'.

In 1943 the laboratory was set up at Los Alamos, New Mexico, whose function was to translate weapon work which had previously been largely theoretical to the practical field. Addressing the Cardinals on his feast-day (St Eugene, June 2), Pius again called on the Powers to respect the laws of humanity in aerial warfare 'at a moment when the spectre of still more horrible instruments of destruction and death affronts men's minds'.

It was in August of that year that the raid by the Allies on the Rome marshalling yards damaged San Lorenzo, and in the following November that the four not very well-aimed bombs, alleged to have been dropped by the fanatical Farinacci, damaged the Governor's Palace in the Vatican.

Two years later, on July 16, 1945, the first atomic bomb was exploded at Alamogordo. Within three weeks, a bomb equivalent to 20,000 tons of T.N.T. had been dropped on Hiroshima, obliterating an area of four square miles, causing between eighty and a hundred thousand immediate casualties and two hundred thousand ultimate deaths. The slightly less fearful attack on Nagasaki followed on August 9.

There was no further papal reference to the new weapons until the Christmas sermon of 1946, some sixteen months later: 'A new factor has recently stimulated the desire for peace and the will to promote it. The power of the new engines of destruction, which modern techniques are constantly reinforcing, to the point of making them appear to horrified humanity as infernal spectres, has put the disarmament problem at the centre of international discussion in a new way and with an unheard-of urgency; to the extent even of arousing hopes of bringing about what past times had vainly dreamed of.' Yet Pius saw little reason to hope for more than a compromise peace.

It was significant that in 1947 the future Cardinal Ottaviani, formerly a professor of canon law at the Lateran Seminary and by that time a highly-placed member of the Secretariat of State, prepared a third edition of his textbook of ecclesiastical public law, written in 1925. In that first edition he had been content briefly to place the 'external' justification of war in the observance of the forms of the *Jus Gentium*. He added that war was never just because it was a suitable means of settling a dispute, for it was quite unable to show on whose side right and reason were. It was just only in that there was an intention to compel the acknowledgement of an undoubted right or an agreement on a doubtful one. A war could never be just for both sides, but the 'wrong' side could err in good faith.

Amending this section in 1947 he uncompromisingly headed it 'War is to be altogether forbidden'. He was clear that it was unthinkable that in practice a just war could still be waged, according to the principles he had previously set out. 'Leaving aside the question of a defensive war (and even this under fixed conditions) fought in defence of the state against actual and unjust attack by another state, there can no longer be a just war which a state may undertake to retrieve its rights.'

(The words 'and unjust' are strictly superfluous, since all attack has been qualified as unjust.) By this time, then, the question had become one of practical interpretation of the theoretical right of legitimate self-defence.

On February 8, 1948 the Pope addressed the Pontifical Academy of Sciences. He quoted St Augustine's *De Civitate Dei* (*xix*, 7) on the horrors of war: 'Whoever considers them must count himself wretched therein, but the man who can contemplate them without anguish of mind is much more miserable, for he has lost human feeling.' Pius applied this *a fortiori* to the present, but without harping on the theme. Sketching the development of atomic theory, he welcomed it as 'a wonderful victory of the mind, drawing humanity on to new paths; what more noble conception? A penetrating of the grand design of divine wisdom.' He had a genuine enthusiasm for the new physics (expressed again to Italian young men in September) but an equal hatred of the arms race, 'inspired by an inspiring mistrust' (Encyclical letter of March 1950). At Christmas of the Holy Year, 1950, he said: 'In a war today arms would be so destructive as to render the world an empty waste [he used the words of *Gen. i, 2*: "*inanis et vacua*"], the desert not of its dawn but of its sunset. All states, all citizens would be involved, all institutions and values imperilled at once.'

But if this was the language of deterrence, it was, he emphasized, to deter both sides impartially. In spite of 'repeated calumnies' of the Church's solidarity with imperialism, she had, he insisted, no notion of East and West as opposed principles: both had powerfully contributed to civilization in the past, and were called to do so in the future.

The first Russian atomic bomb was exploded on September 23, 1949. The Americans tested a 'fusion' bomb in the Pacific in May 1951, and another on November 1, 1952, reported as equivalent to five-to-seven megatons and to have caused an island to disappear. Between times, at Christmas 1951, Pius made a first explicit reference to the deterrent policy, commenting not on its morality but on its effectiveness:

'We too, more than any, deplore the monstrous cruelty of modern arms and pray they may never be used. But is it not materialism and sentimentalism to consider the problem of peace solely in terms of this threat, ignoring the absence of Christian order which is the real guarantee of peace? Hence the discrepancies and inaccuracies about the lawfulness and unlawfulness of modern war, and the illusions of statesmen who count too much on the *existence or disappearance* of modern weapons. The terror they inspire in the long run loses its effect, or will not suffice to prevent the unloosing of war, especially where public opinion has insufficient effect on government decisions.

'Disarmament, or simultaneous and reciprocal reduction, which We have always wished and called for, is no solid guarantee of lasting peace if it is not accompanied by abolition of the weapons of hate, greed and fanatical concern for prestige. In other words, he who ties the question of peace too strictly to that of arms forgets the primary, spiritual danger. A friend of peace, he will arrive too late to preserve it. First we must tackle spiritual anaemia, unawareness of responsibility, lack of Christian order.

'Peace is inseparable from personal liberty, which is today weakened and endangered by mass thinking and organization. When men cry "no more war", can you rely on them? Tomorrow they may cry otherwise.'[1]

Two speeches of 1953 and 1954, both made to doctors, are the high-watermark of Pius XII's thinking about modern war. On October 19, 1953 he addressed the International Office of Army Medical Research:

'We have recently expressed the wish that all war should be punished internationally if it is not absolutely demanded by defence against very grave injustice affecting the community, which cannot be prevented by other means or without giving free play in international relations to brutal violence and unscrupulousness. Not *any* injustice will serve as ground for a defensive war. If the harm involved in the injustice is not comparable to the harm entailed by the

[1] First British atomic weapon exploded October 3, 1952. The first Russian hydrogen bomb, August 12, 1953.

defensive war, then it may be obligatory to put up with the injustice.

'The argument We are developing applies above all to ABC (atomic, biological and chemical) warfare. As to the question whether this can become necessary for self-defence against ABC attack: let it suffice that We have posed the question. The answer must be deduced from the same principles which decide whether war in general is permissible.'

The 'recent' speech to which reference is made is that of October 3 to the Sixth International Congress on Penal Law, which contains this passage: 'In the first place [among things that require an international penal sanction] comes a modern war which is not absolutely necessary for self-defence. . . . The community of nations ought to deal with those criminals, devoid of conscience, who to realize their ambitious plans do not scruple to let loose total war. It is for this reason that, if other peoples wish to protect their existence and their most precious possessions and to deny elbow-room to international malefactors, they have no course but to prepare for the day when they must defend themselves. No state, even today, can be refused this right to maintain itself on the defensive.'

The passage of October 19 is clearly some kind of answer to a question prompted by the passage of October 3. Can ABC weapons ever be justified by the requirements of defence? That it was not a complete answer Pius seemed to show himself aware when he reverted to the matter in addressing another world medical congress in the following September. Meanwhile, in March 1954 the twelve-to-fourteen megaton test had been made which caused injury and one death to a Japanese fishing fleet between seventy and ninety miles away. A month afterwards, at Easter, the Pope repeated his aspiration for the proscribing of ABC war, but again with the proviso 'always bearing in mind the principle of legitimate defence'.

In September he carried the matter further: 'Modern "total war", ABC war in particular—is it permissible in principle? No doubt can remain, especially in view of the horrors and immense suffering provoked by modern war, that to loose it without a just motive (that is, without its being imposed by an evident and extremely grave injustice otherwise unavoidable) would constitute a crime worthy of the severest national and international sanctions. It is not even possible to raise the question of the legality of an ABC war except where it is indispensable for defence in the conditions indicated.

Even then every possible alternative means must be explored and, failing that, the use of weapons strictly confined to defence. *When this use extends so far as to escape the control of man entirely, then it must be rejected as immoral.* Here there would no longer be question of defence against injustice or of necessary safeguarding of legitimate possessions, but of the annihilation pure and simple of all human life within the radius of action. This can be permitted on no grounds.' Adding that, even where ABC war might be a matter of legitimate defence, he would prefer not to see doctors occupied in it—their function being to help and heal, not injure and kill—the Pope concluded: 'This will make comprehensible to you the sense and the justification of Our earlier explanations.'

Pius seems in these passages to be straining to adapt old principles, which he is unwilling to abandon or call in question, to a new situation evolving with appalling rapidity. Attention has been generally focused on the last two sentences of the above paragraph: it has seemed to many (and especially of course to the advocates of unilateral disarmament) that the only relevant situation now is that to which these sentences apply. All nuclear war would escape the control of man, insofar as 'control' means keeping action within the bounds of what is justifiable on the old principles. By March 1962 Father Herbert McCabe, reviewing the symposium *Nuclear Weapons and Christian Conscience*, was able to claim as 'an established theological position' that the waging of nuclear war is among the actions absolutely forbidden regardless of circumstances, and that what is needed is not further discussion but a hammering home of this in sermons. The editor of the symposium, Walter Stein, invokes the two sentences of Pius XII as does Roger Smith in the chapter *The Witness of the Church*.

Pius XII did not again return to the strictly moral question: he concentrated during his last years on denouncing the wastefulness of the arms race, the need for supervision and controlled disarmament, the need for improved international institutions. At Christmas 1955 he approved proposals for ending nuclear tests (as dangerous in themselves), for banning nuclear weapons and for general armaments control as 'a moral duty'. But a year later he said: 'It is manifest that in present circumstances it could happen that war for defence (with hope of success) after every effort to abjure it had proved vain, could not be pronounced unlawful. Nor could a Catholic be a conscientious objector if a freely elected government, in extreme need, by lawful foreign and home policies should take the defensive measures it judges necessary.' Soon after a resolution of the upper house of the Japanese Diet denounced nuclear tests (March 15, 1957) Pius sent a message to Masatoshi Matsushita, an eminent Japanese scholar, in support of it.

In May 1958, not long before his death, he gave audience within the same week to the NATO Defence College and to the Italian army chaplains. To the former he spoke very briefly and avoided the question of the morality of war altogether. To the latter he said: 'For the Church, war is not a nursery of masculine virtues or a stimulus to fertile initiative: it does not contribute to the progress of civilization, even if it sometimes occasions a quickening of scientific and technical progress. It does not remain lawful whatever the conditions. A believer in the great human family should be firmly opposed to any war of aggression. None can question Italy's desire for peace. But war is always a sad possibility; hence Italy must have her army, firmly set against aggression but ready in mind, in technique, in *number and quality of weapons*, for *any* necessary and timely defensive action.'

Pius's last word, then, was a patriotic re-assertion of the right to defence, which did not apparently exclude the use of nuclear weapons; but it can and should be harmonized with the two crucial sentences discussed above.

It is worth adding that on the preceding Easter Sunday in Westminster Cathedral Cardinal Godfrey, whose ear was usually carefully tuned to the Vatican, said: 'We do not believe that it has yet been conclusively shown that there can be no conceivable circumstances in which there might be a legitimate target for even the most powerful nuclear weapon. If this be so, then a nation would be justified in testing such weapons, unless again it be proved that the evil resulting therefrom outweighs the usefulness of the test.'

It was, perhaps, arguably not clear by the time of Pius's death that there was no legitimate 'defensive' use for nuclear weapons. But he had left no doubt that, if it should become clear, he would draw the logical conclusion. On the morality of manufacturing nuclear weapons as deterrents he had said nothing, though he had questioned its usefulness. He had also condemned the whole process of thought behind it—co-existence in fear, which is demoralizing, unstable, the very opposite of a basis for peace. He had insisted that disarmament should be 'spiritual as well as actual' (p. 145). He had enlarged on the wastefulness of the arms race—a waste he felt the more keenly as he found excitement in the peaceful potentialities of nuclear energy. He had insisted as much as anybody in the world on the importance of adequate international institutions—on the uselessness of talk of disarmament unless such institutions were to take the place of armed chaffering. Above all, he had recognized that a situation was possible, even perhaps imminent, in which the use of nuclear weapons would be absolutely and without qualification immoral; and from this, as many believe and have illustrated, the logical step to the immorality of making them is difficult to avoid, unless Catholic moral thinking is to take a most uncharacteristically pragmatical turn.[1]

It has been argued recently[2] that *Pacem in Terris* was a landmark in papal thinking about war: because it no longer viewed the question of disarmament in isolation; because it placed the prevention of international conflicts before their solution; because it made social inequalities and not ideological opposition between East and West the central international problem; because it substituted (or proposed that the Church should substitute) 'prophetic witness to the fundamental immorality and absurdity of war' for 'polishing and applying the theology of the just war'.

It would not be very easy to demonstrate textually this ambitious list of innovations. Of course in a rapidly changing and evolving situation it would hardly be reasonable to expect one pope to anticipate everything that his successor says. Yet the foregoing quotations hardly suggest that Pius XII habitually discussed disarmament 'in isolation'. At Christmas 1951 he enlarged upon the 'illusions' of those statesmen who did so. He constantly set the peace and war problem in the context of improving international institutions. At Christmas 1957 he said: 'The divine law of harmony in the world strictly imposes on all governments the obligation to oppose war with suitable international institutions, to bring armaments under effective supervision. . . . At present the problem is not one of running to the barricades but of forestalling disorders and giving breathing-space to a world that has suffered too much.'

The place Pius XII gave to East-West opposition, and what

[1] Cf. e.g. an elegantly logical discussion in *The Clergy Review*, Volumes XLVII–XLVIII, 1962–3.

[2] e.g. by Dr de Valk in a long paper issued by the Dutch Information Centre during Session III of the Council, DOC (No. 164).

change came with John, may be judged from Chapter 5; their respective attitudes to social inequalities from Chapter 10, pp. 218 *et. seq.* As for the last of Dr de Valk's antitheses: it is plausible to argue that Pius did some 'polishing and applying of the doctrine of the just war', especially in the earlier part of his pontificate, while war was being fought. John reigned for a brief and comparatively homogeneous period, Pius for twenty years over which the terms of the problem were transfigured. Yet Pius insisted constantly and with growing vehemence on the 'fundamental immorality and absurdity' at least of modern war, reserving only the principle of the right of self-defence (and foreseeing the impossibility of applying even that). *Pacem in Terris* does not in fact abandon the latter principle, nor does it assert the former so explicitly as Pius did.

The section of *Pacem in Terris* which deals with arms and war is brief (paragraphs 109-19). This is doubtless deliberate and in line with the general plan of the Encyclical—to discuss peace in the broadest framework and not as a mere antithesis, more or less inadequate, to a state of war. But to keep the problem of armaments in proper proportion and context does not make it any less of a problem. By 1963 it was in one sense at least notably more urgent than it had been in 1958. Receiving the Nobel peace prize in 1963, Professor Linus Pauling estimated the world stock of nuclear weapons at 320,000 megatons. What does this mean? The whole of the last war, including the knocking-out of Japan, involved six megatons of explosives. With the 1963 stock therefore it would be possible to repeat the damage of the last war once a day for 146 years.

With these facts in mind, the treatment of nuclear warfare in *Pacem in Terris* might well be thought rather jejune. As Monsignor Pavan, a chief collaborator in the Encyclical, said to the present writer, 'He might well have said more about this.'

The passage begins by deploring the pile-up of armaments and the burden this puts on the peoples of the world. It deplores the 'balance of fear', the constant chance of war through some 'unexpected or unpremeditated act'. At Christmas 1954 Pius had said: 'The present coexistence in fear holds out only two prospects. Either it will rise to coexistence in fear of God, and so to living together in true peace, or it will sink further into glacial paralysis of international life, with foreseeable consequences. In fact, to go on strangling the natural expansion of people's lives can only lead at last to the outcome it seeks to avoid—war. No people can support the armaments race indefinitely without feeling disastrous repercussions on its normal economic development.'

Three years later he again commented caustically on the wastefulness of armaments piling, 'aggravating the pride of *homo faber* at the expense of *homo sapiens*'.

Pacem in Terris refers explicitly to deterrence only once: '. . . Even though the monstrous power of modern weapons *does indeed act as a deterrent*, there is reason to fear that the very testing of nuclear devices for war purposes will, if continued, have disastrous consequences for various forms of life on earth.'

The second half of this Pius asserted more than once. The first half he was, we have seen, inclined to doubt (p. 148), at least on the long view.

John goes on (par. 112) to call in the name of justice, reason and human dignity for an end to the arms race, properly agreed and controlled reduction of armaments and the banning of nuclear weapons. He quotes in support an early broadcast of Pius, Christmas 1941. But at Christmas 1955 Pius dealt with the topic much more fully. He commented in detail on recent proposals to ban tests, renounce the use of nuclear weapons, and set up international supervision. A brief and graphic scientific account of a nuclear explosion, followed by a word-picture of the scene created, ended with this sentence: 'There will be no cry of victory, but only the inconsolable weeping of mankind which in desolation will contemplate the catastrophe due to its own folly.'

Sketching also the effects of nuclear tests and the character of the proposals for supervision he concluded: 'We do not hesitate to affirm, consistently with Our earlier allocutions, that these three provisions taken together, as an object of international understanding, are a duty of conscience for peoples and their rulers.' He insisted, he added, on the three together because only thus could security be guaranteed: a mere agreement to suspend tests was not enough.

The rest of the arms section of *Pacem in Terris* insists on completeness and sincerity in disarming and the substitution of trust for the balance of fear[1] and exhorts statesmen to approach their task in this spirit.

It may be asked why, if there was so little that was original in

[1] Cf. Pius XII Christmas 1939 and 1951.

this part of *Pacem in Terris*, it made such an impression on the world? More than one reason may be suggested. The first is that Pius XII's pronouncements were spread over twenty troubled years during a good third of which people had little time to read papal utterances even if they encountered them, and not much inclination except to search there for justification of their own policies or condemnation of their enemies. During these twenty years' anxiety and rapid change, Pius made a vast number of speeches to a great variety of audiences, and many of his significant statements are scattered as asides among the thousands of pages, and sometimes expressed in ornate and involved language. John XXIII's single great pronouncement was made at a moment of crucial interest, amid the hopes and fears following on the Cuban crisis and its settlement, the moving into a decisive stage of the nuclear test ban negotiations and other events referred to earlier (p. 141). He wrote too when the First Session of the Vatican Council and his own shrewd handling of its chief crisis had focused exceptional attention on the Church in general and on the papacy in particular, enhancing the already remarkable personal esteem he enjoyed throughout the world. He had a waiting audience in a way that his predecessor had never had. At this highly favourable moment he summed up in one document, direct and terse by papal standards and stamped with his own simple sincerity and unemphatic earnestness, not only the Church's recent teachings on peace but the aspirations of 'all men of good will'. Doctrinally he stood on the shoulders of Pius XII, as he himself made very clear. But his manner of communication to the men of his time was wholly his own, and his moment of communication superbly chosen—not least because it gave to the Encyclical, sadly yet triumphantly, the character of a last will and testament.

8

Lay Status and Station in the Church

THE CHIEF INTEREST of 'Operation Sturzo' (see p. 65) lies in its exceptional character. It was felt to be a crisis. Together with certain episodes elsewhere it generated a shyness of Catholic Action, a suspicion that it carries with it a political flavour. This was explicitly voiced in the Second Vatican Council by Archbishop Heenan, and was doubtless reflected in the fact that, in spite of the prominent part it had played in papal pronouncements in the preceding forty years, Catholic Action was not mentioned in the chapter on the laity in the constitution *De Ecclesia*, and treated with notable brevity even in the *schema* dealing explicitly with the Apostolate of the Laity. Yet since the early twenties the popes have consistently repeated that, though Catholic Action may make its valuable contribution to fitting a man for public life, it has no place in party politics. Nor was this mere accommodation to the restrictions of Fascism. Catholic Action in that specialized form which Pius XI gave it, and which certainly found its prototype in Italy, was defined as 'the participation of the laity in the apostolate of the hierarchy'. It is proposed in this chapter to discuss with some historical considerations the function of the layman in the evangelical work of the Church—a function which certainly has no direct concern with politics. 'Operation Sturzo' represents, for recent times, an extreme point—a danger point; a point reached for special reasons suggested below, and one from which the Vatican promptly receded. The recession has since been notably confirmed.[1]

Pius XII, in his missionary Encyclical *Evangelii Praecones* said,

[1] This sentence was written at the end of 1964. One would feel less confident if writing it now.

'It can certainly be said that the lay co-operation which we today call Catholic Action has existed since the foundation of the Church. Indeed the Apostles and other preachers of the Gospel received no little help from it . . .' and enlarged on his point with a historical sketch reaching from Paul's lay helpers to the great lay saints of the middle ages and to the religious functions of the guilds.

Speaking in the Second Vatican Council on October 24, 1963, Bishop Ancel of Lyons raised an echo of this: 'Many members of the Church, even some priests, seem to think that Catholic Action is a modern invention. Hence it is important to clarify what Revelation has to say on the apostolate of the laity. The *schema* says very little on this point . . .' and he went on to suggest including much fuller texts from the New Testament illustrating the use by Christ and His apostles of laymen.

Both Pope and Bishop are using the term Catholic Action as synonymous with 'apostolate of the laity'. But it could hardly be maintained that the identity is recognized throughout the Catholic world. Many who took the layman's apostolic responsibilities for granted did regard Catholic Action as a modern invention, and vaguely mistrusted it as such.

In a homogeneous Catholic world, which had not outgrown the simple ordering of society into clerics, men-at-arms and tillers of the soil (men of trade and industry were but slowly recognized), the apostolic tasks of the laity, apart from the general one of giving good example and doing works of charity, extended almost solely, where formal education was not general, to helping the overworked priest by catechizing. Additional stimulus was given to this by the Reformation crisis, and Pius V in 1571 approved the Confraternity of Christian Doctrine for organizing the work. The Jesuit sodalities, founded in Rome in 1567, were another Counter-Reformation enterprise aiming, with wide success, at creating solidarity in devotion to Our Lady and apostolic zeal among the laity.

After the French Revolution, though societies like the Association for the Propagation of the Faith (1822) and the Society of St Vincent de Paul (1833) sprang up offering laymen the chance of helping foreign missions or doing apostolic and charitable work among the poor, the emphasis began to pass to defence, to combating anti-Catholic and anti-Christian forces. A Société des Bons Livres founded in France in 1827 received the blessing of Leo XII in an encyclical which began combatively, 'A terrible torrent of filth is caused by the books issued by the diabolical workshops of wicked men. . . .' Phrases like 'calamitous times', 'flood of impiety and wickedness', 'wicked malice of the times', 'insolence and disobedience', 'wicked machinations', 'enormous weight of many disasters' were the commonplaces of papal exhortation during the nineteenth century, only beginning to be toned down under Leo XIII. A papal letter to an Italian Catholic Youth Association in 1868 began crisply with the words *Dum filii Belial.* Two years earlier an Italian Catholic Society had been formed, a precursor of modern Catholic Action, aiming, in the historic heart of Christendom, to 'defend the liberties of the Church and resist the efforts of wicked men', and clearly reflecting far less apostolic zeal than an intransigence largely political. These Catholic associations were told that ecclesiastical authority was 'now in chains' (1876), that new ideas among their members were 'the devil sowing discord' (1877) and that their *raison d'être* was 'to stave off the imminent dissolution of society' (1877). The beginnings of similar movements in other countries, France, Germany, Belgium, Austria, Brazil, in the same decade were greeted in similar language, the Belgian Federation being told in 1873, 'We praise most of all the fact that you are, it is said, filled with aversion for Liberal-Catholic principles, and try to rid men's minds of them as much as you can.'

There were of course varying degrees of justification for this tone, but it was all too indiscriminate, and the papacy had never been further from recognizing that condemnatory rhetoric is subject to the law of diminishing returns. Beneath the universal lamentation there runs a current of conviction that the laity must be 'used' more, but only under the strictest clerical discipline. The majority of the documents here discussed are addressed to members of the aristocracy, who because of their social prestige and influence were useful instruments of clerical policy. The misfortunes of liberal Catholicism in France served only to strengthen the conviction that nothing but disaster could come of allowing the laity to do any independent thinking. The classical extreme expression of this is in the words of Monsignor George Talbot, the curious aristocratic English confidant of Pius IX (1867): 'What is the province of the laity? To hunt, to shoot, to entertain. These matters they understand, but to meddle with ecclesiastical affairs they have no right at all . . .' though in fairness it must be added that Talbot was an unusual cleric talking of an unusual laity, and his words attracted attention only because they were already felt to be silly. Similarly, when the French editor quoted by Père Congar wrote half a century ago, 'It is for the Church to defend the laity, not for the laity to defend the Church,' he was expressing an extreme and obsolescent view; but that Catholic associations should have to be formed for such purposes as 'the defence of the liberties of the Church' was a misfortune which could not fail to colour the atmosphere in which the laity first began to mature. The air was always that of grudgingly yielding, under pressure of events and with liveliest fear of the consequences, ground which was by nature clerical; yielding it moreover not so much for apostolic as for quasi-political purposes.

A mellower tone is detectable in the First Vatican Council's constitution *Dei Filius*: 'All faithful Christians, but those chiefly who are in a prominent position or engaged in teaching, We entreat by the compassion of Jesus Christ and enjoin by the authority of the same God and Saviour that they bring aid to ward off and root out those errors from Holy Church, and zealously help in spreading the light of undefiled faith.' This was quoted with approval by Leo XIII, who himself did much to establish a new tone. He had been viewed with some suspicion, as having liberal leanings, in the Roman Curia of Pius IX's last years. In 1882 he exhorted Catholic writers that 'with gravity and moderation of speech they reprove errors and vices . . . without bitterness, and with respect for the individual; lastly, that they use a plain and clear manner of speech, which the multitude can easily understand'.

Rerum Novarum appeared in 1891, and those who think of Catholic lay activity in primarily social terms, i.e., as 'Christian Democracy' in that loose, non-political sense which Leo tried to impose on the term in *Graves De Communi* (1901), regard the latter Encyclical as a charter, ringing out the nineteenth century with its paternalistic and indiscriminate anti-liberalism and obsession with the Temporal Power. Leo of course was no 'liberal' in any sense which, say, Auguste Comte would have understood, but he had the good sense and realism to see that the best liberal ideals could be valued and taken up apart from aggressive secularism. In this he in some sense anticipated John XXIII. An urgent motive for this discrimination was the growing threat of anti-religious socialism, a more dangerous rival to the Church for the allegiance of the masses. An intransigence based on the memories of 1870 was a perilous luxury; if Catholics continued to sulk behind clerical skirts they left a vacuum in the social and political field which might be filled disastrously. Hence in the first two decades of the new century the pressure of Christian social ideas and movements gradually told even at the Vatican, and by the end of the First World War a large area of Catholic social and political activity had been released from direct ecclesiastical surveillance. This process was not without its difficulties, even its disasters, like the lapse into Modernism of Padre Murri, who had such grandiose schemes for a theocratic Italy. This is not the place to go into the curious involutions of anti-modernism and political integralism under Pius X, a pope who combined saintly zeal and theological rigour with considerable realism and even opportunism in the social and political fields. But in spite of blurring and confusion, the tendency to a clearer distinction between lay apostolate and social-political activity survived, and reached a landmark in the establishment of Don Sturzo's Popular party, Catholic in inspiration but aiming to be firmly non-confessional in spite of the disapproval of such integralists as Padre Gemelli.

The brief history of the *Popolari* well illustrates the difficulty of maintaining the distinction (see p. 15, *et seq.*); Sturzo's party had the worst of both worlds: its non-confessional aspirations alienated the sympathy of the conservative Pius XI, while its Utopian and overloaded programme, reflecting its academic character and political immaturity, alienated practical politicians; its history confirmed the majority of the world's Catholics in their shyness of Catholic parties.

Whatever the merits of Pius XI's attitude to the *Popolari*, his pontificate was dedicated to the task of establishing Catholic Action as synonymous with the lay apostolate and distinct from all party politics. He never tired of reiterating this distinction to Catholics of all nations. It may be thought that in this insistence he had always an eye on the domestic situation in Italy, the need for forestalling any doubts of the Church's exact observance of the Lateran Pacts, and also that he feared Catholic involvement with socialism anywhere; but however this may be, he left no shred of excuse for confusion, in theory at least, between Catholic Action as an organized apostolate directly under the hierarchy and Catholic participation in politics. This does not mean that lay apostles are precluded from taking part in politics, much less that their being lay apostles has no influence on that participation. For Pius XI Catholic Action was the highest medium of political *education*. He was inclined to make a distinction between party politics and politics in the sense of 'the common good' as opposed to 'private and individual good'. He told Italian Catholic men in 1926: 'The common good concerns the *polis*, that is the town, the nation in the fullest sense of the word. . . . Catholic Action, while avoiding party politics, seeks to pursue good and lofty political ends, it seeks to educate politically the consciences of citizens in a Christian and Catholic sense.'

He never tired of insisting that this purpose was a secondary outcome of the primary one, the interior end of the sanctification of souls. Some of his most considered utterances on the subject were addressed to Mexican Catholics, who had no possible chance of getting 'mixed up in politics'. 'The holy apostolate of the laity,' he told them in 1937, 'We have declared continually, is part of the pastoral ministry and the Christian life.' He added that 'publicity and the methods of the circus have no place in it. It looks upon noisy methods as an enemy'. Such observations were clearly not meant for exclusively Mexican consumption.

These clear and lofty expositions of an ideal were often in sad contrast with reality. The practical consequences of this non-political Catholicism under the Fascist régime are harshly described by Jemolo in the passage quoted earlier (p.19). The sort of reaction this excited among intelligent and frustrated youth has also been referred to (p. 62). In subsequent pages (62, *et seq.*) we saw something of Pius XII's efforts to grapple with the overriding problem which, in spite of his predecessor's efforts, had clearly recurred in the post-war, post-Fascist situation: that of keeping the lay apostolate in the strict sense (whose 'noblest form', he said in 1940, was Italian Catholic Action) clearly distinct in practice as well as in theory from the wider forms of Catholic lay activity, and particularly from politics. Since Catholic Action was by definition collaboration with the hierarchy under its strict authority, the distinction was vital if charges of clericalism and disguised theocracy were to be avoided.

Such problems could not be solved nor such misunderstandings cleared up without some radical revision of ideas about the place of the layman in the Church. Jemolo's remarks (p. 19) suggest the impression that a certain kind of 'ecclesiastical layman' creates on the intelligent liberal: what one Italian writer has called 'a steady refusal to take the things of this world seriously' produces a kind of bowler-hatted monk. The remedy is certainly not for laymen of this type to meddle amateurishly in practical politics, least of all as the mouthpieces of the higher clergy. It may be reasonably objected, of course, that special training for apostolic activity does not necessarily produce laymen of this type. The only possible comment is that in some countries at least it tends very strongly to do so. In his Lenten pastoral from Milan in 1962 the present Pope found it pertinent to speak of the *adult* vocation of the laity, of their need for a *virile* spirituality by which they will know how to make their own *characteristic* witness to Christ and His Church in the modern world.

Why is this so? The answer once again can only be found in history: the curious history of the whole conception of the place of the layman in the Church. The primitive Christian concept of the organic community of the faithful, at once an assembly and an hierarchical institution, was thrown out of balance in the later middle ages by the official reaction to such 'democratic' theories as those of Marsiglio of Padua and the mild anticlericalism of the English Franciscan William of Ockham—themselves reactions against exaggerated Roman curialist tendencies which had been criticized severely by the unimpeachably orthodox Bernard of Clairvaux. The opening of Boniface VIII's Bull addressed to Philip le Belle, *Clericis laicos infensissimos esse oppida tradit antiquitas* (It is an old story that laymen are most hostile to clerics) is a famous outburst by an angry autocrat in the heat of a great quarrel. More important perhaps was the fact that about the same time treatises on the nature of the Church began to be written rather as inflated pamphlets, in an atmosphere of polemical reaction, with such titles as *De Regimine Christiano*, *De Ecclesiae Potestate*, *De Potestate Regia et Papali*. This insistence on the hierarchical, organizational aspect of the Church, in itself proper enough, came to be exaggerated and to overshadow the sense of community. The people came to be something on which the Church worked—a passive crowd. No one, asked to reflect, would perhaps have argued this position in so many words, but it was an attitude of mind which powerfully affected ecclesiastical thinking and action. It is revealed or pilloried in many venerable anecdotes, like the one of the ecclesiastical dictionary which under the entry 'Layman' had 'see Cleric'. 'The simple faithful have the same function as the Candlemas lambs: they are blessed and shorn,' said Eduard Le Roy; and in the recent Council debate on the Church, the American Bishop Primeau of Manchester, New Hampshire, carried on the tradition by describing the clergy's expectations of the laity in the words 'believe, pray, obey and pay.'

In practice, of course, the clerical view of and relations with the laity varied very considerably from country to country, not to say from parish to parish, but insofar as the emphasis described above was rooted in accepted theological teaching no priest wholly escaped it. It was the established background to the development of modern Catholic Action. Up to a point Catholic Action itself represented an attempt to break through the tradition. A layman who participates or co-operates in the hierarchical apostolate, however strictly under episcopal control, is no longer, to borrow Bishop Primeau's words again, a 'silent and passive sheep'. But insofar as the emphasis remained on the layman being called or invited to this co-operation and the Church being forced by the pressure of the times so to invite him and 'use' him, it was the old emphasis, the old disturbed balance again. The layman who is baptized and confirmed, leaving aside controversies about his 'participation in the priesthood', needs nothing, it began to be argued, to make him an apostle, though he may be so with differing degrees of formality, of commitment.

If Catholic Action was no more than a mere adaptation to the pressure of the times, a mere acceptance of a 'hypothesis' forced by circumstances on churchmen who still retained a clericalist 'thesis' it would be unlikely to be a very fruitful enterprise. But this of course would be an exaggeration. There was no thesis which excluded the community aspects of the Church or the privileges and responsibilities inseparable from membership. There was only an unbalanced emphasis. What has happened is that the practical developments of lay apostolate prompted by the pressure of necessity have in turn, in the pragmatic way common in history, prompted a development of ideas, a recovery of a richer conception of the nature of the Church and of the place and function of the laity in it. But the development of both practice and ideas has been retarded by resistance traceable to the old outlook.

Take the question of obedience. That obedience to the hierarchy is a duty of both clergy and laity is a general proposition which no sane person will question; and it is a duty that, in matters of apostolic work, is the greater the more closely the layman is associated in the work of the clergy. Where it is simply a question of the layman being guided by Catholic principles in a field in which he is the acknowledged expert, the duty of obedience is more general, and the extent to which the wise church leader will assert himself is more circumscribed. Modern conditions—the spread of education, the growth of specialization and the consequent disappearance of the polymath, whose ranks used to be plentifully sprinkled with clerics—have made these considerations rapidly more pertinent. There may be added reasons for ecclesiastical restraint in special circumstances and because of historical antecedents, notably in politics where, as De Gasperi saw, the appearance of clerical interference or pressure can defeat its own ends by exciting latent anticlericalism.

All this would seem common sense. Yet the *insistence* on obedience in pronouncements about Catholic Action is so constant as to strike the unprejudiced reader as almost obsessive. A good schoolmaster or parent does not have to spend much time talking about obedience—he creates it. If he is voluble about it one begins to look for reasons, and one looks for something wrong in his relations with child or pupil. Over-protestation of the claims of authority is often locking the stable door after the horse has bolted.

It is fashionable to talk of that clerical outlook which has come in for such criticism in the Second Vatican Council as 'the siege mentality'. But there is one respect in which the phrase is inapt. A siege presumably creates esprit de corps without too many lectures needing to be delivered about it.

It is not to be denied of course that in this matter the Church authorities have been given grounds for dissatisfaction at various times, especially during the modern secularization of society and the spread of 'laicism' as it is called on the continent. But it is undeniable that *indiscriminately* hostile reaction to the secularizing process, stemming as it did from an unbalanced insistence on the Church as a legal entity and a subject of rights and privileges, did something to alienate loyalty. Only something: it would be naïve as well as unjust to question that there were evil forces at work bent on frustrating the Church's work. It would be just as naïve to deny that churchmen often made the task of these forces unnecessarily easy.

The words laicism, clericalism and anti-clericalism have just cropped up. Laicism, more commonly called secularism in England (though the Second Vatican Council in *De Ecclesia* was unhappy about both words), has been defined as 'the absence of the religious motive from the activities, institutions and environment of the temporal order' and described as 'a phenomenon typical of the modern age'. The writer[1] goes on to talk of it, using in effect the scholastic, analogical mode of thought, as a disease which has varying degrees of virulence: atheistic laicism; naturalistic laicism (which regards religion as a variable and purely private matter); heretical laicism, which concedes the Church a supernatural mission but allows her no authority, even indirect and moral, in the temporal order; and finally 'laicist tendencies'.

About the first three there need be no delay: they are unacceptable to Catholics. It is the fourth category which is interesting; it is confined to Catholics. Monsignor Pavan describes it as 'any attitude of impatience or negative criticism concerning the Church's interventions in the temporal order.' He adds significantly that this mildest form of the disease is 'perhaps more common in Italy than elsewhere for historical reasons.' It is certainly extremely common for the higher clergy to diagnose it there. 'Laicist tendencies' is a very elastic category—it can be stretched to include almost anything the clergy find inconvenient or unwelcome, and frequently is. Up to 1962, when Monsignor Pavan's little book appeared, it was frequently stretched to embrace many ideas and contentions to which the Council has since given a blessing, and in the minds of a handful of diehards (of whom Monsignor Pavan is conspicuously not one—he was one of the architects of *Pacem in Terris*) it still includes them, Council or no Council.

Is laicism synonymous with anticlericalism? It is rather too readily made so. Laicist No. 1, your militant atheist, will be anticlerical by definition. He will hate the priest because the priest is the minister and teacher of the God whom he rejects. Your laicist No. 2 may be and often is very benevolent towards priests: he is usually the product of a pluralist society in which they can be taken for granted. Your laicist No. 3 is, obviously, the most easily incited to anticlericalism. But a man who is, too easily perhaps, saddled with 'laicist tendencies' may well be no more than an anticlericalist, that is, opposed not to priests but to clericalism. It is true that some practising Catholics are anticlerical simply because

[1] Pietro Pavan, *Laicismo d'Oggi.*

they are busybodies of bilious temperament who find an outlet in a rather morbid interest in church affairs, or because they have personal grudges. This has nuisance value, but little more. But to be opposed to clericalism is a healthy state of mind for anybody at all.

If this raises the delicate question, what is clericalism? a simple answer is far from easy. If it were not for the laws of libel it might be easier to give examples. Perhaps the most comprehensive and significant thing one could say about Pope John XXIII is that he was without trace of clericalism. If anyone should be tempted to think that it is a mere term of abuse without real content, he should be reminded that it is mentioned in the full text of *De Ecclesia* as a thing to be avoided. Anyone who has lived in Rome through the Second Vatican Council knows exactly what it is, but at the same time he knows how refreshingly few of the world's bishops are afflicted with it. It is certainly not unconnected with that unbalanced view of the nature of the Church which dominated clerical thinking for a long time, and which *De Ecclesia* has (we shall see) done so much to correct. It is connected with an insufficient acknowledgement of natural rights, personal and political. This of course lays the term open to being used by the secularist to describe as clericalist any view of the Church's authority that is wider than his own: the late Dr J. N. Figgis in his classic *The Divine Right of Kings* inclined to use it to describe the Church's claim to pass moral judgements in public affairs: he was a laicist of Monsignor Pavan's third type.

Involving as it does a modest and 'external' view of the layman's function, clericalism induces contentment with a very modest standard of religious instruction and training. With these ideas, especially the last, in mind, it cannot be questioned that the *idea behind* Catholic Action was a move away from clericalism, even if it was a move still cluttered by the prejudices of a clericalist past. A laity better instructed in the Faith is less likely to be either clericalist or anticlerical, while any 'laicist tendencies' it develops will be of the healthy sort. This truth and this development were to some extent masked in Italy during the Fascist years, when an ingrowing concentration on ecclesiastical affairs was forced on Italian Catholics.

It was during this period that Cardinal Pacelli's first notable speech on Catholic Action was made, and made outside Italy: at the 1928

Congress of Magdeburg, when he was still Nuncio in Germany. If it naturally followed the lines laid down by Pius XI, it had some striking individual elements: 'What Catholic Action seeks above all to bring to the *organic* structure of Catholic *life* is a *soul*, that is the realization on the part of *each* of the faithful of his or her *status* as a Catholic. . . .' (Italics mine). He also insisted on the proper degree of autonomy both for existing Catholic organizations and for purely cultural enterprises; he dwelt on charity and on 'supernatural optimism'—the last a theme he was often to revert to as Pope, in the dark years—almost as though it were a strenuous counterpoise of mind and spirit against his natural sensitiveness to human distress and bewilderment. Finally he stressed that there was no universally valid form of lay action: the form matters less than the spirit.

Elected Pope, he lost no time in reverting to the theme. His first Encyclical, *Summi Pontificatus*, without mentioning Catholic Action spoke much of lay apostolic work. He quoted St Augustine: 'When you hear Our Lord say "Where I am, there My servant shall be also," do not think only of faithful bishops or of the clergy.' He went on with the passage, which closely likens the head of a household, discharging his duty to teach, encourage and reprove, to a pastor and even a bishop.

The vital question of standards of instruction occupied him early. He said to undergraduate and graduate Catholic Actionists in April 1941: 'The divorce between secular and Christian learning, science and religion, is something the graduate Catholic must dedicate himself to healing. He can do so only by raising his knowledge of Catholic truth to the level of his knowledge of law, history, literature, biology. You cannot face the learned world with a child's religious equipment.' Moral qualities, he reminded his audience, are necessary for the best exercise of a profession; but high standards of scholarship too are needed among Catholic Actionists. Quoting a powerful passage from Augustine's *De Genesi ad Litteram*, he went on, 'If unbelievers see we cannot talk accurately about what we see, how will they respect what we say or write about the unseen?'

Pius had watched this divorce being made absolute in the Rome of his own lifetime. It was symbolized in the gulf between the University of Rome (now strongly secular in tone though, ironically, founded by Boniface VIII) and the various ecclesiastical academies. His own pontificate, especially in the post-war years, can be seen from one point of view as a gigantic personal effort to heal this divorce. It was the motive (in addition to that of courtesy) behind his famous habit of discoursing to every conceivable kind of learned audience on its own subject. He was not pretending to add to their specialized knowledge: he was paying them the compliment of showing a real and not merely polite interest in their subject and at the same time asserting his conviction of the relevance of all things to the Faith. None could have been less 'clericalist' in all this than Pius XII.

The Encyclical *Mystici Corporis* of June 1943 marks a major step in recovering a proper conception of the laity, with its insistence on an organic unity of the Church not confined to the grades of the hierarchy or to charismatics. Yet the note of concession does not seem wholly eliminated: 'Indeed, it is to be observed that, in present circumstances especially, parents and godparents and those among the laity who co-operate with the hierarchy in spreading the kingdom of the divine Redeemer hold an honoured though often humble place in Christian society, and that they too are able, with the help of God, to attain the highest degree of sanctity. . . .' Pius insisted more than once on the need for flexibility and adaptability in organizing the laity. No one was less inclined by temperament to formalism or to mistaking activity for achievement. In October 1946 he wrote to the Patriarch of Venice words which were a criticism of prevalent views as well as a statement of his own: 'We wish that all Catholics would come to recognize in Catholic Action not a closed circle of persons specially trained for specialized vocations, nor indeed an instrument of fruitless strife or ambitious conquests, but rather a friendly group of citizens who have made their own the maternal mind of the Church to save all men and to ensure to society the indispensable leaven of true civilization.'

In this immediate post-war time Pius saw the world as full of problems, but also as calling for that 'supernatural optimism' he had spoken of at Magdeburg: an attribute which had marked the papacy in its great creative days after the collapse of Rome. His speech to the new cardinals in this same year was a programme for the post-war world—a programme in which he clearly saw the laity as playing a new and weightier part for the Church: the laity, he said, should have an ever clearer understanding not only that they belong to the Church but that they *are* the Church, i.e., the community of the faithful. In the following years the Encyclical

Mediator Dei set out solemnly the liturgical foundations of this new estimate of the laity. 'The man who prays is never a nobody,' the Pope once said. It was a view incompatible with 'activism', with straight-jacketing, with forgetting the primacy of the spiritual, with making Catholic Action a super-organization, or its members cogs in a machine.

In the Holy Year of 1950 laity flocked to Rome as never before and listened to the Pope, and the following year set up a milestone in the history of Catholic lay activity: the first World Congress of the Lay Apostolate (October 1951). This illustrated the expansion of lay activity since Pius XI's time and (at a remarkable pace) since the war. It aimed also at co-ordinating without dragooning or suppression a bewildering variety of enterprises. For such an audience it was natural that the Pope, who only a few months earlier had scanned the vast mission field in his *Evangelii Praecones*, should develop his thoughts on the laity expansively. He lost little time in confronting a thesis then much discussed, and set out with both learning and restraint by Père Congar two years later in *Jalons pour une théologie du laicat*: 'It is often said that during the past four centuries the Church has been exclusively "clerical" as a reaction against the crisis which, in the sixteenth century, had tried to achieve the abolition of the hierarchy. The implication is that it is time for the Church to broaden her ranks. So far is this judgement from the reality that it is in fact since the Council of Trent that the laity has come forward and progressed in apostolic activity.' The Pope went on to instance the Jesuit sodalities which he esteemed highly, and the development of women's apostolic work, mentioning by name the Englishwoman Mary Ward and St Vincent de Paul. He instanced also the Catholic movements which had followed on the secularization of Christendom and the separation of Church and State—changes which threw the Church back on her own resources. Again the laity is thought of as filling a gap, acting as a 'reserve clergy'.

This passage has sometimes been taken as a refutation of the charge of clericalism, but it seems that the Pope is rather concerned with adducing historical precedents for lay action in the Church than with passing judgement on the presuppositions behind it. Clericalism is primarily an attitude of mind, and one which had certainly survived the various movements the Pope spoke of. Rather than being modified by these movements it had affected them. It was only beginning to be true at the time Pius spoke that developments in the lay world and in the lay apostolate were weakening the foundations of clericalism by providing new contacts between clergy and laity and new thinking from both sides about their relations.

Pius XII went on to speak to the congress of a triple mission of the Church: to raise fervent believers to the level of the needs of the time; to bring those who hesitate on the threshold to the warmth and comfort of the fireside; to bring back the estranged whom she can never abandon. The clergy, who must stick to their sacerdotal functions, are unequal to the full demands of this triple task. Hence the call to the laity. He offered three considerations on this:

1. Are all equally called to the apostolate? Do not be pedantic. If you see men, for example, supplementing priests in persecuted countries, do not fuss about what organization they belong to. Organization is a good thing, but not if it leads to exclusiveness.

2. The lay apostolate's dependence on the hierarchy admits of degrees. It is strictest for Catholic Action—the official apostolate. Other works can be left more to lay initiative within limits of orthodoxy and general authority. 'When We speak of Catholic Action as an instrument in the hands of the hierarchy, We think on the lines of the Creator using rational creatures as instruments, *avec une douceur pleine d'égards*. But We do not like the expression "emancipation of the laity". It has an unpleasant sound and is historically misleading. Were the great *condottieri* of the Catholic movements of the past hundred and fifty years children? In the realm of grace, moreover, all count as adults. The appeal to the laity is not a consequence of the *failure* of the clergy, who can read the signs of the times as well as any. Collaboration should be the ideal.'

3. The Pope ended with a passage (already quoted) congratulating his audience on refusing to be confined to matters of the sacristy.

As so often with Pius XII when addressing a world-wide audience bringing together many different organizations and traditions, there is a breadth and measured manner about this speech, an appropriate tolerance and realism. When he turned back to the Italian scene, to that Italian Catholic Action which he had called 'the noblest example', his vision concentrated and intensified.

In the year or two following the Holy Year of 1950 he was consumed with zeal for a continuation of its impetus, a spiritual and moral renewal in the world, and this zeal focused at its most incandescent on Rome, not the most promising of targets. He addressed the Romans in February, 1952: 'The Holy Year, which first among you and then in the entire world, produced such a wonderful efflorescence of Christian life, cannot be allowed to pass like a brilliant but ephemeral meteor . . . it is rather a first step, full of promise, towards that restoration in all its integrity of the evangelical spirit. . . . This is the moment to take other decisive steps! This is the moment to shake off that deadly lethargy!' Rome should be 'a pilot city'. There should be a 'climate of general mobilization', a common effort to direct Italy towards 'an integral religious renaissance'. These were the years in which the influence of the Jesuit Padre Lombardi was strong on him. His language often took on an apocalyptic fervour: 'So while the impious continue to spread the seeds of hatred, while they still cry "we will not have Jesus reign over us", another cry will rise, a hymn of love and liberation, ringing with firmness and courage. It will rise from field and factory, from houses and streets, from legislatures and courts, from families and schools.' Three or four times in the same year he returned to the theme of Rome and her moral renewal.

It is impossible to be indifferent to the intensity of Pius's apostolic zeal. That he is concerned with Catholic Action in the strictest sense his predecessor had given it—a spiritual regeneration first and last—is beyond argument. Those who recall him in those early years of the fifties speak often of how his appearance—the almost transparent look, the restless energy of movement, the vibrant voice, the glowing eye—mirrored the consuming spiritual purpose. This was the time at which Luigi Gedda became president of Italian Catholic Action, and it fell to him to translate the Pope's aspiration into terms of Italian practice. None of Gedda's critics have doubted that the aspirations suffered in translation, and never more acutely than in the events which culminated in 'Operation Sturzo' (see p. 65). Gedda had a robust appetite for power and a boundless belief in what could be achieved by organization and 'activism'. He was an integralist under whom Italian Catholic Action earned a reputation for 'a radical incapacity to take the things of this world seriously.'[1] In spite of what the Pope had said

[1] Gianfranco Poggi, *Il Clero di Riserva* (Milan 1963), p. 292.

a decade earlier (cf. p. 167) scholarship, political influence, or experience, professional accomplishment were things to be *used* for tactical and apologetical purposes rather than practised well as themselves a form of example and witness to the living efficacy of faith. A former official of Catholic Action G. B. Scaglia, has put the matter well:

'There is implicit in all Catholic talk about culture a tacit assumption that without exaggeration can be called obligatory. It is the assumption that culture is interesting insofar as it is an effective instrument of defence and attack; that the cultural engagement of Catholics, i.e., their presence and action in the cultural field, has essentially the purpose of defending Catholic principles. This is without doubt a noble purpose . . . but . . . it can be ineffective, if not self-defeating, so long as it makes of the Catholic scholar a parasite who, instead of working alongside others engaged in research, disinterestedly sharing the burden with them, waits for them at the end of the passage, where science may have some point of contact with doctrine, simply in order to supervise and see that the faith is not offended.

'To have authority in the world of thought it is necessary to pay the entrance fee . . . science, culture can be an instrument or better a setting, for the defence of principles, but only provided they are served honestly and positively for their own sake.' (Cf. Chapter 13.)

Gedda's response to the Pope's call for a more dynamic apostolate, a break-away from the enforced too self-regarding mood of Catholic Action under Fascism, was too often in terms of organization and expansion and not enough in terms of real analysis of the Italian religious situation and of the real nature of lay apostleship. A mere subsidiary clergy, giving a pale imitation of the real thing, will not accomplish a task which has defeated the clergy proper. The layman's apostolate must be in the layman's mode, otherwise it will become a screen between the Church and the world rather than an interpreter.

The branches of Catholic Action that were most conscious of all this, and hence most critical of the *linea Gedda*, were the graduates, who were not regarded very warmly by Gedda. The present Bishop of Livorno, Emilio Guano, the Relator for the Council's *schema* on *the Church in the World of Our Time*, and a former chaplain to the *laureati*, put the matter, very restrainedly, thus:

'The position of the graduate section of Catholic Action is a delicate one; on the one hand, we have pledged ourselves to a stricter, more visible discipline; we have accepted the honour and the burden—at times particularly felt—of being directly at the disposition of the hierarchy, and this means caution and restriction which at times cost us dear . . . on the other hand the position of the graduate movement demands from us that we should contribute to stimulating the work of intelligence and Christian initiative, to making evident new experiences and needs that may sometimes be disconcerting: a contribution of candour, deferential yet always filially frank. . . .'[1]

But in Italy during Gedda's time opposition to his 'line' was largely silent and passive resistance. Elsewhere contrary ideas were more freely discussed. During the six years that separated the first World Congress from the second (1951–7), Pius XII combined a degree of understanding of the need for change and of the scale on which lay consciousness was developing with pronounced suspicions of many of the ideas abroad in the field, especially in France (see Chapter 10). Pius's interest in every kind of internationalism was intense, as will be seen later. He was convinced of the need for Catholic organization and action on the international level if the Church's influence on what he regarded as the characteristic post-war trend was to be felt. He said as much in an allocution of July 1952 which was quoted in a letter to Mlle de Camillis, president of C.I.O. (Catholic International Organizations) from the Secretary of State in March 1953.

The hopes he is known to have had of calling a Council may well have been prompted by this line of thought. In the early fifties he did a great deal to encourage and help the co-ordination of Catholic lay activity especially of an international character, notably by creating the 'Pius XII Foundation'. The conference of Catholic International Organizations united a long list of worldwide enterprises dealing with most things from sport and films to child welfare and alcoholism.

But international organizations are more likely to develop ideas and activity independent of national hierarchies. In a letter to the C.I.O. president in March 1955 Pius stressed the need for such organizations to work in harmony with the episcopate. He did not, as we have seen, much like phrases like 'emancipation of the laity', 'lay theology', nor too much talk of 'the priesthood of the laity', and

[1] Quoted Poggi, *op. cit.*, p. 259.

when he canonized Pius X in 1954 he took the occasion in two speeches to the cardinals and bishops present to describe pretty firmly and at length what he considered the limits of lay aspiration. 'Some proud modern spirits provoke serious and dangerous confusion, traces of which are more or less clear in various regions. The awareness, daily more strongly insisted on, of having reached maturity produces in them an agitated and febrile spirit. Not a few moderns, men and women, think that leadership of the Church is not to be suffered by one who is grown up; they not only say it but they hold it as a firm conviction.'

But while he disliked talk of limiting the competence of ecclesiastical authority, Pius did not regard it as incompatible with lay initiative. 'Although the Church refuses to see the sphere of her authority unduly limited, she neither represses nor diminishes thereby the liberty and initiative of her children. The ecclesiastical hierarchy is not the whole Church, and it does not exert its power in external affairs as does, for example, a civil authority, on the juridical plane alone. You are members of the Mystical Body of Christ, grafted on to Him as on an organism animated by one single Spirit, living one and the same life. The union of the members with the head in no sense implies [that they abdicate their autonomy or] that they renounce the exercise of their functions; quite the contrary, it is from the head that they are always receiving their impulses . . . .'

The speech was made to an international congress of women in September 1957. It is interesting to note that, when the speech was eventually printed in the *Acta* of the Holy See, the words in brackets, which had appeared in the *Osservatore Romano*'s report of the occasion, were omitted.

This speech was given only a week before the second World Congress of the Lay Apostolate assembled. Whatever the extent and grounds for the discontent which the Pope clearly sensed in the foregoing passages, the six years since the first congress had seen considerable advance in the ideas and aspirations of the laity; this was particularly marked in English-speaking lands, if only because there it was comparatively novel, whereas in northern European countries with large Catholic minorities it was not. In 1953 Père Congar's *Jalons* appeared and was translated into English (as *Lay People in the Church*) in time for the congress of 1957. In 1955 Monsignor John Tracy Ellis had written an article in the American Jesuit quarterly *Thought* which has been described as a turning-point in Catholic self-analysis. Instead of explaining away the deficiencies of American Catholicism as the result of poverty, immigrant problems and anti-Catholic prejudice, it began to blame American Catholic shortcomings. Catholic higher education was criticized, as Scaglia had criticized it in Italy, for being too utilitarian and apologetic in tone—undervaluing learning and achievement for its own sake. Thomas F. O'Dea's *American Catholic Dilemma* attributed these shortcomings to 'the basic characteristics of the American Catholic milieu': formalism, authoritarianism, clericalism, moralism and defensiveness.

This self-searching soon spread from the academic field into the wider plain of Catholic life as a whole. It was given a sharp stimulus by the 'McCarthyism' debate, which drew world attention to the fact that American Catholicism was a house divided on more than one issue.[1] Cardinal Spellman's readiness to accept the senator as an ex-Marine, enjoying the confidence of the electors of Wisconsin, who was 'doing something about Communism' was not shared by a large number[2] of his Catholic compatriots, least of all by the contributors and readers of *Commonweal* and *America*.

It would be easy to multiply instances of this new spirit in the Catholic Church as early as 1957. America was merely catching up with ideas which had been afloat for long enough elsewhere, but she was doing so with characteristic rapidity and thoroughness, and the importance of this was to be measured by her commitments, financial and other, in Europe and not least in Italy, Rome and the Vatican. Nothing was more likely to make curial conservatives nervous than signs of restlessness among rich and long docile American Catholics.

It was this sort of ferment that lay behind the congress of 1957. The appointed theme was 'The Layman in the Crisis of the Modern World: Responsibilities and Formation', and the elaborately prepared agenda reflected the new ideas. Two thousand delegates represented eighty nations. The Pope began his address with a particular aspect of the familiar hierarchy-laity theme: the question 'does the full-time "professional" apostle, with a canonical mission or mandate to teach the Faith, thereby pass from the lay apostolate to the hierarchical apostolate?'

[1] But it took the Second Vatican Council to turn this into a commonplace, and a favoured topic with such papers as *Time* and the *Saturday Evening Post*.

[2] At least 40 per cent, one Gallup poll showed.

It would be interesting to know in what circles this question had aroused such passions that the Pope judged it necessary to launch a world congress by answering it; no less interesting to know what proportion of his two thousand listeners hung breathless on the answer. Nothing could suggest more powerfully the dehydrated 'ecclesiastical layman' (encouraged of course by an appropriate type of cleric) than the aspiration to be 'up-graded' in this decidedly technical fashion. The Pope's answer to the question, elaborated with exemplary moderation and patience, was 'no!' This answer, far from betraying a desire to depress lay status was of course an assertion of its dignity. However 'professional' the lay apostle becomes, his virtue, his special scope and power derive or should derive from the fact that he *is* a layman, a true intermediary between Church and world, not an imitation cleric. His 'mandate' does not create something different in *kind* from his Christian privilege and responsibility. If those who aspired to this peculiar upgrading thought of it as a means to the 'emancipation' of the laity, their thinking had become extremely involved. Did this view develop out of confusion implicit in the original definition of Catholic Action—the *participation* of the laity in the apostolate of the hierarchy? Participation is commonly used in scholastic language to express not identification but only an analogy. It was noticeable here that Pius XII avoided the word and preferred 'collaboration'.

Having disposed of this *quaestiuncula*, and observed that full-time apostles should not be expected to live on charity but should be reasonably paid, the Pope was free to speak in a wider context, and he did so with a new freedom.

'It would be misunderstanding the nature of the Church and her social character to distinguish within her a purely active element, the ecclesiastical authorities, and on the other hand a purely passive element, the laity. . . . All are free persons, and must therefore be active . . .' and he referred to the Encyclical on the Mystical Body. He explicitly said that the *consecratio mundi* was essentially the work of laymen, and independent of the shortage of priests. 'Let the ecclesiastical authorities here apply the general principle of subsidiarity and complementary aid, and let them entrust to laymen the tasks which they can fulfil as well as or even better than the priest, and let laymen, within the limits of their functions or the limits imposed by the common good of the Church, act freely and exercise their responsibility.'

He took note of complaints about the use of the term Catholic Action to create monopolies, and gave his support to the suggestion that the term should henceforward be used in a purely generic sense to designate all forms of apostolic work, united in a loose federal way. Deprecating the term 'lay theology', he nevertheless urged laymen to study theology, especially in comparative work with other sciences. He urged also co-operation with neutral and non-Catholic organizations, particularly international ones such as UNESCO and those concerned with agriculture in underdeveloped countries. There was an anticipation of the Second Vatican Council: 'We know that there is talk at present of introducing a diaconate conceived as an ecclesiastical function independent of the priesthood. The idea, today at least, is not yet ripe. If one day it becomes so, it will change nothing of what We have just said. . . .'

In his Christmas message of 1957 Pius showed himself conscious of and not convinced by current criticisms of 'the ghetto mentality', and suspicious of such conceptions as a pluralistic society implying a collaboration between Catholics and humanists on the assumption that differences are 'inevitable'.

'If this "human" means, as it seems to, agnosticism where religion and the true values of life are concerned, any invitation to collaboration is equivalent to a demand for abdication, and to this no Christian can consent.'

The final impression left of Pius XII's attitude to new stirrings among the laity and their clerical 'champions' is one of certain inner tensions (or possibly divergent influences) not yet resolved at his death. His personal Christian humanism, the fruit of an eager and enquiring mind, his keen sense of the broadening of horizons in the post-war world, his enthusiasm for most internationalist trends as in harmony with the Catholic spirit, his genuine desire to encourage every generous and zealous impulse, his appreciation of the special needs of, say, Latin America and the mission lands: these were spontaneous and positive forces. But the influence of curial conservatism, which so constantly surrounded him though he was far from uncritical of it, combined with something in his own make-up to prompt the suspicions (not all unjustified) illustrated here. Where he took cognizance of criticism of the Church, even internal criticism, it was usually to refute it. It is not easy to conclude that by the end of his pontificate there was much sympathy in the Vatican for the *ideas* which a generation of change and (in many places) of awakening and renewal had set in currency.

In the six years separating the two World Congresses of Lay Apostolate, rapid progress was evident. Six years later still the Church would be in the middle of Vatican II. As will be seen from e.g., the last quotation above, there was little indication of the way discussion of the layman's place in the Church and related topics would then develop. Yet it could not have so developed apart from the intense activity of Pius XII's days.

In the short pontificate of John XXIII there was little in the Pope's formal pronouncements on this theme to suggest any revolutionary change of outlook at the Vatican. In a letter written at Venice in 1956, Cardinal Roncalli had echoed strongly Pius XII's strictures on 'lay theology', adding some combative words of his own about the indiscriminate use of the 'nickname' clericalist, and the 'intolerance and factious hostility which newcomers heap on the older generation'.

In the Encyclical *Ad Petri Cathedram* (July 1959) the new Pope said that Catholic Action does what the priest cannot do, but collaborating with and obeying the bishops, especially in the mission field. Stressing obedience and unity he added, 'Let them spare no effort, shirk no difficulty that the cause of the Church may triumph.' In *Princeps Pastorum* (December 1959) he repeated these and other thoughts of Pius XII, but added that he thought there should be warning given again and again that practice must be adapted to local conditions and that energy should not be dissipated in too many organizations.

In an address to the young women of Rome a month later he offered an ideal of generous but not tumultuous or inopportune action, not forgetful of interior values. Catholic Action should not fall to the level of any other external organization. Insisting on the primacy of the spiritual, he said, 'this We love to say and repeat', and indeed he did repeat it in three or four subsequent addresses to lay audiences of this kind. Catholic Action should be 'a mirror of harmony', and the enemies of harmony are parochialism, eccentricity and rigidity. To the *Milieux Indépendants* group in May 1961 he spoke first of supernatural motives and fraternal co-operation, and when he spoke of obedience to bishops he put the first emphasis on trust, on the frank exposition of ideas and differences. Saying the same sort of thing to Italian men in 1962 he added, 'the Council's work of renewal will call for the enthusiastic co-operation of the laity'.

It was of course chiefly the utter lack of clericalism in his own make up that did so much to attract and encourage laymen, as it attracted and encouraged everybody. Whatever speeches curial officials might write for him, men felt confident, even on the rare occasions that he stuck slavishly to the text, that they sensed his mind. Yet it is questionable how long such personal magnetism would have counterbalanced the continuing impact of traditional bureaucracy on an increasingly impatient world, had it not been for the master-stroke of the calling of the Council. Pope John may well have grasped that in the years left to him he could hope to make few inroads into Roman conservatism—some at least of those who elected him had done so with precisely that thought in mind. Yet he knew a good deal, especially from his years in France, of how that conservatism was regarded by increasing numbers of non-Italian Catholics who could not be dismissed as mere hereditary anticlericals, children of the *Risorgimento*. Moreover, he was now seeing the Vatican at close quarters himself for the first time in a long life. To call a Council was the one means of drawing ideas from the peripheries of the Church to the centre. It need not be supposed that he expected to approve, or thought it necessary in advance to approve, of all the ideas that might be brought. Arguments will continue as to how far John realized the possibilities of what he was doing. It is true that he appeared to accept the decrees of the Roman Synod as a serious end-product of a supposed radical overhaul of Roman religious life. This was an ideal which had consumed Pius XII, yet he had never held a synod for the purpose. Any unbiased observer must admit that, had he done so, it would probably have been done much better. From this some argued of John, 'Could a pope who accepted the Roman Synod really have had any idea of a general council developing as Vatican II did?'

The argument is hardly convincing. If indeed he hoped for radical change in the Church, it is at least as plausible to suppose that the Roman Synod merely emphasized for him the need to confront Rome with the rest of the Catholic world. This at any rate is what he did, and the results are now history.

What sort of history, in the matter of our present theme?

The ferment in the Catholic lay world of the fifties took various forms. Some, in the spirit of Congar, pinned their hopes on a theology of the laity (as distinct from the 'lay theology' stigmatized by Pius XII). Others had long pinned their hopes on liturgical reform, others on more serious education. None was sufficient, none was unnecessary. But at the basis of all lay the need rightly to value creation, and its earthly summit, humanity, for their own sakes: to distinguish sharply Christian *contemptus mundi* from anti-humanism and clericalism. (It would be absurd of course to suppose that all church officials failed to make these distinctions *personally:* but most of us are one thing when we are living and something rather different when we are drawing up official pronouncements or admonitions.) In too many places clerical and secular learning had been divorced. In Rome itself, where several lines of life coexist without ever crossing, the divorce is an essential element of modern history—of the history of the city since it became the capital of Italy as well as of the Church. The University of Rome was the foundation of the most theocratic of the popes, Boniface VIII. It is a retributive irony that today, in its own enclave on the outskirts of the city, it is a shrine of secularism while the city itself is largely a vast factory of rigidly ecclesiastical learning.

It was in this Rome that the Council assembled. The Roman ecclesiastical attitude to the world outside, both clerical and lay, was quickly manifest. For them the Council was an affair not of the Church but of churchmen, and for nearly a century churchmen had been very efficiently managed from Rome. Here, crammed together in moderately uncomfortable seats in the overwhelming baroque basilica, under a General Secretary who was a superb master of Roman technique, listening to Latin which the defenders of the *status quo* understood far better than anybody else, they could be managed even more easily. As for 'the world', well, if it showed any interest in the Council it could easily be fobbed off. The traditional Vatican attitude to the press was part and parcel of the siege mentality. The press was the enemy. It dealt in nothing but lies, or at best embarrassing truths.

It was all one of the great, historic miscalculations, comparable to that other which had been expressed in the same phrase in 1914; it will all be over by Christmas. From the moment when Cardinals Liénart of Lille and Frings of Cologne, joining hands so to speak across the cockpit of Europe, protested against the prepared lists of personnel for the conciliar committees, the picture of a compliant

Council going through some formal motions before an incurious world (if anyone had ever seriously entertained it) became a mirage. The ideals set out in Pope John's opening speech were to be taken seriously, so the world that had taken Pope John to its heart would take the Council seriously. Rome was full of expert journalists, some of them unbelievers, who once they sensed this and found their editors sensing it, found ways of breaking down the wall of silence and also of equipping themselves to a surprising degree to digest what they ferreted out. There is little doubt that they were vigorously helped in both enterprises by bishops and council consultants, many of whom put their own tactful interpretation on the then draconian rules of secrecy. There were, too, other less reputable ways of getting information.

Extravagances resulted. Bishops and theologians became too easily the heroes or Aunt Sallies of the more exuberant journals. The 'cowboys and Indians' interpretation of the Council became too much the vogue. But the healthiest revolution must have its excrescences. What we had here, in the main, was a contact of the Catholic episcopate with the world, an exposure of the episcopate to the laity which made nonsense *in fact* of the 'hierarcholatry' which, some contended, had overshadowed even the striking advance in the place of the laity since Pius XI's time. It was not an exposure in the sensational newspaper sense, whatever some accounts might suggest. The episcopate as a whole came out of it strikingly well. Some became public heroes. Some became bogeymen. The majority revealed themselves as men of humility and open mind, willing to learn, visibly blossoming in the easy atmosphere of conciliar Rome, making in a few weeks contact with men and ideas not a fraction of which a normal lifetime would have afforded. The old jokes about a bishop never eating a bad meal and never hearing the truth suddenly seemed very stale and inapt. But above all, to the sort of intelligent and unprejudiced layman whose opinion is creative (and many journalists either belonged to or directly influenced this class) a new image of bishops and of the ecclesiastical world swam above the horizon. Englishmen, Americans, Australians, Africans and many others to whom names like Liénart, König, Alfrink, Lercaro, Frings were as unfamiliar as the ideas for which they stood began very rapidly to be familiarized with both. In this odd way even agnostic journalists became, obliquely, lay apostles and ecumenists.

It is right to put this practical revolution first. When the Liturgy was made the first subject of conciliar discussion, many felt a sense of anti-climax, accentuated by the clumsy and long-winded character of the early congregations when procedure was amateurish and exploratory. Few people, even among the bishops, saw liturgical reform as closely hinged to a new conception of the laity. Some even thought of it as no more than new and odd ideas about decorating churches and arranging church furniture and ceremonies, governed by a rigid, rather puritanical attitude to art and music. For this some of the less intelligent, learned or balanced of the liturgical zealots were largely to blame. Yet the liturgy *schema*[1] was the product of the oldest and most learned movement for restoring the reality of religion to the people of God—and for bridging the gulf which had yawned for so long in many places between clergy and people. Hence of all *schemata* it was the one which already in its original form most clearly divided off the 'progressives' who liked it from the 'conservatives' who feared it. With the original drafts of most other *schemata* it was to be the other way round, but the Curia had been so little impressed by the Liturgy *schema* that they had sacked the secretary of the Preparatory Commission.

In some sense the fact that the language issue hogged the stage in the debate, and particularly in the reporting of it, was distorting in its effect; but at least it served to clarify issues in the Council. Latin became the battle-cry of those who saw the Liturgy as doing no more than furnish means of grace to which the laity had a 'right' of approach, mentioned in canon law; vernacular the battle-cry of those pastors who wanted to reclaim millions who had lost interest in this right, by representing it instead as a life-giving, ennobling, privileged activity. If this was an over-simplification, it was the fault of those who strove to preserve Latin less as a symbol of unity than as an instrument of clericalism. There were many, the majority perhaps, who genuinely loved the venerable Roman liturgy, who were yet willing to see changes if they were for the good of souls.

When the *schema De Ecclesia* first came up on December 1, 1962, the heart of the Council was reached, and also the heart of the matter of the laity. What were they? Those cardinals who represented the curial tradition of recent years, according to whose ideas the *schema* had largely been drafted, praised it. But the very first

[1] See Chapter 14.

speaker, Cardinal Liénart, set the tone of majority comment. The Mystical Body was here identified with the Roman Church, he said. It was conceived not as a divine mystery but as a legal institution. Later the Bishop of Bruges, Emile Josef De Smedt, in a famous speech, complained of the presentation of the Church in the *schema* as vitiated by three faults: triumphalism, clericalism and juridicism. All these, he might have added, were vices which had been material not only in widening the gulf between Church and world, between clergy and laity for over a century, but in exacerbating anticlericalism and indifference. The elimination of all three was a prime object of the labours of the Council, resisted by a diminishing number of the original drafters and advocates of the *schema* down to the last few days before it was solemnly promulgated two years later.

Bishop De Smedt enlarged upon clericalism and juridicism. The Church, he argued, was not a pyramid of people, priests, Pope so much as the whole People of God, the organic Mystical Body. The hierarchy's primary function was to serve, and he introduced by way of contrast the term 'hierarcholatry'. Stigmatizing the arid, pedantic terms in which the *schema* discussed who were and were not members of the Church, he said that no mother ever spoke thus, and Holy Mother Church should not be stooping to exercises in minor logic.

These and other no less trenchent criticisms sealed the fate of the document; the debate was prorogued, and when it was resumed in October 1963 a very different text was used—one which had been hammered out between the theological commission and the Secretariat for Christian Unity, a body set up by Pope John to study and further relations with non-Catholic Christians. Moreover, the debating bishops had had nearly a year to think of the implications of the debate. It was no question of 'theological niceties' taking up time that might be better spent on 'modern problems'. It was the vital question of what the Church is, of how she shall see herself and present herself to men not interested primarily, if at all, in her past triumphs and her complex, historic organization, nor in the splendours of her ceremonial or the intricacies of her legal system. The bishops showed their appreciation of this by adopting the revised text for discussion with 2,231 votes against 43, and it was of course much further improved in the succeeding debate.

'A sign and instrument of the intimate union of the whole human race with God.' This was the brief, arresting phrase in which the

Church was now presented. Cardinal Döpfner of Munich, the second youngest cardinal, introduced the new text thus: 'Our aim has been to make the Church known in all the richness of her life and attributes, as she reveals herself in the words of Our Lord in the Gospel and in the preaching of the apostles, especially St Paul. The Church is there presented to us as the chosen People of God, with the men of every country and nation called to be her members; as the sign of salvation raised up in the world; as the Mystical body of Christ, of which Our Lord, as head, is the principle of life, working out salvation among men in history.' It was within this picture, he went on, that the constituent elements of the Church—priesthood, religious, laity—were to be examined.

This is not the place to go fully into the very long debate. Outside attention was chiefly attracted by the chapter dealing with the 'collegial' status of bishops; it became the great 'progressive' aim and was no less hotly resisted by the curial party, and few believed that the motive of this struggle was wholly or even primarily theological. It concerned the future distribution of power within the Church. But the motives of those who wished for a redistribution of power were primarily pastoral, i.e., they aimed to increase the efficacy of the Church's saving mission to men. Cardinal Liénart, deprecating the bandying of texts, said: 'In this context there is no striving for domination; power is defined not in terms of authority but of service, not of personal glory but of the common welfare. . . .' and Cardinal Lercaro of Bologna, the strongest Communist city in Italy, singled out 'generous service with no expectation of reward' as the true core of the presence of the Church in the world.

These pastoral motives were even clearer when the *schema* turned to 'The People of God and especially the Laity'. Eventually, greater clarity was achieved by splitting this chapter into two: The Section on the People of God was made Chapter One, emphasizing that all without distinction from the Pope down share in this title. Such a notion once assimilated would be a heavy blow to clericalism. The new chapter spoke often of the '*universitas fidelium*', enlarging on this with St Augustine's phrase '*ab episcopis usque ad extremos laicos fideles*' (from bishops to the last faithful layman). Among all members of this unified *populus*, since it participates as a whole in the prophetic mission of the Church, the Holy Ghost distributes His gifts as He wills—the sense of faith, the special graces apt for the functions proper to each. Divine gifts, charismata in the stricter or broader sense, are to be welcomed wherever they are found. Those who exercise authority in the Church are to judge of such things, but with a mind not to quench the Spirit, but rather to submit all to fair testing and hold fast to what is good.

The language of *Thessalonians I* recalls the reader vividly to that apostolic age in which the Bishop of Bruges's triple reproach would have been meaningless. In this brief section of Chapter One of the constitution, the biblical foundation of a truly unified conception of the Church is firmly laid—the theological foundation for an ideal of an active, apostolic laity.

The chapter on the laity (No. 4 in the final draft) begins by reiterating that everything said in Chapter One on the People of God applies equally to laity, religious and clerics, adding that the special circumstances of our time demand a deeper examination of the particular character of the laity. At once evident is the departure from the typical language of the many pronouncements on the lay apostolate quoted above: 'Pastors know that they were not instituted by Christ to take upon themselves the whole salvific mission of the Church to the world, but that their proud duty is so to tend the faithful and acknowledge their ministrations and divine gifts [charismata] that all may unanimously co-operate, each in his own fashion, in the common task.'

Any lingering notion of lay action as an emergency measure, as a second best, as something forced on a clericalist Church by the pressure of the times, has disappeared. Instead, a solemn constitution, declaring the nature of the Church, says unequivocally that every Catholic is by definition a co-worker in the vineyard.

Another lingering notion disappears in the next paragraph. An 'inability to take seriously the things of this world' was a criticism levelled at the Catholic Action of the Gedda epoch, and the fault was traced to the fact that in this 'sponsored organization' churchmen, misconceiving the nature of their function in the context, afflicted lay action with churchiness. The constitution first tells the layman that he participates by baptism in the priestly, prophetic and regal office of Christ, and *as such* plays his part in the mission of Christians in the Church and in the world. Then in a long new paragraph added only to the third and final version of the text (the outcome in other words of the Second-Session debate), it says:

'It is the proper mark of laymen to be concerned with the world.

Though members of a sacred order may sometimes be occupied with secular business, even professionally, they are principally and professedly called and ordained to a sacred ministry, while religious by their state of life bear striking witness to the truth that the world cannot be transfigured and offered to God without the spirit of the Beatitudes. The laity on the other hand by the whole tenor of their lives are characteristically if not exclusively called to deal with temporal affairs and direct them towards God. They live in the world, which means that the whole pattern of their existence is interwoven with all manner of the world's business and with the normal condition of social and family life. There God asks of them that, doing their own job, they act like the yeast of the Gospel and contribute *from within* to the sanctification of the world, manifesting Christ to others primarily by the faith, hope and charity clearly showing in their own lives.' If after this the layman thinks he *can* be an apostle without taking seriously the things of the world, he has only himself to blame. If anyone else tells him he can, he has the constitution to point to.

He can point to a good deal more. The next paragraph reminds him of his dignity, in respect of others and of the clergy, whatever his race, class or other circumstances. He has Christ as his brother: can he have any other relationship with Christ's ministers? That is the end of clericalism. *Vobis sum episcopus*, *vobiscum Christianus* (To you I am a bishop, with you a Christian): the bishop must make St Augustine's words his own.

It follows that the apostolate is something to which all are called by baptism and confirmation, and equipped by sacramental charity, though some may in addition be explicitly called to a more immediate co-operation with the hierarchy. (The word 'mandate' is deliberately avoided.) The layman is one with the priest in a common act of worship, witness and service. A gloss on the text here explicitly says 'the intention is to avoid all appearance of clericalism'.

In one of its most eloquent passages the constitution speaks of the participation of the laity in Christ's royal office. The word '*servitium*' is used. It is a true essay in Christian humanism: 'All things are yours, and you are Christ's, and Christ is God's. (I. Cor. iii, 23.) The faithful therefore should recognize the intimate nature and value of the whole of creation, and how it is designed to praise God; thus by the work of the world they will help each other towards a more holy life, so that the world may be imbued with the spirit of Christ and work out its purpose in justice, charity and peace. [A note adds: the value of created things is brought out so that the lay apostolate should not appear as something arbitrarily added to the nature of things.] In the worldwide fulfilment of this task the laity have the principal place.'

If the whole passage puts a resounding end to the charge of 'incapacity to take the things of the world seriously', it does not do so by reviving theocratic pretensions: 'The faithful must learn to distinguish carefully between the rights and duties they have as members of the Church and those which derive from membership of human society. They must work to harmonize these, remembering that a Christian conscience must guide them in all matters, since no human activity can be exempted from God's governance. In our time above all it is vital that this distinction and harmony should be clearly apparent in the activity of the faithful. It must be acknowledged that the earthly city, rightly concerned with the business of this world, is governed by its own principles. At the same time the unhappy doctrine which seeks to build society taking no account of religion, and attacks or destroys the religious liberty of its citizens, is rightly rejected.'

Two amendments introduced into the final text of this section are of the first interest. The text presented for debate in 1963 prefaced the paragraph just quoted with *Matt. xxii*, 21 ('Render to Caesar the things that are Caesar's and to God the things that are God's') and also urged the faithful to resist 'the unhappy separation of religion and the Church from civil matters.' This vague phrase could easily have been taken as a conciliar endorsement of things like 'Operation Sturzo'; as the Commission admitted it 'aroused almost innumerable complaints' (mostly from America) it was left out.

The last sentence originally contained an explicit reference to '*infensus laicismus*'. It was the last echo, faint but clear, of Boniface VIII and his Bull, and out it went—on the odd ground that it would be 'understood with difficulty outside the sphere of French culture'. Is the great figure of the Anagni tragedy only remembered by the descendants of Philip le Belle's subjects? More than this, even the synonym '*saecularismus*' was expunged as an 'ambiguous' term. The intention to remove all stigma of clericalism was pretty determined. In substance, what is rejected is Laicism in the first three senses outlined by Monsignor Pavan. But there is no confusing talk of 'laicist tendencies'. It is pretty safe to say that the more intransigent curialists regard the whole chapter itself as riddled with laicist tendencies.

The final section deals with the relations between laity and hierarchy. The treatment is interesting especially when compared with the copious literature of pronouncements on Catholic Action. The word obedience occurs first after twenty lines which are taken up with listing the rights of the laity. This is entirely in the spirit with which Pope John set out to write *Pacem in Terris* (see p. 141). Those rights to spiritual benefits listed in the code of canon law are repeated, but in much less desiccated language. The faithful are invited to make known their needs to the clergy with that freedom and confidence which becomes the sons of God. They are also reminded that they have the right and sometimes the duty to make their views known, where these are based on knowledge, competence and understanding, for the good of the Church, 'honestly, courageously and prudently, with reverence and charity'.[1]

It is only then that they are exhorted to Christian obedience towards the representatives of Christ, after the fashion of Christ Himself who was made obedient unto death, that he might admit all to the liberty of the sons of God. They should pray for the clergy. The clergy should acknowledge and promote the dignity and responsibility of laymen in the Church, make free use of their qualified advice, confidently entrust them with duties in the service of the Church, leave them scope and freedom of action and even encourage them to set to work spontaneously. While weighing in a fatherly, loving way the ideas, wishes and suggestions of the laity, pastors should carefully recognize the just freedom that belongs to the temporal sphere.

The reader can judge for himself the extent to which this remarkable document embodies an advance in ecclesiastical thought and method. By contrast the *schema* on the lay apostolate, the practical counterpart of the *De Ecclesia* chapter, seemed when it was presented to the assembly, on October 7, 1964, like a man coming blinking out of a cave into strong sunlight: less terse and forceful, overcautious and burdened with the language and disputes of Catholic Action history. Yet it had already been considerably reworked in accordance with written criticism. It had also been

[1] It is to be hoped that this reminder may eventually produce something better than *Objections to Roman Catholicism.*

drastically shortened by order and it was here perhaps that the drafters missed their opportunity by not starting afresh in accordance with *De Ecclesia* and with the ideas which had been aired in two sessions of the Council. As it was, of the sixty-six speeches made during the five-day discussion only half a dozen expressed even qualified approval and many were severely critical.

Several speakers still detected clericalism in the general tone of the document in the surviving inclination to treat lay activity as an adventitious aid, a condescension by the clergy or even a necessary evil, and in the fact that the *schema* had been drawn up with little or no assistance from laymen. The debate revealed even more than had the corresponding one in *De Ecclesia* how strong was the feeling against any form of clericalism, at least outside Italy. A number of Italians complained that Catholic Action was not given a special place, that it was not sufficiently marked off as a special kind of apostolate resting on episcopal mandate and carried out at the strict orders of the hierarchy. But elsewhere the idea was clearly emerging that Catholic Action in this strict sense, insofar as it tends to absorb or control other lay activities or infiltrate its influence through them, is always threatening the proper autonomy of the secular, always tending towards clericalism. Cardinal Suenens reminded the Council of Pius XII's warnings against intolerance and exclusiveness in Catholic Action. Cardinal Liénart touched the heart of the matter when he suggested that the name Catholic Action should be confined *absolutely* to that full-time apostolate in which men submit themselves voluntarily to discipline as comprehensively as do the clergy. The field could then be left clear for defining the rights and responsibilities of the laity without danger of confusion or clericalist tone, as indeed is done in Chapter Four of *De Ecclesia*, while each episcopal conference could take or leave Catholic Action according as to whether it was considered suitable for the territory.

In view of the prevailing tone of Italian contributions much the most remarkable speech of the whole debate came from the young Bergamasque Bishop Santo Quadri, Auxiliary of the Piedmontese diocese of Pinerolo for only a few months. In a speech countersigned by seventy other bishops he said: 'If the laity are to work effectively in the mission of Christian restoration they must be thoroughly acquainted with the origin, nature and value of created things. Material things have their own proper content, make their own demands independently of being any "expression" of a higher supernatural order. If their genuinely human significance is not understood they cannot be "inserted" into the supernatural order. The intimate force of the moral law and the value of created things really lead to God. Directing things to God does not mean suppressing their natural autonomy. A temporal action is and remains temporal while taking on a supernatural significance. This enables the Christian to do more in the temporal order and to contribute to building a society really worthy of man.'

One would give much to know who were the seventy co-signatories of this speech. It must have caused some wagging of heads among the bishop's elder compatriots in the aula. But it was one of the more striking of several signs the Council has offered of new directions in Italy.

Indeed, the conclusion of this chapter must be that, in the matter of the laity, the Council has made commonplaces of many ideas that had appeared only fugitively in the Church's pronouncements before, and whose unofficial development had been watched with suspicion. If Pius XII and his immediate advisers, by hard thinking and against Vatican tradition, adumbrated changes, John XXIII by his personal example set the Church in new and non-clerical directions, but much more decisively by calling the Council he ensured that ideas whose wide acceptance was hardly suspected should prevail, fertilize and fructify at the centre of the Church.

9

Court, Curia and Council

JUST FOUR CENTURIES ago, in September 1565, Pius IV travelled to Perugia. For this journey of scarcely one hundred miles he was accompanied by ten cardinals, each with an entourage of twenty clerics and laymen, and also by the Ambassadors of Austria, France, Portugal and Spain, whose collective following added another hundred or so persons. Next came a great number of prelates of the *famiglia pontificia*: the majordomo, the datary, the sacristan, the secretaries, the privy chamberlains, the chamberlains of honour, each having five or six persons attending him; the adjutants of the chamber, the clerks of the apostolic chamber, the chaplains, a multitude of clerks of every sort, half-a-hundred grooms, the Noble Guard, the Swiss Guard, etc. The whole amounted to about a thousand people.

It was still a feudal prince's progress; yet we are well within a generation of the reforms of Sixtus V, which were to give a *famiglia* and a Curia recognizable today. The papal court grew, like other princes' courts, as a homely mixture of domestic and public functions and functionaries. The use of the name Curia most naturally passed to the papal court when the popes took over the administration of Rome. The Curia of imperial times had been the senatorial palace where the patricians deliberated and furnished the higher direction of public affairs. Among the principalities which gradually emerged from the ruins of the Empire the word Curia came to signify at once the seat of monarchical rule and the royal household, embracing princes of the blood, ministers, great officers. In French and Italian the word came to be spelt two ways (*cour/curie; corte/curia*) to indicate this double aspect which only very slowly became two separate institutions. At the papal court the separation has never become anything like complete.

An indication of the early date of such a papal establishment, at once household and administrative centre, is perhaps found in the story that the senator Pudens on his conversion placed his palace at the disposal of St Peter.

The peculiar feature of the papal establishment was that the chief ministers and advisers were the *presbyterium*, those priests of the city who were attached in stable fashion to ('hinged upon') one of the chief churches or *tituli* of Rome. The consequent expression 'cardinal priest' designated no clearly-defined function, but created the presumption that its bearer would be summoned to aid and counsel the Sovereign Pontiff. The Roman deacons, whose number often varied from the scriptural seven, though they originally had ministerial charge, as a kind of welfare officers, of seven districts of the city, were cardinals in the same sense. Later the Roman *presbyterium* was extended to include the bishops of the sees established in the vicinity of Rome—the 'suburbicarian' sees. These bishops are mentioned under Stephen III (752–7) as ministering in turn at the Lateran, and referred to as 'cardinales'.

The real importance of the cardinals was established once for all, and the use of the name strictly circumscribed, when in 1059 under Nicholas II they became the electoral college for the papacy. It was at this period too, under Leo IX, that the Roman Curia was so remodelled as to become the apt instrument of reform and renewal that helped to create the medieval papacy. Earlier the papal household had changed the nomenclature, functions and faculties of its officers as frequently as other monarchs did. In the tenth century when the office of *vestararius* (master of the wardrobe or treasurer) was held by the notorious Theophylact, his no less notorious wife Theodora was *vestararissa*.

The primitive feudal character of the household survived the reform of the administration, which itself did not prove very enduring. Until the time of Urban VIII (1623–44) the papal household, it seems, was paid in kind, and not until Pius VI (1775–99) was the last distribution of bread and wine made. Down to 1798 the datary used to be given an audience early every morning at which the Pope began his day as was thought proper for the common father by putting his signature to a document granting a favour or dispensation.

Much earlier the abuse and commercialization of this power of dispensation had been a central target of criticism and satire. Within a hundred years of the eleventh-century 'Hildebrandine' reforms, St Bernard was complaining loudly of the business-like activities of the Roman Curia, which continued to attract similar complaints on and off down to the time of Luther, to look no further. The Avignon court in particular was immortalized in the invective of Petrarch, though in modern times Mollat has shown how ably the finances were in fact handled.

The abuses of the cardinalate at the Renaissance period are too well known to rehearse here, and were acknowledged by the Council of Trent (Sess. XXIV, c. 1.). It was the scholarly if somewhat domineering Sixtus V who gave permanent shape to this aspect of the Counter-Reformation, and created the papal administration in the form in which substantially it has survived. In 1586 he fixed the '*plenum*' or ceiling of the Sacred College at 70 (where it remained until Pope John's time) and forbade the election of those who for age or other reasons were unqualified to take within a year the appropriate order.

Two years later, with the Bull *Immensa*, he systematized and fixed the Curia in fifteen permanent congregations. The Congregation of *Propaganda Fide* was added, as we have seen, in 1622.

In June 1908 Pius X, by the Bull *Sapienti Consilio*, did some re-grouping and re-defining of function, and this document, with the *ordo servandus* attached to it, became the basis of the legislation which was enshrined in the Code of Canon Law in 1917.

Three historical stages may thus be distinguished: a first in which the Pope ruled with the aid of a simple council of his *presbyterium;* a second in which the regular consistory of the college of cardinals after 1059 dealt with ordinary business, with special commissions handling more difficult matters; a third since Sixtus V, in which the congregation has been the stable instrument.

A congregation is simply a permanent group of cardinals which, with various grades of assistance, handles some branch or branches of the Church's business. Its decrees require the approval of the Pope, its 'instructions' do not. In questions of competence or of derogation from existing law its pronouncements must be published '*facto verbo cum Sanctissimo*', in consultation with the Holy Father. Its members and officials are bound by professional secrecy, which is strictest in the case of the Holy Office.

This is the oldest of the congregations, being established in 1542 by Paul III as the successor to the Inquisition (whose name it retained for some time). Its purpose was to resist the advance of Protestantism as much as anything: hence it is not surprising that separated brethren and ecumenists feel something short of enthusiasm for it. The Pope is always its Prefect, but the Cardinal Secretary in effect presides over its activities, and has a regular papal audience three times a month. Its Assessor, an important official though not a cardinal (he corresponds to the secretary in other congregations), is received by the Pope once a month. Another important officer is the Commissary, or Inquisitor, who is always a Dominican: the Holy Office is peculiar in being a tribunal as well as an organ of administration. Elsewhere the effect of Pius X's reforms was to remove judicial business from the congregations and confine it to the tribunals (*v. infra*).

The Holy Office is styled 'supreme', and its jurisdiction is not limited by that of any other congregation. Its tasks are to preserve the purity of faith and morals, to judge certain offences considered so heinous as to induce suspicion of heresy;[1] to pass judgement on and if necessary proscribe books which have been denounced to it. It also has competence in certain types of marriage case, and a high reputation for handling these with despatch. Its business is carried out in the most rigid secrecy, which binds not only officials but others involved, and to which the heaviest sanctions are attached. Canon 1555 of the Code sums up laconically: '*Tribunal congregationis S. Officii suo more institutoque procedit sibique propriam consuetudinem retinet.*' (The tribunal of the Holy Office has its own way of doing things and keeps its own customs.)

A few words must suffice to describe the other congregations: The Consistorial is the successor of the body which in the medieval period used to draw up the then much wider business of cardinalitial consistories; nowadays its main function is that which it took over from the suppressed Congregation of Bishops and Religious—the appointment of bishops and the arrangement of dioceses. In 1952 Pius XII put the spiritual care of emigrants (of Latin rite) in its charge.

The Congregation of the Council was the original 'post-conciliar

[1] One of the offences within its jurisdiction is the breaking of the eucharistic fast by priests, and authors used solemnly to discuss whether the reason was that the sacrilege was so grave as to imply heresy. Yet the eucharistic fast has in the space of a few years been reduced by stages to one hour.

commission', set up in 1564 to interpret authoritatively the decrees of Trent. It now deals with general disciplinary matters concerning clergy and people, with catechetics, confraternities, pious legacies, etc.

The Congregation for Religious (more fully, for the affairs of religious sodalities) founded in 1586, is self-explanatory. The Congregation of Rites (1588) deals with matters of worship and with beatification and canonization. In the same year a separate Congregation of Ceremonial was established for dealing with the elaborate details of papal and cardinalitial functions, in or out of the Vatican.

The Congregation of Seminaries and Universities has an interesting history. Sixtus's foundation of 1588 concerned itself only with the Roman *Sapienza* (then the papal university, now a thoroughly secular establishment) and with a handful of other famous universities: Salamanca, Paris, Bologna. Leo XII in 1824 founded a congregation of studies for all schools in the Papal States, but after 1870 its competence was extended to all Catholic universities. The present comprehensive form was given by Benedict XV in 1915. This is an example of progressive centralization whose results have not been entirely happy.

The Congregation of *Propaganda Fide* of 1622 grew out of a commission for promoting reconciliation with the Eastern churches. In mission territories (and in countries like Australia which prefer to continue to be ranked as such) it assumes most of the function of the other congregations, without prejudice of course to the competence of the Holy Office, and since it has a reputation for smooth, speedy and understanding administration, most missionary countries are loath to be 'promoted' out of its jurisdiction.

The Congregation for Extraordinary Church Affairs (which is not to be confused with the Extraordinary Affairs department of the Secretariat of State) was set up in 1814 to handle all questions of episcopal appointments and diocesan dispositions which impinged on civil laws and rights or concordats.

The Congregation for Sacramentary Discipline is a latecomer in the field (1908), while that for the Fabric of St Peter's grew out of a commission set up by Clement VII.

The Congregation for the Oriental Church was created in 1862 as part of *Propaganda Fide*, but made autonomous in 1917. It has exclusive authority (Holy Office again excepted) in some regions and in others performs the functions of the Congregations of Consistory, Council, Religious and Seminaries.

Besides the Holy Office, centralized judicial business is distributed among three Tribunals: the Sacred Penitentiary, restricted since 1908 to the 'internal forum' confessional or otherwise; the Rota which deals largely though not exclusively with nullity cases, and the Segnatura which is principally a court of appeal.

The Roman Curia is completed by a number of offices: the Chancellery, the Datary, the Chamber and much the most important the Secretariat of State. Formally, the office of Secretary of State dates from about the time of the papal journey described at the opening of this chapter. St Charles Borromeo, nephew of Pius IV, exercised (at the age of 23) wide powers some of which had previously belonged to the Cardinal Chamberlain. This tendency of the popes in an age of bitter family rivalries to put their main trust in a blood relation was reflected in the picturesque title of Cardinal Nephew so much disapproved of by historians. It overshadowed for a time the more traditional secretariats, but even before it was abolished once for all by Innocent XII's Bull of 1692 real power had begun to be invested in a Cardinal Secretary of State. The skill of Consalvi enhanced the prestige of the office throughout Europe, and though its scope was inevitably diminished after 1870 it has remained the centre of a power which is great precisely because it is not too strictly circumscribed. The modern extension of papal diplomacy (see p. 124) which the Secretariat controls and for which it trains and supplies the personnel, has enlarged the importance of the office again. It is with the Holy Office a twin pillar of the Vatican system. It is at once a more streamlined and a more flexible instrument than a Congregation. The Secretary of State himself is its only cardinal, and though there are two main departments and one minor one, he has only four principal assistants.

The department of Extraordinary Affairs has its Secretary and Under-secretary while that of ordinary affairs is in charge of a *Sostituto*. Another secretary is in charge of the writing office. Any business likely to have diplomatic repercussions and any not obviously assignable to another congregation naturally gravitates to the Secretariat. A powerful Secretary can use this elastic department to exercise a remarkable degree of control over Vatican policy.

Eugenio Pacelli became Secretary of State in February 1930. When he died as Pope Pius XII in October 1958, and still as Secretary of State, he had relinquished the office for only five of these years—1939 to 1944. The results of this policy have been variously criticized. The Secretariat was the most apt medium through which Pius could exercise unified control over administration without involving himself with too many officials. The present Pope became in effect Pius's principal private secretary. Traditional procedure keeps the congregations in contact with the Pope by assigning regular audiences to heads of departments and others, frequent in proportion to the importance of the department. Thus four audiences a month go to the Holy Office—three to the Cardinal Secretary and one to the Assessor. Only two other congregations have more than one a month: Propaganda, where Prefect and Secretary have one each, and Rites, which has two distinct departments to its work, so that as well as the Secretary, the *Promotor Fidei* (who looks after canonizations) sees the Pope once a month. Three congregations have no regular audience; the tribunals and lesser offices have one a month; the Secretary of State has normally one a day.

Pius XII increasingly in his latter years, and long before his health failed, was wont to put off the heads of congregations from their regular audience by sending a message to the effect that since he had nothing to raise perhaps they could address themselves to the Secretariat. On the other hand, diplomats who did this often found themselves unable to get an answer since the highest surviving officials there were not empowered (or did not choose to regard themselves as empowered) to give one.

The Secretariat of State is the Vatican department that deals most widely with the outside world, since it closely controls the papal diplomatic service. In 1963 this comprised seventy-three *rappresentanze*, a general word which comprises nunciatures, inter-nunciatures and apostolic delegations. The last are not in fact diplomats at all, but merely represent the Holy See *vis-à-vis* the Catholic hierarchy of the country where they reside. The extent to which they interfere in local affairs depends very much on their personality.

Here we have the most closely coherent element in the Vatican system: Secretariat-*Rappresentanze*. It is chiefly responsible for the image of the Vatican as a world Power—subtle, elusive of definition, ubiquitous—that has traditionally excited its enemies to melodrama and its friends to a sometimes undiscriminating awe or enthusiasm. Catholics are generally less affected by these emotions. To them the Church's power is something felt in their daily lives and in the inner places of the soul, or not at all. They are conscious of its external pressures only if they live in a country where its influence over social and political arrangements is temporarily or regularly excessive. If they are intellectuals, liable to impatience with what they see as the limitations of the Roman outlook, it is the Holy Office or the Index of Prohibited Books (or in these days the papal commission on birth control) that fills their horizon. If they live in Rome and see the wheels going round, the whole thing—concept, emotion, awe or revulsion—is inevitably scaled down.

During the period of the Second Vatican Council unprecedented numbers of people have become conscious of Rome and its ecclesiastical machinery, and emotionally involved with it, without achieving understanding of it. This cannot be achieved from books, nor from lightning tours even of well-informed circles and authoritative sources.

It is on the Secretariat and *rappresentanze* that attention should first be focused when considering the much canvassed question of the 'Italianate' Church and the 'internationalizing' of the central administration. Through these the Vatican is internationally most present and at work. The Secretariat is the most flexible and potentially the most comprehensive instrument of papal authority. Under Pius XII this potentiality was realized perhaps to the full, yet with the fullest emphasis on its instrumental character. It was to a Secretariat official that Pius said 'I want executors not collaborators.' Yet there is no department that better illustrates the peculiar character of the Vatican service. This is not merely a matter of being Italian but of being Roman, and not merely of being Roman but of belonging to a particular and narrowly defined Roman tradition.

During the period covered by this book it has been possible to point to half a dozen or so minor officials in the Rome office of the Secretariat, to two or three nuncios, half a dozen apostolic delegates and another half-dozen of their secretaries who are not Italians. But the Secretariat carries a staff of over a hundred and each of the seventy-three *rappresentanze* has a personnel of at least two. Moreover, it is taken for granted by those who live in Rome that under the present system the rare foreign recruits to the service tend to become more Roman than the Romans. Yet in spite of this there is no modern instance of one of them rising to even a moderately high position except Rafael Merry del Val, and even he was reduced to relative obscurity in mid-career. The surest path to advancement begins in the Roman seminary: there indeed is a career open to the right blend of talents, of which boldness of initiative, particularly intellectual, is understandably not one.

It was at the outset of Pius XII's pontificate that Professor Binchy concluded his careful and thorough account of the Lateran Pacts with a chapter on *The Church and the World* in which he contended that world opinion, while welcoming the settling of the Roman Question in principle, had very mixed feelings about it being settled with a Fascist government. This led naturally, he said, to a re-sharpening of interest in the problem of the 'Italianate' church. Before 1870 this had hardly been a problem; though people might question whether one race was necessarily best qualified to deal with all the problems of a universal Church, at least the Pope had his own kingdom, Italy was only a geographical expression and there was no need to regard the Vatican as tied by necessity (as distinct from inclination) to any political system or society.

The imprudent attitude which (we have seen) some Italian clergy adopted towards Fascism emphasized that a new and disquieting situation had arisen. Binchy states it bluntly: 'Catholics in other countries, hearing the noisy jubilation with which this "Triumph of Fascist and Catholic Italy", this "alliance between the Cross and the Roman Eagle" was greeted in the Fascist camp, might well begin to ask themselves whether the time had not come to emphasize the principle of universality which is the essence of Catholicism by introducing it into the administration of the Roman Church. At the present moment that administration is virtually monopolized by men of Italian race; the headquarters of a Church which numbers its adherents among all the nations of the world is staffed almost exclusively by members of a single nation. Now that the nation in question has become a 'dissatisfied' great power, whose predatory ambitions are bound to involve it in conflict with its neighbours, as well as to render it highly unpopular, is it desirable that this monopoly should continue? Above all, the iron grip which the totalitarian machine has fastened on the youth of Italy, with the avowed purpose of securing that future generations shall be thoroughgoing Fascists, is calculated to cause uneasiness among those Catholics (and they include many Italians) who regard the G.I.L.[1] as a highly unsuitable training ground for the future administrators of a supranational Church. Consequently the idea

[1] Fascist youth organization.

that these administrators should be recruited on a much wider basis than at present has received a powerful fillip both from the rise of Fascism and the Lateran agreements. The fact that it is seldom if ever discussed in Catholic publications does not mean that it is not present to Catholic minds; it means rather that such a difficult and delicate problem is not considered suitable for public discussion.'[1]

The fears echoed by Binchy may have been exaggerated, but readers of the earlier chapters of the present work may judge for themselves whether the disappearance of Fascism brought the disappearance of the problem. Some inclined to the view that the Italian is suited by temperament as well as by tradition and training to staff what is after all a supranational rather than an international organization, and that merely to internationalize personnel might do no more than provide a fruitful source of rivalries and discord within the service. This is perhaps to take an unduly pessimistic view of the ability of churchmen to put the Church's interests first, but in any case the matter has never in modern times been put seriously to the test. Nor, as Pius XII ascended the throne, was there the slightest indication that the idea of putting it to the test aroused anything but irritation in the Vatican. Early in 1939 the semi-official *Civiltà Cattolica* wrote on the tenth anniversary of the Lateran Pacts: 'The concern of foreign nationalisms to "de-Italianize" the papal court and to supervise its universal function is founded on nothing but fantasy and prejudice.' But the fantasy and prejudice was very freely indulged in the foreign press, especially of France and Germany.

Binchy of course at the outset of Pius XII's reign was quite unable to rise to the notion of any other type of central administration, supplementary or otherwise; and since he appreciated that a mere recruitment of foreigners at the lowest level was unlikely to have much effect, he inclined to the idea of mild transfusion of foreign blood at the highest level. Experience has shown that isolated foreign cardinals in Curia can fade into the general background as thoroughly as anyone else; the spectacular exception, to be discussed later, is that of Augustin Bea.

The question of internationalizing the Curia and the question of modernizing its procedure should be considered separately, though they could hardly be separated in practice. Pius X had only nibbled at the re-shaping of the Curia, and it was inevitable in the atmos-

[1] D. A. Binchy, *Church and State in Fascist Italy*, pp. 726–7.

phere of the Modernist alarms that the Holy Office should loom largest. A good deal of that heavy and oppressive atmosphere which marks the handling especially of doctrinal problems and new theories and has been the object of such hostile comment in the bolder atmosphere of the Second Vatican Council is the legacy of the unhappy first decade of this century, when the effects of perhaps rather unskilful handling of dangerous views spread far beyond the handful of genuine heretics involved. Men reach the top late in the Vatican, and heads of congregations at, say, the moment when the present Council was mooted were men who had entered Roman seminaries when these were still hushed by the thunders of *Pascendi*.[1] So too were some foreign diocesan cardinals.

Pius XII was Roman born and trained—a classical product of the upper stream of the Roman system. He was also a man of the Secretariat of State and the diplomatic service. He was also a Germanophile, a tireless worker with a phenomenal memory and wide-ranging curiosity, with the temperament and the equipment to by-pass slow, cumbersome custom-bound administration. European history, and English history particularly, is full of the experiments of monarchs seeking to push their 'natural counsellors' to the peripheries of administration and build up an inner core of advisers and executives at once more efficient and more sympathetic. Pius, who set decisive store by his own estimates of men, not always happily, was sensitive to the sometimes stifling pressures of Vatican custom. The least remarked but perhaps the most important sense in which the Pope is the prisoner of the Vatican is that he is caught up in a fixed pattern of ceremony, of language, of complex received practice, of thought even, to resist which would involve for a sensitive man a continuous mental and spiritual strain. The Pope's name is exalted to the utmost in the Vatican, but largely as a means of exalting the complex machine of which he is the head. In practice he is presented with many *faits accomplis* and subjected to much manoeuvring, and his name is far too frequently taken in vain even by insignificant functionaries. The story is often told of John XXIII who, before he became Pope, knew little of the Vatican at close quarters, saying to himself in an awed voice of curial officials 'they have disobeyed the Pope!' Pius XII knew far too much to waste time in such stupefaction. He sought so to arrange things that he would be obeyed where it mattered and that disregard of his will

[1] Pius X's Encyclical condemning Modernism.

would be insignificant in effect. He made no significant changes in the organs of administration: he simply selected the one through which he could most aptly work and rule and contented himself with formal and infrequent recourse to the rest.[1] Many of those who took part in the conclave which elected him were aware of this.

Addressing the Curia for the first time as Pope on April 5, 1939, Pius characteristically gave it a little sketch of its own history beginning with the *Quirites*, and rounded off some generalized compliments about its cohesive structure and 'unhurried moderation' with this memorable purple patch: 'It seems to Us, We say, that the Roman Curia is a diamond unmatched in the brilliance of the multiform splendour of its facets, beautiful with the living and brilliant reflections of all the sacred congregations, set among the jewels of the papal tiara as a symbol of your radiance and your love.' This was perhaps more of a swan-song than an inaugural paean—it has no parallel among the speeches of the ensuing twenty years.

The *locus classicus* for Pius XII's views on internationalizing the Curia is his Christmas sermon to it in 1946. It was not remarkable that during the war years he had been concerned mainly with business for which the Secretariat of State was the apt medium; nor perhaps that he had suspended the creation of new cardinals. A secret consistory had in fact been held on December 11, 1939, which had inspired Cardinal Pizzardo to write to Archbishop Spellman:

> 'Dear Excellency,
>
> Little is wanting to call you Dear Eminence, and thus the beautiful dream of 1932 will be fulfilled.'[2]

In fact it was not fulfilled until 1946. Pius now announced thirty-two new creations, very nearly doubling the Sacred College. He raised it in fact to the *plenum* of Sixtus V, and adduced his awe for this precedent as reason for not distributing more red hats among 'those especially from the Curia and the Roman clergy who, most of all for long service to the Holy See, seemed worthy of it'. After this sop to Cerberus Pius went on: 'We have wished that the greatest possible number of races and peoples be represented, to present a

[1] Nobécourt makes the point that 'secretaries of state had previously served as shields to the Pope, taking rightly or wrongly responsibility for mistakes. By becoming his own Secretary of State he drew on himself and his policy attacks which until then even unbelievers had hesitated to level at the Holy Father.' (*Le Vicaire et L'Histoire*, p. 253.)

[2] R. I. Gannon, *The Cardinal Spellman Story*, p. 283.

lively image of the universality of the Church, which has been illustrated afresh in Rome since the war.

'The Church is essentially supranational—an indivisible and universal whole. It is attempted sacrilege and injury to the human race to try to confine the Church as prisoner of a particular people, or banish her from a particular country.' He also condemned the attempts of liberal humanism to create an alternative unity apart from or in opposition to the Church: this, he argued, had simply led to totalitarianism, and the entombment of human liberty.

The new creations had of course no effect on the central administration of the Church; many were only filling traditional cardinalitial sees. It was reported that someone asked Pius what the effect might be of making thirty-two cardinals of whom only four were Italians. His answer was, 'Well, it might mean that I shall have a foreign successor.' In fact there were still enough Italian cardinals to avert this calamity, though no absolute certainty of course that they would unite to do so. Papal elections apart, the Sacred College hardly ever acted as a unit. Its effective core, the curial cardinals, was still dominated by Italians. Pius showed himself conscious of this: indeed he might almost have read the chapter of Binchy referred to above when he said:

'The integral unity of the Church today more than ever should pervade its visible head, the Sacred College, and all action of the Holy See. But this is chiefly a matter of the spirit rather than of mathematical proportions or statistics. During the long periods when the Italian nation more than others has given the Church her head and many collaborators in her central government, the Church has always maintained intact her supranational character. In fact circumstances have even made this fact a safeguard, e.g. in past centuries when the great European Powers were striving for hegemony. Even after the Lateran pacts the Italian clergy as a whole has, without prejudice to legitimate patriotism, continued to sustain and support the supranational character of the Church. We hope and pray that the younger clergy, especially in Italy but everywhere else too, will continue this tradition, more than ever necessary.

'For Our own part We are anxious to make this house [the Church] ever more solid, more habitable for all without exception. For this reason We want to neglect nothing that can express the supranational character of the Church.'

He returned to the theme, in a slightly more triumphalistic key, when he addressed the new cardinals on February 20, 1946: the unity of the Church, manifest in these elevations, was an example, he said, 'to the poor world, which needs it. The universalism of the Church was not imperialism or exploitation, but a force for cohesion and balance working within man.' He offset the triumphalist note by quoting Pius XI: 'Every social force is of its nature subsidiary; it should serve to sustain its members, not destroy or absorb them.' This, he added, is true also of the Church, without prejudice to her hierarchical structure; and he quoted St Augustine's gloss on the passage of *Isaias*, 'All nations shall come to her': *non enim* de *locis suis migrando venient sed* in *locis suis credendo*[1]—a gloss that many of his Roman listeners no doubt heard with relief.

He continued: 'If at certain times and places one civilization, one racial or social group has influenced the Church more than another, that does not mean she is enfeoffed to it, petrified in a moment of history, closed to further development. Bent over man with increasing attention, listening to his heartbeats, she discerns all his aspirations with all the clairvoyant intuition and penetrating finesse that come of supernatural illumination. Thus the Church follows without pause and without collision the providential path of the times, of existing circumstances. This is the profound meaning of her vital law of continuous adaptation which some, unable to rise to this magnificent conception, have interpreted as opportunism.

'It has been said that, with all modern means of communication, men are more isolated than ever they were. It ought not to be possible to say this of Catholics.'

The effect of the new creations then was mainly symbolic—it expressed what was undoubtedly Pius's great concern, the growing importance of the churches of the non-European world (thirteen non-European ordinaries received the hat): it did not express any great concern to alter radically the balance between Rome and the rest of the world. Pius loved to dwell on the significance of Cardinal Agagianian's position; but in fact this Armenian Uniat prelate had little apart from his beard and his rite to remind his fellow-curialists of the country he had left as a boy; he had lived in Rome ever since.

There was no further consistory until 1953. Pius then created twenty-three cardinals, ten of whom were Italians. Of these latter

[1] They shall not come *from* their own places by migrating: they shall come to her *in* their own places, by believing.

four were curialists and four diplomats nearing the end of their careers. (One of these was his successor, to whom on his twenty-fifth anniversary as a bishop, in 1950, Pius had sent a message pointing out that he had done and continued to do assiduous and useful work!) In spite of these proportions Pius gave at the consistory a slightly milder version of the 'cosmopolitan' speech of 1946.

There were no more consistories, and at Pius's death the situation was such as to alarm those who, for one reason or another, feel strongly about such things. The Sacred College was down to fifty-two. There were only fifteen cardinals in Curia, and only sixteen Italians altogether. But in spite of this, and of Pius's alleged remark in 1946, there was never serious prospect of any non-Italian being elected except the virtually Roman Agagianian.

There have been many speculations about what motives, if any, Pius XII had in allowing this situation to develop. It is generally said in Rome that he had plans for reforming the Curia but did not face the task of implementing them. The strong German influence in his policy would certainly lend colour to this view. It is tempting to surmise that the immense personal effort of the post-war years and eventually his illness consumed the energy that might have gone into the task.

However this might be, John XXIII gave every immediate sign of vigorously setting out to restore the old order of things. After his election he transferred his scarlet skull-cap to the head of Alberto di Jorio, the secretary of the conclave, a very human gesture prophetic of the tone of his first consistory. He is alleged to have said on his first visit to the Secretariat of State, 'There have been too many *sostituti* here for too long.' He was in a position to speak—he had worked under the Secretariat as a diplomat for all but the last five years of Pius's pontificate. He made Domenico Tardini Secretary of State. Within two months of his election he created twenty-three cardinals. Fourteen were Italians, eleven curial men. It was possible to read too much into this: eight of the eleven were aged 74 or over, which took some edge off the excuse he gave that he wished to reinforce an overworked Curia (though indeed men do work very hard at a great age in the Vatican). But in the following year he created eight more, no less than seven of whom were in the Curia, though five of the eight were non-Italians. Ages were again high: three were 74 or over. John continued to have this annual spree until the spring of 1962, and the clerical tailors prayed fervently for his health and prosperity. In March 1960 there were eight hats, though this time only one Italian and curialist. In March 1961, four, with one Italian and curialist. In March 1962, eleven, of whom eight were curialists and four Italians.

No case whatever can be made for John as a re-fashioner of the Curia and the Sacred College—other than in terms of mere arithmetic. He did indeed break through Sixtus V's ceiling at the first attempt, and subsequently blew it sky-high. In four years he created fifty-four cardinals—rather more than the number that elected him. Of these fifty-four *more than half* were curialists. If there had been any purpose in Pius's neglect to promote curialists, John thoroughly neutralized it. Of the fifty-two cardinals that elected him only fifteen were in the Curia—less than a third. Of the eighty-odd that elected his successor thirty-three were curialists.

It was understandable perhaps that he was unimpressed by the arguments against promoting old men: the 77-year-old Cardinal Bea proved to be another spectacular warning against generalizing about gerontocracy. But the same could by no means be said for all the swarm of septuagenarians (and more) that John raised to the Sacred College. Five of them failed to survive him, eight have died since. It is clear that John characteristically thought of the red hat as something which could give pleasure and reward in the twilight of a long if unspectacular career. That, after all, had been to all appearances the reason why he received it himself. But if the Council which brought him his late and chief glory was a stern struggle of the forces of reform against entrenched curial veterans, John himself was about seventy-five per cent responsible. At the beginning of 1963, the year in which he died, forty-six of the eighty-five surviving cardinals were his own creations; of the thirty-three cardinals in Curia, twenty-three were his; of these twenty-three, at a cautious estimate ten were among the established pillars of reaction in the Council, not only as speakers but as organizers and lobbiers. One was a 'progressive' leader; the rest were neutral or too old to be deeply involved.

One of two conclusions is inescapable; either John knew or heeded little of the character of the men he promoted, or he had little idea of what the Council was to mean. Yet the picture was certainly emerging long before his last consistory, at which he created eight curial cardinals out of eleven—among them Browne, Bacci and Antoniutti. John did of course elevate some of the great figures of the Council; König, Döpfner, Meyer, Ritter, Alfrink, Silva Henriquez, Richaud, Suenens, but they were all diocesans and non-Italians, belonging mostly to sees in which the cardinalitial dignity was a regular thing.

A Roman congregation is essentially a committee of cardinals aided by a number of consultors and minor officials. All cardinals are assigned to a number of congregations shortly after their promotion, but it is obvious that those who do not belong to the Curia, and still more those who live outside Italy, can play only a minor rôle in the work, if any at all. In 1963 the Holy Office, the smallest but most important of the cardinalitial committees (eight members) had no non-curial member and no non-Italian except Cardinal Agagianian. Its two chief working officials, the Assessor and the Commissary, were both Italians. Of twenty-five consultors only five were non-Italian, and these five included men like Father Tromp, a leading conservative theologian and the no less conservative and very old and sick Father Garrigou-Lagrange. Of thirteen Qualificators, those charged to study and report on works delated to the Congregation, seven were Italians. Looking through the list, foreigners could certainly be excused for supposing that Italians regarded themselves as the only people qualified to guard the deposit of faith, and that orthodoxy was too likely to be judged by adherence to a particular school, a kind of theological old-boy network.

The Congregation of Extraordinary Ecclesiastical Affairs, which has most to do with business involving other countries and their governments, similarly illustrates the conviction that Italians know best: it had no non-curial cardinal in 1963, and only one born outside Italy—the Chancellor Luigi Copello who is of Italian blood.

The thirty-three curial cardinals occupied at the same date 157 places on Congregations. Some of these were held *ex officio*. The number held by individuals varied widely from a maximum of nine (Micara and Confalonieri) to a minimum of one (Albaredo and Heard). Sixty-six of the places (not far short of a half) were concentrated in the hands of eight men. At lower levels, too, certain names cropped up with extraordinary frequency. That of the Secretary of the Congregation of Seminaries occurred fourteen times in the index of the *Annuario Pontificio* for 1963.

Figures however convey no precise pictures of the way in which an inner circle controls the main lines of Vatican affairs. Nowhere is it more important to know the correct line of approach, which is not always the most direct or most obvious.

Much the most interesting of Pope John's acts in relation to the Roman Curia was one which did not directly touch the Curia at all; his establishment of the Secretariat for Promoting Christian Unity. Officially it was an *ad hoc* instrument to deal with one aspect of the work of the Council, and that not an aspect which the Curia as a whole expected to be important. The conciliar commissions corresponded pretty closely in scope to existing curial congregations: e.g. the Doctrinal Commission to the Holy Office: the Cardinal Secretary of the latter was the President of the former and his right-hand-man Cardinal Browne, O.P., former Master of the Sacred Palace or Pope's personal theologian, was Vice-President. A leading Consultor of the Holy Office, Father Tromp, was Secretary of the Commission. It was hence hardly surprising that the earlier Council documents reflected faithfully the long-established style, tradition and method of the Holy Office and of the Roman schools.

The Commission for Bishops and the Government of Dioceses corresponded to the Consistorial Congregation: that for the Discipline of the Clergy and People to the Congregation of the Council; the Commission *De Missionibus* to the Congregation of *Propaganda Fide*; the Liturgical Commission to the Congregation of Rites. In some cases the names were practically identical: *De Religiosis*, Oriental Churches, Sacramentary Discipline, Seminaries. In other words the agenda and concerns of the Council were originally determined in their main lines by the existing routine administration. This was natural enough on the assumption that the existing machinery was itself not in need of *aggiornamento* (a conviction firmly and almost unanimously held in the Curia) and that it reflected a range of interests proper to the present day (a question not often canvassed in the Curia). The fact that there were other interests was acknowledged chiefly by the setting up of the Lay Apostolate Commission and the Secretariat for Christian Unity. The former could in part be linked with the permanent Pontifical Commission for Radio, Cinema and Television—a link which showed itself in the pedestrian conciliar decree on modern communications media. It showed and is showing more independence of mind in helping to handle the Council's *schema* on 'The Church in the World of the Present Time'.

But by far the most striking of these bodies brought to being by the Council is the Secretariat for Christian Unity. Far from being linked to any existing curial department, it was founded for a purpose arguably the opposite of that for which the chief curial congregation, the Holy Office, had been founded. If the Holy Office represents the nodal point of the Curia and shares with the Secretariat of State an unquestioned predominance in the Vatican, the Secretariat for Christian Unity was the most tangible expression of Pope John's conviction that there were problems the Curia was unequipped to handle. For a variety of reasons, not least of which was the astonishing late flowering of its Cardinal Secretary, Augustin Bea (see pp. 284 *et seq.*), it very quickly created a distinctive and world-wide reputation, an *esprit de corps* and an independence of action for which there is no parallel in Vatican history. If, as seems certain, it survives the Council which occasioned its creation, it will present a very interesting feature of the Vatican scene.

Ideally, of course, the existence side by side of the Secretariat and the Holy Office, the one dedicated to rapprochement with heretics, the other to defending truth against heresy, the one exploratory and inclined to calculated risks, the other defensive and suspicious, the one conciliatory, the other triumphant, should provide the kind of countercheck familiar in political constitutions. But the smooth working of such countervailing forces in, say, the British Constitution rests on the fact that each department understands and accepts the other's function. There has so far been little evidence of such a relationship between the Secretariat and the Holy Office. Pope John threw them together for this purpose when during the First Session in 1962 he ordered that the rejected *schema De Revelatione* should be re-drafted by a commission drawn from the ranks of each. The same procedure was followed with *De Ecclesia*, with results that have been partially examined here.

It has never been pretended by anybody that the collaboration was an easy one—in fact it is no secret that at one stage it produced on at least one side something approaching nervous exhaustion. The doctrinal commission mainly represented the curial tradition, and its leading spirits had all the advantages of complete familiarity with scholastic language and method, with curial procedure, and with the complexities of ecclesiastical legislation. They represented Authority, before which the activities of others, individual or corporate, were on trial. The Secretariat on the other hand stood for an activity in whose very conception flexibility and readiness for compromise (though not of doctrine) were inherent. But it was increasingly clear that behind the latter was the sympathy of the world which increasingly took note of the Council, of many ordinary Catholics and of a growing majority of the episcopate. It has been at the heart of every enterprise in the Second Vatican council which has engaged open-minded sympathies: *De Ecclesia*, *De Revelatione*, *De Ecumenismo*, *De Libertate Religiosa*, *De Judaeis*. It has come to be thought of as the institutional embodiment of the ideas and aspirations which people often rather vaguely lump together as 'the spirit of Pope John' or 'the Johannine revolution'. In composition it presented (1963) a startling contrast to every other Vatican organ. Its twenty full members, half of them bishops, included three Italians, one of them a bishop; there was one Italian among its twenty Consultors. This was certainly not to be explained solely by the fact that it works at a problem hardly present in Italian life. If Italians are to continue to dominate at the Vatican then the implementing of the conciliar decree on Ecumenism will need Italians aware of and trained in ecumenical activity. It would hardly be too much to say that the success of the Johannine revolution or of the Second Vatican Council will be largely measured by the extent to which the Secretariat comes to be an accepted part of the Vatican machinery. So long as it continues to look like a task force encamped at the gates of a beleaguered city, so long will it be clear that there has been no fundamental change in Rome. Nor could the Secretariat survive indefinitely in such a rôle. Its president, once a close confidant of Pius XII and not then thought either especially original or especially advanced, has performed the rare feat of achieving a world-wide reputation in his eighties. But the body over which he presides is precariously established. Several things could happen. It could survive the Council yet be pushed to the peripheries of Vatican activity, come to be thought of not as a body exercising a strong influence on Vatican thinking and policy—a kind of catalyst —but rather as an advanced group pursuing obscure, complex, unrealistic and probably fruitless purposes and negotiations in a world of its own, far from the hard realities of the Secretariat of State and the Holy Office. Like all creations of a single genius, it is vulnerable. The appointment of a successor of a very different kind could emasculate it, or set it by the ears, or deface its image before the world. It is not even now as homogeneous a body as it looks: some of its members are single-minded to the point of fanaticism, others suffer from a mild form of schizophrenia. It remains none the less the only non-curial institution that has exercised a major influence on the central policy and thinking of the Roman Church for a very long time. Whether it can continue to do so in the post-conciliar world is a crucial question, bound up with the future of the Vatican administration as a whole.

As these lines are written that future is still a matter of speculation. If we consider actualities rather than surmised intentions or attitudes, it is neither Pius XII nor John XXIII who has made any breach in the curial system; it is the criticism of the Council, rendered much more explicit by Paul VI in September 1963. One of the clearest ways in which the Curia had revealed its habits of mind was its attitude to the Council. This it regarded as a nuisance to bureaucracy which bureaucracy must dispose of as quickly and quietly as possible. When this did not prove possible at all, there was resentment, with too much facile talk of 'resurgent Modernism', 'a crisis of authority', 'attacks on the primacy' and what-not. Paul VI told his curial audience that for these prejudices they should substitute a conception of the Council as 'a mysterious event under the guidance of the Holy Ghost'. (A strange thing to have to say, but he said it, and later invited a well-known council expert of advanced views to enlarge upon it in a retreat.) In the Curia, the Pope added, the weight of age was making itself felt (he spoke historically). It must be simplified, decentralized, adapted to new functions. He reminded them that St Bernard over eight centuries ago had called for their internationalization. They must not be anonymous in tone or insensitive to general needs; they must not in fact be vulnerable to any of the criticisms commonly made of them. Finally and most to the point, they must be prepared for their functions to be supplemented by bishops, particularly diocesan bishops, summoned at need to advise the Roman pontiff. 'These are Our wishes. We are sure that you share them,' the Pope ended.

This was for reformists a high-water-mark of optimism. Events since have on the whole conspired to induce them to recede from it.[1] A commission to consider reform sits at present under the chairmanship of Cardinal Roberti, a distinguished ecclesiastical lawyer with

[1] Some resurgence of optimism came with the papal announcement at the beginning of the Fourth Session of Vatican II, September 14, 1965, that a permanent episcopal Synod, with proportional representation and only 15% papal nominees, would be set up, and summoned whenever the Pope thought necessary.

the reputation of a moderate. Its recommendations may well appear in print before these present lines. It is hardly rash to prophesy that they will not satisfy all the aspirations of the really ardent reformists. They may not even match the aspirations of the Council's document on church government, due to assume its final form in the session of Autumn 1965. But the principle will have been admitted that it is not sacrilegous, or disloyal, or intolerable temerity to criticize the Vatican administration. This principle was a commonplace in the healthiest and most creative periods of Church history; but it is one which many of the older generation, brought up in the embattled atmosphere of the past century, are liable to rank with the worst excesses of Marsiglio of Padua, or Constance and Basel, if not with that Protestantism in which Professor Gedda saw the root of all present ills. Whether there is indeed a 'crisis of authority' in the Catholic Church, as journalists love to repeat, is a question beyond the scope of this book. If there were, none but a fool would be complaisant about it. But it should not be thought symptomatic of such a crisis that people no longer take seriously the language about Roman officialdom[1] that is customary in, say, the *Osservatore Romano*. It is healthy that what have long been the commonplaces of private conversation among those qualified to judge should be calmly and impartially aired with a view to the advantage of the Church, without the issues being confused or evaded by question-begging allusions to 'washing dirty linen in public'.

This serene ventilation has been an achievement of the Second Vatican Council; the survival of the habit will be a test of the enduring effect of the Council. It will also be much more likely to forestall a crisis of authority than any attempt to revert to former habits and language.[2]

The responsibility of the critics here is at least as great as that of the criticized. Intemperate and uncharitable language, abuse and gossip, a too personal approach: these are part of the price the Church has had to pay for the (largely beneficent) interest the world has suddenly taken in her affairs: when journalists suddenly begin to regard ecclesiastics as they habitually regard film-stars or professional footballers, this is too much for the equilibrium of a certain,

[1] Nobécourt (*op. cit.*, p. 254) justly writes of 'un certain style Vatican, si melliflu qu'il donne trop fréquemment au lecteur le sentiment qu'on cherche à l'abuser'.

[2] A striking example of such serene ventilation was a forthright speech by Cardinal Alfrink in Rome on September 15, 1965, partly a reply to irresponsible Italian press slurs on Dutch Catholicism.

though happily not large, number of ecclesiastics. The capital lesson that needs to be learned in Rome is that if criticism has properly established organs it eventually stops being sensational and begins being effective.

The 'institutionalizing' (to use a barbarous but exact word) of criticism and advice was a question that lay beneath the surface (and never very far beneath the surface) of the dogged, occasionally tedious conciliar debate of 1963 on the collegial status of bishops. Here was a theological issue which was nothing if it remained merely academic: it was idle to discuss the corporate status of the bishops if this was to have no practical expression. Chapter Three of the Constitution *De Ecclesia*, 'On the Hierarchical Constitution of the Church and Especially on the Episcopate', and the *schema* (still to be finally voted at the time of writing) on 'Bishops and the Government of Dioceses' (which deals with the relations of bishops to the Roman Curia) complemented and lent significance to each other. It was clear enough from the distribution of speeches for and against the 'collegial propositions' that the interests of the speakers were not exclusively, or even mainly, theological; but theological ground was good tactical ground to choose for the defence of the existing arrangements, especially since the issue of the debate was made to turn on the question of divine right. The contrary tactic of those who wished not only to assert the collegial status of bishops but press for some organic expression of it was to insist that the doctrine was not new. It had simply been obscured by the fact that Vatican I, cut short after it had fully stated the doctrine of papal primacy in *Pastor Aeternus*, had been unable to develop a comparable statement on the episcopate. Hence a specious character was given to the objections, the 'doubts and scruples', of those who professed to see the assertion of collegial status as an attack on the papal primacy—a 'Gallican invention', as the youthful Bettazzi, Auxiliary Bishop of Bologna, rather satirically put it. (He went on to give an imposing list of Italian theologians, jurists and even curialists and future popes who had espoused the doctrine.)

It was Bishop De Smedt of Bruges who first sounded clearly the underlying realities of the matter: 'Recognition of the collegiality of the bishops will provide the Pope with very effective means of governing the flock of Christ. The bishops will be able to advise the Pope on the apostolate and themselves be able to work in greater unity. . . . It should be emphasized that any desires for the internationalization of the Roman Curia or for other changes in existing policy are not expressions of waning love for the See of Peter but of desire to help the Pope fulfil his mission the more perfectly.'

By contrast, the doubts and uncertainties so monotonously voiced by curial speakers never conveyed, in spite of their command of the language and technique of the *disputatio*, the sense of academic detachment.

This is not the place either to rehearse the question or to follow the Council debate in detail: something should rather be said of the historic background in papal utterances. Popes both in the age of absolutism and in that of the Revolution had been concerned to vindicate their authority over bishops, but chiefly as a defence against state encroachments—a venerable papal tradition, still being upheld by Pius XII in writing to the bishops of Communist China in 1954. Practically every pope from Pius VI to Pius XII can be found to speak of the papal supremacy as a *defence* of the episcopate —something the forgers of the Donation of Constantine would have understood a thousand years earlier, for then bishops had been concerned to bolster papal authority against the overweening claims of metropolitans or princes. Pius IX himself, in the very allocution which followed hard on the Great Definition of 1870, said: 'The authority of the Sovereign Pontiff is great, but it does not destroy, it builds up; it does not suppress, it supports; and very often it defends the rights of Our brothers, the bishops.'

This was entirely in the spirit in which Cardinal Liénart, in the Council debate just referred to, deprecating the tactical bandying of texts, told the fathers pointedly: 'In this context there is no striving for domination; power is not defined in terms of authority but of service, not of personal glory but of the common welfare.' It was eloquent of the ideas and moods that had crystallized in Rome in the century separating these two utterances that the author of the second could be frowned on in the name of 'loyalty' and even be lumped with 'products of democracy and the ideals of the French Revolution'. (Cf. Novak, *The Open Church*, p. 216.)

It has been argued in these pages that Rome often rejected somewhat uncritically these 'ideals', but even Leo XIII, against whom this charge could not be laid, saw that episcopal authority was faring no better at the hands of the political heirs of the Revolution than it had fared under absolute monarchs: it was to the Archbishop of Tours that he wrote in 1888, 'It is Our first duty to take care, uniting Our efforts with yours, that the divine authority of the bishops remain sacred and inviolable.'

John XXIII was not the first modern Pope to think of presenting a new image of the Church in the hope of bringing back strayed sheep to the fold. This was the avowed purpose of Leo's Encyclical of 1896, *Satis Cognitum*. Unity was his main theme, but he dealt also with the unity of Pope and bishops, without however developing the theme substantially beyond the point at which Vatican I had left it. The time was not ripe. He refers to the episcopal college only to insist that the bishops are no more *independent* collectively than individually—a question not at issue in 1963, though some conservatives tried to make out it was.

Benedict XV, in the Encyclical quoted in Chapter 13, and also in an interesting letter of October 1921 to the Apostolic Delegate to the East Indies, was more disposed to emphasize and uphold the authority of the bishop: 'It is certainly permissible for anyone to appeal to the Holy See for an adequate reason; but let no one withdraw from the authority of his Ordinary or refuse obedience to his decrees under pretext of wishing to follow the precepts of the Apostolic See.'

His successor Pius XI is often called an authoritarian, but this is how he interpreted his authority in the Encyclical *Ecclesiam Dei* of November 1923: 'Christ Our Lord not only handed on to the apostles that mission which He had received from the Father. . . . He also wanted the apostolic college to be a perfect unity, its members bound by a very strong chain: inwardly by that faith and charity which "is poured forth in your hearts by the Holy Spirit", outwardly by the rule of one over all, since He gave the primacy among the apostles to Peter. . . .'

The topic of episcopal authority is not prominent in Pius XII's long reign, but in the missionary Encyclical *Fidei Donum* of 1957 he wrote significantly: 'If each bishop is pastor only over the portion of the flock entrusted to him, nevertheless the fact that he is by divine institution and command a legitimate successor of the apostles makes him, *together with the other bishops*, responsible for the apostolic mission of the Church according to those words which Christ said to His apostles: "As the Father hath sent me, I also send you." This mission, which must embrace all nations and all times, did not come to an end with the death of the apostles; it lasts to this day in the persons of the bishops who are in communion with the Vicar of Jesus Christ.'

Three years earlier, speaking in more practical terms to cardinals and bishops present at Pius X's canonization, he said: 'Frequent and mutual communication among bishops is very helpful for the fruitful and effective exercise of the pastoral office. Thus one perfects the other in weighing lessons of past experience; government is made more uniform, the wonder of the faithful is avoided, for often they do not understand why in one diocese a certain policy is followed quite different or even contrary to that of another, perhaps adjacent. . . . To realize these purposes, general assemblies which are now held almost everywhere, are very helpful, and also the more solemnly convened provincial and plenary councils.'

This is hardly the language of one who took it as self-evident that bishops were rubber stamps. But what follows is no less interesting: speaking of the historic tradition of 'close union and frequent communication with this Apostolic See', Pius claimed that it 'arises not from a kind of desire to centralize and unify everything, but by divine right and by an essential element of the constitution of the Church of Christ. The result of this is not detrimental but advantageous to the bishops, to whom is entrusted the governing of individual flocks. For from communication with the Apostolic See they gain light and assurance in doubts, advice and strength in difficulties, assistance in labours, comfort and solace in distress. On the other hand, from the reports of the bishops to the Apostolic See, the latter attains a wider knowledge of the state of the whole flock, learns more quickly and more accurately what dangers are threatening and what remedies can be applied to cure these evils.'

If it be said that this presents a somewhat idealized picture of episcopal relations with the Vatican in the fifties, it is an ideal firmly stated, and one to which the advocates of reform might well have appealed in the sixties; they were merely trying to provide a basis for its better realization.

John XXIII's was not a juridical mind. Though he lacked nothing of the historical sense of Rome and the Primacy, his first instinct was perhaps to think of himself as transferred—become bishop of another see. It was this instinct that gave birth to the Roman Synod. Enough irony has been expended on this; it is important chiefly as reflecting John's conception of the episcopal office. Announcing it he said: 'A Synod is the assembly of the

Bishop with his priests for the purpose of studying the problems of the spiritual life of the faithful, to give or restore strength to ecclesiastical laws for the suppression of abuses, to promote Christian life, to encourage divine worship and religious practice. Fundamentally it is a question of continuing the work of Jesus Christ our Redeemer for the salvation of men, for that special portion of His flock which, aside from the care of all the Churches, is in a special manner confided to Us.' That the synod turned out to be something very different may well in the long run have turned out to the benefit of the Church as a whole. If on this narrower stage John's pastoral solicitude could be swamped in administrative flummery, he may well thereby have been disposed to see that the same should not be repeated on the world stage.

The issue is not yet decided. There are various opinions as to what constitutes a practical expression of episcopal 'collegiality'. That some way of perpetuating the *presence* of the world episcopate at the historic centre of Christendom is an indispensable expression —this is a truth no serious student of recent Church history questions. Here lies the crucial test of the success of the Catholic movements of the sixties. The Church which in a world of primitive communications, a world of countless islands, was a sign and maker of unity, must renew unity in a deeper way in a world which is circled physically in a matter of hours, by sight and sound in a matter of seconds.

10

Social Theories and Conflicts

IN THE YEAR that Pius XII became Pope, the Cambridge Lecturer in History of Political Thought, Michael Oakeshott, publishing a useful compendium of documents of *The Social and Political Doctrines of Contemporary Europe*, had this to say of the Catholic Doctrine: 'As a doctrine it is closer-knit and more systematic than any of the other current doctrines. [These he listed as Representative Democracy, Communism, Fascism and National Socialism.] Its strength lies in its coherence and its rigidity. In virtue of the one it is an example from which modern social and political thought has much to learn; in virtue of the other it appears in the modern world as something of a stranger, and the criticism Catholicism offers of other doctrines is less convincing than its statement of its own. It is, also, the repository of an element of profound importance in the European tradition; it is the only contemporary representative of a genuine Natural Law theory, and it is evidence that this theory is not yet dead. If this doctrine is a stranger in the modern world, it is certainly not an exotic doctrine: authoritarian without the capriciousness of the other authoritarian doctrines, it reminds us of an inheritance we have neglected.'

'There is no opposition,' said Pius XII in his first Encyclical, 'between the laws that govern the lives of faithful Christians and the postulates of a genuine humanitarianism.' This principle, hardly one constantly hymned in ecclesiastical Rome over the past century, he spared no personal effort to uphold throughout his pontificate; on it he based his programme of manifesting the papal concern for every problem of the time. When war came, he argued that it had come because men 'forgot the law of human solidarity which is dictated and imposed by our common Origin, and by the equality of rational nature in all men, no matter to what people they belong.'

He had plenty of precedent for pronouncing on social and economic questions: the fiftieth anniversary of Leo XIII's *Rerum Novarum* occurred in 1941, and in that half-century the body of doctrine to which Oakeshott refers had been built up. But such papal pronouncements are necessarily general in character, and Pius perhaps achieved a higher level of generality than his predecessors. He liked to consider problems on a world-wide scale, and to point to considerations of human nature as a whole for the basis of a solution. It is this large scale of his thinking rather than any markedly original additions to papal teaching that stands out in his social pronouncements. The international problems that the war brought in its train—world hunger, refugees, displaced persons, the decay of colonialism, the flight from the land—here it was that he felt solicitude became him as the Supreme Pontiff. In his handling of particular and local problems he was sometimes less decisive.

It is sometimes said that papal social pronouncements from Leo XIII's onwards are dominated by corporatism. This is even supposed to give them an affinity with Fascist systems. Foolish Catholic pronouncements or dishonest ones like those of von Papen in Nazi Germany's early days have occasionally lent colour to this latter view, but no support for it will be found in papal texts. The principle of subsidiarity, so clearly set forth by Pius XI in *Quadragesimo Anno* and repeated by both the Popes under consideration here, is incompatible with Fascist state corporatism as with other forms of excessive state interference. The free vocational or functional group has been consistently featured in papal teaching as a contribution to what Pius XI called 'the primary duty of the state and of all good citizens—to abolish disputes between opposing classes.' Catholic corporatism is or should be assertion of liberty—it is one of the many lines of that convergence between liberal and Catholic ideals which the unfortunate mood and circumstances of post-Revolution history have conspired to obscure.

Pius XII in his Christmas broadcast of 1942, dealing with 'the internal order of states and peoples' in five principal points, shows many liberal[1] ideals thinly disguised. He upholds the dignity and rights of the human person: the right to sustain and develop bodily,

[1] The popes have of course often spoken against economic liberalism, the doctrine of *laissez faire*, but this would nowadays hardly be regarded as part of the 'liberal' view of life in the general sense intended here.

intellectual and moral life, and to religious training and education; the right to a free choice of a state of life, and to responsible use of material goods. Considering the restoration of juridical order, ruined by totalitarianism, he insists that it should not be tied to or shaped by the programme or interests of a group, party or movement. Courts and judges should take direction from a law clearly formulated and circumscribed, whose norms cannot be diverted by appeal to popular sentiment or utility. The liability of the State and of its dependencies should be clearly acknowledged and enforceable. He insists last and most strikingly on 'a conception of the State Christian in spirit', which he defines as 'morally responsible, serving society, respecting personality'.

Too much generalized talk of 'error' (and of its 'having no rights'—a linguistic confusion) has raised unnecessary barriers between Catholic and secular theory. Oakeshott saw that the opposition was an unreal one. Putting the great cleavage between Communism, Fascism and Nazism on one side and Catholicism and liberal democracy on the other, he wrote: 'To the Liberal and the Catholic mind alike the notion that men can authoritatively plan and impose a way of life upon a society appears to be a piece of pretentious ignorance; it can be entertained only by men who have no respect for human beings and are willing to make them the means to the realization of their own ambitions.'[1]

But even Oakeshott, in stressing the contrast between Abraham Lincoln and Leo XIII on the nature of the State, was stressing an element in Leo's teaching which has proved less essential and enduring than the rest. The Vatican Council decree on Religious Liberty (see p. 292) has for a variety of reasons a good deal of the spirit of Abraham Lincoln in it. It represents a tardy attempt by the Church to grasp the opportunity (again in Oakeshott's words) 'to extract the true metal of the Liberal doctrine from the base ore from which it has never yet been successfully separated'.

It was the fate of Pius XII to be plagued, during the latter half of his pontificate especially, with the socio-religious problems of that country which had given birth to the Revolution, yet in which the bitterest hatred of all that the Revolution stood for has survived; the country moreover, in which class divisions, equally deep and

[1] It is, alas, clear that the German Catholic Church had not seen matters this way in 1933. Nor had many Italian Catholics between 1922 and 1942, cf. Lewi, *op. cit.* Chapter 4.

bitter in recent times in spite of the inheritance of egalitarianism, affected the Catholic Church more perhaps than in any other country. The violence and intransigence of the French Catholic Right has been a sad and unedifying feature of modern history. It has often sought the support of intransigent elements in the Vatican, but has always been just as ready to defy the Vatican and the Pope himself when these have been too open-minded for it. A point of high tension was reached in the years leading up to the First Vatican Council, when the country was torn between the most extravagant neo-Ultramontanism[1] exemplified in the intemperate writing of Louis Veuillot, editor of *L'Univers*[2] and a more restrained but hardly less determined Liberal Catholic movement which was 'inopportunist' about the definition of papal infallibility. After 1870 the social question loomed steadily larger, and the split in French Catholic life was revealed there as much as anywhere. The French Catholic social conscience developed on decidedly paternalistic lines under such pioneers as La Tour du Pin and Albert de Mun;[3] they influenced *Rerum Novarum*, and were at one with Leo's proposals for coming partially to terms with the Revolution—the *Ralliement*. But this met with savage resistance from the French integralists who, here as elsewhere, revealed the shallowness and political motivation of their often trumpeted loyalty to Rome. The Dreyfus affair not only racked the French Catholic body further but provoked a resurgence of anticlericalism culminating in the denouncing by the Republic of the 1801 Concordat and in the laws infamously associated with the name of Combes, the spoilt priest and small-town anticlerical who became Prime Minister.

This complete separation of Church and State brought two results. It revealed and enhanced the real vigour of the French Church. As Brogan has put it: . . . 'the effects of freedom were often bracing; a new missionary spirit was awakened among the clergy and the old bureaucratic attitude became less common. In varied ways the Church tackled the problem of keeping a hold on the

[1] Moderate Ultramontane doctrines, promoting the competence of Rome over national hierarchies in all matters of doctrine and discipline, had been formulated by Bellarmine and later by Fénelon. But French writers especially, under the influence of Joseph de Maistre, exaggerated these grossly in mid-nineteenth century.

[2] Here is an example from as early as 1852: 'It has been said that the Parliamentary system rests on an heretical principle: whatever desire we have to avoid exaggeration, we think that this is not to say enough.'

[3] It was de Mun who summed up the French Catholicism of his day with 'It is easier to fight one's enemies than to get on with one's friends.'

people . . . in every department of life the one great organization that could compete with the French State showed its renewed life. There were no schisms and few scandals. The Catholic Church was now the Church of a minority of faithful and zealous people, not the nominal and official religious organization of nearly all Frenchmen. It did not lose by the change.'

On the other hand, the separation exposed once for all the myth of Catholic France, the Eldest Daughter of the Church. Five years after the end of the Concordat had brought the end of state support for the clergy, vocations dropped by fifty per cent. When the Church had to depend on the offerings and goodwill of the faithful, it languished. Yet from 1910 onwards there was already, growing alongside the old intransigence, a promising new spirit of accepting and tackling existing realities. In Pius X's time two extreme movements were condemned: on the left, Sangnier's *Sillon* (he immediately submitted) and on the right Maurras's *Action Française*, but significantly the latter condemnation was not published, and had to wait until 1926.

For twenty years following the First World War, in which Catholic soldiers lay and clerical had done something to re-burnish the prestige of the Church, Cardinal Verdier, Archbishop of Paris, earned (it was typical of the French Right to bestow it) the title of Red Cardinal equally for his advocacy of working-class needs and for his inflexible maintainance of Pius XI's ban on the *Action Française*. He promoted the building of many churches in the expanding Paris working-class suburbs, including the brilliant pioneer work at Le Raincy by the brothers Perret.[1] The Church assumed leadership in social work: Brogan has written of the period: 'These activities were what an anti-clerical called "the trumps of the clergy", and it was not easy to over-trump them. The established clergy of the Republic, the school-teachers, were not as zealous as their dissenting rivals. It was easier, as was done in one city, to invite the Salvation Army to compete than to compete oneself. Only the Communist party could show comparable vigour in winning and serving the young.'

Verdier was tackling the problem of the new age—that of the industrial masses, among whom Communist vigour had been

[1] Over one hundred churches and chapels were built in the Paris working-class suburbs in the nine years preceding the outbreak of World War II. This compares very favourably with what has been done with a similar problem in outer Rome.

devastatingly successful. The French Right screamed with anger when mention was made of 'de-Christianized France', but the French Right was bourgeois, and the backbone and spirit of the French Church was bourgeois, or so the labouring masses and their champions (including many clerical champions) believed. It was certainly not necessary to be a Marxist to believe this.

So true in fact did it seem to many that they thought the day already past when traditional methods and traditional organization could re-vitalize Catholicism among the French proletariat. Under Cardinal Verdier the work of Canon (now Cardinal) Cardijn spread rapidly through France; yet there were those who thought that these methods remained on the fringe of the problem.

The collapse of 1940 brought a mood of intense self-questioning not least in the French Catholic Church, and in 1941 a Sulpician priest, Père Augros, embarked on a nation-wide enquiry into seminary training. He so impressed the bishops that a year later he became rector of a new kind of seminary in Lisieux, that of the *Mission de France*. Two *Jociste*[1] chaplains who did a course there, Godin and Daniel, presented in 1943 a report to Verdier's successor, Cardinal Suhard, under the title *France—a missionary country?*—a title which sufficiently indicates the conclusions of their own experience. Their practical suggestion was that 'teams' of priests should be freed from conventional duties to work on city missions of a revolutionary kind. Before the year was out the *Mission de France* and the *Mission de Paris* were training recruits; the former was already functioning in some *departements* and in January 1944 the *Mission de Paris* began, with its headquarters in the Eighteenth *Arrondissement*, on the northern edge of inner Paris. It was also in 1943 that the French hierarchy decided to send priests secretly, as civilian workers, to the German labour camps.

It is beyond the scope of this book to describe, much less to pass judgement on, the worker-priests and their efforts. The movement accepted as a premise the failure in France of the normal Church organization to touch the working classes who made up a large proportion of the population. It insisted further that evangelization could not properly aim at drawing them into that organization as it stood. To treat the proletarian Church as a new creation with its own problems, needs and way of life was as necessary, they argued,

[1] Jeunesse Ouvrière Chrétienne. A workers' social movement founded by the Belgian Canon (now Cardinal) Cardijn.

as it was to do the same for African converts in the mission field. The French Church was too plausibly one in which there was no place for the working class; hence the conditions for evangelization were simply not present. Until the conditions of the working class were bettered religion could appear as nothing but pie in the sky, unless a Cartesian gulf between spiritual and material needs was taken for granted. Hence these new apostles talked of 'parachuting' themselves into their mission field, of burning their boats, of farewells without return; they abominated talk of 'experiment', as though they were sociologists slumming. They not only accepted the reality of class distinctions, they even insisted that the class war was a reality which could not be wished away.

A situation in which zealous and intelligent men could hold such views so firmly as to transform their own lives utterly is not one on which the outsider can sit in armchair judgement without fatuity. For the English-speaking reader understanding is especially difficult. Historical circumstance has made the Catholic Church in England especially a working-class affair. The idea of a working population wholly or even mainly estranged from the Church would in our industrial cities seem fanciful, though it may not seem so indefinitely. Not all the problems of the worker-priests are unfamiliar to us, but this partial familiarity can itself be the cause of complete misunderstanding of the French situation. Among us the notion of a bourgeois Church, though it might bring considerable twinges of conscience to the perceptive, could hardly be maintained as completely plausible except by Communist propaganda. The French clergy in the post-war years could talk seriously of the need to *désembourgeoiser* the Church. In 1949 Cardinal Suhard wrote in his Lenten pastoral: 'In too many so-called Christian countries, particularly in France, the Church, in spite of the existence of many ecclesiastical buildings and many priests, has ceased to exist for the majority of people. They no longer have the chance of deciding for or against Christ. A vast accumulation of prejudice has completely distorted the face of the Church in their eyes. The priesthood is still less accessible to them. Therefore it is a good thing that priests should become witnesses again, less to conquer than to be a sign. They have been told that to be a witness does not mean to spread propaganda nor even to stir up emotions, but to keep the mystery of God present. This means so to live that one's life would be inexplicable if God did not exist.' They had to become naturalized, he added, where they had previously been strangers.

Italians are hardly better equipped to understand the peculiar nature of this problem, or were not in the 1940s and early 50s. Something of this unfamiliarity redounds to the credit of the Italian clergy: in many country districts especially they share the poverty and anxieties of their people in a way which would frighten the wits out of some of their foreign critics. It was this solidarity with their people that enabled them to play such a decisive rôle in the Resistance, and in the stabilizing of the post-war Italian state. The fact that this prestige has since been often abused politically should not blind us to its very creditable origin.

Something akin to the French situation is now emerging in the larger Italian cities, but there is still no Paris south of the Alps. Nor do Italians grasp the background to the situation outlined above. The fanaticism of Right and Left within the Catholic Church, the bitter hatreds of integralists and liberal Catholics, reflecting political hatreds, largely escape the imagination of the sceptical and tolerant Italian; among the few things that may rouse him to fleeting fanaticism religion has no place. Hence the fatal ease with which the more temperate Italian integralist mistakes the fanaticism of his French counterpart for zeal and loyalty to Rome—when it happens to be taking that appearance. Recently, for example, with the liturgical decrees of the Second Vatican Council, it has been taking the peculiar form of loyalty to some metaphysical 'Roman Catholicism' which somehow entails defying the Council's dispositions (see e.g. the monthly *Le Monde et la Vie* for October 1964). It is to be regretted that there are still integralists in Rome whose own conduct lends colour and encouragement to this attitude. Archbishop Parente, the Assessor of the Holy Office, a man not suspect of *avantgardisme*, has stigmatized those in Rome who in his own words 'withhold interior assent from the Council's decrees'. But on the whole Italian native good sense has been strikingly revealed in the acceptance of liturgical changes which have been as thorough and logical as any.

It was not long before the activities of the worker-priests attracted unfavourable attention in Rome. On June 20, 1945, Cardinal Suhard, their chief patron and champion, received a communication from the Vatican expressing anxiety about their activities.

Less than two years later, on February 15, 1947, Suhard submitted the first annual report on the worker-priests demanded by the Holy Office. But responsible episcopal reports were not the only kind of information that went to Rome.

In November 1948 some worker-priests upset their bishops by taking part in a World Peace Movement demonstration; but Suhard took occasion of his golden jubilee a few days later (December 5) to defend the *Mission de Paris* in principle. While Suhard lived the movement had a champion both convinced and powerful. He had been a brilliant fellow-student of Pius XII at the Gregorian in Rome, and is said to have refused to discuss the question with anyone in Rome except the Pope himself. Cardinal Gerlier of Lyons, a former successful lawyer and influential in French official circles, was another powerful advocate. So was Cardinal Liénart of Lille.

There was never much hope that the Roman Curia would view the new movement with complaisance. It was calculated in every way to outrage bureaucratic and legalistic instincts, especially from a distance and on the basis of an odd assortment of information, some of it from fanatics. Only an authority which was at the same time a close and sympathetic (though not necessarily indulgent) observer, as versed in the peculiar nature of the problem as the priests themselves though not subject to the same distortions of judgement, could have been expected to be flexible enough without weakness.

Suhard died on May 30, 1949, a black moment in a black year as far as Catholic-Communist relations went (see p. 94). A month later the Holy Office decree on Communism appeared: an interval so short as to lead many to suppose that the Curia had only held back previously out of a desire not to embarrass Suhard. But of course the decree had a much wider field of reference than France, and was not even mainly concerned with the worker-priests. The French bishops decided to interpret the decree broadly, but the worker-priests hardly allowed it to induce them to discretion. They joined, by general agreement, the campaign against French policy in Indo-China in 1950. A month later one of them was wounded in a clash with the police during a World Peace Movement demonstration in Limoges. In July the new Archbishop, Feltin, submitted a further detailed report to Rome.

It was in the autumn of this year that Pius XII's own allusions to the movement began to be clear. In the immediate post-war years the social problems that dominated his attention (and with which it has been suggested he felt most at home) were such as the relief of world hunger, the treatment of prisoners and expatriates, the flight from the land. He had reminded the Roman cardinals in June 1948, when condemning 'laicism', that the essential antidote to it is serious Christian application to social reform. Post-war problems in this field, he said, were peculiar and delicate, and must be treated with world-wide vision. Catholics should not hesitate to join forces with those who are outside their ranks but support the social doctrine of the Church.

This last offered Catholics political scope in democratic countries, though in Italy it was in practice interpreted pretty negatively. Nowhere, of course, was it supposed to extend to Communism. Yet Pius on two occasions, addressing the Italian Catholic Workers' Association (a few weeks after the foregoing speech and also three years earlier in March 1945), gave his blessing to critical co-operation with the undoubtedly Communist-dominated Italian General Trades Union, only stipulating that there should be no identification with an embittered and unchristian class struggle. It is not fear of revolution or of the uprising of the masses, he said on the same occasion, that drives the Church to work for the people: it is love, consideration for human dignity. He was quick too to answer (e.g. Christmas 1949) Communist criticisms that Faith induces indifference to contemporary problems: distress, economic oppression, nationalism.

But from 1949 onwards he increasingly dwelt on the community of interest between workers and bosses, and the iniquities of the class struggle. In May of that year he dilated on the theme to a congress of the *Union Internationale des Associations Patronales Catholiques*. Commenting on his predecessor's conception of Catholic corporatism, the '*organisation professionelle*', in *Quadragesimo Anno*, he commented: 'Nothing seemed to him more fitted to overcome economic liberalism than the establishment of a statute based precisely on the common responsibility of all who take part in production. This put a lot of people on the defensive. Some saw it as a concession to modern political trends, others as a reversion to the middle ages. It would have been wiser to put aside these contrary prejudices and to set about realizing the thing itself with its many practical applications. Now that part of the Encyclical seems to Us an unhappy example of a lost opportunity. Now the fashion is nationalization and state control, countenanced within limits by *Quadragesimo Anno* (but not as the normal rule), for public organs of economy. Economy is not of its nature a state matter—it is a living product of free initiative and co-operation.'

The autumn following Archbishop Feltin's report saw several reactions by Pius XII. In August came the Encyclical *Humani Generis*, generally believed to be aimed largely at a number of French clerical scholars with whom the worker-priests had a mutual sympathy. Three weeks later Pius broadcast to a congress of the *Jeunesse Ouvrière Chrétienne* in Brussels. They should beware, he said, of laicist cultural ideals for the worker; they should integrate the apostolate of the worker with that aimed at modern man in general. There are not two sorts of men, workers and non-workers; you cannot classify souls. Workers suffer from modern maladies as much as anyone else; among them are phantom men, haunting cinemas and sports fields, restless for novelty, for coloured comics, for dance music—too empty to occupy themselves. Not fundamentally hostile to religion, but worse perhaps, incapable of understanding it, '*passant comme un troupeau, les yeux fixés à terre*'. This rather harsh de-sentimentalizing of the proletariat, together with the quotation, from De Musset's *Poésies Nouvelles*, helped to point clearly the target of the speech.

A week later came the Apostolic Exhortation *Menti Nostrae* on the sanctification of the priestly life, which was in its last section even more unmistakable: 'We are sure that you are well aware that among certain priests, not highly distinguished for learning or austerity of life, there has been an alarming spread of revolutionary ideas.' It has been said that those working waist-high in water for long hours on the Arc-Isère dam were not without a certain austerity of life; again one wonders how well-informed the Pope was. He went on to admit the evil of the social conditions which had led priests to 'accept views and adopt a way of life, even in dress and personal appearance, at variance both with their dignity and their office. Even in their sermons and in controversy they are carried away by the hankering after novelty. Thereby they weaken their own faith, and, by compromising their reputation, they impair the effectiveness of their sacred ministry.' He went on to reaffirm the responsibility of the bishops and to direct that episcopal conferences should determine the forms of pastoral activity. 'It is an illusion for a priest to suppose that by using bizarre and absurd methods he will be able to hide the poverty of his own soul and at the same time contribute effectively to the spread of the kingdom of Christ.'

Pius ended by reminding priests that recent papal pronouncements had explained how to deal with the wiles of Communism as well as the evils of Capitalism.

It seems clear that at this point Pius, despite the marked lack of sympathy in his language, was prepared to content himself with warnings and to go on leaving judgement of the concrete situation to the French hierarchy. Unhappily, as Siefer argues, it was from just this point onwards that relations between the Workers' Mission and the bishops began to deteriorate rather than improve.

One of their own number has conceded that the mentality of the worker-priests altered as their commitments widened and deepened. It was not merely that they did not, except in a few cases, work with the parish organization—there were sound arguments for this at least as an interim policy. It was rather that they often seemed able to win the confidence of the workers only at the expense of confirming the latter's contempt for the Church as conventionally understood, as something identified with the class enemies of the workers. The efforts made in the spring of 1951 by the sympathetic Gerlier and by his auxiliary Bishop Ancel, himself a worker, to draw up a directorium for the movement, met with resistance. Siefer concludes: 'As all concerned wanted to avoid an open breach, and there was no legal authority that could enforce such regulations throughout France, the hierarchy desisted from imposing them and just went on awaiting developments. It was the failure to get to grips with the problem at this moment that provided the crucial argument in favour of intervention from Rome two years later' (*op. cit.* p. 57).

From this time the situation got out of hand rapidly. The Holy Office, which had complained severely earlier in the year, now insisted that the number of worker-priests should remain at the existing figure of one hundred, and that annual reports should be sent on each individual. In 1952 uncomfortable publicity for the movement probably upset Rome further. The book *Les Saints Vont en Enfer* by Gilbert Cesbron became a best-seller after two worker-priests had been arrested in the demonstration against General Ridgeway in Paris as he arrived to take charge of NATO headquarters. The hierarchy and doubtless the Secretariat of State were worried about the effect on Church-State relations. The ACO, the Catholic workers organization, was reasonably resentful of its efforts being undermined by priests who were often officials of the

Communist-controlled *Compagnie Générale de Travail.* The French Right capitalized on all these difficulties—unscrupulously true to its worst traditions: a fictitious 'ultimatum from Rome' was spread abroad in the press.

All this must have gone far to move the Vatican to decisive action. In Italy the Communist party was stronger even than in France. As we have seen, the Church had been bending all her efforts since the war to keeping Italian Communism at bay. Nothing could have been more likely to undermine this resistance than the impression that Catholic and even clerical co-operation with Communism was being tolerated in France.

On January 12, 1953 two churchmen living in Paris were made cardinals: the Archbishop, Feltin, and the Nuncio, Roncalli. For the latter the red hat was a signal for departure. He had never been close to the inner circle of power in Rome, and it was clear that he was regarded as inadequate, from the Roman point of view, to the situation in Paris. From the French point of view he was probably the single factor which had prevented the situation from boiling over so far. On February 23 he left Paris, and spent four days in Rome before setting off for the north and for Venice. He was not replaced until Archbishop Marella arrived in Paris in June.

Meantime, on May Day, Pius XII addressed the Italian workers' section of Catholic Action. It was his only explicit reference to the worker-priests since 1950. In the interval he had often condemned the class struggle, though he had also (in speaking to Spanish workers) condemned the 'unnatural situation in which a small group of privileged and very rich exists beside enormous, impoverished popular masses'. Now he told the Italians: 'He errs who thinks he can serve the workers' interests with the old methods of the class struggle, and he deceives himself still further who thinks he must justify his efforts as the only way to go on exercising religious influence over the *mondo di lavoro*.' The last phrase was a pointed translation of the French *le monde ouvrier*, which was the phrase current among the priest-workers and summed up their conception of their task. The 'workers' world' was a world apart—cut off especially from the bourgeois world of traditional Catholicism.

The Roman liquidation process was launched on August 29 from the Congregation of Religious, which circularized all superiors of religious orders in France ordering them to withdraw their worker-priests. This was of course the field in which the bishops could be most easily by-passed. A fifth of the worker-priests were members of religious orders, most of them working in Paris. A few days earlier Cardinal Piazza, Prefect of the Consistorial Congregation, had begun a three-week tour of France. At the end of it, on September 16, he demanded of the French hierarchy a report of their plans to deal with the crisis, and just a week later the Nuncio, Archbishop Marella, announced to a gathering of bishops and superiors that the experiment was to end by order of the Curia.

The big three, Feltin, Gerlier and Liénart, showed clear signs of not relishing the way the matter had been handled, and on November 4 went to Rome to see Pius XII. Ten days later the Vatican announced the revised conditions on which the workers' mission would be allowed to continue. Essentially they amounted to a reassertion of the traditional requirements of the priesthood and the restricting of labour to part-time.

Reactions at the time showed that the majority regarded this as 'the end of the worker-priests'. 'One can reject a solution but one cannot reject the problem,' Père Congar is credited with saying. The reactions of the worker-priests themselves showed equally clearly that they were not convinced that mere zeal for the priesthood explained events. Political pressure, ultimately from the French Right, was behind it all, they believed. But here of course they were vulnerable—it could too easily be answered that their precise trouble was their acquired habit of politicizing every problem.

The last time the *Mission de Paris* met was at the funeral of Henri Perrin in Paris. The scene was movingly described by Georges Hourdin (qu. Siefer, *op. cit.*, p. 81–2).

The *Mission de France* survived, with a new statute, and a new training centre at the ancient abbey of Pontigny; the Prado movement in Lyons under Bishop Ancel (later to become a leading figure of the Second Vatican Council) survived also, as did the Little Brothers of Charles de Foucauld. Père Jacques Loew's mission in Marseilles solved the problem of the mission to the workers more successfully, perhaps because of his personal skill and tact. But by the time of Pius XII's death hope had by no means been abandoned of some relaxing of the measures of 1953. Later pronouncements of Pius continued to urge the improvement of worker-employer relations and to warn against excessive confidence in technology and automation: he seemed to be under the impression that the latter would entail an increase of monotonous machine-minding for workers.

One of the last acts of his pontificate was the suppression of *Témoignage Chrétien*, which in April 1957 had published a defence of the workers-priest by Canon Bonnet, former Chaplain General of the *Association Catholique Ouvrière*, by that time head of the revised *Mission Ouvrière*.

The French cardinals are supposed to have played a decisive part in the election of Angelo Roncalli, their former Nuncio, to succeed Pius XII. Certainly he was exuberantly welcomed in the French press even to the extent of being described as a French pope succeeding a German pope. The first months of John's pontificate hardly lent colour to all this. Even if his pronouncement from Venice in August, 1956 (see p. 98) be taken as an attempt to cancel at Rome the memory of his over-tolerant years in Paris, his early pontificate brought no great comfort to the Left-inclined. April 1959 saw the reiteration and stringent interpretation of the 1949 decree against Communism. Nevertheless, a few weeks after John's election 'Cardinal Feltin let it be known that he now proposed to obtain from the Holy See some fresh clarification and directives regarding the Mission to the Workers, which was in a somewhat uncertain situation as far as canon law was concerned. This intention was natural and obvious, and its realization should have been simple, in view of the new Pope's specialized knowledge of the subject from his time as Nuncio in Paris. . . . [The report] was ready by April and he proposed to lay it before the Pope himself on his visit to Rome, already fixed for the end of that month. Sudden illness obliged the cardinal to postpone his visit to Rome, but the report, which had been read by at least some of the French bishops, was sent on to the Holy Office.

'About this time the Christian Democrat party in Italy was in acute danger from the Left . . . and this had aroused the then Under-secretary of the Holy Office, Cardinal Ottaviani, to issue a drastic recapitulation of the Decree on Communism of 1949. . . . This declaration was seized on eagerly in conservative circles and was immensely reassuring to all the diehards who had been observing with growing dismay the openly popular and conciliatory style of the new pontificate, in which they saw a growing danger for the Church as a mainstay of social order in the world.

'So it was not surprising that the report on the Mission to the

Workers, which had become known in the Vatican long before Cardinal Feltin's visit to Rome early in June, had met with little sympathy. On June 10 (1959) one day before Cardinal Feltin officially submitted his report to the Pope, a plenary session of the Holy Office was called to consider the subject, additional expert opinions on the subject having been obtained in the meantime. Hence not only did the original Paris report encounter an already well-informed group of the Holy Office (and a well-informed Pope) but the astonished Cardinal Feltin was informed on arrival that an adverse decision had been reached. This situation was described by Cardinal Pizzardo himself in the following terms in the letter which arrived in Paris three weeks later, on July 3. "In the audience of June 11, 1959, the Holy Father graciously approved these decisions and when he received your Eminence on the same day he informed you of his thoughts on this point. After he had read the report which your Eminence submitted to him, it seemed right to his Holiness to confirm the decrees of the Holy Office dated June 10 and 24." '[1]

Cardinal Pizzardo's letter was not intended for publication, but did appear in *Le Monde* on September 15. This, claims Siefer, 'was not the result of journalistic detective work, but was due to the shrewd and judicious act of a bishop who was by no means *avant-garde*.' If this time there was no rebellion and no tragedy, the effect on the French Church as a whole, and on future history, was probably much more important. The part played by the French hierarchy and their expert advisers and by the French Press (not least by *Le Monde*) in the Council undoubtedly owes an incalculable amount to this episode. The document had said, *inter alia* '. . . it is surely difficult to regard as completely de-christianized a mass of people that still includes a very large proportion who have received the indelible seal of baptism.'

Liénart, addressing a plenary meeting of the *Mission de France* at Pontigny on September 17, 1959, said, 'I should like to say that, in your fidelity and obedience to the Church, you must remain conscious more than ever of the two realities which form, on the religious plane, the justification of your existence and your work:

'The plain fact of de-christianization is very widespread indeed in France, particularly among the workers, in the sectors entrusted to us. This fact will be studied at the 1960 plenary assembly of the

[1] Gregor Siefer, *The Church and Industrial Society*, pp. 93–4.

Episcopate; and the theme set down there, and emphatically approved by Pope John XXIII, is "The de-christianization of France and what can be done to counteract it."

'The second reality is that it is in the first place the concern of the bishops and priests to provide for the evangelisation of their people . . . therefore, we must all remain faithful to the mission with which the Church has entrusted us, whatever the difficulties we may encounter in accomplishing our task.'

It would stretch coincidence altogether too far to see no cause and effect between this and the fact that Cardinal Liénart was one of the two whose prompt intervention brought the first working session of the Council to an abrupt early close by refusing to accept the prepared lists of candidates for the conciliar commissions. A glance at the notes and bibliography of Siefer's book will moreover reveal that the history of these events in the French Church was followed no less closely and had no less profound an effect in Germany.

There is no means of knowing for certain at present how far Pope John was party to the events of 1959 described by Siefer above. But it is ironic to think that these did as much as anything to determine the mood of the Council which he had then already summoned but whose future course and achievement was at that time undreamed of—indeed would have been forecast quite otherwise on the strength of any analogies with the Roman Synod of January, 1960. It is important to be clear here: it is not being brashly suggested that the French hierarchy came to Rome for the Council in a mood 'to take it out of' the Roman Curia. Their concerns were much more serious than that. The experience of the post-war years in the French Church had been a profound and troubled one. The disciplinary problem posed by the worker-priests, which perhaps could not have found any substantially different solution, was less important to many than the deeper problem of which the travails of the worker-priests were only a symptom—the problem of the deep division in the French Church and of the alienation of so many Frenchmen from the Faith. Integralists could shrug off this last as the fault of everybody except themselves; the bishops had to be more realistic.

The French did not come to the Council with a few bizarre reforming ideas gathered from books; they did not come as fans of any theologian or any liturgical writer; above all they did not come with the hope of going away again as quickly as possible to a domestic comfort as little disturbed as possible by new-fangled practices. They came deeply marked by experience, rendered certain by suffering and perplexity that new ways needed to be explored, and that the existing relations between Rome and the rest of the world needed to be improved if such exploration was to be carried out securely, in peace and with hope of being fruitful.

The bishops had spent many of those troubled years under cross-fire, blamed by Rome for their high-handedness and excessive toleration of novelty, by the worker-priests and their sympathizers for vacillation. It is hardly to be wondered at that they showed themselves deeply committed on such issues as collegial episcopal status and powers, the government of dioceses, curial reform. During the Council debates many French bishops also, making their own a theme hammered at by the Latin American and some other non-European hierarchies, spoke often of the need to restore the image of the Church as the Church of the poor; prominent among them were those who had championed the workers' mission to the last: Gerlier, Liénart, Ancel.

Pius XII had said, 'The Church cannot remain silent before conditions which make difficult or practically impossible the Christian life.' But France was more than half full of people who could not have told you whether the Church had remained silent or not. To make pronouncements to them from ordinary pulpits was like recording with the microphone switched off. It is ironic that the Pope under whom the microphone of the French Workers' mission was finally disconnected should by the extraordinary force of his personality have made the Church's voice heard in places even more inaccessible than the *banlieues* of Paris. Whether the social Encyclical *Mater et Magistra* would have aroused such interest if written by any other pope or under any other circumstances may be questioned. It introduces no new fundamental doctrine. The principle of subsidiary function (see Chapter 3, p. 56), the need for free intermediate organizations between State and individual, the insistence on the dignity of labour and its right to a living share in the enterprise, wider distribution of property—these are all taken over from its predecessors, though developed in contemporary terms. But he showed the most comprehensive acquaintance and sympathy with the features of life in the late fifties and early sixties.

He justified the writing of the Encyclical by pointing to the 'radical transformation' of the economic and social scene in the twenty years since Pius had commemorated *Rerum Novarum:*

'In the field of science, technology and economics we have the discovery of nuclear energy and its application first to the purposes of war and later, increasingly, to peaceful ends, the practically limitless possibilities of chemistry in the production of synthetic materials; the growth of automation in industry and public services; the modernization of agriculture; the easing of communications, especially by radio and television; faster transport and the initial conquest of interplanetary space.

'In the social field we have the development of social insurance and, in the more economically advanced communities, the introduction of social security systems. Trade unionists are showing a more responsible awareness of the major social and economic problems. There is a progressive improvement in basic education, a wider distribution of essential commodities, greater opportunities for advancement in industry and the consequent breaking down of class barriers, and a keener interest in world affairs shown by people of average education. . . .

'Turning to the political field we observe many welcome changes. In a number of countries all classes of citizens are taking a part in public life, and public authorities are taking a keener interest in social and economic matters. We are witnessing the breakaway from colonialism and the attainment of political independence by the peoples of Asia and Africa. Drawn together by their common needs, nations are becoming daily more inter-dependent. There is moreover an ever-extending network of societies and organizations which set their sights beyond the aims and interests of individual groups and concentrate on the economic, social, cultural and political welfare of all nations throughout the world.'

This highly concentrated summary has an alert, empirical air of acceptance which is new in papal utterance, and striking to contrast with the admonitory tones of the age of the *Syllabus.* Speaking of 'socialization' as the characteristic feature of the new age, John uses the term in his own way, detached from doctrinaire political content. (One is reminded of Sir William Harcourt's 'we are all socialists now.')

'The present advance in scientific knowledge and productive technology clearly puts it within the power of the public authority to redress any lack of balance in the economy, and to remedy any difference in economic prosperity which may exist between nations or between different regions in the same political community. It also puts into the hands of public authority the means for controlling fluctuations in the economy and preventing the recurrence of mass unemployment. Hence the *insistent need* for those in authority—since they are responsible for the common good—to *increase the degree and scope of their activities* in the economic sphere. . . .' (Italics mine).

John characteristically stresses that these tendencies are not blind forces at work, but means in the hands of responsible human beings. '. . . a sane view of the common good must be present and operative in men invested with public authority. . . . So long as social action does in fact adhere to these principles within the framework of the moral order, it is not of its nature dangerous or detrimental to the individual. On the contrary, it will in all likelihood help him to develop and perfect his own personal talents. . . .' This, coming though it does from one to whom personal values were everything, contrasts strongly with many traditional glum Catholic commonplaces about the inevitable depersonalization of modern life.

John goes on to consider how the new conditions have enlarged the scope of workers' associations, first championed by Leo:

'Their purpose is no longer to agitate but to co-operate, principally by the method of collective bargaining. But it is worth while stressing here how timely and imperative it is that workers be given the opportunity to exert their influence throughout the State, and not just within the limits of their own spheres of employment.

'. . . it is not the decisions made within the individual productive units which have the greatest bearing on the economy, but those made by public authorities and by institutions which tackle the various economic problems on a national or international basis. It is therefore high time that these public authorities and institutions bring the workers into their discussions. . . .' Again what a distance we are from nineteenth-century Christian paternalism!

Turning to the familiar papal topic of private property and the common good, John promptly recognizes that the terms of the relationship are evolving:

'. . . more and more people today, through belonging to insurance groups and systems of social security, find that they can face the future with confidence—the sort of confidence that formerly resulted from their possession of a certain amount of property.

'Furthermore, *the modern trend* is for people to aim at proficiency in their trade or profession rather than the acquisition of private property. They think more highly of an income which derives from work and the rights consequent upon work than from an income which derives from capital and the rights of capital. And this is as it should be. Work, which is the immediate expression of a human personality, must always be rated higher than the possession of external goods which are of their nature merely instrumental. This view of work is certainly an *indication of the advance that has been made in our civilization.*' (Italics mine.)

It is extraordinary how much more convincing, after this, the traditional commonplaces about property sound, when the Pope adds them. Public ownership, within the rational limits set by the common good, is firmly accepted, so is social security: but '. . . economic enterprises of the State and other agencies of public law must be entrusted to men of good reputation who have the necessary experience and ability and a keen sense of responsibility towards their country. Furthermore, a strict check should be kept on their activity. . . .' There, one is tempted to say, speaks the Italian countryman.

The Encyclical turns later to population problems. They are frankly and clearly stated, though still with some scepticism as to the data about food supply-population ratios.

'We must nevertheless state most emphatically that no statement of the problem and no solution to it is acceptable which does violence to man's essential dignity, and which is based on an utterly materialistic conception of man himself and his life. . . .

'We must solemnly proclaim that human life is transmitted by means of the family, and the family is based upon a marriage which is one and indissoluble and raised, so far as Christians are concerned, to the dignity of a sacrament. The transmission of human life is the result of a personal and conscious act, and as such is subject to the all-holy inviolable and unchangeable laws of God, which a man ignores and disobeys to his cost. He is not therefore permitted to use certain ways and means which are allowable in the propagation of plant and animal life.

'Human life is sacred—all men must recognize that fact. From its very inception it betrays the creating hand of God. Those who violate His laws not only offend the divine majesty, and degrade themselves and humanity, they also sap the vitality of the State of which they are members.'

The text of *Genesis i*, 28, recurrent in papal pronouncements on this theme since *Rerum Novarum*—'Increase and multiply'—is quoted, but also the following words: 'Fill the earth and subdue it.' 'These two commandments,' says John, 'are complementary. . . . A provident God grants sufficient means to the human race to find a dignified solution to the problems attendant upon the transmission of human life. But these problems can become difficult of solution, or even insoluble, if man, led astray in mind and perverted in will, turns to such means as are opposed to right reason, and seeks ends that are contrary to his social nature and the intentions of Providence.'

All this is rather cautiously generalized, but it brings us to the point where the greatest modern private problem for the Catholic conscience converges with one of the greatest of modern social problems. Even were it appropriate for the non-specialist to embark on this intractable topic in a general work such as the present, he would be prevented by the fact that the matter is *sub judice* in the hands of a papal commission; but it would be disingenuous to do less than set out the terms of the question.

The problem is in one sense recent, in another sense much less so. R. F. Trevett is, as far as I know, the only writer to remind the general reader in the context of a Catholic essay on sexual morality[1] that 'there must be and always has been some kind of social and corporate control over the birth-rate. Our medieval ancestors achieved this by a severe restriction of the marriage rate. Certain members of the family were prevented from marrying. The power of the father in a society based on land tenure was so great that he was able to decide which of his children should marry and which should not, and then impose his will on them all. The great religious orders must have housed many who came to them because of such a parental decision. The number of births was roughly determined by the social structure of the peasant state, and the method of restriction, involving stresses, frustration and suffering, was the control of the marriage rate. It is important for Catholics to realize this. Some are too prone to look back on a non-existent, imaginary past, where they believe no sexual problems existed and no effort was made to control the number of births. This leads them to advocate a trust in

[1] *Church and Sex*, Reginald F. Trevett, p. 106.

Providence which is little more than "tempting" God.' It is easy, moreover, to forget how very recently this unpleasant way of regulating populations has become obsolete—where it has.

The fifteenth century *Decretum pro Armenis* listed the traditional ends of marriage in the traditional order; post-Reformation popes were concerned mainly with vindicating the Church's rights over marriage against State encroachment, and it is the classic social Encyclical, *Rerum Novarum*, that returns to fundamentals: 'No human law can abolish the natural and original right of marriage[1] nor in any way limit the chief and principal purpose of marriage ordained by God's authority from the beginning: "Increase and multiply".' Pius XI's Encyclical *Casti Connubii* of December 1930, the *locus classicus* for our subject, quotes this passage from Leo.

It is perhaps useful to remind those who mainly draw their notions of Catholic teaching on marriage from newspaper reports that neither *Casti Connubii* nor any other papal pronouncement consists solely of exhortations to increase and multiply, with the complementary prohibitions. Pius XI's Encyclical, for instance, has fifty paragraphs of positive religious teaching on marriage before it turns to the thorny topic: but at last it does so: 'The conjugal act is of its very nature designed for the procreation of offspring; and therefore those who in performing it deliberately deprive it of its natural power and efficacy, act against nature and do something which is shameful and intrinsically immoral.'

St Augustine is quoted in support:

' "Sexual intercourse even with a lawful wife is unlawful and shameful if the conception of offspring is prevented. This is what Onan, the son of Juda, did, and on that account God put him to death." (*Gen. xxxviii*, 8–10.)

'Wherefore, since there are some who, openly departing from the Christian teaching which has been handed down uninterruptedly from the beginning, have in recent times thought fit solemnly to preach another doctrine concerning this practice, the Catholic Church, to whom God has committed the task of teaching and preserving morals and right conduct in their integrity, standing erect amidst this moral devastation, raises her voice in sign of her divine mission to keep the chastity of the marriage contract unsullied by this ugly stain, and through Our mouth proclaims anew: that any use of matrimony whatsoever in which the act is deprived,

[1] This is an interesting comment on the medieval customs just described.

by human interference, of its natural power to procreate life, is an offence against the law of God and of nature, and that those who commit it are guilty of a grave sin.'[1]

It was about a century since the Surrey clergyman Malthus had drawn attention to the problems likely to be raised by population increases. But in the second version of his *Essay on Population* he had austerely advocated late marriage and continence as a remedy, so that there was a certain irony that during the decade preceding *Casti Connubii* the literary propaganda of Dr Marie Stopes in favour of artificial birth control should have been spread under the auspices of the Malthusian League.

The Encyclical was widely regarded as prompted in part by the statement of the Lambeth Conference a few months earlier, in which the Anglican bishops, having cited total abstinence from intercourse as the most obvious solution of family planning problems, added: 'Yet there exist moral situations which make it obligatory to use other methods. Each couple must decide for themselves, as in the sight of God, after the most conscientious thought, and, if perplexed in mind, after taking competent advice both medical and spiritual. The question they must put to themselves is: Would conception be for any reason wrong? If it be clearly wrong, and if there is good moral reason why the way of abstinence should not be followed, we cannot condemn the use of scientific methods to avert conception.'[2]

Earlier there had been considerable opposition not only ecclesiastical but also civil to birth prevention. Though the Bradlaugh-Besant prosecution which aroused such a stir in Victorian England was unsuccessful, legislation in America was much more effective, and as late as 1957 two states, Connecticut and Massachusetts, still maintained it. But in America also the decade before Pius XI's Encyclical saw the American Birth Control League first flourishing under the presidency of Mrs Sanger, and in 1931 the Federal

[1] The reader may be interested to see Mr Leslie Dewart explaining this passage away in *Contraception and Holiness*, pp. 251 *et seq.* Whatever one's sympathies, it is hard to resist the impression that had this ingenious *tour de force* been employed in the opposite sense, it would have been stigmatized by most of his fellow contributors as a prime specimen of neo-scholastic logic-chopping, medieval mental gymnastics, and so on.

[2] The conference added its 'strong condemnation of the use of any methods of contraception-control from motives of selfishness, luxury or mere convenience'. For other Protestant views, cf. S. de Lestapis, *Family Planning and Modern Problems*, Chapter 3.

Council of Churches in U.S.A. stated that 'the public has the right to expect guidance from the Church on the moral aspects of birth control', and added that 'some form' of control and spacing was recognized as necessary by all Churches and physicians.

As far as the Catholic Church was concerned, the first clue to this was to be found in a brief allusion in *Casti Connubii:* 'Nor are those considered as acting against nature who in their married life use their right in the proper manner, although on account of *natural reasons of time* or of certain defects new life cannot be brought forth.' (Italics mine.)

Two years later Leo Latz, M.D., a Catholic doctor, attracted much attention in America with his *Rhythm of Sterility and Fertility in Women;* so to a lesser extent did Halliday Sutherland with his *Laws of Life* in England.

In Pius XII's pontificate, and especially in its post-war phase, the various advances in medicine, sanitation, insecticides, etc., very rapidly aggravated the problem now known as 'population explosion', especially in the underdeveloped regions of the Third World. At the same time, from a variety of causes, unrest was widely remarked (notably by Pius himself in an address during November of the Holy Year, 1950) in Europe and America with traditional teachings on marriage relations. The following year, in a famous address to midwives (October 29, 1951) he tackled the problem on a broad front.

Having condemned sterilization he went on: 'Today, besides, another grave problem has arisen, namely if and how far the obligation of being ready for maternity is reconcilable with the ever more general recourse to the periods of natural sterility (the so-called "agenesic" periods in woman) which seems a clear expression of a will contrary to that precept. You are expected to be well-informed, from the medical point of view, in regard to this new theory and the *progress which may still be made* in this subject, and it is also expected that your advice shall not be based on mere popular publications, but upon objective science and on the authoritative judgement of conscientious specialists in medicine and biology. It is your function, not the priest's, to instruct the married couple, through private consultation or serious publications on the biological and technical aspect of the theory. . . . But in this field also your apostolate demands of you, as women and as Christians, that you know and defend the moral law to which the application of the theory is subordinated. In this the Church is competent.' (Italics mine.)

The insistence on proper spheres of professional competence here is noteworthy, and should be read in conjunction with what has been said in Chapter 8. It looks forward also to Paul VI's move in 1964 (when the problem had grown further in urgency and been ventilated in an unprecedented manner as the result of the Second Vatican Council) of appointing a commission of enquiry to report on all aspects of the question, and suspending conciliar discussion until this report was forthcoming.

Later in the same address Pius said: 'Serious motives, such as those which not rarely arise from medical, eugenic, economic and social "indications", may exempt husband and wife from the obligatory, positive debt for a long period or even for the entire period of matrimonial life. From this it follows that the observance of the natural sterile periods may be lawful, from the moral viewpoint; and it is lawful in the conditions mentioned. If, however, according to a reasonable and equitable judgement there are no such grave reasons . . . the will to avoid the fecundity of their union while continuing to satisfy to the full their sensuality can only be the result of a false appreciation of life, and of motives foreign to sound ethical principles.'

Pius repeated these observations in 1958 to a Congress on Hematology, quoting also the brief allusion from *Casti Connubii*. Speaking to the Italian *Fronte della Famiglia* a month after the address to midwives, he offered this gloss: 'In Our last allocution on conjugal morality We affirmed the legitimacy and defined the limits—and they are, in fact, very wide limits—of a form of birth regulation which, in contrast to what is known as birth control, is compatible with God's law. It is even to be hoped, although in this matter the Church naturally trusts the judgement of medical science, that doctors will succeed in providing this lawful method with a sufficiently reliable basis, and the most recent information appears to confirm this hope.'

But the hopefulness of the most recent information has fluctuated a good deal in the ensuing seven years, and there seems to be still no agreement among experts.[1] Meantime official teaching has remained stable. Pius XII did not say anything substantially

[1] A few days before these lines were written, a non-Catholic lecturer in obstetrics at a famous London hospital said to the writer, 'I wish to goodness the Pope would come out against the pill.'

different from the lapidary pronouncement of his predecessor; John XXIII (his former secretary has testified) did not directly interest himself in the problem, and left a considerable dossier on it for his successor. It is in fact essentially, in its present dimensions, a problem of the present pontificate, and one that has been aired with a freedom almost without parallel in recent history. There is certainly no major aspect of traditional doctrine which has been so widely called in question in modern times by men who have yet remained in good standing in the Church; and this is particularly remarkable (to many, particularly disquieting) in view of the extraordinary vehemence with which Pius XI pronounced on the subject in 1930. The application of the Natural Law concept in this sphere has been critically scrutinized;[1] the dogmatic status of *Casti Connubii* has been discussed; so has even the primacy of procreation among the ends of marriage. It has been alleged that Catholic teaching might 'change' or 'develop' in this field as it has in those of usury and religious liberty (both disputable parallels). (Cf. Chapter 12). The Council fathers have been openly exhorted to 'avoid another Galileo case' (again a parallel of doubtful felicity). It has been argued that official teaching labours under an age-old 'bias' against physical love, variously traced to St Paul, St Augustine, St Gregory the Great, celibates in general, Manichees and Catharists, and that it is time the Church caught up with modern sensibility in the matter. Some have even advanced a position similar to that taken up in 1930 by the Lambeth Conference—that it should be left to the judgement of married couples how their conjugal relations are regulated.[2]

It would be wrong to suppose that all these ideas are the preserve

[1] Critically in the sense of adversely; hardly in the other sense. There has been some very loose and unhistorical writing on the topic. But here we are up against the sad paradox that those who are hottest in defence of tradition are too often most lukewarm in defence of scholarship. At such a time as this their lukewarmness recoils on them.

[2] There was some irony in the fact that, just as this was being said in autumn 1964, the anonymous and candid writer of the preface to Crockford was offering this explanation of 'the futility of much that (the Established Church) tries to do. The fact is that churchmen as a whole still think that sufficient moral guidance can be obtained by reading the Bible, saying one's prayers and using a little common sense. . . . It is unhappily true that many of the clergy and still more of the laity are not equipped to form a judgement on novel or quasi-novel notions in dogmatics or morals.'

The gods might well grin and ecumenists despair if what Crockford called 'the cult of amateurishness' were to be welcomed in Rome just as it was being bewailed in Canterbury. But in fairness of course Lambeth did say that decision should follow 'competent advice both medical and spiritual', while Card. Suenens, for instance, in his much discussed speech was at the opposite pole from any advocacy of amateurishness.

of a very advanced fringe. Though discussion of the subject was foregone at the last session of the Council, this was not before three of the leading figures of the assembly, Cardinals Léger and Suenens and Patriarch (now Cardinal) Maximos Saigh, had made lengthy speeches in support of a more open[1] attitude to the problem, candid enough to shock and anger many of their listeners.

It is a pity in fact that so much conservative comment inclines to consist of questioning the motives of those who hold more advanced views; this does not make for calm discussion. But at the moment of writing any real discussion is inhibited by the fact that the papal commission still sits.

To conclude by reverting to the more general: Oakeshott, we have seen, in a representative comment by an enlightened and not unsympathetic outsider, spoke of the rigidity and exotic character of the Church's social doctrine. It can perhaps be more readily said for John XXIII than for Pius XII that he felt persistently uneasy about the exotic character and was prepared to draw the logical conclusion and sacrifice the rigidity. His two great encyclicals both handled great social themes, and were themselves exercises in the *aggiornamento* which he offered as a programme to the Second Vatican Council. But the exercises might have remained no more, destined to take their place on library shelves in a busy world, had they not been under the name of one to whom in the end nobody was too busy to give attention. The value of what is addressed to the wide world cannot be realistically measured without reference to the wide world's disposition to listen (which is not the same as saying that it is the business of a prophet to say what the world wants to hear: it never has been). Judged by this test, John XXIII's contribution to papal social teaching is high and secure. When he addressed himself to 'all men of good will', he had already created for himself a vast audience exactly so describable. To borrow a word Siefer uses in a different but related connection, it was *savour* (something the worker-priests had found lacking) that John restored to Catholic social teaching. It was a very personal contribution.

[1] I do not wish to press the word 'open' here further than it would be pressed in describing, say, the Pope's own attitude in submitting the question to a commission of experts.

II

Catholics and Jews

The Apostle of England, Pope Gregory the Great, has a reputation, amply supported by his letters, for championing Jews against injury, including forcible conversion. For Jews on the papal estates in Sicily he advocated an amusing method of persuasion, by promising them reductions in rent. Writing to his agent there he sets out a precise scale for the reductions, and adds: 'We are not acting unprofitably in bringing them to Christ through the hope of having their rents reduced. For even if they themselves come with little faith, there will certainly be more faith in their children who are baptized, so that if we do not gain them we shall gain their children. Therefore any reduction of rent made for Christ's sake is not to be considered a loss.' (Homes-Dudden, *Gregory the Great*, p. 156.) On the other hand Gregory insisted on strict observance of the imperial law by and with regard to Jews, was severe on Jewish proselytizing and on Jews who took Christians as slaves, writing sternly to Queen Brunhilde of the Franks about her tolerating this practice.

More recently another very saintly and learned priest, Father Felix Capello, author of a standard work on the public law of the Church, illustrates succinctly the Roman canonist position at the time of the sixth edition of his work, 1954:

'The Church had adopted a special policy towards the Jews, since they are the one-time chosen people of God, to be converted at the end of time, though meanwhile they hold most tenaciously to the Old Testament. On this account and because of their dispersion among all nations they furnish a very strong argument for the fulfilment of prophecy and for the truth of the Christian religion.

'The Church was wont to tolerate the Jews so long as they did not threaten public security by crimes or scheming. [Father Capello uses the word *conamina*, which in this context might best be translated as 'trying it on'.] She left them freedom of worship, while ensuring that they should not be a nuisance to Christians nor hinder and disturb them in the practice of their religion.' (Capello, *Summa Juris Publici Ecclesiastici*, pp. 222–3.)

The Bishop of Terracina in Gregory's time shut the synagogue on the pretext that the singing there disturbed people in nearby churches. Gregory ordered him to give the Jews another building in the city. (Homes-Dudden, *op. cit.*, p. 154).

Capello goes on: 'To avoid however the danger of perversion of Christians and for moral and social reasons she never allowed them to mix fully or to dwell with Christians, and indeed preferred to assign them special parts of the city. Sometimes she even ordered them to wear distinctive clothing.' (*Op. cit.*, *ibid*). The strict ghetto system dates in fact from the Counter-Reformation. The medieval 'Jewry' was not a strict legal affair; even after the Third Lateran Council had forbidden believers to lodge among infidels the law was slackly and intermittently enforced. Paul IV, with the pleasantly-named Bull *Cum Nimis Absurdum* (1555), enforced segregation, and the Roman ghetto dates from the following year. Christians were not allowed to employ Jews as doctors or nurses. A general attitude of suspicion and contempt existed. It was not thought necessary to spare the feelings of Jews, at least publicly. Even Innocent III's Constitution of 1199, generally considered the *Magna Carta* of papal policy towards the Jews, was given the title *Licet Perfidia Judaeorum*.

Capello continues: 'It is falsely alleged that this policy of the Church provoked hatred and unbridled cupidity among the Jews: It is clear from the writings of the Fathers how the Jews from the very beginning pursued Christians with implacable hatred; whence many ecclesiastical laws were drafted to protect Christians from the hatred and rapacity of the Jews. The Church never promoted anti-semitism, and history shows that she continually reproved persecution of the Jews.' Jewish historians, though naturally in a rather different tone, have agreed at least that the Church's legislation was generally defensive rather than aggressive in purpose. Well-known preachers sometimes railed against the 'insolence' of the Jews. In some places, especially in Rome, they were on occasion compelled, rather unfeelingly, to attend sermons, 'with the idea' as Capello quaintly says, 'of forcing them not to conversion but to the fulfilment of their duty of knowing the truth'. Capello's answer to liberal criticism of this was the *argumentum ad hominem:* 'What about Catholic children who are forced to attend non-Catholic schools?'

Official policy and extravagant clerical rhetoric, crudely oversimplified by listeners, often led to popular violence and calumny, and established a bad popular tradition. In western Europe to some extent the heart went out of religious anti-semitism, as out of much else religious, with the Peace of Westphalia, but it survived to play a considerable part in the anti-semitism of the modern liberal age.

The American Constitution gave normal rights and privileges to Jews, and the French emancipated them in 1791. Napoleon's victories temporarily spread this emancipation, though the Emperor himself was no lover of Jews, whom he expected to conform thoroughly to the Napoleonic pattern. The emancipation process largely went *pari passu* with the advance of liberalism in the nineteenth century, though notably slowly in England. It made no headway at all in Russia and other eastern European countries, where huge ghettos were periodically devastated by fearful pogroms.

The advance of liberalism was an equivocal benefit to the Jews. Where it was accompanied, as in Germany, by advancing nationalism it bred a new and harsher anti-semitism, political, economic and sometimes racial, though exploiting surviving religious prejudice. Lewi (*The Catholic Church and Nazi Germany*, p. 270) is able to quote as examples of this last two Catholic publicists and even two bishops, one of them that Martin of Paderborn who was prominent at the First Vatican Council as a leader of the extremist Ultramontanes and a close associate of Manning. But he is silent about how representative or isolated they were. (It is not necessary to add that it is regrettable that they can be pointed to at all.)

In Germany after the unification of 1870 anti-Jewish feeling coalesced into a regular movement, an Anti-semitic League being founded in 1880. The origins of German and Austro-Hungarian Christian Socialism were tainted with it, but though it lasted till the end of the century and produced a classic of anti-semitic literature in Houston Stewart Chamberlain's *Foundations of the Nineteenth Century* (destined to have its full effect a generation later) it resulted in no official anti-Jewish measures like the anti-Catholic *Kulturkampf*.

French anti-semitism reached a peak with the success of Edouard Drumont's *La France Juive* in 1886. Drumont also disliked Protestants and foreigners, but the non-Aryan was his Public Enemy Number One: As with Marr's *Victory of Judaism over Germanism* in Germany thirteen years earlier, economic depression contributed to Drumont's success. Moreover, as Denis Brogan, hardly to be suspected of reaction, has said: 'For all his talents and for all the French appetite for verbal savagery, Drumont would not have become either a hero or a villain if there had not been plenty of fuel for his fire.' (*Development of Modern France*, p. 275.) Victims of anticlerical fanaticism could occasionally point to Jews as its authors.

Drumont founded a newspaper, *La Libre Parole*, at the time of the Panama scandal; more important, just in time for the arrest of Captain Dreyfus, of which it gave advance hints. It was the Dreyfus affair too that laid the foundations of Maurras's fame. There were noisy anti-Dreyfusards among the French clergy, but there was also a Catholic Committee for the Defence of Justice formed in the Jewish officer's interest, while Picquart, the leading figure in the Revision, was a conservative Catholic. The issue was, of course, a much wider one than the Jewish question, but the Church paid heavily for the indiscretions of the Right when M. Combes rose to power on the floodtide of revisionism.

After the First World War the Jewish people could claim to be enfranchised all over the world for the first time since Constantine. Yet the vague idea of the Jewish-Freemason international conspiracy, often supported by weird and wonderful literature such as the *Protocols of the Learned Elders of Sion*, became part of the climate of the early twentieth century. It was held fiercely and actively only by minorities of cranks, such as the Catholic League for Patriotic Politics in Germany (see Lewi, *op. cit.*, p. 6) but larger numbers were more or less affected. The presence of a number of Jews among the leaders of the Communist revolution stimulated anti-semitism, as it aggravated in some quarters horror of Communism.

Less than this would have been needed to keep the flame alive on the French Right. The Vichy government promulgated an anti-semitic statute in 1941, and the deportation of Jews from both occupied and unoccupied France began a year later. The papal Nuncio Valeri protested but without effect. The Catholic theological faculty at the University of Lyons stigmatized the law as, 'injurious to a class of Frenchmen' and, significantly, as 'an act of religious discrimination contrary to a French tradition established for a century and a half'. This, if a little kind to the French radical tradition, was yet a late and noble fruit of Leo XIII's *ralliement*. The other side of the coin was shown in the sequel of 1947, when one Xavier Vallat, former commissary general for Jewish affairs, on trial for war crimes at Riom, defended himself from complicity with the racial anti-semitism of the German occupying power and claimed to draw his inspiration from what had been the teaching of the Church for centuries. A member of the high court asked him if he had ever heard of St Paul's 'there is henceforward neither Jew nor Gentile nor Greek', or of Pius XI's 'spiritually we are all Semites', but he simply repeated that he was inspired by a doctrine with 'a deep foundation in our historical traditions, and which has its guarantee in the doctrine of the Church itself'.

If this passage could have been put at the head of the Second Vatican Council's chapter *De Judaeis*, the latter might have had a smoother passage.

Not long after the Vichy law mentioned above, Pétain, it seems, instructed his ambassador at the Vatican, Louis Bérard, to sound out reactions there to his anti-Jewish measures. Bérard produced nothing concrete from the Vatican, but in support of his surmises gave Pétain a little lecture on the difference between the Church's respect for the human person and that of Rousseau and Condorcet, who did not recognize original sin. How this was supposed to justify deporting Jews only an integralist Frenchman could explain.

Nobécourt (*Le Vicaire et L'Histoire*, p. 209) asks: 'In what world were they living, these people—ambassadors, marshals, prelates? Did they not know that 150,000 persons had marched to liquidation behind the German troops?' But he reminds us that several French cardinals and bishops protested vigorously against the Vichy legislation.

To return to Germany. The rise of National Socialism did of course bring a novel, pseudo-scientific anti-semitism based on the work of Chamberlain and others and chiefly developed by Von Guenther, Hitler's *Mein Kampf* and Rosenberg's *Myth of the Twentieth Century* (the latter condemned by the Holy Office in 1934) while the cruder popular anti-semitism of Julius Streicher appeared in *Der Stürmer*, founded in 1922.

The story of the persecutions of Jews which began with Hitler's advent to power is, to older people at least, as familiar as it is horrible; its pre-war phase culminated in the pogroms of 1938 following the assassination in Paris of a German diplomat by a young Jew.

The recent work of Guenther Lewi, not friendly but formidably documented, gives a sad picture of German Catholicism in the years of Hitler's rise to power and up to the Second World War. Like all minorities with a certain sense of insecurity (the memory of the *Kulturkampf* had bitten deep), it was feverishly anxious to appear as patriotic as its neighbours. Its leaders were authoritarian, conservative, mostly academic in background, short of either knowledge or skill in politics, not closely organized and united only in their aversion to the customary bogies of the extreme Catholic Right—liberalism, freemasonry and Bolshevism. Ready for many concessions and sacrifices in preserving the essentials of Catholic communal life—schools, organizations—they were shortsighted and unsure in discerning which concessions were useful and which disastrous. Hardly any of them showed the least insight into the true nature of National Socialism. Politically inclined to sympathy with a 'strong' government which was loudly anti-Marxist, anxious not to be left out of the 'national awakening' which Hitler proclaimed, eager to support claims to *Lebensraum*, treaty revision, etc, they stifled what doubts they felt (and there was plenty of ground for doubt) by the thought that the régime could be 'purged of its neo-pagan elements'. Thus initial reserves, prohibitions even, against the party gradually gave way as the weakness and divisions of the Catholic Zentrum and Bavarian People's parties increased.

Lewi's strictures first appeared in the American Jewish Committee's *Commentary* in February 1964, but shortly afterwards Cardinal Döpfner, preaching in Munich on the anniversary of Pius XII's election, spoke hardly less frankly: 'During the years when we were confronting National Socialism, there were certainly regrettable decisions, unfortunate fundamental attitudes and individual reactions within the Church. We ought not to barricade ourselves before competent historical enquiry; we wish honestly to acknowledge the weaknesses of the Church leaders, the Catholic associations, the Catholic people. Our generation, and particularly the young, are sceptical of all whitewashing apologetic. . . . From the facts of the past it behoves us to draw a lesson for the present and the future. On the other hand, great things, heroic things had their place in the Church in those years, thanks to bishops, priests and laymen; and these we can look back on with acknowledgement and admiration' (quoted by Nobécourt, *op. cit.*, p. 50).

The Zentrum had as Chairman from 1928 a conservative canon law professor, Monsignor Ludwig Kaas. Other clerics advanced in the party under him, and its interests and tone became more narrowly confessional and authoritarian. This helped to drive many Catholics, in spite of episcopal exhortations, to join the growing and more dynamic Nazi party. In March 1933 the urgency of coming to terms with Nazism (which logically meant abandoning the Zentrum) was accepted, and the Concordat of the following July was the outcome. Pacelli's own subsequent apologia for this (see p. 43) is accepted in principle by Lewi: the agreement was an extreme example of the concordat conception. The phrase 'spark of hope' used by Pius illustrates this. But it seems clear, that whatever he (then Secretary of State) thought about it, there was considerably more than a spark of hope in most German Catholic breasts: something more like excessive optimism, if not credulity.

The Concordat was, as we have seen, the culmination of a policy which Pacelli had pursued since his first days in Berlin. Cardinal Döpfner in the sermon already quoted said: 'The Holy See could scarcely have avoided it, but it is true, as I remember very well, that many of us were bewildered and crestfallen to see it concluded.' The cardinal was a student at the German College in Rome at the time.

The two chief intermediaries in the negotiations were Monsignor Kaas, who eventually left Germany for Rome and became Pius's close friend and adviser on German affairs, and the equivocal Von Papen. The Nuncio in Berlin was Cesare Orsenigo, who does not seem to have been by a long chalk the most illustrious or strong-minded of Vatican diplomats. Orsenigo's position was not an easy one: but it is eloquent of his mentality and background that he should have demanded for the priests interned in Sachsenhausen camp, in addition to facilities for Mass, breviaries and a priest to give the last sacraments, 'that they should not be cremated, since cremation was in fundamental opposition to the rules of the Church'. (15 March, 1940. See Friedlander, p. 65.)

Lewi, who explicitly disclaims impartiality, surmises that Pius XII's statement that 'the German government asked the Holy See to conclude a concordat', is literally true, but that this was done on the prompting of Monsignor Kaas, which had previously been agreed on during his visit to Rome. He does however admit that others hold the opposite view. However this may be, it was certainly an odd business to see one who up to a few days before had been the head of the chief Catholic party concluding a concordat with a pagan totalitarian régime. Sir Robert Clive has testified that he was told at the Vatican that the Holy See was not particularly interested in the Centre Party. It went the same way as the *Popolare* had gone in Italy, though hardly for the same reasons since in all conscience it was 'confessional' enough.

The German hierarchy's part in the negotiations was eventually reduced to their being represented by their most pro-Nazi member, the Archbishop of Freiburg, Gröber, later known as 'the brown bishop'.

If there were misgivings on the Catholic side they were paralleled on the other side: many Nazis thought that too much had been conceded to Rome. But one parallel was lacking: the Holy See intended to keep the Concordat, Hitler did not. The wolf had successfully[1] maintained the disguise of granny. Now he could sharpen his teeth.

The next six years were years of tribulation. Within a year, the murders of Klausener, Probst (German Catholic leaders) and Dollfuss; the German bishops negotiating from weakness through three Nazi-inclined representatives; Pius XI angry; Von Bergen counselling Berlin to discuss nothing until Pacelli should return (from Buenos Aires) to exercise a moderating influence. What became increasingly clear was that those things to preserve which the German Church had accepted Nazism were precisely the things the Nazis had no intention of letting them preserve. The Church was trying to do the impossible—to reconcile contradictory loyalties. The government was merely doing what it had always intended to do.

Lewi, I have said, disclaims impartiality. His scholarship is painstaking, but his feelings are clear enough when all he has to say of the caricature of the Pope in *The Deputy* is that it is 'a bit stylized'. He even describes the Encyclical *Mit Brennender Sorge* as 'conciliatory,' which certainly entails a strained interpretation of it.

[1] Successfully, that is, to the point of achieving the agreement, which had its political value in Germany and abroad during the vital early years. The Vatican on the other hand possibly thought that the régime would not last and that the Concordat would be there when it had gone. So it turned out, but much happened in between.

Nobécourt speaks of its 'clarity and vigour' creating an irreparable gulf between the Church and Nazism. Pacelli, whom Pius XI admitted was its real author, shortly afterwards explained the Vatican's intentions: '. . . to repair the damage and put an end to the troubles which, in present-day Germany, arise from the fact that public authority and the party which sustains the state are tied to ideas and forces which openly or in fact intend to enslave the Church and destroy the Christian faith.'

The Encyclical certainly was not lost on the Nazis, but too few German Catholics were any longer in the frame of mind to profit by it, as Lewi seems to demonstrate. They were much less so once war had broken out and the war mood had taken possession. The force of patriotic fervour in wartime is something Lewi either cannot or will not grasp, but that it took some extravagant forms in Germany need not be disputed. On the first anniversary of the outbreak of war, a pastoral letter by the fire-eating pro-Nazi army bishop, Rarkowski, drew a candid comment in a Vatican broadcast: 'The German episcopate has so far avoided taking a position on this war that would transcend their pastoral duty towards the faithful. If the army bishop has read or heard what the Head of his Church has repeatedly and unequivocally said about the injustice done to Poland, he must be aware of the discrepancy between his position and that of the Holy See. Many Catholics do not at all share the political and historical viewpoint of the army bishop, but are convinced that Hitler's war unfortunately is not a just war and that God's blessing therefore cannot be upon it. . . . It almost looks as if the army bishop sometimes finds it easier to align himself with the Nazis than with his church.' Unfortunately the broadcast had no official status, and its only known effect was to draw a protest from the German Foreign Office.

Lewi's case against the German Church in the Jewish question is that with one or two heroic exceptions like Provost Lichtenberg no one spoke up for Jews unless they were converts. This was true of the Kristallnacht pogrom of 1938 already referred to. When the Final Solution was determined on in 1942, Bertram of Breslau protested in the name of the hierarchy, but only, it seems, against the projected compulsory divorce legislation which aimed to separate non-Aryans or part-Aryans from Aryan married partners. Von Preysing of Berlin urged vigorous action on his fellow bishops. To quote Lewi: 'The point of departure should be concern for the

Christian Jews, but beyond this one should speak clearly about the outrages inflicted upon the Jews generally. We do not know how many bishops acted upon Preysing's request.' What we do know, and what Lewi astonishingly does not mention either here or elsewhere in his book, is that Von Preysing also wrote to the Pope and was sent, on April 30, a very long letter which is perhaps the capital document so far known in this whole matter. (See appendix.)

This was a private letter: publicly, Pius's preoccupation with neutrality always made him stop short of names, but the broadcast of the preceding Christmas (1942) had so clearly alluded to Germany in the well-qualified judgement of Ambassador Von Bergen that he devoted an exceptionally long and thoughtful despatch to it. He warned the Reich that Pius's sympathy and understanding of Germany, born of his long acquaintance, was being strained to the limit. ('He is perhaps the only high personality in the Church who tries to understand the new Germany and to do it justice; but as head of the Church he cannot go beyond the limits imposed on him.') Allowance must of course be made here, as in reading the whole of Friedlander's book, for the diplomatic language and technique used by Von Bergen, a civilized man whose job must often have seemed to him very much like holding a tiger by the tail. Von Bergen said in the same despatch: 'Theoretically the Pope's (Christmas) pronouncements about religion have a general import and are directed in the first place against Bolshevism. Nevertheless, in an incomprehensible way the declarations that Stalin has meanwhile made on the subject of religious liberty in Russia, and which Roosevelt has received so joyfully and exploited for propaganda, have had here the effect of morphine. They contrast the permission given to the Polish Jesuits to establish themselves in Moscow with the exclusion of Catholic priests from the Ukraine and the removal of crucifixes in Bavaria. There is no doubt therefore that the Christmas messages are addressed equally to Germany, as an appeal and also perhaps as a warning.'[1]

Von Bergen had sent many bromides to Berlin since the Concordat, but the pressure of events was making him more candid. Later, when the government had further aggravated the situation

[1] Paul Dezza, S.J., writing in *Osservatore della Domenica* in June 1964, quoted Pius XII as saying in December, 1942: 'Yes, the Communist danger does exist, but at this time the Nazi danger is more serious. They want to destroy the Church and crush it like a toad.'

by deciding no longer to consider newly-occupied territories as subject to normal diplomatic exchanges, he told Ribbentrop: 'Pius XII is as little open to threats as we are. If a struggle is forced on the Church, he reckons with the possibility of many Catholics leaving the Church, but he is intimately convinced that the majority will remain loyal to their faith and that the clergy will be ready for the most extreme sacrifices. In spite of everything . . . he would like to avoid the struggle, if only to prevent a terrible conflict of conscience for millions of Catholics.' Hitler, it has been said, held the German Catholics as hostages, they held the Pope as a hostage. There is something in it.

The papal broadcast here under discussion followed closely on one of the high points of tension at the Vatican in regard to the Jewish question. There was never any real doubt of what Pius XII *thought* about anti-semitism. In his first Encyclical, though he did not mention it explicitly, he went out of his way to say that 'In the midst of the disruptive contrasts that divide the human family . . . the teaching and work of the Church can never be other than that which the Apostle Paul preached: "Here is no more Gentile and Jew, no more circumcised and uncircumcised; no one is barbarian or Scythian, no one is slave or free man; there is nothing but Christ in any of us." ' If the words primarily meant that entrance into the Church did away with such differences, they also meant that to set store by such differences was a mark of paganism, of the 'old man' which the converts must put off.

At Christmas 1941 Pius spoke of the comfort it had been to 'console, with the moral and spiritual assistance of Our representatives abroad and with Our own subsidies, a huge number of refugees, expatriates and emigrants, also among the "non-Aryans".' The use of the term, and in quotation marks, was a rebuke to those who had popularized its use. The previous September, we have seen, Bérard, the Vichy ambassador, had written to Pétain about the anti-Jewish statutes. Lewi says that he 'was able to report . . . after lengthy consultations with high Church officials, that *the Vatican* did not consider such laws in conflict with Catholic teaching.' What Bérard actually sent was three or four thousand words of somewhat garbled history and general philosophizing about the matter, prefaced with the words: 'I shall say nothing which I have not verified with the most authorized representatives of the Church's government.'

What we have here is an extreme example of that Roman habit of elastic use of the term 'Vatican' to suggest support for anything one wants to put over. It would not have been difficult for Bérard to fish about among Vatican personnel and find enough support for the mildly anti-semitic line diffusely developed in his letter, which was quite enough to satisfy the not very acute Pétain. This is to suppose that Bérard was prepared to go even to this trouble to justify his vague sentence. We can be certain that, if he had had the slightest hint of reason for suggesting the Pope's own complaisance, he would have done so. But the most consistent thing about Pius XII was that he was a complete stranger to the kind of narrow minded and chauvinist integralism which lesser ecclesiastics could often easily be induced to voice. If Pius failed to give tongue about the sufferings of the Jews, it was certainly not because he endorsed the diplomatic involutions of Bérard. The Vatican archives may, of course, hold the key to Bérard's letter, if there is one.

On July 30, 1942, Myron Taylor's assistant in Rome, H. C. Tittman, sent this telegram to the Department of State:

'In my recent reports to the Department, I have drawn attention to the fact that the absence of any public protest by the Holy See against the Nazi atrocities is endangering the moral prestige and undermining faith in the Church and in the person of the Holy Father himself. I have several times officially pointed out this danger to the Vatican; certain of my colleagues have done the same but without success. The answer is invariably that the Pope in his speeches has already condemned outrages on morality in wartime and that to be more specific could only worsen the situation.

'Yesterday the Brazilian Ambassador to the Holy See came to see me to ask if I was ready to join in a concerted démarche (not collective but rather simultaneous) to persuade the Pope to condemn publicly and in specific terms the Nazi atrocities in the German-occupied regions. M. Accioly told me that he had already received the necessary instructions from his government to take part in such a démarche and that he was trying to obtain the co-operation of the representatives of Great Britain, Poland, Jugoslavia, Belgium and of as many South American countries as possible. . . .

'Although I strongly doubt that the Pope can be persuaded to take the desired initiative I cannot see what harm such a démarche could do and I think it would serve to reinforce the individual appeals so far made.

'If the department thinks it desirable that I should take part, I shall be glad to receive instructions as soon as possible.'

Receiving the required instructions, Tittman sent a note to the Secretary of State Maglione on September 14. Drawing attention to the Nazi treatment of civil populations, which had been universally condemned by free peoples, he added, 'I am authorized by my Government to underline that a similar condemnation of these atrocities by the Holy Father could help to impose some restraint on the Nazi régime.'

The governments above mentioned together with Uruguay sent similar notes, and on September 26 Myron Taylor himself followed this up with some details supplied by the Jewish Agency in Geneva; he said he would be grateful to know if the Vatican had any information confirming these, and added, 'If so, I should like to know if the Holy Father has any suggestions for practical measures by which the forces of civilized public opinion can be used to prevent the continuation of these atrocities.'

It was an odd way of putting it. If Hitler had ever been amenable to the forces of civilized public opinion, he had surely stopped being by the autumn of 1942. He might have said with Macbeth:

'I am in blood
Stept in so far, that should I wade no more
Returning were as tedious as go o'er.'

However, Tittman informed his department on October 6 that the Pope was apparently giving serious attention to the question, though opinion was divided in the Vatican about the wisdom of the Brazilian move: 'The Holy See is apparently still convinced that an open denunciation by the Pope of the Nazi atrocities, at least as far as Poland was concerned, could have no more result but the violent death of a great many more people. Nevertheless, Monsignor Montini has told me that the moment may come when, in spite of so grave a prospect, the Holy Father will feel obliged to speak.'

The background to the reference to Poland was that, on August 24, Monsignor Paganuzzi, a military almoner of the Knights of Malta, had managed to get a note and documents from the Secretariat of State to Cardinal Sapieha, Archbishop of Cracow. Sapieha read the papers and tore them up saying: 'Thank the Pope. Nobody knows better than the Poles that he has our interests at heart. But if I were ever to publish this paper or if it were found on me, the heads of all the Poles would not suffice for the reprisals that Gauleiter

Frank would order. It would not be just a question of Jews. He would kill all of us. What would be the use of saying what all the world knows? It is natural that the Pope should be with us. But there is no need to make his condemnation public if it serves to aggravate our ills.'

Speaking of the Jews, the cardinal added, 'The saddest thing is that we have to leave these unhappy, isolated people without help. There are people dying who have not even the comfort of a word. We cannot, we must not speak if we are not to shorten their days. We live the drama of these wretched people, and none would wish to help them more than us, but it is an impossibility. It is all the same, Jews and Poles—they have taken everything from us, bread, liberty . . . there remains at least life and the hope of seeing the end of our Calvary.'

It is permissible to doubt Tittman's surmise (Friedlander, *op. cit.*, p. 120) that this weighed less with Pius than the fear of eventual reproaches by defeated Germans. The doubt is reinforced by the now well-known story first told by Lamberto Furno in the Italian weekly *Vita* for April 8, 1964. For a weekly audience in August 1942, either two days before or twelve days after Sapieha's remarks, to be given to a German group including soldiers, Pius prepared a speech 'very vigorous and written directly in German', denouncing the Nazi atrocities as requested. An hour before the audience he was still reading the text and reflecting. To a person who was very close to him he read it in a vibrant, emotional and indignant voice. He turned to concentrate for a final decision and then, without warning, let go of the papers, saying these exact words: 'I have the duty of simplifying things, not of complicating them.'

The very professional language in which this decision was subsequently conveyed to the diplomats concerned by the Secretariat of State (see Friedlander *op. cit.* pp. 120, 122) certainly disguised most effectively the anguish of soul which had produced it, but this is not perhaps remarkable. The following Christmas Pius said in his Christmas message that humanity ought to vow itself to the cause of 'the hundreds of thousands who, without the least fault of their own, sometimes merely because of their nationality or race, are condemned to die or slowly to decay'. We have seen what Von Bergen thought of this.

Maglione, meeting Sir D'Arcy Osborne, the British Minister, at a reception soon afterwards, said, 'You see that the Holy Father had taken notice of your Government's recommendation!' Pius too, it seems, expressed surprise that his remark had not been regarded as explicit enough: to Tittman, for instance, a few days after Christmas, he said that the passage obviously referred to the Poles and Jews, and that he could not have mentioned the Nazis without mentioning the Bolsheviks; he 'indicated by his attitude', Tittman added, that he thought the allied stories had an element of exaggeration for propaganda (Friedlander, p. 128). This 'indication' may well have expressed Tittman's irritation rather than the Pope's meaning. Nevertheless it would be interesting to know whom Pius had discussed the matter with between the agony of August and the diplomacy of December. Answering Von Preysing's letter the following April, he was clearly still perplexed and ready to leave the matter to the hardly less perplexed German bishops (see appendix).

To Eduardo Senatro, *Osservatore Romano* correspondent in Berlin, Pius made the oft-quoted remark, 'Do not forget, my dear friend, that there are millions of Catholics in the German army. Shall I plunge them into conflicts of conscience? *They have taken an oath: they owe obedience.*' The italicized words are quoted by Nobécourt, but not, oddly, by Lewi. If Pius indeed uttered them, it is hard to understand how he, an expert canon lawyer, could have done so if he really knew what was going on in Germany.

The following autumn the Nazis set about rounding up the Roman Jews, who numbered in round figures eight thousand. More than half of these were sheltered in religious houses, a few in the Vatican, more by Italian neighbours. About one thousand were taken off to Auschwitz. Earlier the Pope had supplied a loan from the Vatican treasury of fifteen kilograms of gold to make up the fifty the Jews were ordered to raise under pain of having eight hundred hostages taken. The rector of the German church in Rome, Bishop Hudal, wrote to the German commander saying that he had been told from the Vatican that arrests had begun and asking that they should stop: 'I fear that otherwise the Pope will have to make an open stand which will serve the anti-German propaganda as a weapon against us.' The arrests did not stop, though they were limited for the reasons just given.

These facts are set down here because they have not, so far as I am aware, been previously given consecutively in any English publication. If a settlement of this vexed question is possible at all it requires first a publication of Vatican documents. Friedlander, whose book consists mainly of documents from the Foreign Office of the Third Reich, is the first to admit that these need to be complemented by relevant Vatican documents. In the ordinary course of events these will not appear until the 2040s. In February 1965 it was announced in Roman papers that a Vatican White Book was shortly to be published dealing with the relations between the Holy See and the Third Reich between 1933 and the end of the war. Simultaneously, it was promised, the Bavarian Catholic Academy's historical section would publish the entire corpus of notes exchanged between the Secretariat of State and the Reich between 1933 and 1939.[1]

In the meantime the issue is not furthered by repeating what nobody denies (though Lewi rather minimizes it): the charity of the Holy See and of many Catholics of all ranks towards the Jews; nor by solemn and laborious articles proving that Pius XII did not invite the Berlin Philharmonic to give a concert in the Vatican during the war. (See *Civiltà Cattolica*, mid-April, 1965.)

For Lewi, the question is already judged; though his main concern is with the German Church, he ends by condemning Pius XII too, if not the whole Catholic conception (see Chapter 12). He sees the issue as one of moral integrity. Pius in his first Encyclical had said, 'We feel We owe no greater debt to Our time than to testify to the truth with apostolic firmness. . . . In the fulfilment of this Our duty We shall not let ourselves be influenced by earthly considerations nor be held back by mistrust or opposition, by rebuffs or lack of appreciation of Our words, nor yet by fear of misconceptions and misinterpretations.'

'These noble sentiments,' thinks Lewi, 'remained an empty formula in the face of the Jewish tragedy.' But none of the reasons Pius listed here can be seriously advanced as deciding him against speaking on the German atrocities. What decided him, mistakenly or not, was the belief that if he spoke more people would suffer, not less. Moral integrity has its claims. It is easy to understand those for whom these claims are paramount. The dilemma is a real one. But to confuse scruples about exposing other people's lives with 'reasons of state' hardly contributes to solving it. Cardinal Döpfner has said all that can so far be said, perhaps all that it will ever be

[1] The Rome Correspondent of *Le Monde* was, on February 13, 1947, sure that he was 'not revealing a secret' in saying that the Curia was preparing a White Book, and that 'surprises could be expected'.

possible to say: 'The retrospective judgement of history perfectly authorizes the opinion that Pius XII should have protested more firmly. There is nevertheless no justification for doubting the sincerity of his motives or the authenticity of his profound reasons.'

It is said that when an American general apologized to Pius XII for the clatter made by tanks in passing the Vatican, the Pope answered, 'Any time you liberate Rome you can make all the noise you want.' When Jewish refugees, returning from captivity, sought audience of him on November 29, 1945, he spoke to them first with a backward glance: 'Your presence, gentlemen, is an eloquent reflection of the psychological changes, the new directions that the war has brought to maturity. The gulfs of discord and hate, the folly of persecution, which were created among peoples and races by false and intolerant doctrines, opposed to a human and Christian spirit, have devoured many innocent victims, including non-combatants. The Apostolic See, faithful to the principles of natural right inscribed by God in every human heart, revealed on Sinai and perfected in the Sermon on the Mount, has never left in doubt at any moment however critical that it repudiated those ideas which history will list among the most deplorable and dishonourable travesties of human thought and feeling.'

There was a germ here of new thinking even for Catholics. Pius went on to look forward. Saying that he took this Jewish visit as an expression of gratitude for the way the Church's charity had transcended egoism and racial passion, he went on: 'Doubtless in a world only slowly and against many obstacles confronting world problems the Church, remembering her religious mission, must maintain a wise reserve about particular questions of political and territorial character. But this does not prevent her proclaiming the great principles of humanity and brotherhood which must underlie the solution of such questions.'

Here was a neat side-stepping of the Zionist question,[1] without diluting the benevolence of the first half of the speech. The same synthesis was due to prove less easy to maintain in the Vatican Council. Pius concluded, 'You have suffered the wounds of hatred, but in your trouble you have also felt the gentle benefits of love: a love not fed by earthly motives but by a belief in that heavenly

[1] A fortnight earlier the British-American joint committee had been set up to enquire into the condition of Jewish refugees in Europe and the future possibilities of Palestine. More than half the Jews of Europe had been destroyed in the war.

Father whose sun shines on all of whatever language or race, and whose grace is open to all who seek the Lord in spirit and in truth.'

Less than a year later, on August 3, 1946, delegates from the Supreme Council of Arab Palestine were at the Vatican: Pius showed his mettle as his own Secretary of State: Peace, he said, was impossible without truth, justice, respect for rights and for 'certain acquired positions and traditions. . . . Hence, having received recently complaints and appeals from different parts of the world, inspired by different motives, it is superfluous for Us to tell you that We condemn all recourse to force and violence from whatever quarter, as We have already condemned repeatedly in the past the persecutions which a fanatical anti-semitism launched against the Jewish people. But it is clear that this impartiality which We impose on Our Apostolic Minister . . . cannot mean indifference.'

The Israeli state was proclaimed, after fierce fighting, on May 14, 1948. In October of the same year, and again at Christmas, Pius proposed the internationalization of Jerusalem.

But it was away from politics and from the cautious channels of diplomacy and official language that new currents of feeling now flowed. The spirit of Cardinal Döpfner's sermon, of lessons to be learned from the errors of the past, animated the new Germany. There had been Catholics and Jews who had suffered together. Some at least saw the need for rooting out the remains of ancient prejudice, for going beyond the neat, cold generalities of Canon Law treatises in dealing with a people who had been treated with a monstrous inhumanity unparalleled in history. What was felt in Central Europe was felt in America, where nearly half of the world's remaining 11,000,000 Jews lived and followed zealously the interests of their European and later Israeli brethren.

During the war Catholic Hungary had proposed an anti-semite law into which religious arguments were allowed to intrude: the ancient charge of 'deicide' was linked with the modern conspiracy charges. Cardinal Seredi, the Primate, rose in the senate and nobly protested: 'Should your hearts, seized by race-hatred, drive you to vote for this law, hear my words—words which the Lord Himself suggests to me at this fateful moment. In truth I say to you: all the tears, all the victims, all the massacred martyrs will accuse you when your time comes to give an account before the Lord of your infamous act of this day. Remember the warning of Bernard of Clairvaux: "Do not touch the Jews for they are the apple of God's eye." In the name of Almighty God I shall vote against this infamous law.'

The rejection of the deicide charge and the collective curse was one of the Ten Points drawn up at the Seelisberg Conference in 1947. This was organized by the French Jewish scholar Jules Isaac, who had studied anti-Jewish elements in Catholic tradition. (See *Commentary*, January 1965, p. 20.) He had audience with Pius XII in 1949 and asked for phrases offensive to Jews to be removed from Catholic prayers. Pius agreed to order new and less offensive translations but would not alter the originals.

A number of currents combined to create in the years before the Vatican Council a growing movement for destroying what remained of anti-semitism in the Catholic tradition. In 1961 Cardinal Liénart of Lille said in his Lenten pastoral: 'It is not true that the Jewish people bear the first and only responsibility for the death of Jesus. The deepest cause of His death upon the cross is the sins of men. We are all responsible; the Jews were only our delegates. Nor is it true that the Jews are deicides . . . nor that Israel, the chosen people of the Old Testament, has become an accursed people in the New. Indeed, the religious destiny of Israel is a mystery of grace, and we Christians ought to ponder it with respectful sympathy.'

Cardinal Liénart is a biblical scholar, and his words focus attention on another powerful impulse in the new attitude to Judaism: the advances in biblical studies with their effect on theological thinking. For centuries the Church had taught that the Old Testament was a preparation for the Gospel, full of 'types' of Christianity. Her liturgy was full of the literature of Judaism. She recognized that Christ was of the House of David, that St Peter and the apostles were Jews. Yet all this was taken as consistent with discriminating against Jews in the Christian era. It could only be so on the assumption that they shared the guilt of their ancestors (or that official minority of their ancestors) who had rejected and crucified Christ; that they shared also the blindness and hardness of heart which had caused this crime and been confirmed by it.

A profounder understanding of 'salvation history' made theologians more impatient of these inconsistencies, and reinforced impatience with a past which had nourished the inconsistencies and so compromised Catholicity with anti-semitism.

Monsignor (now Cardinal) Journet of Fribourg wrote in 1956: 'We call Jesus the Lamb of God who takes away the sins of the world: that is, of the entire world and not merely of the Jews. To say then that He came to take away sin is to assign the *causa finalis* of His death on the cross; hence it is impossible to place the primary responsibility for it except on sin which is common to all men. The part in this universal responsibility proper to the crowd at Jerusalem was in the main that of ministerial causes. . . . But it is another thing to turn into a slogan the mystery of sin at work in the condemnation and crucifixion of Jesus, to speak of the 'deicide' Jews as the greed of princes or the ambition of the mighty or the passion of the mob have done in the past, so that they might put the Jews outside the law. This a Christian can remember only with sorrow, indignation and tears.' This should be compared with the self-defence of M. Xavier Vallat (p. 250).

John XXIII was of all men the most natural to incarnate this new spirit. A diplomat for most of his working life, he was yet as far from the calculations of professional diplomacy as it was possible to be. The natural kindliness, neighbourliness, aversion from fanaticism of the Italian was with him supernaturalized. Similarly, his Secretariat for Christian Unity offered a natural conciliar vehicle for revising a bad tradition here. A former member of Pius XII's German entourage, Augustin Bea had every personal and national reason for taking the lead in what was increasingly seen as not a mere corollary of ecumenism but a basic element in it. His secretariat was set up on March 25, 1960. On the following June 13 Jules Isaac submitted a dossier to the Pope; out of these events was born the plan for a Council declaration. A first draft was drawn up in 1961, and the ranks of opposition within and without the Church were drawn up not long afterwards.

An appalling incident at the beginning of the Council threw a lurid light on the reality of the problem. A substantial book, expensively produced in great numbers, was distributed to all the fathers of the Council. Under the title *Complotto contra la Chiesa* (Conspiracy against the Church) it interpreted the Council and the movements of reform within the Church in terms of the worst kind of anti-semitism—as a Jewish plot to overthrow Christianity. It was even known where this vicious rubbish was printed, but no light was ever thrown on its authorship, though speculation was plentiful and some of it very plausible. The enterprise was typical of the stupidity which seems inseparable from integralist fanaticism. It made an excellent contribution to the defeat of its own purpose. It underestimated absurdly the intelligence and good sense of the bishops, who, if they could read Italian, needed only to glance at it to see the spirit that inspired it. Many of them remembered it when the Council turned its attention to the Jewish question, and saw the point of the proposed declaration *De Judaeis*.

This happened at the beginning of November 1963, after the death of Pope John, but Cardinal Bea then and subsequently made the point that the declaration had been Pope John's own wish, communicated to him personally. The document stressed the connection between the Catholic Church and the Jews, the chosen people of the Old Testament. The culminating point of the divine plan of salvation was the coming of Jesus Christ, son of David, of the seed of Abraham. The responsibility for Christ's death lay on the whole of humanity. The personal guilt of the Jewish leaders who brought about His crucifixion cannot be charged to the whole Jewish people either of His time or of today. It was therefore unjust to call the Jews deicides or to consider them as cursed by God. There was no biblical basis for hatred or persecution of the Jews. It was unjustifiable to disdain, hate or persecute them. Catechists and preachers should do everything in their power to promote respect and understanding for the Jews.

Introducing it in the Council, Bea began by saying that, though it had begun life two years earlier, 'Unhappy political conditions' had held it up, though it was entirely religious in purpose. The Secretariat had earlier stated more explicitly: 'It cannot be called pro-Zionist or anti-Zionist, since it considers these political questions entirely outside its scope.'

Bea anticipated some of the objections, such as that the decree called in question the events narrated in the Gospels. It was all the more necessary now, he said, to imitate the charity of Christ and His apostles in view of the appalling sufferings caused by anti-semitism over the past generation.

Jewish reaction was voiced by Dr Nathan Goldmann, President of the World Jewish Congress: 'Such a declaration would be a historical event of supreme and fundamental significance for the whole Christian world. It would be a step of vital importance towards the removal of age-old misunderstandings, wrong thinking and hostility which have set peoples and faiths in conflict against one another and have caused the Jewish people two thousand years of suffering, persecution and at last appalling tragedy. The heart of world Jewry will therefore be uplifted and refreshed by this new hope of an era of understanding, tolerance and harmony so profoundly needed for the peace and welfare of mankind.' (See *The Tablet*, November 16, 1963, p. 1245.)

This generous welcome was not echoed in some quarters in Rome. In spite of Cardinal Bea's eloquent advocacy the document did not get off to a propitious start in 1963. At that time the whole ecumenical *schema* was still being met, to put it kindly, with the suspicion customarily accorded to novelties in Rome. But it was clear the chapter on the Jews was meeting a special kind of opposition—the kind that was likely to create difficulties for the Secretariat of State. This threw into relief the whole question of the relation of the non-curial Secretariat to the Curia in general and to the chief, or foreign office in particular. It was not merely that the Arab States, among whom lived Catholic minorities, were likely to resent the Declaration, but also that the governments who had profitable relations with the Arab world were likely to resent these being upset. Here was an issue that journalists could get their teeth into: a short document, no metaphysics, deceptively simple issues and a strong spice of politics flavouring the theology whatever the intentions of the theologians. Here was trouble developing in a way likely to escape the control of the Secretariat of State's careful and unobtrusive way of handling things. They could have had no better incentive for resenting the 'amateurism' of Cardinal Bea and his team. Yet when it came to tinkering with the document in the interests of diplomacy, the boot was on the other foot, as the Archbishop of Westminster was to point out bluntly in the Third Session (speech of September 29, 1964).

The document was merely given an airing at the end of the Second Session; its advocates hoped to have it accepted by vote, along with the Declaration on Religious Liberty, as a basis for discussion. But their opponents were simply too clever for them. Cardinal Bea accepted this with a good deal more Christian resignation than most other people. Only his fellow curial cardinals showed more.

In the interval between Sessions Two and Three the world was treated to the odd spectacle of Coptic Christians and Nasser mouthpieces exclaiming in chorus against the idea that the Jews were not deicides. This and a good deal more pressure had its effect—nobody quite discovered how. The Pope diverted much attention from the crisis (one which as an ex-Under-Secretary of State he was likely to appreciate) by visiting the Holy Land, Arab and Israeli, and meeting His Beatitude of Constantinople.

When the declaration reappeared it was clear that Nasser and the Copts and the rest had been mollified; the Jews of the world, of whom there were far fewer, had not. Islam was now included in the document, and there was no explicit reference to deicide. The revised version was clearly the work of men who had more important things to worry about than the Ecumenical Council.

Mere habit caused public opinion to consider this as just another conservative-progressive issue. It was obviously not, as the debate showed: a much greater weight of middle opinion was behind this document. Cardinal Lercaro might insist, and rightly, on its primarily religious and spiritual character, but many were anxious to support it for other reasons, quite unconnected with Middle East politics. The Americans were the most eager to exorcize the ghost of anti-semitism once for all: practically every leading American churchman had publicly committed himself to the Declaration. The Germans were no less anxious. In the debate of September 28–9, favourable speeches swamped opposition. Only the Syrian curial Cardinal Tappouni (speaking for the other orientals) and the indestructible Ruffini put up resistance. Moreover the supporting speeches generally called roundly for a restoration of the original text. Thirty-four bishops from every part of the world spoke in this debate. Practically the only criticisms made of the text were that it did not go far enough, and that it had been mishandled in the interval since its first appearance. To the historically-minded this was a moving spectacle: a world-wide Catholic repudiation of a vague tradition, never active except among a minority but tingeing the minds of the many. It was an *aggiornamento*, but it was also a return to life-giving sources. With a vision born of suffering, it went back behind the rectitude of Innocent III and the magnanimity of Gregory the Great to the apostolic age in which men saw as of habit and felt in their bones the whole design of God.

The day after the debate had ended and the text had been sent back with seventy-odd amendments for consideration, the Premier of Syria criticized the Declaration, and even the raising of the matter, which could not, he said, be a purely religious question. The President of Lebanon organized a telegraphic round-robin among local bishops, professing to see Zionist politics in the Declaration. There was a great deal more lobbying at the Vatican, which led to a further slightly desperate attempt to divert the chapter along with its fellow on religious liberty; it was at this moment only that the Jewish question became, obliquely, the subject of a trial of strength between the conservative caucus and the leading reformist cardinals. Obliquely, because it was no longer the text but principle and procedure that were involved. Even so, it was the sprightly Bea's personal swift action which decided the issue, contrary to what most reports said.

The document which at last appeared as a result of the debate was the best version of the three, and also extended the hand of friendship to all non-Christian religious. Nothing but delaying tactics could hold it up further. They did not. On November 20, 1964, the Council voted the document by a majority of 1,893 to 99. It remains only to be promulgated in autumn 1965.[1]

To John XXIII, it is a monument more lasting than bronze. But not the only one.

[1] It is sad to record that this was not finally achieved without further obstinate resistance by a tiny but tenacious minority, most of whom lacked even the excuse of living in Arab regions, but whose objections derived rather from a narrow and excessively scholastic approach to the Bible and to theology (cf. Chapter 13). Their efforts to obtain substantial changes in a document already overwhelmingly approved by the general congregation of the Council (efforts it is hard to think of as anything but insolent) were firmly resisted by the drafting commission, though minor changes of expression were made which many continued to regret. But the record of this obstinacy, preserved in the textual history of the document, may perhaps chiefly throw into relief the generous spirit which moved the Council as a whole.

12

Separated Brethren and Religious Liberty

CATHOLIC-JEWISH RELATIONS were not alone in receiving a profound shake-up during the travail of war. Catholic-Protestant relations underwent it too. But this was rather the acceleration of a movement already afoot.

For a variety of reasons, ranging from Christian zeal and charity through good sense to mere politicizing, it had become clear to many by the end of the seventeenth century that religion as a source of division and war was a poor substitute for religion as a principle of unity. Not all concluded that the solution was to do without religion. Grotius (cf. Chapter 6, pp. 125 *et seq.*) whose religion was of the kind generally called 'undogmatic but profound', was hardly more interested in international law than he was in the restoration of Christian unity. It was his biggest disappointment that his efforts in this field, begun in 1614 and continued down to his death in 1645 were so misunderstood, and he prayed for unity in his will. He hoped to induce James I to take the lead, and to this end corresponded with James's Swiss-French court theologian, Isaac Casaubon but, as Casaubon knew better than any, the atmosphere of James's court was anything but ecumenical. Casaubon's previous career in France, incidentally, throws an interesting light on the aspect of the sixteenth-century religious scene which receives least prominence in political histories: he was much courted by both Catholics and reformers as a scholar, and no less suspect to both sides as a waverer.

The Peace of Westphalia set a seal of sorts on the religious divisions of Europe, but what might be called the immaterial rather than the spiritual unity of Europe was not destroyed: the new learning often threw a bridge across political frontiers; so did the arts.

The necessity for such a bridge, and the kind of bridge needed, varied. In England the Reformation was politically an outright success, at least over Rome. In France it was, in the same terms, a failure. In Germany it was more like a drawn battle.

There was nothing ecumenical about the 'Elizabethan compromise' of academic convention. It is true that the Anglican Church had no Messiah comparable with the great continental or Scottish ones, but only a series of cunning impresarios and a vernacular reformer of genius. True also that writings like those of Hooker reveal the continuity of learning. The Anglican Church was structurally political rather than theological from the outset, but for that very reason it was for long extremely intolerant of theological deviations—a maker of martyrs. The Civil War was, in part at least, fought to vindicate the right to deviate for anybody except papists. This was the most Erastian[1] of all Churches, established on an increasingly tight little island by a political unity of which it became itself the cement.

By contrast Germany was a political patchwork of over three hundred states. There was local Erastianism, consecrated to some extent by the Peace of Augsburg: *cujus regio ejus religio* was toleration for the princes by the Emperor rather than for the people by the princes. But though it took two generations and the horrors of the Thirty Years' War to ratify the principle at the level of high politics, it did mean that virtually from the beginning Catholics and Lutherans at least lived side by side, in whatever degree of peace, speaking the same language and living by the same broad culture. Catholic priests did not have to go to foreign colleges to be trained. By the time the unified German Protestant state was formed, this state of affairs was more than two hundred years old.

The Reformation and Counter-Reformation faithfully resurrected an ancient tradition of sectarian rudeness. Christopher Dawson quotes a rubric which used to appear in the Greek liturgy: 'On this day the thrice accursed Armenians begin their blasphemous fast which they call *artziburion*, but we eat cheese and eggs in order to refute their heresy.' (*Judgement of the Nations*, p. 118). It is hard to decide whether this illustrates Dawson's generalization that 'behind every heresy lies some kind of social conflict', or Manning's that 'all conflicts are at bottom theological', or no

[1] Thomas Lüber or Erastus gave his name to the doctrine which claimed for the State entire coercive power in ecclesiastical matters. He was born in Baden in 1524.

generalization at all, but it is easily paralleled from post-Reformation history. In this atmosphere Grotius's was perhaps a voice crying in the wilderness. The typical intellectual reaction to the wastefulness of religious war and the tedium of religious pamphleteering was the fashion for Deism, the 'religion of all sensible men', which has had a history less organized but more tenacious than that of any Church except the Roman.

Among those who remained faithful to institutional Christianity, the situation in Germany, product of the 'drawn battle', was especially interesting.[1] To take a few vivid illustrations of the 'draw': Of the cathedral of the Saxon town of Bautzen, dedicated to St Peter, two-thirds have since the middle of the sixteenth century been devoted to Lutheran worship, the rest—the chancel—to the Mass. The division is by a grill. '*O Salutaris*' from one side, '*Ein feste burg*' from the other, and the sanctuary lamp glimmering through; an odd expression of *cujus regio ejus religio*. Martin Giebner, the distinguished convert parson, was baptized and sang as a choir-boy on one side, and half a century later said his first Mass on the other. The *Simultankirche* (used for both services) has long been a familiar thing, a famous example being the chapel of Neumann's rococo masterpiece, the former palace of the Prince-Bishops of Speyer at Bruchsal. Thus there was no difficulty (in contrast to most similar occasions in England) when the Catholics of Lindau had their church burned down in 1930, about their returning to share the next-door pre-Reformation church with the Lutherans.

The situation bred many anomalies. In Saxony and Bavaria a Catholic king was *summus episcopus* of a Lutheran State Church. When Napoleon suppressed the twelfth-century Cistercian abbey of Salem he handed over the buildings and estates to the Protestant Margrave of Baden, a Zahringer, most of whose subjects in that district at least are Catholics. The church became a parish of the diocese of Freiburg, whose bishop long afterwards vetoed a proposal by the Protestant prince Max (a most zealous guardian of the building) to restore a cell of Cistercians there. The prince did eventually bring the Cistercians back to the shores of Lake Constance, and to his estates, at the little pilgrimage church of Neu-Birnau, and he is said to have walked in the procession at the re-opening in the late twenties.

[1] I owe much in the succeeding paragraphs to conversations with Monsignor Höfer and Father Cuthbert Smith.

With much of this Pius XII must have been familiar from his long sojourn in Germany.

To go back a little, the advance of Prussia, especially in the western German lands after 1815, caused something of a Catholic retreat. Catholics tended to retire from public life and develop a sense of inferiority—something which was later to affect the Zentrum, whose parliamentary strength was always out of all proportion to its intellectual and cultural impact. This weakness was, as we have seen, disastrous at the time of the advent of National Socialism. The Zentrum was not originally a specifically Catholic party but a party of toleration: it tended towards anti-Protestantism and anti-imperialism through its accretions of Poles, Alsatians and others. Yet these and subsequent migrations within the German-speaking territories had in the long run an important effect in breaking down further the principle of *cujus regio ejus religio*.

It remains true that down to the First World War relations between Protestants and Catholics worsened rather than improved with the growth of the Reich. 1914–18, it appears, brought a sharp change: war conditions, especially in the services, brought sometimes startling habits of co-operation. Afterwards, a factor which had long distinguished the German situation began to weigh more heavily: the presence side by side in such universities as Tübingen of Catholic and Protestant theological faculties. (It is hardly necessary to dwell on the contrast with the situation at Oxford and Cambridge.) It was in the late twenties that Dr Simon, the professor of theology in the Catholic faculty, who was also Rector of the University of Tübingen, began private conversations with his Lutheran opposite numbers. It was thus that an ecumenical dialogue began in Germany between Protestants and Catholics.

The Tübingen conversations were soon imitated—for example at Bielefeld by Alfred Bozi, a rich, highly cultured Protestant industrialist and magistrate. At Meitingen the priest Max Joseph Metzger, who was beheaded by the Nazis in 1944, founded the *Una Sancta* movement whose remarkable work in many parts of Germany is now over a generation old, and whose co-operative Protestant-Catholic review, once forbidden by the Holy Office, is now permitted. Metzger was convinced that dogmatic differences were far less important in keeping Catholics and Protestants apart than the spiritual attitude on both sides, and in the autumn of 1939 he wrote a letter to the newly-elected Pius XII to that effect. It is not known whether the letter was actually received by the Pope.

What tended to make Germany the home of ecumenism *par excellence* was the fact of a unified Lutheran tradition largely predominant, and having a solid doctrinal tradition. Dialogue was much easier between Catholics and such a Church. It existed elsewhere, but often under less realistic conditions. Of all this Pius XII must have been well aware, though his background and training were hardly such as to dispose him to keep ecumenical problems at the forefront of his interests. On the other hand, no pope ever took more seriously his office as common father of all men nor, as we have seen, could he have been more interested in world social problems, of which religious disunity was undoubtedly one. His very success in Germany, the impact he had on German life, had its oblique ecumenical value. He made people more aware of the Church and represented it himself in a remarkably effective way. His emphasis was always on the essential links of Germany, through her Catholic history, with Rome and the Mediterranean world. St Boniface was the central figure of many of his addresses, and St Boniface above all represented Rome. In his first Encyclical he wrote: 'The denial of the fundamentals of morality had its origin in Europe in the abandonment of that Christian teaching of which the Chair of Peter is the depositary and exponent. That teaching had once given spiritual cohesion to Europe. But cut off from the infallible teaching of the Church, not a few separated brethren have gone so far as to overthrow the central dogma of Christianity, the divinity of the Saviour.' Yet earlier, in his first broadcast on March 3, he had said, '. . . We think too of those outside the fold of the Church who, We are sure, will willingly believe that in this solemn hour Our prayers call down God's help on them too;' and he used the phrase *omen pacis*, clearly intending it in a sense far beyond the merely political.

Pius did not revert to these themes until after the war. In the meantime, in his beloved Germany, the Nazis began to forge bonds of common suffering between priests, Lutheran pastors and others in the concentration camps. The effect of this has been often described—an effect which was widened and deepened by the post-war soul-searching. For instance many ex-army officers, seeking a stabilizing force in the general collapse, looked to Christianity in a general way; but as prosperity revived and a materialist outlook with it, the need for Christian union was more strongly felt.

In 1945 the Braunshardter Conferences were inaugurated. Bishop Staelien of Oldenburg and Dr Simon, by this time Provost of Paderborn, under the patronage of Archbishop Jaeger of Paderborn (now a cardinal and leading member of the Secretariat for Christian Unity) invited a dozen Lutheran theologians to meet a dozen Catholic ones to discuss questions of theological terminology. The chairman of the Lutheran party was Dr Schlink, of the Catholic party Dr Simon, later succeeded by Dr Höfer. From 1948 onwards these meetings, lasting four or five days, took place at least once a year and often twice, alternately under Catholic and Lutheran auspices and with the full approval of the Holy Office and of the German Evangelical Synod. They were and are thoroughly scholarly and scientific in character.

A different kind of Catholic ecumenism developed in France under the inspiration of the Abbé Paul Couturier, whose emphasis was on common prayer for unity, while in 1945 Father Charles Boyer founded the *Unitas* association in Rome, whose review of the same name was also published in an American edition by the Graymoor friars. The capital contrast between Germany and other countries remained that between a movement widely taken for granted and one regarded with varying degrees of suspicion and having some of the psychological disabilities of a persecuted minority. This was notably so in England. The Malines conversations, between an unrepresentative minority of the English establishment and continental theologians under Cardinal Mercier's leadership, were viewed by the English Catholic hierarchy with an intense hostility and suspicion undiluted by any sense of English Catholic responsibility in this field. The English attitude to continental ecumenical zeal in the first half of the present century has been summed up by Archbishop Mathew: 'It is difficult to imagine that an Abbé Portal or any other enterprising Frenchman will ever be able to explain the English to one another.'

This expressed the attitude of the majority of Anglicans no less than that of Catholics. The notable advance of Catholicism in England during the nineteenth century had been mainly due to the access of reinforcements (Irish and converts) likely to increase rather than diminish the traditional coolness of relations with the Establishment. Newman rightly holds a great place in the esteem of ecumenists; yet Newman, preoccupied with the dangers of Liberalism, spoke of the Church he had left as a department of state, a collection of officials depending on the civil power, which could not be used to combat the spirit of the age except as a drag on a wheel. In *The Present Position of Catholics in England* he explained why he did not share the current expectation of the conversion of England, of which Wiseman had been the most exuberant exponent. The main obstacle was to be found not in Protestant arguments but in Protestant tradition, which dominated all but Tractarian and rationalist minorities and was 'the intellectual and moral language of the body politic'. What was catholic in Tractarianism directed a historical appeal, not to the living Church, but to the primitive centuries. Anglo-Catholicism later was, as Ronald Knox shows in *A Spiritual Aeneid*, to have an essential spice of naughtiness about it—'flirting with Rome'. Thus he wrote in 1917. Re-introducing the book thirty-three years later, in Pius XII's Holy Year, he was to write: 'The plain fact is that, while England led the world, and the Church of England was effectively the expression of its national life, there was a monumental quality about the partnership which, do what you would, laid hold of the imagination. Now that the hegemony is in dispute between two other world Powers, one wholly irreligious and the other, seen at its best, a babel of Christianities, the case is altered. Anglicanism, through no fault of its own, has become sectarian.'

If Knox had lived longer he might well have come to see that it was just this development that provided an impulse to ecumenism. If 'sectarian' means 'not forming the intellectual and moral language of the body politic', then Catholicism too has become sectarian in the vast majority of places, whatever outward forms may suggest to the contrary. Failure to grasp this is one aspect of 'triumphalism'. The problems it raises, in Italy for example, have been hinted at earlier.

It has also been suggested that the late forties in Rome were not, in any field, a period of what the Italians call *aperturismo*. Many things combined to reinforce the sense of siege. The conservative-minded saw the Church, scarcely delivered from the totalitarianism of the Right, in danger of succumbing to the power, naked in some places, insidious in others, of the Left. The Left increasingly became, in the minds of many unimaginative administrators, the sum total of things that threatened the integrity of the Church. So had the spiritual heirs of de Maistre a century earlier lumped all they disliked under the label of 'the Revolution'. It is difficult to avoid the impression that ecumenism, with its new impetus derived from the war, was regarded widely as such a threat.

Pius XII, whose own conservatism was offset by a much wider outlook and intellectual curiosity than that of his Curia, as a whole, was under heavy pressure during those years. Yet he was never in danger of losing sight of the world beyond the Leonine wall and the covers of the Codex. If he saw the civilized world as 'locked in a titanic struggle' with Communism, he drew the conclusion that a counterforce of love was needed to 'unite in a league as wide as the world itself all those between whom high ideals, nobility of sentiments, shared suffering have forged links much stronger and closer than the differences which divide them.' Seeing 'insincerity' as the major evil of the time, he addressed his appeal against it not only to Catholics but 'to all of those who share with us faith in Christ and in a transcendent God.'

On June 5, 1948, the Holy Office issued the following *monitum:* 'Since it appears that in some places, contrary to Canon Law and without permission of the Holy See, joint meetings of Catholics and non-Catholics have been held to discuss matters of faith, all are reminded that canon 1325 section 3 forbids these meetings, without permission, to laity, clerics and religious. Much less is it lawful for Catholics to summon or establish such conferences. Bishops should strictly enforce such prescriptions, especially in regard to conferences called ecumenical. And since joint acts of worship have taken place both at such meetings and at other times, we repeat the warning that all *communicatio in sacris* is forbidden altogether by canons 1258 and 731 section 2.'

A *monitum* of course does no more than draw attention to the state of the law, which was consistent with fruitful ecumenical activity e.g. in the Braunshardter Conferences. Yet people unacquainted with the nuances of Roman procedure might have been tempted half a year later to contrast the tone of this *locus classicus* with a passage from Pius XII's Christmas message, in which he enunciated the programme for the Holy Year of 1950: the Great Return.

The fourth of the various classes who were to make this great return were the dissident Christians, the 'many, believing in Jesus Christ, separated from Us for various reasons. With unspeakable groans the Spirit, which is in the hearts of all good men, lifts today with an imploring cry the prayer of Our Lord "*Ut Unum Sint*".

Rightly anxious at the boldness of the united front of militant atheism, men ask today more loudly the question they have long asked: Why still schisms, still separation? When will there be harmonious union of all the forces of the spirit and of love?

'If at other times the invitation to unity has gone out from this Apostolic See, this time We repeat it more warmly and paternally, feeling compelled by the petitions of so many believers scattered through the world, who after such sufferings turn their eyes to this See as to the anchor of salvation for the whole world. For all those who adore Christ (not excluding those who in sincere though vain expectation adore Him as promised by the prophets but not yet come) we open the Holy Door and at the same time the hands and heart of that fatherhood which the Redeemer has committed to Us.'

It was not perhaps completely unintelligible if the anxious, the spiritually hungry and war-scarred wondered what exactly was the relation between the chief Roman Congregation and its Prefect. That the Pope eventually became conscious of the anomaly seems clear from the very much longer Instruction on the Ecumenical Movement which appeared from the Holy Office on December 20, 1949. This time it paid the movement at least the compliment of devoting to it a great deal more space and a rather more sympathetic preamble; it began in fact by echoing Pius's testimony to the prevailing hunger for unity; it was glad to see grace stirring many dissidents to 'come back to unity'. But attempts, individual or collective, to reconcile them are not always based on sound principles or lacking in danger. Hence,

1. Bishops should (since reunion is primarily the Church's business) bend their energies to (a) helping people to return to the Church and (b) protecting the faithful from the dangers of the ecumenical movement. They should appoint qualified invigilators especially over ecumenical literature both Catholic and non-Catholic, where this is to be published, sold or read by Catholics.

2. Bishops should lay down the law. They should be mistrustful of the 'irenic', of the habit of saying that 'more unites us than divides us', especially among the ill-instructed. They should discourage ways of talking which raise false hopes, such as saying that encyclicals expounding the Mystical Body, the nature of the Church and the necessity of 'return' to it are not *de fide*; or that the Church has not in dogmatic matters the fulness of Christ but can be perfected

from without. They should firmly insist and ensure that historians should not exaggerate Catholic faults and conceal Protestant ones, nor emphasize the accidental in Protestantism in such a way that the essential, defection from the Catholic faith, is hardly seen or felt. Catholic doctrine is to be propounded whole and entire, without ambiguity: whether on justification, on the constitution of the Church, on the Primacy or on the fact that the only reunion is return. Outsiders should be taught that the good they have will not be lost but perfected in the Church, but should not be left with the impression that their return will bring anything substantial to the Church.

3. Mixed meetings and conferences are to be treated with extreme caution and vigilance. Their only virtue is to spread among non-Catholics knowledge of Catholic doctrine hitherto lacking: to Catholics they bring only danger of indifferentism. Only 'very suitable' priests are to be assigned to such conferences. (What made them very suitable was, fortunately perhaps, not further specified.) The faithful should not attend them without special permission, and only select types should be allowed. Where profitable results are not to be hoped for, the faithful should be kept away and associations dissolved or quietly snuffed out. Because experience shows that larger meetings of the kind produce little profit and more danger, they should only be allowed after the most searching enquiries. To discussions between Catholic and non-Catholic theologians only those priests should be sent who have proved themselves suitable both by learning and by firm adherence to the principles and norms laid down in the matter by the Church.

4. All such meetings are subject to the directions of the *monitum* of June 5, 1948, of which all are reminded. Group catechetical instructions are not forbidden, even those in which non-Catholics take occasion to explain their teachings in order to find out clearly how they agree or disagree with Catholic teaching. Nor does the *monitum* apply to meetings not concerned with faith or morals but only with general principles of natural law, Christian social order, etc., but even here Catholics must not approve or concede anything not agreeing with divine revelation or with the Church's teaching even her teaching on social matters. For local meetings bishops are granted henceforword a three-year delegation to give the necessary papal permission, on three conditions: (a) that there shall be absolutely no *communicatio in sacris*. (b) that the negotiations are

supervised and directed; (c) that annual reports to be sent to the Holy Office of where such meetings have been held and what experience they have yielded. The same concession applies to theologians' conferences, but here the Holy Office requires reports of the agenda, the speakers and those present. For interdiocesan, national or international conferences special permission direct from the Holy See is still required even before arrangements can be initiated.

5. The *Our Father* or other opening or closing prayer approved by the Church is allowed.

6. Episcopal conferences should see to more effective supervision and a uniform policy.

7. Religious superiors should see their subjects conform to the papal and episcopal line.

All this understood, the instruction concludes, we should press ahead and keep before the faithful the noble work of reunion.

Interesting discussions of this document must have taken place, for example at subsequent Braunshardter Conferences. The detached observer, reading it nowadays, might be tempted to contrast it too exclusively with the recent decree of the Second Vatican Council on Ecumenism, not least in its conception of what ecumenism is. This would be to read history backwards. The Instruction must be seen as a document of its time, though of course it rests on certain timeless principles. Equally, in accordance with the scope of the present work, the time must be judged by the document.[1]

The Instruction has been described (in 1960) with perhaps some holy disingenuousness, as 'the official charter, so far, of Catholic ecumenism', and as bringing encouragement to Catholic ecumenists (G. H. Tavard, *Two Centuries of Ecumenism*, pp. 230 & 231). Certainly it represents an advance on anything that had gone before in the matter of concrete concessions. Some recognition of the fact that Catholic-Protestant relations are the complex resultant of historical forces in each country is discernible in the fact that bishops are given some rein in dealing with these relations. More notably still, from the vantage-point of the Second Vatican Council debates, some initiative is urged on episcopal conferences, though partially negative. There is also recognition that the simultaneous

[1] It should be added that an *Instructio* is a departmental document not strictly requiring papal approval.

recitation of the Lord's Prayer is not fraught with perils unspeakable, as had previously been widely thought.

The rest is probably best explained by reflecting that disciplinary pronouncements are aimed at checking abuses, and hence tend to sound conscious exclusively of them. (The *monitum* was in fact aimed to anticipate the Amsterdam assembly of the World Council of Churches, which had been firmly put at arm's length by Pius XI in his *Mortalium Animos* of 1928.) Catholic ecumenism has at times been ill-served by the extravagances on its fringe, though conservative Catholics are sometimes more aware of these than of the clarity and firmness which leading ecumenists show. (Cf. e.g. Gustav Weigel, S.J., *The Ecumenical Movement: a Catholic Approach*, esp. Chapter 3.)

What emerges in the Council's decree on ecumenism is the understanding of it as a purpose, a state of mind governing without compromising religious thinking and practice. The difference between the decree of 1964 and the Instructions of 1949, especially the difference of tone, is simply the measure of the achievement of Pope John and the Council.

Before turning to that we should consider two other brief references of Pius XII to Protestantism. Speaking to the second great International Congress of the Lay Apostolate in 1957 (cf. Chapter 8), he referred to Latin America, and spoke of four great menaces threatening the Church there, in this order: 1. the invasion of Protestant sects; 2. secularization; 3. Marxism—a most active element in the universities and trades unions and 4. a disquieting spiritism. Speaking to Dominican tertiaries a year later he repeated these ideas, but this time described the Communist advance as even more menacing than Protestant proselytism.

No attempt is made here to consider Catholic-Orthodox relations, but a word or two may be said of Pius XII's references to the subject. Two important Eastern centenaries fell during his reign, for each of which he wrote an encyclical. The first, *Orientalis Ecclesiae*, commemorated the fifteenth centenary of the death of St Cyril of Alexandria, praising him as a hammer of heretics and a pillar of the papacy, which he certainly was, though historians have not agreed to regard him as a model either of tact or of precision of theological language. Pope Celestine had more than once to restrain him. Pius took this occasion to express his hope for the return of the Eastern churches to the fold. 1951 was the fifteenth centenary of Chalcedon and in the letter *Sempiternus Rex* he spoke of the Oriental Churches whose bishops so finely vindicated Christian doctrine there, but which were now so long and so wretchedly cut off from the unity of the Mystical Body of Christ. 'It is holy, wholesome and the will of God that all should return to the one fold of Christ We would like them to be clear that Our thoughts are of peace and not of affliction. We have proved this, we may boast in the Lord. Following Our predecessors We have worked for their return: to make it easier. We have safeguarded their lawful rites, We have fostered studies concerning them, We have promulgated laws in their interest, We have established a Congregation in the Roman Curia for their affairs. We have made the Armenian patriarch a cardinal. In our war work, inevitably inadequate, We have made no distinction between them and Catholics. Let those then whom misfortune has cut off from this Apostolic See (for which to rule is to serve) this divinely erected and unshakeable rock of truth, follow in the footsteps of Flavian, Chrysostom, Marcian and Pulcheria and pay homage to it without delay. Many benefits will accrue to the Christian world. We know of ancient accumulated prejudice, but faith can move mountains. The way will be smoothed by that calmer investigation, without anger or partisan spirit, which is common now compared with past times.'

Pius spoke of the greater urgency of unity against the united forces of the enemies of Christ, the sufferings of whose victims cry out to us. Communism and the Orthodox were often linked in his utterances. He reacted more than once (e.g. at Christmas 1948) to attacks and abuse from Orthodox under Communist control. 'We know of the servile dependence that some representatives of the confession known as Orthodox show towards a system whose final aim, repeatedly avowed, is the banning of all Christian religion.' On the other hand, in his letter of July, 1952 to 'the most dear Russian peoples', he spoke of his 'special affection for those who, although by the vicissitudes of history separated in great part from the Apostolic See, yet retain the name of Christian amid great difficulties'. He recalled the charity of Benedict XV and Pius XI to Russia after World War I, and reminded them of his own refusal to be pressed into lending approval to the war against Russia.

When we turn to consider Catholic ecumenism under Pope John, we reach ground on which above all the personal factor was decisive. If he is the ecumenical pope *par excellence*, the root was in an ecumenical personality. To say this is not to insist excessively on contrast between him and Pius XII. It is certainly not to imply a greater solicitude for the healing of schism in the one than in the other, nor a less firm conception of the unity and unicity of the Church.

What is best described in the homely metaphor of breaking the ice is of literally the first importance in the ecumenical field. Of course, if ice-breaking becomes too exclusive a concern, we move into what the siege mentality loves to call 'false irenicism'. The Second Vatican Council's decree does indeed warn against false irenicism; but if this becomes too much of a bogey there is no progress towards *eirene*, peace. In the atmosphere of the late forties and early fifties, particularly, it did become too much of a bogey. Now, it is something of an anomaly that the side which is negotiating from strength should be more loud in sounding the trumpet against false irenicism than the side which is negotiating from weakness. The anomaly is not dispelled by insisting that the former has the responsibility of guarding the deposit. The *depositum fidei* is not something like squirrels in a sack, likely to escape at a moment's relaxation of vigilance. If it is so thought of, the reasons are historical, and relatively recent accidents, rather than unshakeable logic.

A certain confidence, a certain absence of tension, a certain ease and generous breadth quite distinct from vagueness is, one is tempted to say, the proper ornament of an infallible Church. It is the one sort of triumphalism we can afford and which none will resent. It clearly marked the men of exceptional stature at the Second Vatican Council. During the period defined above, one senses its lack. To equate this with lack of charity is to personalize it in a way neither just nor illuminating. In thinking of Pius XII it is worse—it is ridiculous. But in Rome it was an *ambiance*, a style, a recent inheritance against which, it seems to me, Pius more than once showed himself restless, but from which it was inevitably hard for him to act in complete independence. Those who have read thus far may think that a number of things, in recent and less recent history, contributed to this *ambiance*. A further temptation is to add that there was too *exclusive* a preoccupation with the 'disturbance of the simple faithful', who were too often the culpably ill-instructed faithful, whether the fault was the Church's, or the Liberal or Fascist state's, or the fault of individuals.

There was a lack of trust, a recoiling from the most legitimate risks, that was hardly compatible with the 'confidence we have through Christ towards God'. It was the life of people in a fortress, which is not a normal life.

John entered the keep of the fortress very late in life—far too late to take on any tinge of a mentality to which he had always been basically a stranger. One suspects, if it is not irreverent to say so, that his chief delight in being Pope was to give vent to a disposition which, while rooted like an oak in faith and goodness, unaffectedly immersed in the supernatural, was not only wryly detached from all the conventions of clerical bureaucracy but gifted by nature and grace with the effortless generosity that leads from strength. He could shrug off small blunders, he was never manacled by the fear of them. There were problems with which he was unequipped to wrestle, and some of these he solved by jovially taking wing.

In the Encyclical *Ad Petri Cathedram* (June 1959) he could insist as uncompromisingly as anybody on the marvellous spectacle of unity which distinguishes the Church from all other bodies and reflects the will of her Founder (noting in passing that it was consistent with legitimate and fertile differences of opinion on the undefined); but somehow the words had no chilling effect for the outsider—they rather lent point to the spontaneous outpouring of courtesy and charity which followed: '[The Church's] prayers can stir and warm your hearts, you who are separated from this Apostolic See. You will allow Us to call you, with ardent desire, brothers and sons. Allow Us to nourish the hope of your return—a hope We cultivate with fatherly affection.' And characteristically he sought and found an early precedent for this feeling in the words of Bishop Theophilus in the turbulence of fifth-century Alexandria, words which throw a somewhat flattering light on that enterprising prelate. John's concern for unity, his ecumenical spirit, was a natural personal goodness and power to charm supernaturalized and universaalized. No less important, it was institutionalized, first in the Secretariat for Christian Unity and finally and vitally in the Council.

It was again characteristic that, a few months after founding the Secretariat, he took occasion of the fifteenth centenary of Leo the Great, one of the giants of papal history, a distinguished and virile mind and perhaps the most distinguished pen among the popes, to dilate on the unity theme. John had one certain link with Leo—both understood the value and manner of leading from strength without bombast. Their spirit spanned the ages, including those recent ages in which the permanent substance of papal power had taken on outer aspects that Leo would hardly have understood. The Encyclical on Leo, *Aeterna Dei Sapientia*, is an indispensable key to John's conception of the scope of the Vatican Council—hardly less so than his more famous opening speech.

It was however in the latter that he startled his hearers into attention by speaking of the 'zealous persons, whose voices often reach our ears, but find no echo in our heart.' His criticism of them was that they 'behave as though there were nothing to learn from history, the mistress of life'. And history is indeed one of the weakest disciplines of the Roman schools. It is hard to overestimate the silent contribution made in recent times by adult historical scholarship to the lessening of tensions between Christians. It was Leo XIII, first opener of the Vatican archives, who said with caustic wit to Gasquet, the English Benedictine historian and Cardinal, that if the evangelists had been writing today they would have found the denial of Peter and the betrayal of Judas being blue-pencilled for fear of offending the dignity of the apostolic college. But Leo's was a voice that found little echo in the wilderness of the late nineteenth century. It did not find much in Gasquet.

The decree *De Oecumenismo* is one of the achieved things of the Second Vatican Council. It is easy to underestimate its importance by concentrating too much on its two annexed declarations, on the Jews and on Religious Liberty.[1] That the latter is crucial and difficult need not be denied. It was a Spanish bishop, Moralejo of Valencia (a Spaniard with a knowledge of England), who said that the chapter was a necessary preliminary to the Decree rather than an appendix. But equally we overestimate the importance of the Ecumenism Decree if we forget how completely all the concerns of the Council are unified by an ecumenical impulse. The Church, Revelation and the Bible, Liturgy, Oriental Churches, the Training of Priests are the chief examples.

The interest of Bishop Moralejo's statement just quoted lies especially in the fact that he belongs to what is regarded as the most 'confessional' of the surviving larger European states. Does 'confessionalism' admit of degrees? During the discussion of the Second Vatican Council's proposed declaration on Religious Liberty the Roman professor Pavan defined the confessional state as one which recognizes religious liberty for all citizens and for all religious

[1] Subsequently issued separately as *De Ecclesiae Habitudine ad Religiones non-Christianas*, Section 4, and *De Libertate Religiosa*.

communities, but at the same time assigns a juridical position of privilege to one determined religion. Clearly England with its established Church would come within this definition, yet to most Englishmen the term confessional state probably conjures up images of *autos da fé* or Spanish policemen harrying members of the British and Foreign Bible Society. Only in very recent times has the confessional state become the exception rather than the rule, so much so that it now tends to be equated in the minds of many with the totalitarian state. This Monsignor Pavan defined (from the religious standpoint) as one which formally recognizes the right to religious freedom but tends in a thousand ways to empty it of content.

The characteristic modern alternative is the lay state, which recognizes for all citizens the same religious freedom, juridically and constitutionally. This is historically a product of the Revolution, which was often (though not always) violently anti-religious; hence the liberal conception of religious freedom has suffered all the ambiguities and adversities of liberal conceptions in the past two centuries. No liberal idea was greeted with more hostility by the Church. To try to obscure this is useless—we can at best try to understand it.

Gregory XVI in *Mirari Vos* described the idea that 'liberty of conscience and of worship is the right of every man which should be proclaimed and asserted by law in every rightly-constituted society' as a '*deliramentum*', a piece of nonsense. Pius IX, in *Quanta Cura*, made this stricture his own, adding that the claim derived from an altogether false idea of government and was gravely prejudicial to the salvation of souls.

These documents are extreme examples of how a polemical way of viewing a question, restricting it to the moment, can obscure it. Concentrating on the violent anti-religious and anti-clerical aspects of the Revolution, they see the claim to religious liberty as a claim to withdraw from *divine* authority, a claim that the State should so to speak license such withdrawal, underwrite indifferentism. This, which no pope could but condemn, may well have been the intention of some revolutionaries: it is no necessary part of the conception of religious liberty.

Divine authority is absolute. This means simply that no man, unless inculpably ignorant of divine law, can disregard or defy it without sin. He retains, of course, the power to act sinfully, but it is senseless to talk of the right to sin. What a man has naturally and retains under all circumstances is the right to choose freely: only if his act is thus free has it any moral significance, good or bad. It may also be a choice of what is objectively erroneous but to a sincere conscience appears as right. All this is consistent with the absolute character of divine authority, because even that authority is exercised in the concrete conditions of history, among men.

The function of earthly authority is to safeguard human rights. These certainly do not, when they are fundamentally human or 'natural' as the traditional phrase is, derive from earthly authority: but since the latter is concerned with the rights of the community as a whole, it may be entitled to restrict the exercise of human rights in cases where the public interest is involved.

All this presents no difficulty so long as we are concerned with conscience in the sense of interior conviction. That the assent of faith is a free and rational act is an essential part of Catholic teaching, whatever practices may at moments of history have made light of it. The 'interiorization of morality' was, as Gilson has pointed out, the distinctive contribution of Christianity to our moral thinking. The interior act is ultimately inviolable, and simply not the business of external authority, though it is the business of external authority by education to try to ensure that such interior activity shall be healthy. Faith is a free interior assent that even the Church cannot *command*, much less civil authority.

But religious liberty as discussed in the Second Vatican Council was not, as the proponents of the Declaration frequently reminded us, simply liberty of conscience. It was not a declaration about the individual's moral or religious judgements, his relations with his God. It went out of its way to list a number of interior attitudes which it was not intended to countenance: scepticism, irreligion, indifferentism, shelving of the problem of forming one's conscience.

In other words, the liberty under discussion was not emancipation of man from the power of God. It was concerned with the free exercise of religion in society, whether by the individual or the community, and with interference with that free exercise whether by the individual or the community, that is, the law.

There is no need to waste time in showing that such freedom has not been taken for granted as a right in European history. What concerns the Council is giving expression to what the advocates of the Declaration regard as the logical outcome of a modern process of re-thinking.

In earlier times the matter was discussed in terms of 'toleration'. The idea of toleration rests upon the assumption that the true religion (or what its adherents take to be the true religion) disposes of the power to suppress false religions, or restrict them. The question of toleration is the question how far and in what circumstances this power may or should be withheld. The difference of emphasis will be appreciated.

The question has not always been stated clearly. Half a century ago the writer of the article on Tolerance in the French *Dictionnaire Apologétique de la Foi Catholique* wrote: 'Ecclesiastical intolerance may be an unpopular word, but the reality is in sympathy with all that is highest and most generous in us. It speaks of conviction and confidence, where tolerance speaks of scepticism and despair; it is a proof of strength, where tolerance shows only feebleness and impotence; it inspires a saving zeal, where tolerance commits us to a self-centred indifferentism. The Catholic Church can hate no one, nor pass by with indifference a single unfortunate. She is the most intransigent, the most intolerant of churches, but also the most loving. In the expression of a French archbishop, "the Church has the intransigence of truth and charity".'

This spirited but confused piece of rhetoric is chiefly interesting as an expression of early twentieth-century French integralism. Of course a body which believes it possesses divinely-revealed truth is intolerant of divergences from that truth in the sense that it cannot suppose that they also may be true. It appears that the rhetorical Frenchman is saying no more than this, but he is saying it in a singularly unfortunate way. It is more significant to find the sober Father Capello writing that civil toleration in a Catholic state has no reason except the avoidance of greater evils and is to be measured precisely by the degree of its *necessity*. 'Whence if a lesser extent of tolerance suffices, i.e. a more restricted degree of liberty, only this and nothing more can or should be conceded.' (*Op. cit.*, No. 285).

Clearly this view does not rest upon the assumption of any *right* to religious freedom. To grant it is simply a matter of expediency to be judged by circumstance. Thus the revocation of the Edict of Nantes would be justified on the grounds that the conditions which had brought it about no longer obtained (even if it were not argued further that the Edict had in the first place arisen from the 'irreligion' of Henry IV). Canonists commonly answered objections with the tag 'error has no rights', which begged the question whether a man in error might have rights.

The brilliant African Archbishop Zoa of Yaoundé alluded clearly to this in a speech made on behalf of seventy other African bishops in the Second Vatican Council. It is absolutely necessary, he said, that religious liberty be doctrinally and not merely pragmatically justified, both in a positive way by recalling the absolute dignity of the human person created according to the image of God, and the reverence especially due to him in religious matters; and also negatively by solemnly rejecting the idea that the so-called right of coercion might in future circumstances be suitably revived. We must speak about religious liberty, said Zoa, in such a way that every man, as such, will be able to agree with our assertions.

Clearly if a man has a right to religious freedom, the public authority has a duty to uphold this right where it does not conflict with the public interest, though to decide where this conflict exists may in practice be difficult.

It is curious to find the 1954 edition of Capello's standard work stating the canonist position in so bald a fashion, since it was then nearly a year since Pius XII had given an address which attracted worldwide attention to the theme. Pius was himself a Roman canon lawyer, but he was also a pope of international experience, absorbed in the post-war problems of international relations and world co-operation. Earlier in 1953 another canonical expert, Cardinal Ottaviani, a former Roman professor of the subject, had stated the canonical position in a typically vigorous and uncompromising article. In the autumn of 1953 the fifth national congress of Italian Catholic Jurisconsults met in Rome, taking as its theme '*Nations and the International Community*'. They sought audience of Pius XII, and he paid them the compliment of a long and deeply-considered address in which his central theme was the religious position foreseeable in the Community of Nations. What was envisaged, he understood, was that 'internally and for its own citizens every state will regulate religious and moral affairs by its own laws; nevertheless everywhere in the Community's territory citizens of member-states will be allowed their own ethical and religious beliefs and practices, insofar as these do not contravene the penal laws of the state they happen to be living in. How must Catholics judge this?' Presupposing that no state or community can order or authorize what is contrary to religious truth or morality

Pius asks, how far could a Catholic state be a party to a community rule of toleration?

His answer is of the first interest: 'In determined circumstances God may give us no mandate, *even no right* to repress what is erroneous or false. A glance at facts shows us that error and sin exist in the world in ample measure. God reproves them—He yet lets them exist. Therefore the principle that tolerance of evil is itself immoral *cannot be absolute*, and tolerance may be indicated by the *higher norms* of the general welfare. [He cites in support the parable of the wheat and the cockle.]

'That which does not conform to truth and the moral law has *objectively* no right to exist, to propagate itself, to act; but to refrain from impeding it by state laws and coercion can be justified in the interests of a *higher and wider good*.' (Cf. p. 72).

What seems to be happening here is that the Pope, confronting the practical question of religious relations in a possible international community, is seeing that the traditional notions of toleration will not suffice to determine them but will need further development. The international community authority will need to have its religious policy morally clarified; what the Pope clearly sees is that the Community will inevitably be what we now call a pluralist society. Certainly it will not have, says Pius, any right to order or authorize (i.e. lend its authority to) what is contrary to religious truth and morality. But how will it be determined in such a community what is or is not contrary to religious truth? Plainly the community as such will have no competence or authority to determine this.

Enlarging on this Pius seems to fall back here and there on the language of Capello, but the difference is in fact significant. The words I have italicised above are crucial. Once it is admitted that in certain circumstances there may be even no *right* to repress, the basis of the classical doctrine of toleration is undermined. It really makes no sense to talk of no right to suppression of error if there is not some right belonging to those in error.

Pius later shifted his treatment back to the ground of conscience: He made rather broad claims for the history of Catholic tolerance of 'a good conscience' (invincible ignorance) from the time of Constantine the Great. He also mollified the integralists with a brief triumphalistic passage: In early Christian times, he said, there had never been any hesitation in choosing between ' "incense for the idols and blood for Christ", but the temples of the idols are now in ruins, while all repeat the ancient creed before the tombs of the martyrs. So much for what is religiously false.'

All this was profoundly true; nevertheless the essential breach in the recent tradition of teaching on tolerance had been made or, it might be better to say, the essential confusion cleared up.

One of the foundations of Christian thought, firmly rooted in the Gospels, is that the absolute State in the strict sense is incompatible with Christianity. For absolute means unbound to any law but its own will. History has dictated that the Church should spend an undue proportion of her time asserting this principle against usurpations of her own authority by the State—whether the Catholic State which recognized her position in general terms but was directed to keeping it within bounds (or encroaching on it—this often depended on the point of view); or the non-Catholic State which gives a preferential position to a 'false' religion; or the liberal State which gives preference to none but inclines to impatience of all; or the totalitarian State which at best regards religion as an instrument of policy.

The first of these four types of Church-State tension is the one with which the Catholic Church has historically been most familiar; and it is in terms of this type that her canonists have retained the habit of thinking, even where one or more of the other three types have at various times supervened. Hence it seems to many that, in proportion as canonists have dictated policy, the Church has inclined to show an undue tenderness towards states that paid lip-service to her own privileged position, even when they have been careless of human rights in general. At the other extreme, she has sometimes been blind to the presence of a genuine solicitude for human rights (e.g. in 'liberal' states) where this has been accompanied by an insufficient regard for her own privileges.

The sixteenth of the propositions condemned by Pius IX's *Syllabus of Modern Errors* was this: 'Men can find the way of salvation, and arrive at it, in the exercise of any religion.' As a statement of the relative value of religious systems, this is clearly something that Pius IX had no alternative but to condemn. It is a statement of indifferentism, and hence a denial of the authenticity of the Church's divine mission. But as a statement of how God can and might work in given circumstances, in a society where religious unity had been lost and invincible ignorance abounded, the proposition is quite unexceptionable.

Nearer to our subject, and a harder nut to crack, is proposition 79: this rejects as false the contention that 'civil liberty of worship and full power of public expression of opinion does not lead to the corruption of the public mind and morals and spread the pest of indifferentism'.

Perhaps the best one can say about this is that it is no more than an expression of conviction, perhaps immature in the 1860s, about the likely effects of a certain type of government action. Leo XIII can be seen gradually shedding the conviction under the influence, for example, of what he saw of the growth of the Church in America. Pius XII was led to a reassessment of the traditional doctrine of toleration by way of the practical problem of religion in an international community. This simply threw into relief the pluralist character of all modern society, international or national, and its social mobility. Pius was certainly helped in his reassessment by his sympathy (expressed in his first Encyclical) with the liberal and essentially Catholic notions of the equality of rational nature and the dependence of civil authority on divine authority and law.

Under John XXIII these ideas are thought out to their logical conclusion, and the conciliar Declaration is the term of the process. There has been a good deal of rather unnecessary bother about the standing of a 'Declaration', which is a term not previously familiar in conciliar literature; what might be insisted on is the literal significance; the throwing of light. The document itself states explicitly that the Church's function is to spread the light, and implies that she should do so on the matter of religious liberty too. This is the moment to do so, because it marks the term of a long evolution of the Church's teaching on human dignity and her pastoral care for men's liberty. Substantially these have been constant, but the element of progress is represented by two distinctions, made more slowly in the Church and finally clarified by John XXIII: first, the distinction between false ideologies and the practical experiments or institutions developed under them; the latter may be acceptable though the former are still firmly rejected. (This of course is simply a reference to the passage of *Pacem in Terris* which attracted widest attention. See p. 112.) Second, the distinction between religious errors and the person erring in good faith, by virtue of which the rights belonging to human nature and dignity must still be acknowledged and fostered though the errors are inflexibly rejected.

Because of this progress the Church is today in a position where she can give the broadest patronage to human liberty, though relativism, indifferentism and the idea of a conscience independent of God be still rejected. The faculty to offer to God a *liberum et rationabile obsequium* is the crucial test of human dignity and freedom. Today the danger is less that of false liberty than of no liberty at all, so recent popes have re-stated traditional doctrine insisting on religious freedom as the primary human right whether it arises from a true conscience or from an erroneous or ill-instructed one.

John's personal note sounds again in the section following, which provides a gloss on the traditional principle that no one should be forced to embrace the faith. A high ideal of respect for human integrity, one might say of delicacy of approach, is laid down—'abstention from all coercion or *pressure*, *direct or indirect*'. Even the disarming suggestions of Gregory the Great are ruled out here (see p. 246).

As Cardinal Meyer pointed out in the debate on the Declaration, it does, while amply discussing the ground, theological and even philosophical, for liberty of conscience, concern itself ultimately with the limitation of political competence; this is a limitation which the Church should recognize in all contexts, convenient or not, the cardinal added.

American influence in the Declaration is of course strong and any form of establishment at the federal level has always been clearly impracticable, apart from any theory, in America. (It has existed, along with considerable intolerance, in individual states.) In places with a different tradition these limits on the religious responsibilities of the State caused heart-searching. Cardinal Ottaviani demurred at the idea that the state is 'incompetent to choose a religion', as though this implied that any degree of establishment, or even any concordat, was out of court. It is certainly true that many American personalities associated with the Council have a strong emotional dislike of both, but the Declaration cannot be adduced against either. It asserts of course the State's incompetence to choose a religion on behalf of any of its subjects, but not its incompetence to recognize (as does for example the Irish Constitution) a religion as that of the vast majority of its subjects and even to make dispositions for public order accordingly, without prejudice to the fundamental rights of others.

The mention of public order raises what the architects of the

Declaration admitted was their hardest task—to determine what restrictions of religious liberty, or rather what interventions of public authority against it, could be justified on the grounds of public interest and order. Some varied problems were raised: polygamists in Utah, Jehovah's Witnesses, anti-vaccinationists, aggressive Protestant sects in Spain, and a variety of solutions put forward. To find a criterion for legitimate intervention which will not be open to distortion and abuse is not easy.

It has sometimes been suggested that the Spanish bishops played a leading part in the opposition (some of it, to say the least, ingenious) to the Declaration. During the Third Session of the Council it was reported that a meeting of forty-five Spanish bishops ended with forty of their number leaving the room banging the door after them. It was widely assumed that the forty were the opponents of the Declaration, the remaining rump its only supporters. Accurate information subsequently made clear that the reverse was true.

13

Bible, Bureaucrats, Bishops

IN A SERMON some twenty years ago Ronald Knox had this to say:

'You have a friend, I dare say, whose house is full of beautiful things, whose library is stocked with the rarest and choicest editions, and yet he himself, because he has inherited and not collected them, seems to move quite unimpressed in the world of beauties you envy; the books are coated with dust, the pictures badly hung, and all the best things seem to be kept in some sort of reception room, swathed in dust-cloths and chilly from long disuse of the hearth. He is surprised, perhaps, even impatient, at your enthusiasm, and hurries you on to see the next of the two dozen things he really does value, and these not for their intrinsic worth but because some story hangs by them: this is an interesting heirloom, that came into his possession in a rather curious way, that watch went with him all through such and such a campaign—he seems to have eyes for nothing else.

'I sometimes feel that we Catholics are a little like that in our use of the Bible. We have a score or so good fighting texts at our fingers' ends: Thou art Peter . . . Who so eateth My flesh . . . What God hath joined . . . and so on. We learned them from the catechism and it's useful to know them because we may want to use them at any time; they are regular landmarks in the history of controversy. And for the rest, the whole treasure-house of the Gospels is there at our elbow and somehow we never seem to have more than a nodding acquaintance with it; it doesn't seem to sink in. Seeing we see but dimly; hearing we hear abstractedly and only half understand.' (*Mystery of the Kingdom*, pp. 10–11.)

Knox was no crusader—it is hard to imagine him as part of any movement. There is the more weight in this gentle but pointed diagnosis: one which Knox had no doubt brought into the Church with him but which a quarter of a century inside the Church had given him, the most fair-minded and candid of men, no reason to change.

Catholic biblical scholarship had not indeed had a very happy existence in the two generations preceding Knox's entry into the Church at the end of the First World War. It flourished best at a serious academic level in Germany where, as we have seen, Catholic theological faculties existed side by side with Protestant ones in the national universities. Unhappily many of these universities, such as Tübingen, displayed the nineteenth-century weakness for interpreting the Bible according to the assumptions of German Liberal Protestantism rather than according to the mentality of the biblical authors, and even admirable Catholic work was not always untouched by this prevailing weakness. In Belgium and in France work of high academic level was achieved in a wholly Catholic environment.

Landmarks in modern Catholic biblical studies were the foundation in 1890 of *L'Ecole Pratique d'Etudes Bibliques* by the Dominican M. Lagrange in Jerusalem; the Encyclical *Providentissimus Deus* three years later; the establishment of the Pontifical Biblical Commission in 1902. All typified the spirit of Leo XIII. The Commission was indeed a supplementary organ of Vatican control, but its original personnel indicated that it was intended to be constructive rather than merely negative in purpose.

Unhappily this progress received a severe set-back with the Modernist crisis which culminated in Pius X's reign with the decree *Lamentabili* and the Encyclical *Pascendi* of 1907.

To regard Modernism as simply a manifestation of enlightenment and progress and anti-Modernist legislation as just another example of Roman obscurantism is of course to show either prejudice or complete misapprehension. Modernist leaders were men who had some standing as scholars, but scholarship fifty years ago was a good deal less scrupulous about axe-grinding than it is today, and the Modernistic principle was the negation of scholarship: It was the reading of philosophical prejudices into texts, including the texts of scripture. Von Loewenich, though sympathetic to Modernism and violently opposed to the methods by which it was dealt with, admits 'it must be justly conceded that Pius X was speaking not only for the interests of his own Church but also for Christianity as a whole.

Modernism was really in danger of ending up in immanentism[1] pure and simple.' (*Modern Catholicism*, p. 72).

But among integralists who, when they turn from abstractions to persons are not given to nice discrimination, the condemnations of 1907 launched something like a reign of terror against all ecclesiastical learning, and particularly biblical learning. The theological espionage of the organization known as *La Sapinière* (briefly but graphically described by J. Levie, S.J., in *The Bible, Word of God and Words of Men*, p. 73) was revealed by a fortunate accident at the beginning of World War I, and prompted Benedict XV to include in his first Encyclical an excellent sharp passage. After repeating his predecessor's condemnation of Modernism he added, 'No private person should set himself up to exercise *magisterium* in the Church, whether in books, newspapers or sermons. In matters in which difference of opinion is possible, without prejudice to Faith, where the Apostolic See has interposed no judgement, it is open to anybody to say what he thinks and to defend it. But from such discussions all intemperance of speech should be excluded as gravely offensive to charity. Nor should anybody think himself entitled to accuse those who hold other opinions than his own of doubtful faith or of indiscipline.'

The mood and methods the Pope condemned here did not disappear, and did much to hamper the proper participation of Catholic scholars in the spectacular advances of biblical scholarship between the wars. These were particularly impressive of course in the field of archaeology and related sciences, which revolutionized the approach to the Bible. Protestant scholarship was affected no less—it too grew up and became less affected with the nineteenth-century prejudices. The Biblical Commission on the other hand took on a tone altogether more negative than that in which it had been conceived.[2] Yet both Pius X and Pius XI took steps to raise the standards of teaching in scripture; the former founded the Biblical Institute and projected the revision of the Vulgate; the latter put this project in train.

Contacts between Catholic and Protestant or Jewish biblical scholars increased. It is said that Augustin Bea, when lecturing at

[1] Immanentism is a position which can be arrived at by those attempting to reconcile orthodox Catholic exegesis with an agnostic-scientific approach; the outcome can be a pantheistic view of God as omnipresent in the universe but not a transcendent being.

[2] Cf. Levie, *op. cit.*, p. 57.

the Biblical Institute in Pius XI's time, was invited to take part in an international and inter-denominational conference, and went somewhat fearfully to Pius to ask whether he ought to go. He was told 'Of course you must.'

Pius XII's reign opened with a spectacular Vatican intervention in the biblical field which was something of a reversal of the long-prevailing trend. An Italian priest, Dolindo Ruotolo, author of a thirteen-volume pious but decidedly unscholarly commentary on Scripture which the Holy Office put on the Index, gave vent to his mortification in a violent pamphlet with the title 'A Very Grave Danger for the Church and for Souls: The Critical-Scientific System in the Study and Interpretation of Sacred Scripture, its Disastrous Deviations and Aberrations.' This he published under the pen-name Dain Cohenel.

The Biblical Commission in a letter to the Italian hierarchy dated August 20, 1941, severely chastised the tone and content of this pamphlet. Cohenel was a negligible fanatic and is of little interest except as provoking this letter which, mainly a refutation of his extravagances, was also a partial preliminary sketch for the Encyclical *Divino Afflante Spiritu* which Pius XII issued on September 30, 1943.

Perhaps no important papal announcement has ever been made at a moment less propitious to ensure it attention. The world was still in the throes of war, the Germans had recently occupied Rome. *Humani Generis*, which treated only incidentally of biblical questions and appeared in the very different atmosphere of August 1950, received a great deal more publicity. Yet Catholic biblical scholars have united in regarding *Divino Afflante Spiritu* as their Magna Carta, and recent events, especially those of the Second Vatican Council, have brought it into focus as probably the greatest single achievement of Pius XII's reign and one of his assured titles to a place in history.

There is no need to do more here than offer a brief summary and direct the reader's attention to the text and to the many expert commentaries on it. We need only insist on its importance in the perspective of Pius's pontificate as well as in the wider perspective of modern scriptural scholarship. This is sufficiently indicated by noting that in an official collection of papal pronouncements on Scripture ranging from mid-fourth century to the present and filling 250 pages, Pius XII takes up no less than sixty-seven.

Written to commemorate the fiftieth anniversary of *Providentissimus Deus*, *Divino Afflante Spiritu* begins with a historical section describing the aims and achievements of Leo XIII and succeeding popes (briefly set out above); but Pius launches the central section by saying that 'the position of biblical studies has greatly changed during the past half-century.' Excavation (hardly begun in Palestine when Leo wrote), the discovery of papyri and codices, more exact study of the early Fathers, have given new dimensions and stimulus to biblical study; so have the remarkable advances in ancient languages and philosophy. St Augustine is adduced as a champion of these scholarly methods in an age which enjoyed fewer advantages than ours. (The question of the authority of the Vulgate is touched on.) These aids should support the contemporary scholar in his search for the author's meaning and for theological content. 'The faithful want to know what God has told us in Holy Scripture.' Modern scholarship had deepened our insights into the meaning of inspiration. The interpreter must 'go back in spirit to those remote times,' with the help of history, archaeology, ethnology and so on—searching out the ancient writer's proper mode of expression. If today many problems persist, the general effect of this more scholarly approach, says the Pope, has been to restore rather than diminish confidence in the history of the Bible.

The final section, pastoral in intent, calls urgently on bishops, priests and educators to pass on the fruits of this new and better understanding of the Bible to the people of God.

Not the least striking (to some startling) feature of *Divino Afflante Spiritu* was that it gave carefully qualified approval to Catholic use of the type of criticism known as *Formgeschichtliche Methode* or Form Criticism, which though used in a destructive and inadmissible way by its most famous non-Catholic exponents such as Bultmann and Dibelius was, in the opinion of responsible scholars, capable of fruitful adaptation. (See e.g. Duncker in *Catholic Biblical Quarterly*, January 1963, pp. 27–30.)

To keep the remaining pronouncements of Pius XII's reign in proportion it must be remembered that by taking so positive and open a stand in *Divino Afflante Spiritu* he was not abdicating the Holy See's right to pass judgement on the productions of biblical scholarship or to give future direction. This would make nonsense of the *magisterium* of the Church. Nor can there in the nature of things be any guarantee that every new utterance will be a further 'liberalizing' step. Humanly speaking a number of factors may exercise a determining influence at any time: the current state of opinion, the Pope's own studies and cast of mind, the character of the advice he takes. Pius XII himself pointed out how few scriptural texts have been the subject of infallible pronouncements.

Three more considerable pronouncements on biblical matters belong to Pius XII's reign:

1. A letter from the Biblical Commission to Cardinal Suhard in 1948. Here the appropriate commission of experts is answering, with papal approval, questions submitted by the cardinal concerning the dating of the *Pentateuch* and the interpretation of the first eleven chapters of *Genesis*. It was generally taken by scholars as confirming the predominantly positive trend of *Divino Afflante Spiritu*.

2. An instruction of the Holy Office offered general directions for a more effective teaching of Holy Scripture.

3. The Encyclical *Humani Generis*, concerned mainly with certain current theological opinions, reiterated earlier warnings concerning biblical studies and added a further one against an overstrained interpretation of the Suhard letter.

The official position at Pius XII's death was apparently a satisfactory one. Pius had made history by laying down lines along which Catholic biblical studies could progress in a way at once scholarly and serene, and hence ecumenical. But beneath the surface there were uneasy stirrings. Roman integralism was not inclined to leave the scholars, or the Biblical Institute in particular, in peace for long. The authorities of the Biblical Institute, complaining of this sniping, were more than once assured by at least one high curial official that the minor functionaries who were the culprits had been told to shut up and not meddle in biblical matters. It was vain. Yet while Pius XII survived the murmurings remained subterranean.

Rather more than a year after the election of John XXIII, on February 17, 1960, the fiftieth anniversary of the foundation of the Biblical Institute was celebrated in the Vatican Palace by a solemn and ceremonial audience at which twenty-three cardinals were present, including the newly-elevated Cardinal Bea, a former professor of the Institute. To John XXIII was offered a commemorative volume of biblical miscellanea by the chiefs of the Institute, including S. Lyonnet, one of the deans.

The Pope told them in his address that scientific seriousness was their first and highest title of honour. This included not presenting working hypotheses as definitive conclusions, but it certainly also included, he stressed, making the utmost use of modern instruments of scholarship. This sounded like a tranquil inheritance from the previous pontificate. But it was the calm before the storm.

Rather ironically in view of popularly accepted categories, it was a Spanish member of the Institute's staff who unwittingly brought down a load of trouble on the Institute's head. He published in the sober pages of the *Civiltà Cattolica* in September 1960 an article with the title 'Whither Catholic Exegesis?' He contrasted the position taken up by Pius XII in *Divino Afflante Spiritu* with those often taken up by Catholic scholars at the beginning of the present century—to the Pope's advantage obviously, but without personal animus. He went on to argue that though the great Encyclical had gathered up a number of scholarly threads from the preceding generation it had set a new tone of confidence. The writer was disposed to defend *Humani Generis* from the charge of being a backward step; there was plenty of ground for reiterated calls to prudence, especially in the field of popularization. He concluded by answering his own question: Exegesis was proceeding along the lines laid down by Pius XII.

The reader need not be troubled with the details of the hysterical war dance that this harmless article provoked. What a very distinguished cardinal who is also a biblical scholar thought of it may be seen referring to Appendix II. The rector of the Biblical Institute was to speak later of 'an all-out attack upon *Divino Afflante Spiritu*'. One of the protagonists of the attack accused an Institute official in conversation of having 'exploited Pius XII's ignorance'. This remark was illuminating not because it was plausible but because it threw a light on the real integralist attitude to the Holy See.

The timing of this new all-out attack suggested estimates of Pius and John quite at variance with what have become the conventional ones. The assailants undoubtedly had powerful and well-informed friends in the Vatican, and seem to have felt some confidence of getting clear away with what amounted to a defiance of the late Pope's pronouncements.

But three events occurred at the beginning of 1961. At the beginning of February Cardinal Pizzardo, Prefect of the Congregation of Seminaries, publicly dissociated himself and his Secretary from the attacks on the Biblical Institute. (Two of the leading attackers were officials of the Congregation.) On March 2 the Rector of the Institute was appointed to the Council's Theological Commission. Three days later the Pontifical Biblical Commission agreed to write in the name of all its consultors, to the Institute deprecating the attacks. It was widely believed that the Pope himself was behind at least two of these moves.

On the other hand, two of the most respected and long-serving teachers at the Institute were removed from office. (They were to be reinstated later, during the Council.)

On June 20 following the Holy Office issued a *monitum* against excesses in biblical criticism, but in very general terms; it added another warning against rashness in stigmatizing the opinions of others, and a note to the effect that the *monitum* had been issued with the approval of the Biblical Commission. This last was an innovation in procedure.

Pope John was inclined to shrug off partisanship in these quarrels. '*Sono tutti buona gente*', (they're all good folk,) he would say, and draw attention to the admirable view from his window. But that things lodged in his mind and contributed to cumulative impressions became pretty clear when he opened the Council. It is safe to say that there was no ecclesiastic resident in Rome whose mind, as he heard the now famous words about 'prophets of gloom' and 'the medicine of mercy' did not go back to the events just described.

Now it was this speech that set the tone of the Council, quite a different one from what had been expected at the outset and very different from what integralists everywhere had hoped. To the integralist mind a Council was an abstract notion bearing little relation to the reality of the twenty historical Councils.

The Pope's speech pointed explicitly to this lack of historical sense: 'They behave as though they had learned nothing from history, which is none the less the teacher of life—and as though at the time of former Councils everything was a full triumph for the Christian idea of life and for proper religious liberty.' The purpose of the Council, John went on to say, was not the reiteration of familiar fundamentals: what was expected was 'a step forward towards penetration of doctrine and formation of consciences, in perfect conformity to the authentic doctrine, which however should be studied and expounded through the literary forms of modern thought. One thing is the substance of the ancient doctrine of the *depositum fidei*, and another is the way in which it was presented.'

The full impact of this speech can only be understood in relation to the impact on the learned world of the disputes just described. These were known only vaguely if at all to busy bishops within the Church; beyond the Church they were widely known to scholars, as Cardinal Liénart had pointed out. It was believed that the trouble-makers had enjoyed too much official sympathy. Some non-Catholics at least had been confirmed in the conviction that Rome was the leopard of indelible spots. This 'scandal' was one of the things both the cardinal and the Institute officials had drawn attention to.

Now it seemed clear that the Pope had simply been holding his fire. Here was a declaration against the spirit of integralism made at a moment when it would have the maximum effect on the Church through the assembled episcopate, do most to reassure the non-Catholic Christian scholarly world (for many of the observers at the Council were either distinguished scholars themselves or else in close touch with the world of biblical, theological and historical scholarship) and attract the widest attention in the world at large, on whose behalf the press were listening.

It was on this day, thought many, and not on the day of *Pascendi* that the ghost of Modernism was at last laid. For the evil of heresy is not merely that it maims the heretic but that it poisons the air, so that honest men cannot breathe in peace and only fanatics feel free. This was perhaps an over-optimistic judgement, but it was a resounding tribute to one of the most memorable papal utterances of all time.

A disturbance bred of pettiness and false zeal had, in the oblique way of Providence, contributed to history. It was to do so still further. In the First Session of the Council, the chief discussions, inside and outside the council hall, centred on the *schema* concerning Revelation. By comparison the debate on the Liturgy never reached a high temperature. Liturgical reform might be thought vital to an integral renewal of the Church, and opposed, especially on the language issue, by a variety of people who were far from being integralists. But it remained an issue on which neither side could plausibly be regarded, either by the other or by the world at large, as sinning against the light. The same was not true of the lengthy statements of the Catholic position on Scripture in the *schema De*

Revelatione. Nowhere was it more clear that those who had devised the original document expected it to be underwritten practically without discussion. They saw three parties: themselves, the guardians of the deposit; the scripture scholars, who were sent to try them; the bishops, who could not be expected to know about these things. The Council could with a little skill be turned to good account, to put paid once for all to the insolence of the learned.

A strained interpretation? Yet at one point, just before the vote on the acceptability of the *schema*, one speaker rose to suggest that it be rejected in favour of 'a solemn declaration on the Holy Scriptures'.

It did not take long to convince the uncommitted mass of bishops that their function in the Council, one of witness to the truth, could be carried out more effectively than by acting as rubber stamps. But if they were to act otherwise they needed to know something of the issues. Most of them had studied Scripture at a period when the light shed by *Providentissimus Deus* had been blacked out by the Modernist crisis and not yet restored by *Divino Afflante Spiritu*. To learn they must turn to men of authority. They did so in great numbers, and found, sometimes faintly to their surprise, that they were turning also to men of integrity, even of holiness—not noisy, not obstructive, but evident. They discovered in fact that integrity was not the same thing as integralism. Men who had previously been the bogeys of integralist controversy were seen in three dimensions and to their great advantage. In this way the extravagances of 1960–61 which Pope John had mysteriously tolerated, recoiled upon their perpetrators. Bishops who could not grasp the arguments for or against Form Criticism, but were sensible enough to realize that somebody had to, could recognize integrity and dedication to learning when they saw it and heard it. Decisive perhaps was the gradual swing of American opinion, in which the late lamented Cardinal Meyer, himself a biblical scholar, emerged in an increasingly determining rôle.

It was thus that a majority was created in favour of rejecting a *schema* on Revelation which would have made real debate impossible: a formally insufficient majority whose insufficiency the Pope swiftly supplied. This remains clearly the watershed of the Second Vatican Council. No issue had had quite the same simple clarity, though it was concerned with the most complex and specialized matter on the Council's agenda. 'Excessively professional and scholastic, not pastoral, excessively rigid, theologically immature, incomprehensible to non-Catholics, unsympathetic to scientific research in theology and exegesis, too evidently reflecting certain schools of thought': with language of this sort the bishops of the Church led the Council in a new and unexpected direction from which it has never since been seriously diverted.

One of the charges given to the Church by her Founder is that of guarding the deposit of Faith. This certainly includes the power to decide what books belong to the canon of inspired writings, the power to interpret these authoritatively, the power to decide what shall and shall not be taught as Catholic doctrine, what theological status shall be given to theories, speculations, the various propositions in which the development of doctrine is embodied. It must also entail the power to determine what are matters of Faith and what are not. Humanly speaking these are formidable responsibilities. We should feel no confidence in anybody who claimed to discharge them by purely natural means. But of course, the specific character of the Church's claim is that she discharges them under divine guidance and hence is invulnerable to error in doing so.

It is equally important to add, what is fully common teaching, that the bishops, including the Pope, must make full use of ordinary means in discharging their teaching office. In the best periods of the Church's history this had been a powerful intellectual stimulus. Though there have always been some temperamentally inclined to obscurantism, and they have been at intervals unduly articulate, the Church has on the whole held sound learning and hard thinking in high honour.

Today it is important as never before, not only that she should do so but that she should appear to do so. Reverence for the expert may sometimes assume exaggerated, even religious forms, but it is a very real and deep force in modern life. A Church which was thought not to take account of it would suffer in her mission.

It does not of course follow from this that the Church must give even provisional welcome to every learned novelty. There is an obvious distinction between new facts and modifications of fact based on scholarly evidence which there can be no question of rejecting, and hypotheses, theories, methods of approach about which often even common sense will suggest reserve. It is clearly appropriate for the Church authorities to act as a filter for speculation in fields that concern them, to insist that we do not commit ourselves to what is inadequately based. In this she is serving the interests of scholarship as well as of revealed truth. But it gives no edification if there appears to be imperfect sympathy between men of piety and integrity who have devoted their lives to the scientific study of the Bible and the administrators who should be drawing on the riches of this knowledge to their own and the general advantage.

John XXIII aimed at presenting a new and fair image of the Church. Part of it was that the divinely constituted *magisterium* should appear as magisterial. It has certainly done so.

14

Liturgical Revival

IF IT BE thought that the Church of the present century has emerged in somewhat mottled tones from some of these chapters, there is one aspect of the period from which a much brighter picture can be seen—the crucial one, for the Church's inner life, of liturgical revival and reform. When the Second Vatican Council's Constitution on the Sacred Liturgy was promulgated in December 1963, it was not difficult to see in it the climax of a century and more of scholarship and apostolic effort in which, from the outset of the present century, the papacy had increasingly taken the lead. If some Council documents confronted bishops with novel and even unwelcome ideas, no aspect of Catholic belief and practice had been more thoroughly studied in modern times than liturgy, and the literature is both voluminous and accessible. If popes have warned against the vices attendant on liturgical revivalism—antiquarianism, pedantry, intolerance, puritanism—they have insisted that participation and joy in public worship, liturgical prayer, is the authentic way in which man turns to God as a member of Christ's Mystical Body—as one with the living unity of the baptized.

Popes had fairly regularly asserted their authority in liturgical matters from at least the time of the Quartodeciman controversy under Pope Victor I (189–99). The Quartodecimans were those Eastern Christians who kept Easter on the 14th Nisan, whatever the day of the week.

A famous letter of Innocent I to the Bishop of Gubbio in 416 shows the Pope insisting on received Roman practice against a more primitive one locally preserved. The Roman liturgy, celebrated for its simple and lapidary character, spread through Europe through the energy of Charlemagne; though this Commander of the Faithful had no scruple in embellishing it in accordance with Frankish taste, the efficiency of his *missi dominici* (royal visitors) and the organizing and editorial power of the Englishman Alcuin imposed a liturgical revival through the Frankish dominions.

Yet in the middle ages local usage and accretions proliferated, and there were many provincial and even diocesan variants of the Roman rite, to say nothing of course of the separate Eastern liturgies. Many distortions of the original spirit and purpose of the liturgy had developed in the middle ages. As early as the thirteenth century there is evidence, in England for instance, of masses gabbled through to distracted and irreverent congregations who grasped little of what was happening.[1] There was little active participation, communion was infrequent. The design of many churches militated against the solidarity of clergy and people in the liturgy; so, in some respects, did the development of ecclesiastical chants, and other music. There was considerable development of popular devotion which, while it has been too harshly criticized by purists, often did much to dissipate the attention and energies of the layman.

A movement towards greater uniformity was already evident by the end of the middle ages and was facilitated by the advent of printing. The Council of Trent at its last session (December 1563, exactly four centuries before the present Constitution) directed the setting up of a commission for liturgical reform, one of whose members was Goldwell of St Asaph, the only English bishop at the Council. Revision of the breviary went on during the 1560s and the Bull *Quo Primum* of 1570 (Pius V) made a reformed missal obligatory for all who could not show a continuous local usage of two hundred years or more.

Further revisions of liturgical texts have been made by subsequent popes. One of the manifestations of Gallicanism was the production of independent liturgical texts, which went on down to the time of Pius IX.

Many of the issues of recent liturgical reformism had been raised earlier: e.g. the propriety of private masses and the desirability of frequent communion in Benedict XIV's *Certiores Effecti* of 1742, the proper fulfilment of choral office in his *Cum Semper* of 1744, Christian iconography in his *Sollicitudini* of 1745.

The same pope's *Annus Qui* of February 1749, addressed to the

[1] See Chapter 7 of *Church Life in England in the Thirteenth Century* by J. R. H. Moorman (the present Bishop of Ripon).

bishops of the Papal States, exhorted them to see that scandal should be forestalled in the Holy Year of 1750 by restoring decorum and cleanliness in their churches, by seeing to the reciting of the divine office chorally in the proper way, at the proper hours and with the proper chants, and by excluding everything theatrical and profane. This long and discursive Encyclical, with its copious historical documentation and tone of civilized reflection and argument, is interesting to compare with the more magisterial and legal-sounding utterances that became the regular thing a century or so later. It also gives incidentally a very full picture of liturgical musical practice at mid-eighteenth century. Benedict quotes Aelred of Rievaulx's *Speculum Charitatis* to show that even in the twelfth century Cistercians were complaining vigorously of current, mainly Cluniac, practices; but he also fair-mindedly quotes John of Salisbury as defending them. By nothing, he warns his suffragans, is a church more immediately judged than by the way services are carried out.

It is eloquent of the age that he shows little disposition to widen explicitly the scope of his exhortations beyond the bounds of the Papal States: to the Empire, for instance, which was about to enter on the golden age of that 'worldly' mass music of Mozart and Haydn which the German Cecilian Society would a century later stigmatize harshly as 'sacrilegious'.

A number of subsequent papal pronouncements, from Pius VI's *Auctorem Fidei*[1] to Gregory XVI's *Commissum Divinitus* are aimed against usurpations of papal authority in matters liturgical and against mistaken reforms. Pius IX went so far in 1874 as to tell the Uniat Ruthenians that some of the attempts to 'purify' their rite were laying snares for their faith and aiming to lead them into schism.

In 1833 the Bishop of Le Mans's secretary, a young priest called Prosper-Louis-Pascal Guéranger, bought the secularized abbey of Solesmes and re-established a small Benedictine community there. He had already written articles on liturgical reform, and the rest of his life was devoted to making Solesmes a centre of that reform, and establishing other centres in France, Spain and England. He died in 1875, four years after the publication of his chef d'oeuvre, *L'Année Liturgique*.

In France, as well as Solesmes, Ligugé, Marseilles and the

[1] Aimed against the Synod of Pistoia, cf. *infra*, p. 313.

Parisian abbey of Rue de la Source; in Belgium, Mont-César and St André at Lophem-lez-Bruges; in Germany, Maria Laach; in England, Farnborough under Abbot Cabrol, all were power houses of the modern liturgical revival. But the work was by no means confined to monasteries, and the scholarly work which was integral to the revival transcended denominational frontiers; the Cistercian Cardinal Bona had made lasting contributions to liturgical learning in the seventeenth century; so had that pioneer of modern critical history, the Benedictine Mabillon. In the nineteenth century scholars of such different backgrounds as Ranke and J. M. Neale, Duchesne and Edmund Bishop had added to liturgical learning, while the Bradshaw and Surtees Societies institutionalized the work of the pioneers after whom they were named.

Leo XIII encouraged the work of Solesmes in a letter to the Abbot, in 1901, but it was under Pius X that the papacy fully espoused the cause. Solesmes was of course chiefly famous for the restoration of plain chant,[1] but in his classical *Motu Proprio Tra le Sollicitudini* of November 1903 Pius made it clear that this aim was only part, though an integral part, of 'one pastoral care not only for this Holy See . . . but also for individual churches: maintaining and promoting the beauty of the house of God. Here the august mysteries are celebrated, here the faithful gather to receive the grace of the sacraments, to assist at the Holy Sacrifice of the altar, to adore the Most Blessed Sacrament and to be united at the Church's common prayer in her public and solemn liturgy.' Two years later came the decree on frequent communion. Though Pius was able to entitle it *Sacra Tridentina* and call to his support a chapter of that Council's twenty-second session, the decree was a witness to how Catholic practice had declined.

General practice, not least in Rome itself, lagged behind reforming zeal and papal direction, as Pius XI witnessed in 1928 (*Divini Cultus*) when he reiterated Pius X's musical dispositions with more practical

[1] Godfrey Diekmann, OSB, draws attention to the almost casual way in which the liturgical revival emerged on to the official stage: 'It is generally admitted that the pastoral liturgical renewal of today had its effective beginning in a talk by Dom Lambert Baudouin at a national Belgian Catholic Congress in 1909, a talk which was considered irrelevant to the purpose of the Congress by the organizers and was finally allowed to be delivered under the auspices of the "Art and Archaeology" section. Similarly, the principle of "active and intelligent participation" which proved such a decisive factor in promoting the liturgical movement, during its nearly forty years of desert wandering, derived from a *Motu Proprio* dealing with music.' (*Concilium*, February, 1965, p. 35.) It may be added that this was not altogether to the advantage of the revival.

measures for their realization. It was also part of the Milanese Pope's dynamic attitude to the mission field that he strongly encouraged native liturgical arts there. This did something to compensate for the stodgy academism which weighed heavily on Church art and architecture in Europe in general but in Rome in particular, at the time. Fascist contributions to church building were especially pompous and uninspired.

Pius XII in his first encyclical pledged himself to follow his predecessor's 'generous decisions' about adapting native culture and customs for liturgical purposes. This was part and parcel of the worldwide outlook which, after the stresses of war, was to characterize his pontificate, and was to play its part in preparing an open-minded response by the Church to the aspirations of African and other nationalism in the post-war period. Pius also showed himself consistently a believer in the value of established differences of rite, though especially after the advance of Communism in Eastern Europe he was compelled to follow Pius IX's example and keep a sharp eye on attempts to exploit these differences to loosen the bonds of Uniats with the Holy See (cf. the Encyclical *Orientalis* of 1945).

The recall to the fundamentals of religion prompted by the war, and the effect of persecution in driving many Catholic communities in on themselves, induced much stress on the need for the sanctification of Sunday, and hence for better understanding of and more intense participation in the mass, the sign and expression of unity.[1] As early as 1940 Pius had said to the young men of Italian Catholic Action: 'To take full part in the mass means to take part in the entire sacred action. It means to be one with those "*circumstantes*" whom the priest presents to God in the memento of the living—those who with the priest offer the sacrifice of praise for themselves and theirs, for their redemption, for their health and well-being. [The allusion is to the canon of the Roman mass.] You should remember that this "sacred action" includes, after the offering of the Victim, His consumption, that is the communion of the celebrant and the faithful. The *Acts of the Apostles* (ii, 42) witness that the first Christians were assiduous in hearing sacred instruction, in the breaking of bread, and in prayer.' (A.A.S., 1940, p. 498).

[1] Cf. Diekmann, *op. cit.*, p. 38: 'It was in army and war-prison camps, when reduced to the bare essentials of worship, in a personal encounter of priest and lay soldiers stripped of all external props, that the reality of the liturgy and the meaning of Church were discovered anew by thousands. To this discovery the pastoral-liturgical renewal of the post-war years largely owes its dynamism.'

But he was always sensitive to the risk of getting liturgical concerns out of proportion. In the letter he wrote to Von Preysing in 1943 (see Appendix) he said: 'You know that the Holy See has considered the liturgical questions which have been raised among you to be important enough to merit its attention. But we must admit that we attach far more importance to protecting Christian consciences against all the poisons that threaten them. What use would it be to make the liturgy of the Church more beautiful if, outside the church, the thoughts and actions of the faithful in their daily lives became alien to the law and love of Christ?'

A little later, in June of the same year, the Encyclical *Mystici Corporis* had a vital section on liturgy as the nourishing process of the Mystical Body of Christ, expressing and sustaining the vital unity with the Redeemer: though Pius at the same time warned against the fashion of belittling private prayer, vocal or mental. Two years later, speaking to Roman parish priests and Lenten preachers, he voiced his reservations about liturgical reform as a panacea for spiritual ills: 'When we look about us at humanity and ask ourselves if it is disposed to receive this reality [of the priesthood of the New Testament] the answer, alas, for many, cannot be affirmative. The supernatural world has become foreign to them, it means nothing. It is as though in them the spiritual organs of knowledge of such deep and saving truths were atrophied or dead. An attempt has been made to explain such a state of soul by defects in the Church's liturgy. But We do not believe that it would be sufficient to purify it, reform it, render it more sublime, to see if those who are today in error would find again the way of the divine mysteries. Those who reason in this manner show that they have a very superficial concept of spiritual anaemia and apathy. It has incomparably deeper roots.'

The letter *In Cotidianis Precibus*, also of 1945, expressed the link between liturgical and biblical scholarship and his desire to promote both: it announced a new translation of the psalter made direct from originals by scholars of the Pontifical Biblical Institute.

In the Encyclical *Mediator Dei* of November 1947 all these themes were gathered up. The preamble linked it with *Mystici Corporis:* In the liturgical revival 'Bolder relief was given to the fact that all the faithful make up a single and most compact body with Christ for its Head, and that the Christian community is in duty bound to participate in the liturgical rites according to their station.' Pius pointed to the character at once scholarly and spiritual of the revival, and spoke of previous papal concern. *Mediator Dei* is commonly called the Magna Carta of liturgical reform, but Pius stresses that not the least of his motives is to 'take proper steps to preserve it at the outset from excess or outright perversion'. Of his right and duty to do this there is to be no question: the Pope is very much the apex of the liturgical manifestation of the Mystical Body. He is the vicar of Christ the Priest, who is the teacher of public worship. That this charge was taken up from Christ in the apostolic age is demonstrated from the New Testament.

Exterior worship is a sign and instrument of unity, but it is sterile without interior worship; conformity is not enough. There should be no false antithesis erected between 'objective' and 'subjective' piety; a proper balance should be maintained between the doctrine of *ex opere operato*, which correctly states the intrinsic, divinely conferred efficacy of the sacraments, and *ex opere operantis*, which defines the necessary dispositions of the recipient.

Worship is intimately linked with hierarchy and priesthood, which is not handed down indiscriminately to all men but conferred on designated men by the 'spiritual generation' of Holy Orders, which is not mere delegation. Here lies the root of hierarchical authority over the liturgy. The Pope repudiates a use of the tag *lex orandi lex credendi* which would make it mean that worship is a kind of proving ground for truths to be held by faith. A variety of influences, he goes on, have gone to the development of liturgy—doctrine, sacramentary discipline, extra-liturgical devotion, the arts; the establishment of the Congregation of Rites has provided since the sixteenth century an instrument of control.

Pius speaks harshly of the temerity of innovators who introduce vernacular, transfer feasts, delete 'unsuitable' Old Testament passages, without reference to authority. He censures also antiquarianism and puritanism, instancing the addiction to the 'table' altar, the exclusion of black vestments, of wounded and suffering Christs and other images from church, the exclusion of polyphony. 'This way of acting bids fair to revive the exaggerated and senseless antiquarianism to which the illegal Council of Pistoia gave rise.' The Synod of Pistoia, summoned by Scipio de' Ricci, bishop of that diocese, in September 1786 in response to the efforts of Leopold of Tuscany to assume control of the Church in his domains, included among its abortive Gallican-Jansenist proposals a number of liturgical changes, including a vernacular usage. But Pius in the above stricture is more concerned with the spirit and status of the Synod than with its detailed proposals, some of which were defensible.

The Encyclical goes on to give a résumé of Eucharistic theology, with this conclusion: 'The faithful should be aware that to participate in the Eucharistic sacrifice is their chief duty and supreme dignity, and that not in an inert and negligent fashion, giving way to distractions and day-dreaming, but with such earnestness and concentration that they may be united as closely as possible with the High Priest. . . . The fact however that the faithful participate in the Eucharistic Sacrifice does not mean that they also are endowed with priestly power. It is very necessary that you make this quite clear to your flocks.' With this proviso, however, the Encyclical stresses the solidarity of priest and people in the offering, and favours various modes of 'participation'—dialogue, singing hymns, joining in sung mass. Yet Pius remains realistic in his estimate of the very varying possibilities of participation, and opposed to experiments dictated by whim or doctrinaire notions. Again, while giving every encouragement to communion at mass, he will have no nonsense about 'no masses after communion', and trounces the suggestion that thanksgiving after communion is superfluous. He vindicates too the doctrinal and liturgical basis of adoration of the Blessed Sacrament.

Turning to the divine office, the prayer of the Mystical Body, he enjoins that the people should participate where reasonable, and notably in the vespers of great feasts [a Roman tradition] which should not be sacrificed to the cult of pleasure.

He charges bishops to check the practice of closing churches between liturgical services, and speaks up for a reasonable allowance of extra-liturgical devotions, while recognizing that Christian life does not consist in their multiplication. He ends by some fairly brief references to the liturgical arts and to the need for liturgical training.

This résumé of *Mediator Dei* hardly suggests that the Magna Carta was a *carte blanche*. Pius clearly looked upon the liturgical movement as a thing excellent in general purpose which was yet a constant potential source of extravagance; it was a view which did not lack the support of evidence. Yet Pius's contributions to the practical advancement of liturgical revival were of the first consequence. He has often been called a 'Marian pope', but his exaltation of the mass and the Eucharist was no less insistent, and his measures to facilitate liturgical practice more memorable. In the nine years that separated *Mediator Dei* (1947) from the no less weighty address to the International Conference on Pastoral Liturgy at Assisi in 1956, he restored the Easter Vigil to its primitive hour and form (February 1951), partially relaxed the Eucharistic fast (January 1953), gave qualified approval to the idea of priests communicating instead of saying private masses when attending liturgical conferences (November 1954), acceded to the demand for transferring the other Holy Week services to evening (November 1955), simplified the rubrics of the breviary and the missal (March 1955), and set up a commission for more general reform (March 1956), whose work was to issue in a decree of the Congregation of Rites of July 25, 1960, nearly two years after his death. This document of nearly 150 pages of the *Acta Apostolica Sedis* is the culmination of the boldest series of liturgical innovations by a pope in modern history; their part in preparing the ground for the Second Vatican Council's Constitution and the radical discussion which preceded it cannot be exaggerated. The Constitution was thereby enabled to appear as a logical completion of recent policy in a way no other conciliar document did. This in spite of conservative opposition which often invoked, selectively, *Mediator Dei.*

Pius prefaced his remarks to the Assisi Congress of 1956 with a review of these recent measures of his own. What he went on to say was again much marked by the note of warning, against narrowness of view, against incomprehension, against specific errors. In the mass, he said, only the celebrant or *true* concelebrants sacrifice—*not* the others present, whether clerical or lay. One mass at which a hundred priests are present is *not* the same as a hundred masses; the practice may be tolerated at liturgical conferences so long as it does not encourage this error. In episcopal consecration, too, the co-consecrators must say the words, not just identify themselves with the consecrator-in-chief; internal intention is not the decisive factor. This is clearly a postscript to *Mediator Dei* for those who had 'not yet acquiesced' in this point.

On the Real Presence he recalls the literal meaning of the New Testament passages and of Trent, XIII, 1. Christ did not say, 'This is a sensible appearance that signifies the presence of My body and blood'. There must be no attenuations of the Real Presence doctrine that are 'not for the masses', and that would leave in the tabernacle only species preserving a so-called real and essential relation with the true Lord who is in heaven. He quotes Trent against those who deprecate processions, adoration, Holy Hours, Forty Hours' Devotions, and even reservation, and quotes with approval the Holy Office instruction of 1952 which enjoins reservation 'regularly at the high altar . . . and in an unmovable tabernacle at the centre'. He discerns a tendency to less esteem for the presence and action of Christ in the tabernacle. The advantages of mass facing the people are no good ground for this. 'The liturgical movement should not be content to *let* people come to the tabernacle—it should bend itself to attract them.' But Diekmann has pointed out that the Encyclical did stress other kinds of presence: 'Pius XII's statement in *Mediator Dei* on the presence of Christ in every liturgical action (A.A.S. 39,[1] p. 528) has probably had more theological impact than anything else in that document. We had become so accustomed to speak of Christ's "Real Presence" in the Eucharist that unwittingly we considered His other modes of presence as somehow unreal or figurative.' (*Op. cit.*, p. 38).

The divinity of Christ should not, says Pius, remain at the periphery of liturgical thought. Christ is not merely a mediator, He is also equal to the Father and the Holy Ghost in the liturgy.

The attitude of the liturgist to the past should avoid the extremes of blind attachment or total contempt. Account should be taken of the differing attitudes of the faithful—some have to be restrained, some remain indifferent or hostile. The Church, finally, 'has grave reasons for maintaining the unconditional obligation of the use of Latin for the celebrant'.

Two Holy Office *monita* wind up the liturgical story for Pius XII's reign. In February 1958 there was a warning that some had been adding prayers and readings to the mass on the pretext of revivalism and 'participation', and deleting others. Bishops were reminded of their supervisory duties (can. 1261/1) and clerics that only the Apostolic See can modify the liturgy (cc. 1257 and 1259/2). Also, prayers and pious exercises need the Ordinary's licence (c. 1259/1). Attention was further called to can. 770: 'infants are to be baptized as soon as possible', the practice of delaying has appeared, mixed up with odd ideas about the lot of unbaptized infants. Later in the same year came an admonition that some vernacular translations of the Holy Week liturgy had been printed which omitted the words '*Mysterium fidei*' (the mystery of faith) from the words of

[1] i.e. 1947.

consecration of the chalice, and that some priests had been leaving them out. This was contrary to canon 1399/10 and to the admonition of the preceding February.

In liturgical as in other matters, it is not a homogeneous picture that emerges from a review of Pius XII's utterances. He was firmly behind the essential aspiration, to restore the idea of the Christian community and of its self-awareness in the great acts of public worship. Yet his conviction that the liturgical revival was 'the Spirit passing through the Church' was consistent with a good deal of mistrust of many aspects of the 'movement', scepticism of exaggerated hopes of its effects, and a desire to keep a tight curial restraint on it. The re-thinking involved in liturgical revival carried with it the development of a special language, and for this he seems to have had a decided distaste: he was generally inclined to put novel terminology either actually or virtually in inverted commas. He was by temperament not personally fond either of crowds or of ceremonial, and his scepticism of 'movements' was part of that profounder scepticism which is often, in distinguished minds, the obverse of a profound faith. But his lack of emotional attraction lends all the greater weight to his intellectual assent to the central matter.

This has been stated moderately and succinctly by Father C. Davis:

'The task that faces us in the liturgical apostolate today is to persuade the faithful to take again a fully active share in the celebration of mass. If our efforts are to bear good fruit and not do harm, the faithful must answer the priest, join in the singing and perform their ritual actions, not because we have told them to do so but because they have become aware of the value of all this for their Christian life and have learnt to want it and seek it as fulfilling a spiritual need. Only in that way shall we canalize into the new forms of celebration the devotion, often intense, which they already have to the holy mass. The vital factor is always, not the practical details of ritual technique, but the spiritual consciousness of our people.

'Now, the enrichment we are seeking to give them is a reawakened sense of the assembly of Christians as a sacred reality: the inadequacy we are trying to overcome is a loss of the understanding of the assembly as a basic reality of the Christian life.' (*Theology for Today*, p. 258.)

Pius rarely if ever used the word 'assembly', but enough has perhaps been said to show that he insisted on the 'basic reality' outlined here. Father Davis also puts in perspective Pius's criticism of some liturgist contentions:

'We all know how Pope Pius XII reacted strongly against the mistaken depreciation of "private" masses into which some had been led. There is no need to enlarge upon the point here. Such masses are not only fully justified doctrinally but also have a definite and honoured place in the life of the Church. The increase in their frequency has enriched our understanding of the liturgy, making us better aware that the mass, the sacrifice of Christ, is a gift to the Church and that in the liturgy the action of Christ, mediated through His minister, comes first and precedes our response. Nevertheless, the prominence given to this form of mass led to a neglect of awareness of the assembly. Priests forgot their rôle as president of the assembly when the faithful were present and the faithful thought of themselves as assisting at mass rather than as taking part in it, as being outside rather than inside the eucharistic celebration. Thus the assembly was broken up into individuals; and the communal character of the celebration was further damaged when low mass, a form adapted for celebration without a congregation, was taken over for use as a public celebration. Hence the need to right the balance and stress again the part of the assembly. . . .

'The need to avoid any depreciation of masses without a congregation must not make us overlook the fact that such masses have a meaning only against the background of regular eucharistic assemblies in the Church. The fact that the mass is the sacrifice of the Church, the public worship of the Church, demands that it be regularly celebrated with an assembly of the Church, so that all the members of the Church can take part in it personally. It can also be celebrated without a congregation by a minister representing the Church; but it would be an odd kind of Church in which public worship was carried out only in a vicarious fashion.' *Ibid*, pp. 265 and 267.

Pius clearly conceived his relation to the liturgical movement as spur and rein at once—the correct conception at that stage in which a great deal of pastoral zeal, learning and enthusiasm were being sifted into ecclesiastical ordinances, and in which enthusiasm sometimes outran not merely discretion but discipline. If this sometimes resulted in liturgical ordinances having a ring of excessive legalism, then clearly those who had invited the restraining hand shared the blame; moreover liturgical enthusiasts can themselves speak in a very peremptory and intolerant way when they forget that (as Father Congar calls to mind) 'reforms spring up in the name of the *meaning* of things as against undue concern about rubrics and observances'. (*Laity*, *Church and World*, p. 32.)

Nothing was more striking about the conciliar debate on liturgy and the forging of the constitution than the way in which in a few months a century-old process of revival was lifted finally out of the phase of 'wandering in the desert', out of the realm in which the word 'movement' (with its overtones of persecuted minorities) belongs and set down in the serene air of the Church in council—the Church realizing herself anew and with a fresh depth. Here there can be no disputing what was John XXIII's greatest contribution; to provide the liturgical revival with this serene setting, ecumenical in every sense.

It is a commonplace that the liturgical revival is 'pastoral' in purpose, and nothing was more certain to attract John to it; the pastoral dominated all other aspects of his conception of the supreme office. 'The various initiatives of a pastoral character which mark this first stage of my papal apostolate have all come to me as pure, tranquil, loving, I might even say silent inspirations from the Lord. . . .' (*Journal*, August 14, 1961.)

Speaking while taking possession of the Lateran a few days after his election he said:

'The chalice upon the altar and the venerable rites which unite the consecrated bread and wine in a single sacrament mark the high point, the sublime peak in the union between God and man and the perfection of our Christian profession.

'In Our many dealings with Christian people, there is a saying of Bossuet, one of the great modern geniuses of Christian learning, that we find often coming back to Us: "There is no perfection in Christian life or practice apart from participation in the eucharistic banquet". The catechetical teaching We spoke of before leads to it naturally, and all the zeal of the pastoral spirit is dedicated to it.

'We intend to make this clear from the very first days of Our pontificate by presenting Ourself to the world above all as a pastor. . . .

'The picture of your Bishop and your priest that We would like you to carry with you always is one of him standing at the altar, distributing the Body and Blood of Our Lord, for this is the living substance of the religion We profess—the *Nobiscum Deus:* God within us. . . .' A.A.S. 1958, p. 918.

His first Easter homily, in March 1959, was a lengthy eulogy of the Holy Week liturgy. It was striking to see him entering one of the great basilicas for a Good Friday ceremony, with his bustling stride, without fuss, benign yet recollected; or making his cheerful and talkative way through a Lenten Sunday service, whether in one of the historic station churches or in one of the stark new working-class parishes of the peripheries. Here indeed the assembly gathered in close unity with its chief pastor.

To those in the mission field he wrote: 'Unity in prayer and in active participation in the divine mysteries in the Church's liturgy contributes with special effect to the wealth of Christian life both of the individual and of the community. It is furthermore a marvellous means of education in that charity which is the distinctive sign of the Christian; a charity which is alien to every social, linguistic and racial discrimination, that stretches its arms and its heart out to all, whether enemies or brothers.' (Encyclical *Princeps Pastorum*, *A.A.S.* 1959.)

He even told the President of Turkey of his 'true and lasting joy in the fact that We introduced into the Church, in conjunction with Latin, the first indication of understanding of the new times—the reading of the Gospel in the Turkish language, then renewed and restored. . . .'

On the anniversary of his election he spoke to the Roman people of 'new actions' suggested by modern life combining with ancient traditions to restore the worship of God, and when the work of preparation for the Council was launched it was not surprising to find him giving a firm mandate to the liturgical preparatory commission.

When the Commission's *schema* eventually appeared, opposition to it varied in motive. There were those who seemed to think that Pius XII's vindications of the Holy See's prerogatives in liturgical matters precluded an ecumenical council (summoned after all by the Holy See) handling them except in the most general and gingerly way. A clause to this effect was actually inserted in the final draft of the Preparatory Commission's *schema after* it had been passed by the Central Commission and before the bishops received it: the kind of device of which more was to be heard in the coming three years. *Mediator Dei* was often quoted in the debate, but mainly by opponents of reform for the purpose of deprecating a 'too daring' approach to liturgy by the Council—as though this canonically summoned and historic assembly was no more than a kind of blown-up version of the Synod of Pistoia. This was all eloquent of the odd ideas of Church government that had grown up in certain circles in the lop-sided period since 1870. The eventual answer to it of course was the existence of the Constitution, duly ratified by the Pope. But Article 22 of this document dealt briefly with the question of authority:

1. Regulation of the sacred liturgy depends solely on the authority of the Church—which means on the Apostolic See and, as laws may determine (*ad normam juris*), on the bishop.

2. In virtue of authority conceded by the law, the regulation of the liturgy within certain defined limits belongs also to various kinds of bishops' conferences legitimately established.

3. Therefore no other person, even if he be a priest, may add, remove or change anything in the liturgy on his own authority.

This, it has been pointed out,[1] 'stands in sharp contrast to canon 1257 which, before Vatican Council II, summed up the development of liturgical authority in the Latin Church: "It pertains to the Apostolic See alone to order the sacred liturgy and approve the liturgical books." ' The same writer adds that 'pontifical documents subsequent to the Code of Canon Law have, if anything, asserted an even greater reservation of power', and cites both *Mediator Dei* and the decree of the Congregation of Rites of September 1958.

The article must accordingly be read in close connection not only with the rest of the Constitution, which gives such prominence to restoring the concept of the people of God grouped liturgically around their bishop, but also with the relevant parts of the Constitution *De Ecclesia*, which restores a balance to the ecclesiastical structure by completing the unfinished work of 1870.

Pragmatically this extending of a measure of initiative to local authorities supplied a need that the debate itself had thrown sharply into relief. *A priori* it is clear that there is no field in which a central bureaucracy is more inevitably handicapped in legislating for the world-wide Church, and the differences revealed in the debate amply confirmed this. There could be no substitute for a close and imaginative grasp of the needs provoked in concrete communities by rapid social and psychological change. The matter was well put

[1] By F. R. McManus in an interesting article, *The Juridical Power of the Bishops and the Constitution on the Sacred Liturgy* in *Concilium*, February 1965, p. 20.

from one point of view by the Auxiliary Bishop Ancel of Lyons, famous for his apostolate among the workers in that city: he urged 'those bishops who had no pastoral charge' (the reference was clear enough) 'to try to understand the plight of pastors who were faced with situations in which the Church was considered moribund, and appreciate their longing for a liturgical renewal. Bishops who still enjoyed the security of large, docile congregations were asked not to close their eyes and hearts to the needs of those living in de-Christianized areas, where the mere pouring in of money would be of little use. He could speak for a large number of priests who were frequently seeking his counsel and encouragement in their attempt to revitalize the Church and awaken a spiritual awareness in the lives of their people. Two criteria ought to govern those who would adapt the liturgy: they must have a profound knowledge of and feeling for the liturgy; and they must understand the local psychology. No adaptation would be worthwhile unless it took these two things into account.'[1]

The Liturgical Constitution was the first but not the last Council achievement to afford a perspective of episcopal thinking that had not been discernible in reports of the debate which gave it birth. These might have led the superficial observer to imagine that the whole discussion raged about the abolition of Latin or the hygienic puzzles raised by communion under both kinds. There was never any question of abolishing Latin, except in the minds of a handful. The language issue was in any case never an easy one—in many countries it raised enormous difficulties. But to make Latin, factitiously, the touchstone of loyalty to Roman tradition (playing on the genuine love of the cultural heritage of western Christendom shared by the majority) was a tactic in the interests of those who through training and background handled Latin with complete facility. To make it a touchstone of concern for souls was beyond human ingenuity.

Full, conscious and active participation belongs naturally to the liturgy and is the right and duty of the baptized: on this broad principle the Constitution bases its dispositions. Liturgy is to be a compulsory major subject taught by qualified professors. Innovation is to have organic unity with the past. The communal is always to be preferred to the private. There are to be no distinctions of persons during the liturgy except those arising out of rank and

[1] Summarized by Rynne, *Letters from Vatican City*, p. 111.

function within the Church. The didactic function of the liturgy is to be ensured by a noble and unencumbered simplicity. There are to be more and better scripture readings. Sermons are to be mainly scriptural and liturgical in source. Bible services are to be encouraged, especially where there is no priest available. Though Latin remains the staple in the West, vernacular is to be introduced as authority deems beneficial. In the adapting of regional customs and way of life to liturgical usage, the generous concessions reflect the characteristic outlook of the document. Aspiration to restore the liturgical rôle of the bishop is tempered with realism towards the indispensable rôle of the parish. In the spirit of Pius XII, the liturgical spirit is seen as a sign of the times, to be institutionalized adequately in every diocese. Detailed provisions in the various sectors of the liturgy reflect faithfully these general aspirations. The full pattern of these will not of course emerge until the radical revisions laid down by the Constitution have been completed, but the considerable practical changes already becoming familiar have quite failed to justify the fearful premonitions of integralists and the milder trepidation even of moderate men.

In the liturgical arts there is a longer and rougher road to travel. Music has been longest the object of solicitude, and though there is no feeling of assurance that the Church's incomparable musical heritage is yet safe from the fervid philistine and the pious iconoclast, there is an improving understanding (reflected in official pronouncements) of what is needed and of the distinction between the regularly and the occasionally justifiable. In the less flexible matter of church building and decoration, the limits of what legislation and administrative exhortation can do are woefully (or perhaps one should say happily) narrow. It is significant perhaps that Rome, the very source of this, has produced in the past generation the choicest monuments of dull, indecisive and even repulsive church building that the world has to show. A similar equation between bureaucracy and mediocrity could be easily illustrated elsewhere. Where churchmen have managed to engage the enthusiasm and kindle the imagination of architects without reading them lectures, the results have been far happier and occasionally splendid. Perhaps it is only when the liturgical revival has progressed far enough to make even artists conscious of a place (and that a special and honoured one) in the community of God's people that we may expect a corresponding revival of religious art.

15

Conclusion

'THERE ARE MOMENTS, M. Gaubert, when I ask myself whether God did not bury the Church when he buried Pius XII.' The remark is made by a character in the novel *Paris—Le Monde by* Roger Bésus, one of several recent works which show that French integralism is still alive and kicking.[1] Pius XII has also enjoyed the doubtful benefit of the advocacy of the Belgian novelist Alexis Curvers, whose *Le Pape Outragé* regards Hochhuth's play as the culmination of an Enterprise of Subversion aimed against the Church through Pius. 'This last witness to order instead of to fables was a nuisance . . . it was a question of eliminating him by any means possible.'

This kind of conspiracy mania is not the monopoly of the extreme Right, but it finds there its most arresting exponents. The obverse side of M. Curver's conspiracy is the 'myth' of John XXIII. Louis Salleron, reviewing the book in *Carrefour*, summed up this charge: 'We progressive Catholics have invented a John XXIII in our own image. Maligning him as we maligned his predecessor, but by heaping praises on the one and calumnies on the other, we have made of John XXIII a pope who wanted to introduce democracy into the Church, make an *aggiornamento à la sauce tartare*, build a Christianity detached from the heritage of centuries.'

For one of M. Bésus' characters, again, the Council is 'folklore', 'matter for newspaper tittle-tattle'.

It has been suggested here that while the contrasts between Pius and John are real enough, many issues are falsely stated in terms of such contrasts. Still more are the violent oppositions of these ecclesiological romances to be dismissed as humbug. John XXIII,

[1] See the excellent article 'Les Nouveaux Inquisiteurs' in *Informations Internationales Catholiques*, November 1, 1964.

it has been argued here, was by nature and temperament a pluralist, Pius something of a paternalist. The latter often by intellectual integrity digested and stated liberal principles for which he perhaps felt little emotional affinity. Nostalgia for a papal theocracy but recently lost surrounded Pius in his youth. He grew up in a Rome whose prevailing atmosphere was still that in which the laity were a minority governed by priests: Catholic lay action had originated and grown, largely in his own lifetime, in this strongly paternalist and clerical environment. It was all something out of which he had to think his own way.

John XXIII was a northern peasant. He had served in the army. His impressionable years had been spent under the absorbing influence of a distinguished liberal bishop, a rich character: Radini-Tedeschi. He had done three turns of diplomatic service, all in countries which in various ways had habituated him to the clergy taking a back seat: as a minority among the Orthodox in Bulgaria; in lay dress and obscurity in Istanbul; dealing with an anti-clerical political tradition in France.

Yet there was no clerical 'thesis' of Pius to which John offered the 'hypothesis'; Pius had reason for insistence on the fundamentals of authority and obedience. The need is perhaps recurring. John had other things to emphasize, no less fundamental.

The papacy has been slow over the centuries to learn the lesson pointed by De Gasperi. Pius XII accepted it after the failure of 'Operation Sturzo', though not with ease; the unease was partly a matter of temperament, more a historical legacy he had to outgrow.

The Church is often reproached simultaneously, or in rapid succession, with not minding her own business and with being indifferent to the world's business. These reproaches often cancel out, but clericalism can merit both. The true nature of lay action in the Church has only slowly emerged; it is a field in which the best practical guidance has not really originated in Rome, but it is the nature of the Roman Church that, wherever things originate, they must come to a head at Rome. Pope John provided occasion for this: with the Council especially, but also with *Mater et Magistra* and *Pacem in Terris*. The constitution on the Church provides the solid foundation for the layman's status, for theological thinking is in the end more important than pragmatical.

The Church's fear of Communism and mistrust of socialism enhanced mistrust of the layman for long after the war: *Punti Fermi* was the classical exposition of this, and of the concomitant leaning towards clericalism. The tendency was persistent to treat political issues, in which the layman should be able to judge and act for himself, as doctrinal issues; there was no sound ground between secularism and clericalism. Yet the conventional picture of the Church running Italian politics by telling people who not to vote for is a very partial and superficial one: rather it is arguable that over the past decade the leading figures in Italian politics—especially Aldo Moro, first as Secretary of the Christian Democrats then as Prime Minister—have been engaged in educating politically the Italian Church.

During the post-war years of Pius XII's reign Communism was wreaking enormous damage on the structure of the Church in eastern Europe; while in the West there seemed real danger of people progressively succumbing to its appeal. Both these things were attenuated under John—the first by the slowing down of the post-war impetus of Communist expansion and consolidation, of which the last fling was the crushing of the Hungarian rising; the second by the growth of prosperity in the West.

Western and eastern versions of the Communist problem came to be seen as separate. This did not imply that essential Communist doctrines were to be viewed any differently in one place or the other, but that the actual situations perhaps ought to. Need to make the best of a bad job in the East—a need the Vatican diplomatic tradition was thoroughly equipped to meet—began to have its echo in the West too by Pope John's time, and this has continued. The present Holy Father has adopted towards the much-discussed dialogue with Communism an attitude in every sense realistic: recognizing that in places where Catholics work among a majority of Communists, contacts, discussion, even some degree of common trades union action may be inevitable, but insisting on knowledge, firmness and vigilance in those who embark on dialogue.

It is in the sphere of international relations that continuity of thought between Pius XII and John XXIII seems most evident, and the limitations imposed by an Italian horizon least disabling. In the one case perhaps we can see an intellectual vision, sharpened by the experience of war, of the need to give political expression to the brotherhood of man, which might also offer the papacy occasion for a renewed world rôle; in the other, a deep personal instinct which overrode every limiting factor and tradition. But excessive contrast would be a distortion: the unifying factor was charity—the deep sense of the mystical unity of those baptized in Christ, and further, of the unity of all men created by God for Himself. Here too lay the root of the profound horror of war shared by the two popes—something which carried them far beyond the traditional and no longer adequate categories of Catholic thinking on war. Here certainly both were in the van of progress: conventional political thinking has arguably trailed after them. This is a burden which Paul VI has taken up vigorously: his sense of the human community is strong: it took him into Asia. It has found its most recent expression in the establishment under Cardinal König of a Secretariat for improving contacts with non-religious peoples. We have seen an Italian elder statesman, Pietro Nenni, head of a party once viewed with intense suspicion at the Vatican, if not actually proscribed, travelling to New York, with the papal blessing, to address a UNO conference on the significance of *Pacem in Terris*, and being received in a long private audience soon after his return.[1]

This New York conference on the great Encyclical went far beyond war and peace—to the roots of peace, in social harmony. In this new phase of the Church's long and closely-woven history we are aware of a tension between a theoretical proclamation of the brotherhood of man and a leaning towards anathema inherited from a more homogeneous and theocratic age. The priest, the bishop who must be constantly condemning, remains inescapably a remote figure, not a friend but a monitor. Brotherhood and the breathing of fire may be bound in the same document—it is more difficult to bind them in the same life. The difficulty is immensely enhanced in a world in which the Church has lost the useful asset of inspiring awe—in which her magisterial voice is no longer a voice of thunder. The integralist is essentially the man who fails to grasp this. He sees only weakness and decay in the realism which recognizes the de-christianization of the world and the need, not for new doctrines but for new moulds and a new demeanour.

Whatever may be said of those who surrounded him, Pius XII had a mind far too acute and searching to miss these distinctions or overlook these needs. But it seems that he was only feeling his way towards practical expedients when illness and exhaustion slowed the pace of his re-thinking. Moreover, his great sense of authority

[1] A later and more striking move of Paul VI in this field was of course his flying visit and speech to the United Nations Headquarters in New York on October 4, 1965.

combined with his personal experience to make him deeply mistrustful of systems or experiments rooted in the defiance of authority.

In one thing John was most clearly 'sent by God': by pitching papal authority in a lower key, counterpointing it with a simplicity and deceptive casualness which his very physical appearance and manner and speech decisively helped to create, he fell miraculously into harmony with the prevailing mood, in the world of his short reign. That he thereby lowered the prestige of that authority would be a bold contention in the face of recent history: for every seminarian or journalist who has defended extravagant and shallow views by taking John's name in vain, a hundred statesmen, a thousand mature scholars, as many non-Catholic religious leaders and a hundred times as many ordinary people have been brought to think of the Church more deeply, more sympathetically, more reverently, more seriously. For every old Italian lady who (let us suppose) voted Communist in 1963 because she thought the Pope had said it was all right, a hundred people in Italy and a thousand elsewhere were shaken in their assurance that the Church had no more to say to the modern world. If the last of the Council's *schemata*, whose stumbling beginnings emphasized the loss of communication, emerges from the forge as successfully hammered as did *De Ecclesia*, that assurance may be shaken still more happily.

There is no need to defend Pope John by denying that his brief, eventful pontificate brought problems, even risks in its wake. Those to whom this is a damning criticism reveal an odd conception of the Church's function and an odder one of her history. As the German Jesuit Von Galli put it stimulatingly to a Stuttgart *Katholikentag* in 1964, such people think too much of the Rock of Peter and not enough of the barque of Peter. The second metaphor reminds us that 'Christ did not institute the Church in order to deliver us entirely from anxiety. He did not institute it so that we should have a slick answer to everything and, finally, He did not institute it as a sort of pillow on which we Catholics can rest while the others get on with the work.' There is an element of exaggeration here of course, but it is a legitimate counter-exaggeration. There are risks against which the Church is our insurance, and risks that loyal membership of the Church precludes our taking. But we should know what they are, and not extend the list.

A document of Pius XII's reign which now seems almost exclusively conscious of risks is the Holy Office instruction on ecumenical activities. But, as was suggested in Chapter 12, it is not possible to pass judgement on Pius XII's attitude to the non-Catholic world simply on the basis of this document and its related *monitum*. His contribution to closing the gap between the Church and the rest of human kind was made in other ways—in his active promotion of biblical scholarship and liturgical reform; in the international field; above all perhaps in the long, intense personal effort to enter into the activities and difficulties of the men of every kind and calling who visited the Vatican in such numbers in the post-war years. If the world, and the non-Catholic Christian world especially, responded so promptly to the personality of John XXIII, and to the possibilities opened up by the Council, it was partly at least because of a consciousness of Church and papacy which had grown continuously during Pius XII's reign.

That consciousness certainly included a recognition of the importance of the Church and the papacy in a world which had so largely lost its moral and spiritual bearings. In the decade following the war men were not disposed to underestimate the power of an authoritative voice. But they needed to feel certain that it spoke with the accents of their own time. This need did not derive (if we speak of serious levels of opinion) from contempt for the past. There has been no time in history at which men have more industriously and meticulously delved into the past. But they did not do so because they felt that the past was something to which they could ever return; rather because they felt the speed and inevitability with which a new world was being born, and hence an urgent need to secure contact with their roots. Few gave more frequent expression than Pius XII to the sense of a new world being born out of the travail of war and technical progress. He made a gigantic personal effort to grapple with it. But where that effort stopped short and was supplemented by workmanlike bureaucracy trained in a restricted school, the world was often acutely conscious of anti-climax.

It was here that the heart of the revolution of the next pontificate lay. John caught and retained his predecessor's sense of a crisis in the Church's history. He might have been expected (was expected by many) to regard it as something which an octogenarian need not tackle. He could fall back on the triumphalist cliché: the Church has weathered many crises; she will be here not only when I am gone but when her enemies have fallen and been forgotten.

But what of those millions who, though not her enemies, had themselves forgotten her? To the integralist, crisis means only danger; but the oldest definition of crisis is 'danger plus opportunity'. To those who, reared in the spirit of the '*non expedit*', thought of the Church first as the rock-fortress, an ecumenical council was a vast and expensive device for courting trouble. The main achievement of the First Vatican Council had been, in a world of revolutions, to close the ranks round the infallible Pope, much as de Maistre had advocated. What was to be gained by opening them?

Elsewhere, the experience of the Church's leaders had been very different. In many countries they lived much more closely at grips with the realities of modern life: with secular culture, with non-Catholic Christianity, with problems raised by the spread of higher education, problems of communication with those inside or outside the Church who are the heirs—and the willing heirs—of modern progress in all its phases. To such bishops the crisis was a very different matter. There was danger, but it was much more subtle and various. It would be quite false of course to suppose that the bishops of France, of Belgium, of Holland, of Austria, of Germany are insensitive to the dangers of false doctrine: a little reflection on the horrible history of the past thirty years will show the absurdity of this. The danger of false doctrine points to the necessity of guarantees of orthodoxy—of being assured that here on earth the Church embodies God's guidance in the irrefragable certainties of Faith. These things are not inventions of Roman bureaucracy, nor matters of taste or temperament. They are the stuff of Catholicism, and clearly enough present in the New Testament.

But if it is legitimate enough to think of the Church from one point of view as a fortress against error, this is not the predominant conception of it that emerges from the Gospel. The parables of the leaven, of the sower, of the mustard seed, these illuminate the character of the apostolic mission, the challenge, always renewing itself, to the ministers of Christ's word. Many approached the Second Vatican Council convinced that the chief danger is that the Church should seem to ignore this challenge; should seem to turn in on itself at a time when the task of the missioner, the seeker after souls, is more immediate and acute in the historic capitals of Christendom than in the distant lands of strange men and cults.

Pope John combined a shrewd assessment of his own limitations (we should call it Christian humility) with a crystal, candid trust in divine providence and a robust if unacademic sense of history. He was constitutionally incapable of thinking of crisis without its element of opportunity. But it was not opportunity for some Promethean effort of his own. The Church was led throughout the world by bishops whose functions had been left ill-defined since crisis cut short the Council of 1870—a time when danger was allowed to swamp opportunity. A sufficient number of these were men of originality, force, learning, boldness of imagination as well as of spirituality and zeal. John saw enough of them to weigh them in the balance against those, more familiar, 'whose voices sound often in Our ears but find no echo in Our heart'. To give those distant voices a chance to sound more strongly: there was no need to look further for a justification of the Council, since this was the simplest way to make men more comprehensively aware of the Church. Criticism of the Church's current 'image' sounded in many places, even among those whose loyalty to the Church was wholly above suspicion. They were often exaggerated or based on insufficient knowledge; but they were not all fanciful, to be brushed aside in the name of defence or conservation, as though critic were synonymous with aggressor.

There is an important distinction to be made between the concept of conservatism in relation to doctrine and in relation to practical matters. All ecumenical councils since Constance at least have argued whether they should discuss doctrine or reform, and in what order. (John XXIII settled this question firmly in advance—a valuable exercise of the papal prerogative.) The desire for change generally begins in the practical sphere. It is often a sign of healthy discontent, of mental vigour; equally, reaction against it, rhetorical deploring of novelty, is often no more than mental laziness and hardening of the arteries. If this masquerades as a concern for orthodoxy, for the integrity of faith, then it is dishonest. But the masquerade can only deceive because it can and has happened that reforming zeal modulates into heresy, that fury with existing practice turns into advocacy of error. The Church must maintain sound doctrine, but this does not consecrate the teaching methods or the leading ideas of any particular age. Theology seeks the understanding of the deposit of Faith, and the insights, the understanding of every age have their contribution to make to this.

Our own age is an age of professionalism, it is often said. At its best this means that those who do not pay the utmost attention to fact, to accuracy of method, to high scientific and technical standards are generally disesteemed as wanting in seriousness. It means an age in which incredible resources of technique, ingenuity, accumulated knowledge are brought to bear upon any enterprise on which men really set their hearts. A Church which commands the allegiance of 550,000,000 and sets itself the most exalted of enterprises cannot afford to neglect these resources. If distinguished scholars, advanced in views perhaps but of unquestioned zeal and loyalty, are treated unimaginatively and suspiciously, if there seems to be a gulf between expert knowledge and popular ignorance bridged only by an uneasy episcopate, then it will seem that the Church is paying no more than lip service to these ideas.

It is an extraordinary irony that the name of Pius XII, one of the keenest, most insatiable minds in the history of the papacy should have been invoked in support of the kind of integralism that the Second Vatican Council has largely routed: that M. Bésus should be able to get away with the silliness of making one of his characters resist the blandishments of a pro-Council newspaper by invoking Pius XII in his prayers. This can only mean that the free flow of ideas between Rome and other parts of the Catholic Church (and of the world at large) has been inadequate.

Some kind of regular senate of the world episcopate in Rome has been canvassed as the remedy.[1] Might not the difficulties of neutrality in the war years have been fewer if such an international body had been an established thing, an institution that nationalist fanaticism had to reckon with? At least bishops who put patriotic or even party fervour before the interests of truth and of general justice would have been more clearly put in the wrong. Might not the problems of lay action and political implications have been settled less equivocally and more consistently for the Church as a whole, and the Church's position made clearer and firmer in particular countries? Might not the Church's contribution to the growth of the international community have been more positive; social principles better applied; disasters like the worker-priest affair averted; Catholic ecumenism more coherently and courageously developed; standards of learning raised all round and such a business as the campaign against the Biblical Institute rendered impossible?

Of some of these things at least Pope John was conscious. But his historical standing does not need the support of exaggerated claims

[1] Now established by the present Pope. Cf. p. 211, note.

for far-sightedness and cunning. Simplicity, directness were what the situation of his day supremely demanded and what he was supremely equipped to supply. He wrote in his diary: 'It is commonly believed and considered fitting that even the everyday language of the popes should be full of mystery and awe. But the example of Jesus is more closely followed in the most appealing simplicity, not dissociated from the God-given prudence of wise and holy men. Wiseacres may show disrespect if not scorn for the simple man. But those wiseacres are of no account; even if their opinions and conduct inflict some humiliations, no notice should be taken of them at all: in the end everything ends in their defeat and confusion.'

John XXIII developed a sound technique for taking no notice of wiseacres. He tried to bring about some simplification of language: it is there in the encyclicals, most of all in *Pacem in Terris*. He tried to impose it on the Vatican newspaper, and his successor has tried even more persistently. This is a herculean labour, showing little result for great effort.

But even when he stuck to his brief the tradition of papal rhetoric could not blur the sharp, homely image of John. In a Council which was his creation it seemed wholly natural that bishops should complain forcefully of the inflated and remote language of Conciliar *schemata;* no less natural that they should reject formalism, excessive schematization, academic frigidity, legalistic pomp; the whole paraphernalia of the tribune, the office and the lecture room. These things are the props of everyday administration and training; but you do not summon the Church's leaders from the round earth's imagined corners to listen to what they could read in a thirty-year-old manual, a commentary on the code of canon law or a letter from a minor functionary. That the Council administration took some time to grasp this was the best proof of what a divine grace the Council was; and if supernatural grace abounded in the assembly, whatever the clash of convictions, there was also much natural grace, borrowed from the genial begetter of this historic concourse.

On this chord of grace, natural and supernatural, we may close. Here Pius XII and John XXIII were securely united. No historic institution lives by a succession of faceless heads; history is the accumulation of fruitful contrasts, the dialectic of human nature's infinite variety. Such truisms are no less true of the papacy: in the

Church of God the continuity is of grace, and the manifestation of grace is most luminous in and through the variations, the quirks even of character. In their wholly different ways Pius XII and John XXIII were richly endowed with grace natural and supernatural. Caricature, mythologizing, cynicism, sentimentality, even the conventions of hagiography have failed to obscure this. History—the history of what to the human vision seems one of the half-dozen decisive moments in the life of the Church on earth—will surely ratify it.

APPENDIX I

CATHOLICS AND JEWS

Letter from Pius XII to Monsignor Preysing, April 30, 1943, from *Pie XII et le IIIe Reich — Documents* by Saul Friedlander, pp. 129 *et seq.*

(see p. 255)

'First of all, venerable Brother, We wish to thank you for the kind greetings you have sent Us—either personally or in the name of your clergy and your diocese—on different occasions, notably in December for Christmas and the New Year, and for the anniversary of Our election to the supreme pontificate. We know from how loyal a heart they come, a heart filled with the spirit of faith. We send you Our special thanks—you and the people of your diocese—for your devout prayers. In your letter of February 27 last you assured Us of your urgent prayers, having in mind "how rarely God had laid so heavy a burden on a pope's shoulders at the beginning of his pontificate, with this fearful world war and all the sins and evils that are its consequence". To be sure, prudence must guide Us when we make comparisons between the present and the past, and We have not the least wish to underestimate the preoccupations and misfortunes which have weighed down the shoulders of Our predecessors. Nevertheless, the sincere purpose of the Pope to stand out with full impartiality before all the powers of this world in the vast and bewildering conflict that confronts them, and at the same time carefully to protect Holy Church from its consequences—rarely had this presented the Holy See with so heavy a trial as at the present time. Most preoccupying to Us, however, are "all those sins and evils that are the consequence of war", as you so aptly express it. The development of the cruel technique of war, subject to no restraint, makes unbearable to Us this prospect of reciprocal massacre that shows no sign of coming to a close. Day by day We receive information of inhuman acts that have nothing to do with the real necessities of war, and which fill Us with horror and alarm. Recourse to prayer made before God who sees all things, close to the tabernacle of our Redeemer, alone enables Us to find the moral strength to overcome the impact of such acts upon Us.

The Nazi attitude towards the Pope's efforts to bring about a less inhumane conduct of the war

'For your part, you must have become acquainted with the terrible experience of war in that most painful form of aerial bombardment. Once again We tell you and the faithful of your diocese how much We deplore the destruction of St Hedwig's Cathedral during the last Berlin raid. The faithful should know that We have a daily prayer and a special blessing for all, who on that day, of either side, fell victim to aerial bombardment. We are doing what lies in Our power to mitigate the evils of the war, and We labour without respite so that the civilian population should be spared as much as possible; neither do We let Ourselves be daunted by the meagre chances of success. It is not Our fault if total equity *vis-à-vis* problems presented by the war obliges Us, now that it is Germany which suffers the more from aerial attacks, to undertake a discreet mediation—independently of the fact that the German authorities, consequent on the presence in Rome of the Archbishop of New York, or rather consequent on rumours which have circulated about his visit to Rome, made it publicly known that Germany was not interested in the Pope's efforts to secure a more humane conduct of the war. In Our striving to achieve this more humane conduct we have an equal solicitude for all victims of the war, for all who thereby suffer materially or morally. And all such victims, in Germany as elsewhere in the world, set their hopes in Our help.

'We were most anxious that Our Prisoner-of-war Information Service should profit Germany as it does other nations. This service has developed to its present proportions because of requests made to the Holy See for its intervention, requests which often other authorities had been unable to meet. Along with Our other war charities it has been able to do much good, and We thank God for it. We are unable to understand what motives could have persuaded the German authorities to forbid these Pontifical services access to German territory. This prohibition has been particularly felt here, where We have so many communications concerning German prisoners, sent to Our service for transmission to their families in Germany. We have at last been successful, but in a roundabout way and with the greatest difficulty. Since autumn 1942 requests for information about missing persons, or prisoners on the Russian front, in particular at Stalingrad, have been coming in from Germany in ever increasing numbers. They bear witness to an overwhelming distress. For Our part, no effort is left undone to secure news of prisoners who are in Russia, but unfortunately we have had no success at all up to the present.

The German bishops' pastoral letters

'We are grateful to you, venerable Brother, for the clear and frank words addressed by you, on various occasions, to your people, and through them to the public at large. We have in mind, among others, your declaration of June 28, 1942, on the Christian concept of rights; on "Dead Sunday", November last, on the right of every man to life and love; We think specially of your Advent Pastoral, which was also adopted by the west German ecclesiastical provinces, on the sovereign rights of God, and on the rights of the individual and of the family.

'Let it not be thought that bold stands taken by the Bishops can injure your country in the eyes of world opinion, when they thus insist, in the face of their government, on the rights of religion, the Church, the human person, in favour of those who are defenceless and oppressed by this show of public strength, whether the victims be children of the Church or not. Far from compromising your country, this courageous defence of right and of humanity will earn, both for your country and for yourselves, the respect of world opinion, and in the future it could prove to your advantage.

'As Supreme Pastor of the faithful, it is Our care that the faith and convictions of your Catholic people remain pure from compromise with principles and actions contrary to the law of God and the spirit of Christ, or which even set them to scorn. To take a recent instance, it was a consolation to Us to learn that Catholics, notably those of Berlin, had given proof of great charity towards the sufferings of "non-Aryans". Let this be an occasion for Us to express Our paternal gratitude and Our profound sympathy for Monsignor Lichtenberg in his imprisonment.

'How distressed We are only to consider how these ideas will be able to make their way into the mentality of Catholics too, especially of the young, progressively, perhaps almost unconsciously, through the pressure of habit and of unremitting propaganda. You know that the Holy See has considered the liturgical questions that have arisen among you to be sufficiently important to merit its attention. But We must admit that We attach far more importance to protecting Christian consciences against all these poisons that threaten them. What use would it be to make the liturgy of the Church more beautiful if, outside the Church, the thoughts and actions of the faithful in their daily lives became alien to the law and love of Christ?

Reasons for the Pope's reserve

'With regard to pronouncements by the bishops, we leave to pastors in their individual circumstances the responsibility for deciding whether and in what manner the danger of reprisals and other forms of pressure, as well maybe as other circumstances arising from the length and psychology of the war, recommend them to show reserve—in spite of the reasons there would be for intervention—for the sake of avoiding greater harm. This is one of the motives which impels Us too to set limits to Our public pronouncements. The experiment We made in 1942, in permitting the free reproduction of pontifical documents for the use of the faithful, justifies Our attitude, as far as We are able to see.

'We have spoken at length on these matters, not because you need Our exhortation in order to act, but partly because We are aware of your courage and your great concern for the honour of Holy Church, and partly because We know you assess the situation coolly and prudently. Christ's representative must travel an ever more difficult and rocky path if he would hold a right balance between the contradictory demands of his pastoral charge.

'We turn Our mind to those measures against the Church of which you have informed Us in your letter: confiscation of ecclesiastical property, the seizure of your seminary at Hedwigshoehe, restriction or prohibition of the apostolate among Polish deportees in Germany, or of the religious instruction of Polish children, prohibition of entering into marriage for the Poles, etc. All this ever has been and remains but part of a vast plan which aims to stifle the life of the Church in territory under German rule. The most hard hit, as you know, is the Catholic Church in the Warthegau. We feel most deeply for the unutterable distress of the faithful of those parts, all the more since every attempt at intervention with the government on their behalf has come up against a harsh refusal. If We have restrained Ourselves until now from openly denouncing the situation affecting the Church, it is because of the considerations We have spoken of above, and above all, in the particular case of the Warthegau, the fear that what yet remains of pastoral life would be threatened in its turn.

'We are relatively well informed of the situation and fortunes of priests in concentration camps, among whom Poles are by far the most numerous. If in any way the possibility presents itself, every priest, and his companions in captivity, should be made to know they are the objects of Our deepest sympathy, that in these times of cruelty and suffering few misfortunes are so near to Our heart as theirs; and that We pray earnestly for them every day.

'We have before Us the text of a note addressed by the German episcopate to the Reich government. You can see now for yourself how slight would be the chances of success for a confidential appeal to the government. Nevertheless, however things may fall out, this note will serve to justify the bishops in the eyes of the world, when the war is over.

Action of the Holy See on behalf of the Jews

'For Catholic non-Aryans, as well as for those of the Jewish faith, the Holy See has undertaken charitable works on both material and moral levels, in the measure of its responsibility. This action has demanded much patience and disinterestedness on the part of those agencies which carry out Our various forms of relief in meeting the hopes—one might well say the pressing needs—of those who sought Our help, and also in order to negotiate successfully the diplomatic difficulties which cropped up. We do not wish to speak of the very large sums of money which We have spent in American dollars to ship emigrants overseas. Those sums were readily given for people in distress. They were given for the love of God, and We have done well to look for no appreciation in this world. Yet Jewish organizations have sent the Holy See their warm thanks for its rescue work.

'In our Christmas message We said a word about what is actually being done against non-Aryans in territories under German rule. It was a brief word, but that was readily understood. It is superfluous to tell how much Our love and fatherly solicitude are greater than ever today towards non-Aryan or semi-Aryan Catholics, children of the Church like the rest, now that they are faced with moral distress and the falling away of the very props of life. Unhappily, as things are, We can afford them no practical help beyond that of Our prayer. Nevertheless, We have decided to raise Our voice again on their behalf, as circumstances suggest or permit.

Nazi education

'We have only recently heard some most consoling facts about the unshakeable loyalty of German Catholics to their faith and their Church. Looking beyond immediate grounds for hope or anxiety, there remains for Us one grave question concerning the future. It is this: how will Catholic youth, the coming generation, after complete subjection to the influence and education of a closed system, one alien to Christianity, arising from the Party organization and the already known prescriptions of the future *Volkesgesetzbuch*, be able to keep its Catholic faith and transmit it intact? Our consolation is to be found alone in the promise of Scripture: "God is faithful, and will not permit you to be tempted beyond your strength, but with the temptation will also give you a way out, that you may be able to bear it." (*I Cor. x, 13.*)

'As an earnest of this "way out" we give to you, venerable Brother, to your fellow labourers in the apostolate and to all the faithful of your diocese, "under the sign of the Cross"—as you yourself expressed it in your pastoral letter for last "Pope's Sunday", the Apostolic Blessing for which you asked, with paternal affection, and all Our heart.'

APPENDIX II

BIBLE, BUREAUCRATS, BISHOPS

(see p. 301)

Letter from Cardinal Lienart to the Rector of the Pontifical Biblical Institute.

Reverend Father,

Thank you very much for sending me your memorandum about the article which Monsignor Romeo published at the beginning of this year in the magazine *Divinitas*, the organ of the Pontifical Academy of Theology in Rome.

It seems to me a very grave matter that, on the pretext of defending the Encyclical *Divino Afflante Spiritu* of Pope Pius XII, a Roman prelate should make a stand against the immense efforts of Catholic exegesis towards establishing on solid foundations, in the face of adverse criticism, the true value of the Old and New Testaments. It seems to me a very grave matter that a Review edited by a Roman Pontifical Academy should, by publishing this article, publicly oppose the teaching given by another Pontifical Institute especially charged by the Holy See with biblical teaching—an Institute, further, whose professors consider it an honour to pursue their researches in accordance with the authentic Catholic tradition and the directives of the Popes.

Little do they realize how these scholarly quarrels are far from being confined to Rome itself. They have repercussions throughout the universal Church and cause distress, I should even say scandal, to bishops and priests who are most devoted to the study of the Scriptures. For it is the whole of current Catholic exegesis which is attacked and rendered suspect, with no regard to what love of truth, or love of one's neighbour, may require.

They also have repercussions in the other Christian Churches which have at least kept their attachment to Sacred Scripture. These domestic quarrels and their repercussions can only dissuade them from being reconciled with us and from seeking after lost unity around the Successor of St Peter. They are harmful to the present efforts of His Holiness Pope John XXIII to reveal the Catholic Church in all its purity and beauty to the eyes of those who look at it from outside.

This is to tell you, Reverend Father, how much I share with you the trial inflicted on the Pontifical Biblical Institute and through it on the whole of Catholic exegesis. I authorize you to make free use of this letter for the good of the cause.

Bibliography

Adams, J. C. and Paolo Barile, *The Government of Republican Italy*, New York, 1961

Ahrmann, Matthew (ed.), *Race, a Challenge to Religion*, Chicago, 1962

Aigran, R. (ed.), *Liturgia*, Paris, 1931

Aradi, Zolt, *John XXIII*, New York, 1959

Arcy, M. C. d', *Christian Morals*, London, 1937

Balducci, Ernesto (ed.), *La Presenza della Chiesa nel Mondo d'Oggi*, Rome, 1964

Barile, Paolo (see Adams, J. C.)

Bartoli, Domenico, *Da Vittorio Emanuele a Gronchi*, Milan, 1961

Beales, A. C. F., *The Catholic Church and International Order*, London, 1941

Béguin, Olivier, *Roman Catholicism and the Bible*, New York, 1963

Binchy, D. A., *Church and State in Fascist Italy*, Oxford, 1941

Brogan, D. W., *The Development of Modern France*, London and New York, 1939

Callaghan, Dan, *The Mind of the Catholic Layman*, New York, 1963

Capello, M. (ed.), *Summa Juris Publici Ecclesiastici*, Rome, 1954

Cardinale, I., *La Sainte Siège et la Diplomatie*, Tournai, 1962

Chartre, Henri, *Christianity and Communism*, London, 1960

Cianfarra, Camillo, *The Vatican and the War*, New York, 1954

Colombo, D. (see Gheddo, P.)

Covatta, L. and G. Rondi (ed.), *E Venne un Uomo di Nome Giovanni*, Milan, 1963

Davis, C., *Theology for Today*, New York, 1962

Dawson, Christopher, *The Judgement of Nations*, London, 1943

" " *Progress and Religion*, New York, 1929

Dumont, C. J., *Approaches to Christian Unity*, New York, 1959

Fitzsimons, J. (ed.), *Manning, Anglican and Catholic*, London, 1951

Fogarty, M. P., *Christian Democracy in Western Europe*, London, 1957

Friedlander, Saul, *Pie XII et le IIIe Reich*, Paris, 1964 (published in U.S.A. by Alfred A. Knopf)

Gannon, R. J., *The Cardinal Spellman Story*, New York, 1962

Gheddo, P. and D. Colombo, *Opera Missionaria ed Ecumencia di Giovanni XXIII*, Milan, 1963

Giovannetti, Alberto, *L'Action du Vatican pour la Paix*, Paris, 1963

„ „ (Italian edition), Rome, 1960

„ „ *Pio XII Parla alla Chiesa del Silenzio*, Milan, 1958

Gozzini, M. (ed.), *Concilio Aperto*, Florence, 1963

Graham, Robert, *Vatican Diplomacy*, Princeton, 1959

Granzow, Brigitte, *A Mirror of Nazism*, London, 1964

Guzzetti, Battista, *Chiesa, Communismo e Socialismo*, Milan, 1961

Halecki, Oscar, Pius XII, New York, 1954

Hales, E. E. Y., *Pio Nono*, London, 1954

„ „ *Revolution and Papacy, 1769–1846,* London, 1960

Häring, B., *The Joannine Council*, Dublin, 1963

Hochhuth, R., *The Representative*, London, 1963

Homes-Dudden, F., *Gregory the Great*, London, 1905

Jaeger, Lorenz, *The Ecumenical Council, the Church and Christendom*, London, 1961

Jalland, Trevor, *The Church and the Papacy*, Naperville, Illinois, 1944

Jemolo, A. C., *Church and State in Italy, 1850–1950,* Chester Springs, Pennsylvania, 1960

John XXIII, Pope, *Journal of a Soul*, London and New York, 1965

Joyce, G. H., *Christian Marriage*, London, 1933

King, Archdale, *Liturgy and the Roman Church*, Milwaukee, 1957

Klinger, Kurt (ed.), *A Pope Laughs*, New York, 1965

Knox, Ronald, *The Mystery of the Kingdom*, London, 1952

Kung, Hans, *Council, Reform and Reunion*, New York, 1962

Latourette, K. S., *Christianity in a Revolutionary Age*, New York, 1959

Lavedan, Pierre, *French Architecture*, London, 1944

Lefebvre, Gaspar, *The Spirit of God in the Liturgy*, London, 1959

Leslie, Shane, *Cardinal Gasquet*, London, 1953

Lestapis, S. de, *Family Planning and Modern Problems*, London, 1961

Levie, Jean, *The Bible, Word of God and Words of Men*, New York, 1961

Lewi, Guenther, *The Catholic Church and Nazi Germany*, New York, 1964

Lichten, Joseph L., *Pius XII. A Question of Judgement*, Washington, 1963

Loewenich, W. von, *Modern Catholicism*, New York, 1959

Lombardi, Riccardo, *Concilio per una Riforma nella Carità*, Rome, 1961

Neuvecelle, J., *The Vatican*, Great Meadows, New Jersey, 1955

Nobécourt, Jacques, *Le Vicaire et l'Histoire*, Paris, 1964

Novak, Michael, *The Open Church*, New York, 1964

Oakeshott, M., *The Social and Political Doctrines of Contemporary Europe*, Cambridge, 1939

Ottaviani, Alfredo, *Institutiones Juris Publici Ecclesiastici*, Rome, 1925, 1954

Padellaro, Nazzareno, *Portrait of Pius XII*, London, 1956

Papal Teachings: *The Church*, Boston, 1962

„ „ : *Directives to Lay Apostles*, Boston, 1963

„ „ : *The Lay Apostolate*, Boston, 1961

Pavan, Pietro, *Laicismo d'Oggi*, Rome, 1962

Pawley, B., *Anglican View of the Council*, New York, 1962

Pellicani, A., *Il Papa di Tutti*, Milan, 1964

Pichon, Charles, *Histoire du Vatican*, Paris, 1942

Poggi, G., *Il Clero di Riserva*, Milan, 1963

Pontifical Biblical Commission, *Enchiridion Biblicum*, 4th ed., Rome, 1961

Putz, Louis J. (ed.), *The Catholic Church in the U.S.A.*, Chicago, 1956

Rè, Niccolo del, *La Curia Romana*, Rome, 1952

Romeo, Antonio, *L'Enciclico Divino Afflante Spiritu e le Opere Nuove*, Rome, 1960

Rondi, G. (see Covatta, L.)

Rynne, Xavier, *Letters from Vatican City*, New York, 1963

„ „ *The Second Session*, New York, 1964

Siefer, Gregor, *The Church and Industrial Society*, London, 1964

Siri, Giuseppe, *Ortodossia, Chiesa, Fedeli, Mondo*, Genoa, 1962

Smith, Howard K., *The State of Europe*, London, 1950

Spadafora, F., *Razionalismo, Esegesi Cattolica e Magistero*, Rome, 1960

Stern (ed.), *Nuclear Weapons and Christian Conscience*, London, 1955

Tardini, Domenico, *Pio XII*, Vatican, 1960

Tavard, G., *Two Centuries of Ecumenism*, Notre Dame, Indiana, 1960

Taylor, M. (ed.), *Wartime Correspondence between President Roosevelt and Pius XII*, New York, 1947

Thomson, Donald J., *The Emerging Layman*, New York, 1962

Trethowan, Illtyd, *Christ in the Liturgy*, London, 1951

Trevett, R. F., *Church and Sex*, New York, 1960

(Various), *Pius XII*, Vatican, 1956

Vermeersch/Creusen, *Epitome Juris Canonici*, Malines, 1963

Walker, R. F., *Pius of Peace*, Dublin, 1946

Webb, Leycester, *Church and State in Italy, 1947–1957*, Melbourne, 1958

Webster, Richard, *Christian Democracy in Italy, 1860–1960*, London, 1960

Weigel, G., *The Ecumenical Movement: Catholic Approach*, New York, 1957

Weldon, T. D., *States and Morals*, London, 1946

Wesseling, Theodore, *Liturgy and Life*, London, 1938

Index

Adzhubei, Mr & Mrs, 108, 109, 115
Agagianian, Card., 204, 205, 207
Albaredo, Card., 207
Alexander VI (Pope, 1492–1503), 121–2
Alfieri (Italian Ambassador to Vatican), 36, 37
Alfrink, Card. (Utrecht), 56, 181, 207, 212
Ancel (Aux. Bp. of Lyons), 157, 229, 231, 235, 322
Antonelli, Card. (Secretary of State), 77
Antoniutti, Card., 206
Augros, Père, 223

Bacci, Card., 206
Basel, Council of (1431–49), 212
Bea, Card. (Secretariat for Christian Unity), 56, 200, 206, 209, 265, 266, 267, 297, 300
Beck, Col. (Polish Premier), 31, 33
Bekkers (Bp. of s'-Hertogenbosch), 56
Benedict XIV (Pope, 1714–58), 123, 308, 309
Benedict XV (Pope, 1914–22), 12, 88, 127, 195, 215, 282, 297
Bérard, Louis (Vichy Ambassador to Vatican), 250, 256, 257
Bergen, D. von (German Ambassador to Vatican), 12, 23, 27, 28, 253, 255, 259
Bertram (Bp. of Breslau), 254
Bethmann-Hollweg, Theobald von (German Chancellor), 12
Bettazzi (Aux. Bp. of Bologna), 213
Biblical Commission, Pontifical, 296–302
Biblical Institute, Pontifical, 297–302, 312, 332, 341–2
Boniface VIII (Pope, 1294–1303), 71, 162, 167, 180, 187
Bonomelli, Emilio, 82, 83, 84
Borgongini Duca, Msgr., 37, 38
Bourne, Card. (Westminster), 89
Boyer, Fr. Charles, 275
Brady, Duchess, 22, 23
Braunshardter Conferences, 275, 277, 280
Browne, Card. (Holy Office), 206, 208
Bulls, Papal:
  Clericis Laicos (Boniface VIII), 162
  Cum Nimis Absurdum (Paul IV, 1555), 247
  Immensa (Sixtus V, 1588), 193
  Quo Primum (Pius V, 1570), 308
  Sapienti Consilio (Pius X, 1908), 193

Capello, Fr. Felix, 246–8, 288–90
Cardijn, Canon (later Card.), 223
Casaubon, Isaac, 270
Catholic Action, 21, 60–70, 82–4, 91, 102, 156–72, 176–8, 185, 188–9, 230, 311
Cavour, Count (Piedmontese Premier), 77
Celestine I (Pope, 422–32), 281
Central Preparatory Commission, *see* Vatican Council, Second
Chalcedon, Council of (451), 281
Chamber, the, of the Curia, 196
Chamberlain, Neville, 28, 29
Chancellery, the, of the Curia, 196
Charrière (Archbp. of Lausanne), 56
Charles-Roux (French Ambassador to Vatican), 23
Christian Unity, Secretariat of, *see* Secretariat
Churchill, Winston, 128, 129
Ciano, Count Galeazzo, 27, 38
Civiltà Cattolica, 77, 97, 200, 261, 301
Clark, Gen. Mark, 52
Clement VII (Pope, 1523–34), 195
Clement XI (Pope, 1700–21), 123
Clement XIV (Pope, 1769–74), 123
Clermont, Bp. of, 45
Colombo, Card. (Milan), 105
Colombo, Don Carlo, 98
Combes, M. 249; — Laws, 54, 221
Commissions (Vatican II), *see* Vatican Council, Second

Communism, Holy Office Decrees on, *see* Holy Office
Comte, Auguste, 159
Concordats:
with Bavaria (Pius XI, 1925), 11, 13
with Germany (Pius XI, 1933), 22, 43, 44, 252–3
with Italy (Pius XI, 1929), 60–8, *and see* Lateran Pacts
with Napoleon I (Pius VII, 1801), 73, 74, 75, 123, 221, 222
of Vienna (Nicholas V, 1448), 73
of Worms (Calixtus II, 1122), 73
Congar, Père, 159, 169, 174, 179, 231, 319
Congregations, of the Curia:
for Bishops and Religious, 194
of Ceremonial, 195
Consistorial, 92, 194, 195, 208, 231
of the Council, 96, 194, 195, 208
for Extraordinary Church Affairs, 195, 207
for the Fabric of St Peter's, 195
Holy Office, *see* Holy Office
for the Oriental Church, 195, 208, 282
of *Propaganda Fide*, 50, 122, 193, 195, 197, 208
for Religious, 195, 208, 230
of Rites, 195, 197, 208, 313, 315, 321
for Sacramentary Discipline, 195, 208
Secretariat of State, *see* Secretariat
of Seminaries and Universities, 195, 207, 208, 301–2
Confalonieri, Card., 207
Consalvi, Card. (Secretary of State), 73, 74, 75, 77, 123, 124, 196
Constance, Council of (1414–17), 212, 331
Constitutions (Vatican II), *see* Vatican Council, Second
Constitution *Licet Perfidia Judaeorum* (Innocent III, 1199), 247
Copello, Card. L. (Extraordinary Church Affairs), 207
Cortesi (Nuncio in Warsaw), 31
Coughlin, Fr., 50
Couturier, Abbé Paul, 275
Crucé, Emeric, 126
Curia, *see* Congregations

Declarations (Vatican II), *see* Vatican Council, Second
Decrees (Vatican II), *see* Vatican Council, Second
Dei Filius, Constitution (Vatican I), 159
Divini Cultus (Decree of Pius XI), 310
Dollfuss, Engelbert, 253
Döllinger, Dr Johann, 11
Döpfner, Card. (Munich), 56, 105, 184, 207, 251, 252, 261, 263
Drumont, Edouard, 249
Dupanloup (Bp. of Orleans), 75, 77

Ecumenical Movement, Holy Office Instruction on, *see* Holy Office
Edict of Nantes, Revocation of (1685), 123, 288
Eisenhower, President, 144
Encyclicals:
Ad Petri Cathedram (John XXIII, 1959), 178, 284
Aeterna Dei Sapientia (John XXIII, 1961), 285
Annus Qui (Benedict XIV, 1749), 308–9
Auctorem Fidei (Pius VI), 309
Casti Connubii (Pius XI, 1930), 240–4
Certiores Effecti (Benedict XIV, 1742), 308
Commissum Divinitus (Gregory XVI), 309
Cum Semper (Benedict XIV, 1744), 308
Diuturnum Illud (Leo XIII), 71
Divini Cultus (Pius XI, 1928), 310
Divini Redemptoris (Pius XI, 1937), 89, 90, 94, 117
Divino Afflante Spiritu (Pius XII, 1943), 298–304, 341
Ecclesiam Dei (Pius XI, 1923), 215
Evangelii Praecones (Pius XII, 1951), 156–7, 169
Fidei Donum (Pius XII, 1957), 215
Graves De Communi (Leo XIII, 1901), 159
Humani Generis (Pius XII, 1949), 228, 298, 300, 301
Humanum Genus (Leo XIII, 1884), 88
Immortale Dei (Leo XIII, 1885), 71
In Cotidianis Precibus (Pius XII, 1945), 312
Mater et Magistra (John XXIII, 1961), 103, 105, 235–8, 325
Mediator Dei (Pius XII, 1947), 169, 312–16, 320, 321
Mirari Vos (Gregory XVI), 76, 286

Encyclicals—*continued*
Mit Brennender Sorge (Pius XI, 1937), 22, 44, 89, 253–4
Mortalium Animos (Pius XI, 1928), 281
Mystici Corporis (Pius XII, 1943), 168, 176, 312
Non Abbiamo Bisogno (Pius XI), 17, 19, 21
Orientalis Ecclesiae (Pius XII, 1945), 281, 311
Pacem in Terris (John XXIII, 1963), 98, 99, 105, 108–18, 129–33, 136–42, 152–5, 165, 188, 292, 325, 327, 333
Pascendi (Pius X, 1907), 201, 296, 303
Pastor Aeternus (Pius IX), 213
Princeps Pastorum (John XXIII, 1959), 178, 320
Providentissimus Deus (Leo XIII, 1893), 296, 299, 304
Quadragesimo Anno (Pius XI, 1931), 88, 89, 97, 103, 219, 227, 228
Quanta Cura (Pius IX, 1864), 87, 286
Qui Pluribus (Pius IX, 1846), 87
Quod Apostolici Muneris (Leo XIII, 1878), 88
RerumNovarum (Leo XIII, 1891), 88, 103, 159, 219, 221, 236, 239, 240
Sapientiae Christianae (Leo XIII), 71
Satis Cognitum (Leo XIII, 1896), 215
Sempiternus Rex (Pius XII, 1951), 282
Sertum Laetitiae (Pius XII, 1939), 79
Sollicitudini (Benedict XIV, 1745), 308
Summi Pontificatus (Pius XII, 1939), 59, 167, 218, 256, 261, 274, 292

Fanfani, Amintore, 98, 102, 103, 106
Farinacci, 17, 37, 146
Feltin, Card. (Paris), 117, 226, 228, 230, 231, 232, 233
Florit, Card. (Florence), 105
Frings, Card. (Cologne), 56, 180, 181

Galeazzi, Count, 83, 84
Gargitter (Bp. of Bressanone), 56
Garrigou-Lagrange, Fr., 207
Gasparri, Card. Pietro (Secretary of State), 13, 18
Gasperi, Alcide de (Italian Premier), 16, 22, 24, 25, 62, 65, 81–5, 97, 98, 164, 325
Gasquet, Card. (Vatican Librarian), 12, 13, 285
Gedda, Dr Luigi (Head of Italian Catholic Action), 63–5, 68, 69, 82–4, 171, 172, 173, 185, 212
Gemelli, Fr., 18, 20, 160
Gerlier, Card. (Lyons), 136, 226, 229, 231, 235
Giebner, Martin, 272
Gioberti, Vincenzo, 47
Giolitti, Giovanni, 15, 131
Giovannetti, Msgr., 33–6
Gladstone, W. E., 127
Godfrey, Card. (Westminster), 151
Goldmann, Dr Nathan (President, World Jewish Congress), 266
Gracias, Card. (Bombay), 105
Gregory I, the Great, (Pope, 590–604), 246, 268, 293
Gregory VII (Pope, 1073–85), 13
Gregory XVI (Pope, 1831–46), 76, 124, 286, 309
Grober, (Archbp. of Freiburg), 253
Gronchi, Giovanni, 98, 100
Grotius, Hugo, 125, 126, 270, 272
Guano, Emilio, (Bp. of Leghorn), 172
Guarantees, Law of, 37
Guéranger, Abbot of Solesmes, 309–10
Guerry, (Archbp. of Cambrai), 56

Hague Conferences (1899, 1907), 127
Halifax, Lord, 28
Heard, Card., 207
Heenan, Card. (Westminster), 156, 267
Henriques, Card. Silva, 207
Himmler, Heinrich, 39
Hitler, Adolf, 22, 23, 24, 27, 29, 31, 33, 37, 128, 250–4, 256, 258
Hobbes, Thomas, 121, 125
Holy Office, 93, 99, 105, 193–8, 201, 207–10, 225, 226, 229, 232, 233, 250, 273, 280, 298, 316
Holy Office Decrees, Instructions, *Monita*, etc:
on Communism (1949), 93–7, 103, 119, 232
on Ecumenical Movement (1949), 277–81, 328–9
on Scripture, teaching of (1961), 300, 302
Hull, Cordell, 52

Ilichev Report, 118

Innitzer, Card. (Vienna), 23
Innocent I (Pope, 401–17), 307
Innocent III (Pope, 1198–1216), 13, 19, 86, 123, 247, 268
Innocent XI (Pope, 1676–89), 123
Innocent XII (Pope, 1691–1700), 196
Isaac, Jules, 264, 265

Jaeger (Archbp. of Paderborn), 275
James I (King of England), 270
Jesuits, 11, 26, 47, 77, 123, 255
Jeunesse Ouvrière Chrétienne, 223, 228
John XXIII (Pope, 1958–63), *passim, and see* Roncalli
Jolif, Fr. Yves, 117
Jorio, Card. Alberto di, 205
Journet, Card. (Fribourg), 264
Jus Gentium, 125, 126, 146

Kaas, Msgr. Ludwig, 252, 253
Kellogg-Briand Pact, 128
Kennedy, President, 101
Khrushchev, Nikita, 107–9, 141, 142
Knox, Msgr. Ronald, 276, 295, 296
König, Card. (Vienna), 56, 105, 181, 207, 327

Lagrange, Fr. M., 296
La Malfa, Ugo, 106, 112
Lambeth Conference (1930), 241, 244
Lamennais, F., 76
Lamentabili (Decree of Pius X), 296
Lateran Council, the Third (1179), 247
Lateran Pacts (1929), 17, 18, 20, 25, 26, 37, 42, 50, 160, 199, 200, 203
Lay Apostolate, World Congress of:
  First (1951), 69, 169, 173, 178
  Second (1957), 173, 174, 178, 281
Léger, Card., 245
Leo I, the Great (Pope, 440–61), 284, 285
Leo IX (Pope, 1049–54), 192
Leo XII (Pope, 1823–29), 157–8, 195
Leo XIII (Pope, 1878–1903), 48–50, 71, 88, 124, 158, 159, 214, 215, 219, 220, 221, 237, 240, 250, 285, 292, 296, 299, 310
Lercaro, Card. (Bologna), 56, 136, 181, 184, 268
Lichtenstein, Msgr., 254, 337
Liénart, Card. (Lille), 56, 105, 180–4, 189, 214, 226, 231–5, 264, 303, 341–2
Liturgy, Constitution on the Sacred (Vatican II), *see* Vatican Council, Second
Lombardi, Fr., 82, 171

McCarthy, Senator, 53, 57, 175
Maglione, Card. Luigi (Secretary of State), 27, 30, 31, 34, 35, 37, 38, 40, 258, 259
Maistre, Joseph, Comte de, 76, 221, 276, 330
Malines Conversations, 275
Manning, Card. Henry (Westminster), 248, 271
Marella, Archbp. (Nuncio in France), 230, 231
Martin (Bp. of Paderborn), 248
Mathew, Archbp. David, 275
Matteotti, Giacomo, 16
Maurras, Charles, 222, 249
Menti Nostrae (Apostolic Exhortation of Pius XII, 1950), 228
Mercier, Card. (Malines-Brussels), 55, 275
Messineo, Fr., 97–9, 102
Metzger, Fr. Max Joseph, 273
Meyer, Card., 207, 293, 304
Micara, Card., 207
Mindszenty, Card. Josef (Budapest), 92, 95
Modernism, 14, 15, 160, 201, 211, 296–7, 303–4
Montini, Giovanni (later Paul VI), 14, 83, 99, 124, 129, 162, 258, *and see* Paul VI
Moralejo (Bp. of Valencia), 285
Moro, Aldo, 102, 103, 106, 326
Moscicki (President of Poland), 31
Mundelein, Card. (Chicago), 23, 27
Murri, Padre, 15, 160
Mussolini, Benito, 15–24, 27–31, 36–9, 84

Napoleon I, 73, 75, 76, 112, 123, 248, 272
Nenni, Pietro, 81, 97, 98, 102, 103, 106, 327
Newman, Card., 77, 275–6
Nicholas II (Pope, 1059–61), 192

O'Connell, Card., 51
Ollivier, Emile, 77
'Operation Sturzo', 65, 69, 81, 82, 98, 156, 171, 187, 325
Ormesson, Wladimir d' (French Ambassador to Vatican), 38
Orsenigo, Cesare (Nuncio in Berlin), 252
Osborne, Sir D'Arcy (British Minister to Holy See), 259

Osservatore Romano, 13, 24, 28, 31, 37, 38, 44, 94, 97–106, 115, 119, 174, 212, 260
Ottaviani, Card. (Holy Office), 53, 99, 146–7, 232, 289, 293

Pacelli, Eugenio (Secretary of State, later Pius XII), 11–17, 20, 22–5, 27, 50, 89, 142, 166, 196, 252, 253, 254
Pacelli, Francesco, 17
Papen, Franz von, 219, 252
Parente, Archbp. (Holy Office), 225
Partito Popolare, 15, 19, 160
Paul III (Pope, 1534–49), 194
Paul IV (Pope, 1555–9), 247
Paul VI (Pope, 1963–), 56, 98, 162, 211, 243, 326, 327, *and see* Montini
Pax Romana Congress (1957), 136, 140
Penitentiary, Tribunal of the Sacred, 196
Penn, William, 126
Pesaro, Bp. of, 103
Pétain, Marshal Henri, 250, 256, 257
Piazza, Card. (Consistorial Congregation), 231
Pius IV (Pope, 1559–65), 191, 196
Pius V (Pope, 1566–72), 157, 308
Pius VI (Pope, 1775–99), 192, 214, 309
Pius VII (Pope, 1800–23), 74, 75, 123, 124
Pius IX (Pope, 1846–78), 47, 48, 58, 74, 77, 87, 89, 106, 158, 159, 214, 286, 291, 308, 309, 311
Pius X (Pope, 1903–14), 14, 124, 160, 174, 193, 194, 200, 215, 222, 296, 297, 310
Pius XI (Pope, 1922–39), 15–29, 34, 54, 61, 62, 84, 88, 89, 156, 160–1, 167, 169, 181, 204, 215, 219, 222, 240, 241, 244, 250, 253, 254, 281, 282, 297, 298, 310, *and see* Ratti
Pius XII (Pope, 1939–58), *passim*, *and see* Pacelli
Pizzardo, Card. (Congregation of Seminaries), 202, 233, 301
Preysing, Card. von (Berlin), 94, 254–5, 260, 312, 335
Primeau (Bp. of Manchester, New Hampshire), 163
Punti Fermi, 100, 101, 102, 105, 117, 325

Quadri, (Bp. of Pinerolo), 189

Radio, Pontifical Commission for ——, Cinema and Television, 208
Rarkowski, Bp., 254
Ratti, Achille, 22, *and see* Pius XI
Ribbentrop, Joachim von, 34, 35, 256
Richaud, Card., 207
Richelieu, Card., 122
Risorgimento, The, 15, 25, 47, 48, 61, 64, 66, 71, 77, 81, 106, 124, 179
Ritter, Card., 207
Roberti, Card., 211
Roman Synod (1960), 179, 216, 234
Roncalli, Angelo Giuseppe (later John XXIII), 40, 98, 99, 101, 178, 230, 232
Roosevelt, Franklin D., 23, 50–2, 255
Roosevelt, Mrs F. D., 52
Rota, the, of the Curia, 196
Ruffini, Card. (Palermo), 268
Ruotolo, Dolindo, 298

Sacra Tridentina (Decree of Pius X), 310
Saigh, Card., 245
Saint-Pierre, Abbé de, 126
Sangnier, Marc, 222
Sapieha, Card. (Cracow), 258, 259
Saragat, Giuseppe, 81, 97, 106, 112
Satolli (Apostolic Delegate to U.S.), 50
Scelba, Mario, 105
Schemata (Vatican II), *see* Vatican Council, Second
Schlink, Dr, 275
Scripture, Holy Office Instruction on, *see* Holy Office
Secretariat for Promoting Christian Unity, 183, 208–10, 265, 275, 284
Secretariat of State, 195–8, 201, 202, 205, 209, 210, 259, 261, 267
Seelisberg Conference (1947), 264
Segnatura, of the Curia, 196
Segni, Antonio (Italian Premier), 99, 100
Seredi, Card. (Budapest), 263
Simon, Dr (Rector of Tübingen), 273, 275
Siri, Card. (Genoa), 102, 105
Sixtus V (Pope, 1585–90), 191, 193, 195, 202, 206
Slipyi, Archbp., 107
Smedt, Emil Josef de (Bp. of Bruges), 56, 183, 185, 213
Smith, Al (U.S. Presidential Candidate), 49, 50
Spellman, Card. (New York), 23, 50–3, 175, 202, 336
Staelien (Bp. of Oldenburg), 275
Stalin, Joseph, 89, 108, 129, 255
Stephen III (Pope, 752–7), 192

Sturzo, Don, 15, 16, 61, 65, 83, 160, *and see* 'Operation Sturzo'
Suarez, Francisco (Jesuit theologian), 126, 145
Suenens, Card. (Malines-Brussels), 56, 189, 207, 244, 245
Suhard, Card. (Paris), 42, 94, 223–6, 300
Syllabus of Modern Errors (1864), 12, 48, 75–7, 85, 87, 101, 107, 236, 291–2
Synod of Pistoia (1786), 309, 313–14, 321

Tambroni, 100, 102
Tappouni, Card., 268
Tardini, Card. (Secretary of State), 20, 21, 29, 36, 40, 105, 205
Taylor, Myron C., 51, 52, 257, 258
Tisserant, Card., 42
Tittman, H. C., 257–60
Togliatti, Palmiro, 97
Tra le Sollicitudini (*Motu Proprio* of Pius X), 310
Trent, Council of (1545–63), 169, 193, 195, 308, 310, 315, 316
Tromp, Fr., 207, 208
Truman, President, 52
Tübingen Conversations, 273

United Nations Organization, 128, 131, 136–40, 142, 327
Urban VIII (Pope, 1623–44), 122, 192
Urbani, Card. (Venice), 105
Utrecht, Peace of (1713), 123, 126

Val, Card. Rafael Merry del (Secretary of State), 14, 198
Valeri (Nuncio in France), 249
Vallat, Xavier, 250, 265
Vatican Council, First (1869–70), 58, 87–8, 155, 159, 213, 215, 221, 248, 330, 331
Vatican Council, Second (1962–5), *passim*, especially 58, 74, 104–7, 110, 155, 179–83, 190, 208–11, 243, 265, 302, 325, 330, 332
  Commissions:
    for Bishops and the Government of the Dioceses, 208
    Central Preparatory, 105, 182, 320
    De Missionibus, 208
    for the Discipline of the Clergy and People, 208
    Doctrinal, 208
    for the Lay Apostolate, 208
    Liturgical, 208, 320
    for Oriental Churches, 208
    for Religious, 208
    for Sacramentary Discipline, 208
    for Seminaries, 208
    Theological, 302
  Constitutions, Declarations, Decrees, *Schemata :*
    Apostolate of the Laity, the, 156, 157, 184–8
    Bishops and Government of Dioceses, 213
    Church and the Modern World, the, (*De Ecclesia*), 85, 86, 156, 165, 166, 172, 182–3, 188–9, 208, 209, 210, 213, 321, 328
    Communications, Modern, 208
    Ecumenism (*De Ecumenismo*), 210, 280–5
    Jews, the (*De Judaeis*), 210, 250, 266–9, 285
    Liturgy, Sacred, 182, 303, 307, 308, 315, 319–23
    Religious Liberty (*De Libertate Religiosa*), 74, 75, 210, 220, 267, 285–7, 292–4
    Revelation (*De Revelatione*), 209, 210, 303–4
Verdier, Card. (Paris), 222, 223
Veuillot, Louis (Editor of *L'Univers*), 221
Victor I (Pope, 189–99), 307

Weber (Archbp. of Strasburg), 56
Westphalia, Peace of (1648), 120, 123, 126, 248, 270
Wilhelm II, Kaiser, 12
Worker-priests, 223–35
Wiseman, Card. (Westminster), 276
Wyszynski, Card. (Warsaw), 94, 95

Zoa (Archbp. of Yaoundé), 289